W9-AGX-265

DATELINE: TORONTO

Books by Ernest Hemingway

ACROSS THE RIVER AND INTO THE TREES

BY-LINE: ERNEST HEMINGWAY

THE DANGEROUS SUMMER

DATELINE: TORONTO

DEATH IN THE AFTERNOON

A FAREWELL TO ARMS

THE FIFTH COLUMN AND FOUR STORIES OF THE SPANISH CIVIL WAR

FOR WHOM THE BELL TOLLS

GREEN HILLS OF AFRICA

IN OUR TIME

ISLANDS IN THE STREAM

MEN WITHOUT WOMEN

A MOVEABLE FEAST

THE NICK ADAMS STORIES

THE OLD MAN AND THE SEA

SELECTED LETTERS

THE SHORT STORIES OF ERNEST HEMINGWAY

THE SNOWS OF KILIMANJARO AND OTHER STORIES

THE SUN ALSO RISES

TO HAVE AND HAVE NOT

WINNER TAKE NOTHING

Ernest
Hemingway

DATELINE: TORONTO

The Complete *Toronto Star* Dispatches, 1920–1924

EDITED BY
WILLIAM WHITE

CHARLES SCRIBNER'S SONS / NEW YORK

Library of Congress Cataloging-in-Publication Data

Hemingway, Ernest, 1899–1961.
Dateline: Toronto.

I. White, William, 1910– . II. Toronto daily star.
III. Toronto star weekly. IV. Title.
PS3515.E37A6 1985 814'.54 85-14439
ISBN 0-684-18515-6

Published simultaneously in Canada by
Collier Macmillan Canada, Inc.—Copyright under
the Berne Convention.

1 3 5 7 9 11 13 15 17 19 H/C 20 18 16 14 12 10 8 6 4 2

Printed in the United States of America.

Dedicated to the Memory of

HARRY L. NOLDER, JR.

—William White

Contents

Foreword by Charles Scribner, Jr.

One of the important facts about Ernest Hemingway is that virtually all his life, from the time he was a boy to the day he died, he thought of himself as a writer—nothing else. That image of himself created his ambition, directed his will, and supplied his greatest satisfaction.

It was in high school that Hemingway's idea of himself as a writer began to take definite shape. The pretension was reasonable: words came easily to him, and he had a natural sense of style for putting them together. One of the results of his years at the Oak Park and River Forest High School was this realization of his talent. In his senior year he wrote lively reports for the weekly school paper and short stories for its literary magazine. That is not an unusual combination of genres for a schoolboy, but Hemingway never gave it up. Throughout his career he wrote stories and news reports.

The experience of seeing his work in print was as pleasing to him as it is to all writers, but in him it became an addiction. He was always on the lookout for material to use in a story; he was a magpie in that respect, industriously and almost by reflex action storing away in his memory colorful bits and pieces of life. His classmates referred to him as "our Ring Lardner," the highest compliment they could pay him, and at that time by no means inappropriate. When the time came for him to think about college, it could have been no great surprise to anyone that he chose instead a job as cub reporter on the *Kansas City Star*. He knew he had a bent for journalism and the job was in line with his secret ambition.

Hemingway's six-month stint on the *Star* has been described as an apprenticeship. Valuable in many ways, it provided him with rules for style which were compatible with his own writing instincts. He learned how to dig out the facts of a story and he toiled to describe them simply and directly. He also learned to recognize a good story when he saw one. His image of himself had now developed into the reality of being a professional writer; status—and that particular status—was very important to him.

It is clear that as a writer Hemingway would develop still further beyond the lessons he had learned in Kansas City. He would end up creating a style capable of representing events and truths that lie outside the scope of journalism, and to do that he had a certain amount of unlearning to do. His companions in journalism were impressed not only by his energy on the job, but also by his interest in literature off the job.

Leaving the *Star* for wartime ambulance service in Italy interrupted his writing, but the variety and vividness of the memories then stored up show that he was still seeing everything with the eye of the reporter.

The first crisis in his career occurred when he got back home. Fired with desire to be a "real" writer, an important writer, he found that the stories he wrote then were rejected over and over again for a whole year.

It must be startling for readers familiar with Hemingway's later work to read his productions of that period. Stilted in language, these stories seem utterly unlike what we know he had it in him to write. He was clearly getting nowhere. In the straits he was in at the time, it was providential that he managed to obtain a free-lance assignment on the *Toronto Star*. Almost a chance event, this was one of the most fortunate opportunities that ever came his way. For a writer, there is no substitute for being published and read. The *Star* gave him an appreciative readership and kept him writing on a regular basis. Between February 1920 and December 1924, he wrote over one hundred and fifty pieces for the *Star*, ranging from amusing sketches of everyday life close to home—medical fads, tips to campers, political satires, and the like—to firsthand observations of later experiences as a foreign correspondent in postwar Europe.

One of Hemingway's passions was to get the inside story, the "true gen," and there was a touch of punditry in his journalism whenever he could set the record straight—whether it had to do with the superiority of one boxer over another, or the "true facts" about something like rum-running into the United States. Even though he was still in his twenties, this "persona" is probably the first appearance of the subsequently famous "Papa Hemingway" figure—that voice of experience and much-traveled source of inside information. In the *Star* pieces he was certainly heading in that direction.

Another characteristic that one sees in them, as in his later writings, is the uncanny knack for dialogue. He frequently introduced conversations to give his news stories a dramatic dimension.

The comic element of the Toronto articles may surprise those who know only his novels and stories. It is not that Hemingway lacked that vein, as the character of the old lady at the bullfight in *Death in the Afternoon* makes clear. But in most of his serious writings he chose not to be humorous, perhaps because humor reminded him of his journalism, or perhaps because he felt that *his* humor was not compatible with high literature.

When Hemingway and his wife, Hadley, traveled to Europe in December 1921, he regularly sent back to the *Star* human-interest stories describing postwar conditions. The reader is also able to share Hemingway's first experience of bullfighting, the sport that came to be so important in his writing, and there are of course many spirited accounts of Paris in the Twenties, when artists and writers were breaking new ground. Hemingway would soon become one of the most important of these innovators, but at the time he was listening and learning.

The *Star* sent him to two international conferences: the International Economic Conference in Genoa and the Lausanne Peace Conference. Later he reported on the war between the Greeks and the Turks and described the haunting plight of the stream of refugees from Thrace.

But his days with the *Toronto Star* were numbered. When he returned to Toronto shortly before the birth of his first son, John, there was a falling-out between him and the *Star*'s city editor, Harry Hindmarsh. The latter obviously regarded him as spoiled, and set out to clip his wings. In the stiffness of some of Hemingway's last news reports for the *Star* on Sudbury coal and other subjects, one sees that when forced to adopt a less personal style, Hemingway went to the other extreme of impersonality. He did not take kindly to editorial restraint.

By now his energies were almost entirely devoted to imaginative fiction, and his artistic star was rising. Still, throughout his life he would continue to accept journalistic assignments whenever they led him to places that interested him. He covered postwar Italy for *The New Republic*, the Spanish Civil War for the North American Newspaper Alliance, China for *PM*, the Royal Air Force for *Collier's*, and the bullfights of the "dangerous summer" of 1959 in Spain for *Life*.

In reading these articles, one must remember that Hemingway did not write them as works of literature. In later life it would infuriate him if his reports and dispatches were mentioned in the same breath as his novels and stories. But he wrote so well that some of his journalistic pieces can stand on an equal footing with his literary work. In fact, he himself promoted a number to that rank when he put together collections of stories.

And again, he wrote so well that the pieces collected here make delightful reading even now, more than half a century after they were written. For readers of Hemingway, these stories will hold as much interest as his letters of the same period. Indeed, the most agreeable way to read this book is as a series of letters home from an enthusiastic, articulate, and perceptive friend—one who probably has a great future as a writer.

Charles Scribner, Jr.

Introduction

By 1924 the by-line "By Ernest M. Hemingway" had become familiar to readers of the *Toronto Star Weekly* and its companion publication the *Toronto Daily Star*. From February 14, 1920, until September 13, 1924, Hemingway's pieces appeared in the *Star Weekly*, and from February 4, 1922, until October 6, 1923, he also contributed to the *Daily Star*. They were journalism, not short stories or imaginative fiction, but they played an important part in the development of a major American author.

When Hemingway began to write for the *Toronto Star*, he was completely unknown: his work had been published only in high school periodicals, in Oak Park, Illinois, and in the *Kansas City Star*, where he was an anonymous cub reporter. By the time his last article was printed in the Canadian newspaper, he had published only a few short stories and two little books in limited editions, *Three Stories & Ten Poems* (Paris, 1923) and *in our time* (Paris, 1924); however, his literary career had started. Yet before this career began, Hemingway's work with the *Toronto Star Weekly* and the *Toronto Daily Star* gave him a chance to make a living from his writings, while still in his twenties; an opportunity to see more of the world, especially Europe, at first hand while covering political, social, and military activities; and a few important years, while he was still impressionable and growing, to flex his not-yet-literary muscles. From these years in Toronto, and reporting for Toronto readers as their foreign correspondent, came the creative writer and the author of some of the finest short stories and novels of our time.

In reprinting these 172 identifiable articles—most of them signed "By Ernest M. Hemingway"—I have relied on the original published texts in the weekly and daily *Toronto Star* editions. As is the usual newspaper practice, the manuscripts were destroyed shortly after they were set in type in the print shop, so we shall never know exactly what Hemingway wrote, and what the Toronto copyreader added, deleted, or changed. I have not "corrected" Hemingway in the way Emily Dickinson's early editors "corrected" her poetry, though I have changed typographical errors made by linotype operators and missed by proofreaders; and where editors have missed Hemingway's notorious misspellings, such as in German place-names, I have silently spelled the word correctly. To have left it in its original wrong form would have achieved nothing. Though the *Star* editors or copyreaders may have added commas in Hemingway's sentences, I have changed punctuation only on a few occasions where necessary for clarity or understanding or identity. In a very few cases I have added a word in square brackets for the same reasons. In the rare cases of doubtful grammar, I have made no changes. Hemingway may well have been writing idiomatically, or, even then, before he had fully developed his narrative style, valuing the way in which he said a thing more highly than grammatical niceties.

As for the titles, they were almost always newspaper headlines written on the *Toronto Daily Star* or *Star Weekly* copydesks according to the place and space of the articles on the newspaper page. They were rarely, if ever, by Hemingway himself. Thus, for bibliographical and historical purposes, I have put the original headings in the Table of Contents, and I have given the pieces more convenient and shorter titles in place of headlines. I have deleted all subheads in the stories. They, too, were not written by Hemingway but usually by the copydesk purely for typographical reasons to break up the large pages. In datelines on all out-of-Toronto news stories, I have retained the names of cities from which they were filed but removed the dates, for the more important dates of publication in the *Star* appear immediately below the titles.

"By Ernest M. Hemingway"—the "M." was not dropped until later—appears on all but thirty-five of the dispatches, a few times misspelled, and twice "E. M. Hemingway." One piece is by-lined "Hem." On twenty-four occasions the articles were unsigned; W. L. McGeary, librarian of the *Toronto Star*, to whom we are deeply indebted, has used office records and other verifiable evidence to attribute many of these to Hemingway. I am also greatly indebted to Randall Scott Davis of La Crescenta, California, for discovering and identifying fourteen unsigned Hemingway contributions to the *Toronto Star* and the *Star Weekly* and two contributions with the by-line "By A Foreigner." In addition, Hemingway used as a pseudonym the name of his then-newborn son, John Hadley, six times, usually because he had other signed pieces in the same issue of the *Star*. For the same reason he once used the by-line Peter Jackson, an invented name.

Unsigned pieces and those with by-lines other than "By Ernest M. Hemingway" or "By E. M. Hemingway" are noted in the Table of Contents. I have included one short piece entitled "Miss Megan George Makes Hit: 'A Wonder' Reporters Call Her," published in the *Daily Star*, October 6, 1923, which Professor Carlos Baker has attributed to Miss Isobel Simmons of Oak Park, Illinois—because it carries Hemingway's by-line.

Here, arranged chronologically between the covers of one volume for the first time, are all of Hemingway's writings for the *Toronto Star*. Twenty-nine of these articles appear in my own *By-Line: Ernest Hemingway* (Charles Scribner's Sons, 1967). In spite of the novelist's well-known resistance to efforts to collect his newspaper articles, no apology need be made for his reporting as reporting. Given Hemingway's own rules for seeing what he saw and putting his pieces together in his own way, sometimes in an unorthodox way, it is fine stuff of which the *Toronto Daily Star* and the *Toronto Star Weekly* were proud. And much of it, over sixty years later, can still be read both as a record of the early Twenties and as evidence of how Ernest Hemingway learned the craft of writing.

William White

DATELINE: TORONTO

Circulating Pictures

☆ THE TORONTO STAR WEEKLY
February 14, 1920

Have you a coming Corot, a modern Millet, a potential Paul Potter or a Toronto Titian temporarily adding whatever the new art adds to your home? If not it is possible to obtain one of the finest works of the moderns for a limited time for a mere fraction of its value.

The Circulating Pictures movement had its genesis in Toronto with Mrs. W. Gordon Mills of 63 Farnham Avenue, who last spring approached one of the foremost Canadian artists with the proposition that she might borrow a picture or two for the summer months. The artist, who is one of those that have introduced anger into art, readily consented and together they discussed the possibility of starting a circulating picture gallery. A number of young married women of Toronto enthusiastically took up the idea and now a gallery of circulating pictures is in full swing, or rather circulation.

According to Mrs. Kenneth T. Young, of 152 Bloor Street West, the circulating gallery is at present a very close corporation. After being asked by a writer for the *Star Weekly* for a story on the new application of Harvey's principle of circulation, she talked it over with the other circulatees and they decided that the publication of their names or the names of the artists would give a taint of commercialism to the entire scheme which would quite spoil it. It wouldn't be nearly so enjoyable to have one or two colorful joyous pictures in your home if you knew that any other responsible person might have them too. Imagine the élan to be derived from the public library if only a dozen or so persons were allowed to make use of it.

The reporter learned, however, that the principle under which the circulating gallery is operating is this: the young matrons select the pictures they wish from the rich, semi-starving or impecunious artists, depending upon the degree of the artist's modernity and his facility with advertising, and pay ten percent of the picture's assessed value. They then have possession of it for six months. The present scheme has been for each of the young women to have two pictures and after their kick—to use a slang phrase—has worn off, or after it has become so intensified as to make an exchange advisable, to trade with her nearest fellow member of the gallery.

For example, a picture by one of the artists, who, to quote Mrs. Mills, "has introduced anger into art," might be so potent if hung in the living room that it might be exchanged after only a few days, perhaps at the husband's request.

Another might be so powerfully pastoral in motif that the husband might be as easily controlled by it as the cobra by the fakir's pipes. Such a picture might remain in the home indefinitely, doing yeoman service on the occasion of such domestic incidents as teething, the purchase of spring hats or the discovery of an overdrawn account.

Then there is the painter's side of it. By this arrangement he receives something at least. His pictures are viewed by many more people and at the end of six months he receives them back ready for sale. But commercialism must not enter in.

A Free Shave

☆ THE TORONTO STAR WEEKLY
March 6, 1920

The land of the free and the home of the brave is the modest phrase used by certain citizens of the republic to the south of us to designate the country they live in. They may be brave—but there is nothing free. Free lunch passed some time ago and on attempting to join the Freemasons you are informed it will cost you seventy-five dollars.

The true home of the free and the brave is the barber college. Everything is free there. And you have to be brave. If you want to save $5.60 a month on shaves and haircuts, go to the barber college, but take your courage with you.

For a visit to the barber college requires the cold, naked valor of the man who walks clear-eyed to death. If you don't believe it, go to the beginner's department of the barber's college and offer yourself for a free shave. I did.

As you enter the building you come into a well-appointed barbershop on the main floor. This is where the students who will soon graduate work. Shaves cost five cents, haircuts fifteen.

"Next," called one of the students. The others looked expectant.

"I'm sorry," I said. "I'm going upstairs."

Upstairs is where the free work is done by the beginners.

A hush fell over the shop. The young barbers looked at one another significantly. One made an expressive gesture with his forefinger across his throat.

"He's going upstairs," said a barber in a hushed voice.

"He's going upstairs," the other echoed him and they looked at one another.

I went upstairs.

Upstairs there was a crowd of young fellows standing around in white jackets and a line of chairs ran down the wall. As I entered the room two or three went over and stood by their chairs. The others remained where they were.

"Come on you fellows, here's another one," called one of the white coats by the chairs.

"Let those work who want to," replied one of the group.

"You wouldn't talk that way if you were paying for your course," returned the industrious one.

"Shut up. The government sends me here," replied the non-worker and the group went on with their talking.

I seated myself in the chair attended by a red-haired young fellow.

"Been here long?" I asked to keep from thinking about the ordeal.

"Not very," he grinned.

"How long before you will go downstairs?" I asked.

"Oh, I've been downstairs," he said, lathering my face.

"Why did you come back up here?" said I.

"I had an accident," he said, going on with the lathering.

Just then one of the non-workers came over and looked down at me.

"Say, do you want to have your throat cut?" he inquired pleasantly.

"No," said I.

"Haw! Haw!" said the non-worker.

Just then I noticed that my barber had his left hand bandaged.

"How did you do that?" I asked.

"Darn near sliced my thumb off with the razor this morning," he replied amiably.

The shave wasn't so bad. Scientists say that hanging is really a very pleasant death. The pressure of the rope on the nerves and arteries of the neck produces a sort of anesthesia. It is waiting to be hanged that bothers a man.

According to the red-haired barber there are sometimes as many as one hundred men on some days who come for free shaves.

"They are not all 'bums' either. A lot of them take a chance just to get something for nothing."

Free barbering is not the only free service to be obtained in Toronto. The Royal College of Dental Surgeons does dental work for all who come to the college at Huron and College streets. The only charge made is for materials used.

Approximately one thousand patients are treated, according to Dr. F. S. Jarman, D.D.S., head of the examination department of the clinic. All the work is done by the senior students under the direction of dental specialists.

Teeth are extracted free if only a local anesthetic is used, but a charge of two dollars is made for gas. According to Dr. Jarman, dentists in general practice charge three dollars to extract a single tooth. At the Dental College you can have twenty-five teeth extracted for two dollars! That should appeal to the bargain hunters.

Prophylaxis, or thorough cleaning of the teeth, is done at the college for from fifty cents to a dollar. In private practice this would cost from a dollar to ten dollars.

Teeth are filled if the patient defrays the costs of the gold. Usually from a dollar to two dollars. Bridgework is done under the same system.

No patients are refused at the Dental College. If they are unable to defray the cost of the materials used they are cared for just the same. The person who is willing to take a chance can surely save money on dentistry.

At Grace Hospital across Huron Street from the Dental College, there is a free dispensary for the needy poor that gives free medical attention to an average of 1,241 patients a month.

This service is only for the "needy" poor. Those of us who are poor, and are not adjudged needy by the social service nurse in charge, have to pay for the medical service. According to the figures at the Grace Hospital, over half of the cases treated last month were of Jewish nationality. The others were a conglomeration of English, Scotch, Italian, Macedonian and people of unknown origin.

Free meals were formerly served at the Fred Victor Mission, Queen and Jarvis streets. But the authorities at the mission state that there is almost no demand now. Prohibition and the war solved the "bum" problem and where formerly there was a long queue of "down-and-outs" lined up to receive free meal tickets, there is now only an occasional supplicant.

If you wish to secure free board, free room, and free medical attention there is one infallible way of obtaining it. Walk up to the biggest policeman you can find and hit him in the face.

The length of your period of free board and room will depend on how Colonel Denison [police magistrate] is feeling. And the amount of your free medical attention will depend on the size of the policeman.

Sporting Mayor

☆ THE TORONTO STAR WEEKLY
March 13, 1920

Mayor Church is a keen lover of all sporting contests. He is an enthusiast over boxing, hockey and all the manly sports. Any sporting event that attracts voters as spectators numbers His Worship as one of the patrons. If marbles, leapfrog, and tit-tat-toe contests were viewed by citizens of voting age, the mayor would be enthusiastically present. Due to the youth of the competitors the mayor reluctantly refrains from attending all of the above sports.

The other night the mayor and I attended the boxing bouts at Massey Hall. No; we didn't go together, but we were both there.

The mayor's entrance was impressive. He remained standing for some time bowing to his friends and people who knew him.

"Who is that?" asked the man next to me.

"That's the mayor," I replied.

"Down in front!" called out the man next to me.

The mayor enjoyed the first bout hugely. During it he shook hands with everyone around him. He did not seem to know when the bout stopped, as he was still shaking hands when the bell rang for the end of the last round.

Between the rounds, the mayor stood up and looked over the crowd.

"What is he doing—counting the house?" asked the man next to me.

"No. He is letting the sport-loving people look at their sport-loving mayor," I said.

"Down in front!" shouted the man next to me in a rude voice.

During the next two bouts the mayor recognized a number of acquaintances in the crowd. He waved to all of them. He also shook hands with all the soldiers in uniform present, shaking hands with some of them two or three times to make sure.

Scotty Lisner was taking a bad beating in the next bout. The mayor's eyes never strayed to the ring, but he applauded vociferously—whenever the crowd did.

He turned to his right-hand neighbor.

"Lisner is beating him, isn't he?" said the mayor.

His neighbor looked at him piteously.

"I thought Lisner was the better fighter," said the mayor, satisfied, looking eagerly around for someone to shake hands with.

At the end of the fight the referee consulted with the three judges and hoisted a hand of Lisner's opponent as a sign of victory. The mayor stood up.

"I'm glad Lisner won!" he remarked enthusiastically.

"Is that really the mayor?" asked the man next to me.

"That is His Worship, the Sporting Mayor," I replied.

"Down in front!" yelled the man next to me, in a rough voice.

It looked as though the mayor enjoyed the last bout best of all. Of course, he didn't see it, but he discovered several people he had not shaken hands with, and also there was a great deal of booing and cheering. Sometimes the mayor would absent-mindedly boo when the crowd cheered but he always righted himself instinctively at once. He seemed able to shift a boo into a cheer with the same ease and grace of shoving a Ford into low gear.

At the close of the fights the Mayor absent-mindedly said, "Meeting's dismissed," and dashed for his motorcar, thinking he was at a City Council meeting.

The mayor is just as interested in hockey as he is in boxing. If cootie fighting or Swedish pinochle or Australian boomerang hurling are ever taken up by the voters, count on the mayor to be there in a ringside seat. For the mayor loves all sport.

Popular in Peace—Slacker in War

☆ THE TORONTO STAR WEEKLY
March 13, 1920

During the late friction with Germany a certain number of Torontonians of military age showed their desire to assist in the conduct of the war by emigrating to the States to give their all to laboring in munition plants. Having amassed large quantities of sheckels through their patriotic labor, they now desire to return to Canada and gain fifteen percent on their United States money.

Through a desire to aid these morally courageous souls who supplied the sinews of war we have prepared a few hints on "How to Be Popular Although a Slacker."

It were wise, of course, for the returning munitioneer to come back to a different town than the one he left. Citizens of his own city might have misunderstood his motives in exposing himself to the dangers of the munition works.

The first difficulty to be surmounted will be the C.E.F. [Canadian Expeditionary Force] overseas badge. This is easily handled, however. If anyone asks you why you do not wear your button, reply haughtily: "I do not care to advertise my military service!"

This reply will make the man who was out since Mons and is brazenly wearing his button feel very cheap.

When you are asked by a sweet young thing at a dance if you ever met Lieut. Smithers, of the R.A.F., in France or if you happened to run into Maj. MacSwear, of the C.M.R.'s, merely say "No," in a distant tone. That will put her in her place, and, besides, it is all that any of us can say.

A good plan is to go to one of the stores handling secondhand army goods and purchase yourself a trench coat. A trench coat worn in wintertime is a better advertisement of military service than an M.C. [Military Cross]. If you cannot get a trench coat buy a pair of army shoes. They will convince everyone you meet on a streetcar that you have seen service.

The trench coat and the army issue shoes will admit you at once into that camaraderie of returned men which is the main result we obtained from the war. Your far-seeing judgment in going to the States is now vindicated, you have all the benefits of going to war and none of its drawbacks.

A very good plan would be to learn the tunes of "Mademoiselle from Armentières" and "Madelon." Whistle these religious ballads as you stand in the back platform of the streetcar and you will be recognized by all as a returned man. Unless you are of hardy temperament do not attempt to learn the words of either of those two old hymns.

Buy or borrow a good history of the war. Study it carefully and you will be able to talk intelligently on any part of the front. In fact, you will more than once be able to prove the average returned veteran a pinnacle of inaccuracy if not unveracity. The average soldier has a very abominable memory for names and dates. Take advantage of this. With a little conscientious study you should be able to prove to the man who was at first and second Ypres that he was not there at all. You, of course, are aided in this by the similarity of one day to another in the army. This has been nobly and fittingly expressed by the recruiting sergeant in these words: "Every day in the army is like Sunday on the farm."

Now that you have firmly established by suggestion your status as an ex-army man and possible hero the rest is easy. Be modest and unassuming and you will have no trouble. If anyone at the office addresses you as "major" wave your hand, smile deprecatingly and say, "No; not quite major."

After that you will be known to the office as captain.

Now you have service at the front, proven patriotism and a commission firmly established, there is only one thing left to do. Go to your room alone some night. Take your bankbook out of your desk and read it through. Put it back in your desk.

Stand in front of your mirror and look yourself in the eye and remember that there are fifty-six thousand Canadians dead in France and Flanders. Then turn out the light and go to bed.

Store Thieves' Tricks

☆ THE TORONTO STAR WEEKLY
April 3, 1920

If you enter a department store carrying a bag of candy, an umbrella or wheeling a baby carriage you may become an object of suspicion. After you have entered if a clerk or floorwalker calls out "Two-Ten" you may know that the suspicion has crystallized and that you are regarded as a potential shoplifter.

Shoplifting or unorganized stealing by amateur thieves is one of the big problems of the merchandiser, according to the head of one of the biggest department stores in Toronto. Department stores lose three percent of their sales through thieving from the counters, this merchant states.

The candy bag, umbrella and baby carriage tricks are some of the standard schemes of the shoplifter. The facility with which they can be worked makes anyone possessing the properties for the trick a suspicious character to the department store clerk.

In the operation of the candy bag for obtaining merchandise, a woman stands along the counter displaying rings and cheap jewelry as though she were waiting for someone and dips into her candy bag. Her hand goes from the candy bag to her mouth. But on the downward trip something from the counter goes into the bag. The movement is so simple and unsuspicious that it is almost impossible of detection. Hence the lynx-eyed manner in which the candy-bag toter is scanned.

There is nothing subtle about the umbrella method. It merely consists in entering the store with an empty umbrella and leaving with a full one.

Two women, a baby and a baby carriage are requisites for the success of the baby-carriage trick.

One woman wheels the baby carriage and does a bit of shopping. The other removes articles from the counter, telling the clerk she wishes to show them to another woman who is with her. Whatever is taken is placed in the baby cab under the baby, who is an unconscious accessory both before and after the fact.

The woman returns to the counter while the clerk's attention is distracted and says that she has replaced the article. Flat bolts of lace are the things most often taken in this way. With a pile of them on the counter the clerk cannot tell if they have been replaced. With baby seated happily on the loot, it is calmly rolled out of the store.

"Two-Ten," which sounds to the uninitiated like the call for a cash girl, clerk or floorwalker, is the signal given by anyone in the store when they see a suspicious-looking person enter. It means "Keep your eyes on her ten fingers."

In addition to amateur merchandise stealers, the big stores are confronted with the problem of organized gangs of thieves who work department stores throughout the States and the Dominion. Four is the usual number for a shoplifting team.

They arrive in a town and wait until clerks are advertised for by some big store. Two of the quartet take positions as clerks and the rest is easy. It is simply a matter of how much of the contents of the store they can deliver to the outsiders who play the role of customers.

These professionals have such a variety of artifices that they are very successful. The great success of their scheme, however, lies in its essential simplicity.

Floorwalkers and store managers have one almost infallible way of detecting theft among the clerks. It is an application of the old platitude, "A guilty conscience needeth no accuser." If a clerk follows the floorwalker with her eyes it almost invariably develops that she is stealing. She must watch the floorwalker to prevent his surprising her in some irregularity—and if she does watch him she is gone.

Although women make up the majority of offenders at amateur shoplifting, boys also do quite a bit of thieving. Pocket knives and perfumes are the most common articles taken by the younger generation. They are readily vendable.

It is interesting to note, too, that the head of the Toronto Juvenile Court recently asked one of the Toronto stores to take Ford ignition keys off their counters. Boys were buying them and then unlocking parked Ford cars and taking them for joyrides.

"There are no such people as kleptomaniacs," said a department store head. "At least, we have never run into a genuine klep. All of the people who steal from us have stolen the stuff because they wanted it or the money it would bring.

"The thieving is divided into two classes, amateur and professional. The amateurs are usually given another chance and released. We try to send the professionals to prison. But never in all my experience with thousands of shoplifters have I encountered a kleptomaniac."

Trout Fishing

☆ THE TORONTO STAR WEEKLY
April 10, 1920

Spring is only spring to the majority of the city dwellers.

There are no more coal bills, but the little car needs a couple of new casings. We won't trade it in after all this year. There is an Easter hat and a spring suit for the wife and the old kelly [hat] will have to do another season.

The kids are playing marbles and jumprope in the street, and in the evening when the office toiler walks home from the car line he has a wordless feeling that things aren't right. He feels that he wasn't meant for this, and that somehow if things had gone differently he wouldn't be doing just this. But that doesn't last long, for shortly he is home.

To those that are beloved of the Red Gods, spring is more than that. It is the opening of the trout-fishing season.

If you are a common or garden variety of angler you have a vision of a deep, dark hole where the waters of the creek disappear in a black swirl under the bole of an overhanging tree. Someone is crouching out of sight on the bank and looping worms onto a hook. That is you. Then you gently swing the gob of worms out onto the water and lowering the tip of your rod let the bait sink into that swirl under the cedar. The line straightens with a jerk. You strike and swing the steel rod back over your head, then there is a struggle and the trout is flopping on the bank behind you.

For that kind of fishing you need an outfit that costs about nine dollars and a half. A good steel rod nine and a half feet long will set you back about five dollars. A half-dozen three-foot gut leaders will be a dollar. Twenty-five yards of excellent bait line can be purchased for another dollar. Any reel will do around two dollars as you don't need to do any casting with it. A box of number four Carlisle hooks, one hundred in a box, won't be more than a quarter.

With that outfit you are equipped for bait fishing on any type of stream that you have to "horse" the trout out of. Horsing is a technical term for that free arm motion that causes the trout to suddenly desert the stream he has been born and raised in and go for a flying trip through the air. It is the only method of landing trout in streams that are so brushy and clogged with snags that it is impossible to play them.

Worms are the bait for the early part of the season. Use plenty of them and keep your bait fresh.

Some bait fishermen will say that a leader is an affectation and tie the hook directly to the line. But a leader will mean bigger fish. A leader is invisible in the water and the old sockdologers that will barely sniff at a bait on the end of a line will hit a seemingly unattached gob of worms like a flash.

At this time of year the trout are in the holes in the smaller streams. The drains through culverts on the nearby streams often harbor the very largest trout. In the evening and in the early morning trout will be feeding in the shallows—but the deep pools and hollows under the banks are the very best bets in the daytime.

The bait fisherman's best time is the early spring. The fly fisherman comes into his own in the later spring and summer.

Just now he is contributing to the prevailing unrest of labor owing to a vision of a certain stream that obsesses him.

It is clear and wide with a pebbly bottom and the water is the color of champagne. It makes a bend and narrows a bit and the water rushes like a millrace. Sticking up in the middle of the stream is a big boulder and the water makes a swirl at its base.

A man in hip boots with a landing net hanging under his left shoulder by an elastic cord is standing in the rushing current and studying what appears to be a big red morocco pocketbook.

The man is the fly fisherman, and what he is looking at while his fairy light wand of a rod rests straight up in the top of his hip boot is his fly book. A snipe lights on the boulder and looks inquiringly at the fly fisherman and then flies jerkily up the stream. But the fly fisherman does not see him for he is engaged in the most important thing in the world. Deciding on his cast for the first day on the stream.

Finally he bends on two flies. One on the end of the leader and one about three feet up. I'd tell you what flies they were, but every fly fisherman in Toronto would dispute the choice. With me though they are going to be a Royal Coachman and a McGinty.

The fairy rod waves back and forth and then shoots out and the flies drop at the head of the swirl by the big boulder. There is a twelve-inch flash of flame out of water, the flyfisher strikes with a wrist like a steel trap, the rod bends, and the first trout of the season is hooked.

Those are the two kinds of trout fishing. Ontario affords the very best of both kinds. I would go on and write some more. But there are too many trout fishermen in Toronto. The city would be paralyzed. Imagine the havoc in offices and families if they all left the city tomorrow.

Everything would be tied up, from the streetcars to the Parliament House.

Besides, I can't write any more just now. I'm going trout fishing.

Tooth Pulling No Cure-All

☆ THE TORONTO STAR WEEKLY
April 10, 1920

To the mind of the man in the street the practice of medicine is swayed by a series of fads. A few years ago we all had appendicitis. More recently we all were the unwilling victims of tonsils and adenoids. Still more recently it seemed to the layman that blood pressure controlled all things. At present it seems that all the ills that flesh is heir to can be traced to our teeth.

But that does not mean that to achieve health we must become an appendixless, tonsilless and toothless race. Removal of any of those centers of infection is the very last thing to do. We ran through the appendix and tonsil period and now to the layman it seems that we are in the midst of an era of X-rays and tooth pulling.

It is a fact that there is in the United States an organization of dentists known as the One Hundred Percent Club, who extract every tooth where the root is infected. On the other extreme are the dentists who try and save every infected tooth.

The middle course of saving all the teeth that are possible to keep, and only extracting when it is the only possible plan, in the sane one, according to a leading Toronto dentist.

"All movements swing like a pendulum," he said. "They go to one extreme and then return to the other. The only safe plan is to use common sense and sanity."

According to the Mayo brothers, world-famous surgeons of Rochester, Minnesota, ninety percent of all infections of the body are located above the collar. In the Mayos' hospital all teeth with infected roots are extracted simply to eliminate the possibility of infection.

Infection starts on the outside of a tooth in a little gelatinous globule. This may not be removed by the toothbrush, which would merely pass through the clot of germs and separate them but not remove them.

The waste products which this colony of active germs produce form lactic acid which, with the germs, dissolves the tissue and eats its way up the tooth. The germs finally enter the roots where a pocket is formed which the dentists call a rarefied area.

It is these pockets at the root of the teeth which contain millions of disease-breeding germs which the dentists locate through the X-ray.

The X-ray is not infallible, according to the dentists. Too many dentists accept the X-ray picture as final and order the tooth pulled. The X-ray should only be one step in the diagnosis. It may show almost anything, depending upon the angle from which it is taken and the skill of the dentist who is reading it.

As soon as a pocket is discovered at the root of the tooth, the hundred percenter orders the tooth pulled. He does this because it has been discovered that in these pockets are germs which enter the circulation and go to every part of the body. They are called selective germs. That is, each one has some particular part of the body which it affects.

The pus pocket at the root of the tooth may send germs out into the blood which will attack the kidneys, heart or spleen. The pus which forms in the pocket burrows back into the tissue, providing a better opportunity for the germs to circulate and eventually reaches the gum, where it forms what is known to the layman as a gum boil.

To one dentist, as soon as the X-ray reveals an infected area, the only course to follow is to have the tooth out. The careful dentist, however, ascertains whether the root of the tooth is dead or not. If the root is alive he does not have the tooth pulled, but by a system of drainage and irrigation clears up the infection at the root, syringes out the pocket and saves the tooth.

The greatest weapon in combating infection is general good health. There was an era of germicides. Many mouthwashes were manufactured to be used to kill the germs in the mouth. We were supposed to rinse our mouths with some well-advertised wash and leave it like a battlefield after the assault with dead germs lying in heaps.

It is an absolute fallacy to suppose that we can kill the germs in our mouths with germicides, according to the dentist. There is nothing that we can put into our mouths strong enough to kill germs that will stand ten minutes' boiling. The germ will always be with us.

Living a healthy life, keeping up our resistance, keeps the germs under control. They are like seed which is planted in different kinds of soil. If the soil is rocky and arid they cannot take hold. But if it is soft and favorable they flourish. Living a healthy life is the way to combat all disease.

Lieutenants' Mustaches

☆ THE TORONTO STAR WEEKLY
April 10, 1920

Two returned men stood gazing up in infinite disgust at a gang of workmen tearing down a building on King Street.

"They've been pecking at that for two weeks," observed the first, who wore a maple leaf with the First Division insignia in his lapel as he spat into the street.

"War ain't taught them nothin', Jack," said the other veteran, looking up at the workmen knocking the bricks out one by one. "Stokes gun would do up that job in no time."

"Or they could mount a six-inch how at the corner and it sure wouldn't take two weeks to finish the job," Jack suggested.

"We ain't efficient ourselves, Jack. None of them we've named are the real house wreckers. It ought to be bombed. Have a couple of eggs dropped on it at night when the streets are clear. They'd flatten her. I seen Jerry come over—" Bill was getting reminiscent, so Jack changed the subject.

"No, Bill. We didn't get nothing permanent good out of the war except the lieutenant's mustaches. Plenty of them about."

"And from the look of the big stores on Saturday, the women are mighty well applying it that Canadians are storm troops," countered Bill.

"They ain't the only ones as knows that, either. Why, I remember once at Vimy—" It was Bill's turn to choke Jack off.

"Here's our car. Say Jack—" They clung to the arms and legs of the crowd on the rear platform. "They got these out of the war all right enough. Remember 40 hommes ou 8 chevaux?"

"I rather well do. Why once on leave train we was—" Bill interrupted quickly, shouting above the roar of the tram.

"Ran into a not half bad one the other night, Jack. Out to my sister's there was a young fellow. Returned boy he was; had kind of a sentimental turn. He looked kind of familiar but I couldn't quite place him. I was in the other room readin' the paper and he was talkin' with my sister's friend. 'Betty,' says he mournful like, 'this is the way I feel,' and he recited that thing by this Kipling bloke. 'Me that has been what I've been. Me that 'as seen what I've seen—' you know how it goes. Well, when he come to the place where it goes 'Me that stuck out to the last—' I recognized him. Know who he was?"

"No. Who was he?" Jack shouted back.

"Used to be batman to the R.T.O. at Boulogne," grunted Bill, as a milling passenger stepped on his pet corn.

Fashion Graveyards

☆ THE TORONTO STAR WEEKLY
April 24, 1920

Big department stores cannot obtain insurance against changes of styles. If they did not devise some scheme to protect themselves against shifts in the public taste, merchandisers would be constantly in danger of being crowded with unsalable "Hyline" coats, "Pinchback" suits or other passing favorites.

Anyone who has tried to purchase a particular model of coat which happened to be suitable but at present is out of style, knows that it is impossible to do so in the big city stores. Do the departmentals and men's furnishing houses sell all the goods they buy? What becomes of the old styles and the unsuccessful styles? Those are the questions the would-be purchaser asks.

The answer is that all good styles when they die go to the country. Because they cannot get insurance against changing fancy of the city public, every large furnishing house has an outlet established in some smaller city in the mining district, bush or country.

In some towns like Sudbury a furnishing house advertises that all their goods are direct from Toronto. They are, too, but the Sudburian or Cobaltese who imagines he is buying the latest Toronto models is really purchasing all the unsalable clothes of one of our furnishing houses.

In towns as near as Sudbury clothes would be only a little way out of style. Far back in the wilds is where the real old-timers will be vended.

There you will see a little false-front store advertising a New York, Toronto or Chicago connection, whose very latest creations will be "Mack Machinaw's, the Kind They Are Wearing on Broadway," or "Be in Style, Wear Peg Top Trousers."

Those little stores on the edge of things are the real graveyard of dead styles.

Trout-Fishing Hints

☆ THE TORONTO STAR WEEKLY
April 24, 1920

Sporting magazines have fostered a popular fiction to the effect that no gentleman would catch a trout in any manner but on a fly on a nine-foot tapered leader attached to a double-tapered fly line cast from a forty-five-dollar four-and-a-half-ounce rod.

There is reason for this putting of trout fishing into the class of a rich man's diversions. Outdoor magazines are supported by their advertising. The advertisers are putting out expensive goods suited to the under-stocked, over-fished streams of the Eastern United States where only fly fishing is allowed. So the sporting writers pound their typewriters in praise of the fine and far-off fishing of streams like the Beaverskill and Esopus, whose fame is built on the catches of twenty years ago and take every opportunity to stigmatize the bait fisherman.

The old-timer, firmly implanted in the seat of the scornful, reads the twaddle of the American trout-fishing critics and smiles. He knows the comparative value of bait and fly. He knows that at certain seasons the fly is a far more killing lure than any natural bait. And he knows that on some streams the fly will catch only small trout. He also knows that bait fishing for trout with light tackle and a leader is as sportsmanlike as fly fishing, that it is the only practical method on thousands of streams and that day in and day out through the season it will catch infinitely larger trout in exactly as sportsmanlike a way as fly fishing.

Worms, grubs, beetles, crickets and grasshoppers are some of the best trout baits. But worms and hoppers are those most widely used.

There are three kinds of earthworms. Two of them are good for trout fishing and the third is absolutely useless. The big night crawlers come out of their holes in the grass in the night, and enough for a good canful can be easily picked up after dark with the aid of a flashlight. They are really too large and thick for trout bait and are much better for bass, but are far better than nothing.

Common angleworms are easy to get in the spring but are sometimes impossible to find in a long dry spell in the summer. They can be dug after a rain and kept alive in a big box full of earth until they are needed.

A large quantity of worms can be transported a long way by keeping them in a small tin pail full of moist coffee grounds. Coffee grounds stay moist and keep the worms much better than earth, which dries and does not absorb the water evenly. Too much water will kill the garden hackles as quickly as not enough. Worms kept in coffee grounds will be clean and fresh for fishing.

Pale yellowish worms which are found under manure piles look like angleworms, but are really a distinct species. They have an offensive odor and taste and trout do not like them.

The novice at trout fishing with worms needs to know a few general rules, but in the main he must work out his own destiny as every stream differs. The following rules are applicable everywhere, however.

Always approach a hole cautiously so as not to frighten the trout.

Never let your shadow fall over a hole.

Use plenty of bait and keep the point and shank of your hook covered.

Remember that the most difficult places to get your bait into are the most likely to contain big trout. Other people will have fished the easy holes.

Watch the line at the tip of your pole. As soon as it straightens the least bit, strike with your wrist. Don't wait for a jerk before striking.

Always drop your bait a little before the head of a hole and then lower the tip of your rod so that the current will roll your bait naturally into the hole.

Little wrinkles like those make the difference between getting a small and foolish trout who will strike at anything out of a hole and fooling some big old-timer that will only strike at a bait that is absolutely natural.

Worms are best used on the small, brushy creeks, full of logs and deep holes that must be fished from the banks. They are superior to grasshoppers on streams that must be fished from the bank because if there are hoppers in the grass along the stream they are stirred up by the fisherman and a number usually land in the stream. The trout will take a free hopper swirling down the current every time in preference to one attached to a leader.

On streams that can be waded grasshoppers are the premier bait. They are cast exactly as a fly, except that you try and minimize the snap to avoid whipping off the bait.

Trout rise to a hopper far more readily than they do to a fly, and they are bigger trout. If you want to insure catching big trout, put three good-sized hoppers on the hook. Put the hook in under the chin of the grasshopper and carry it back through the thorax. A triple hopper bait is too large for the smaller trout to hit, and tempts the old whangle berries.

The big difficulty about fishing the grasshoppers has always been the difficulty of catching them. The classic way is to get up early in the morning before the sun has dried the dew, and catch the hoppers while they are still stiff and cold and unable to hop more than a feeble foot or two. They are found under the side of logs in a clearing and along the grass stems.

Any fisherman who has chased a lively grasshopper in the heat of the day will appreciate the method of catching them invented by Jacques Pentecost, an old-time north shore trout fisher.

In a clearing or around an old lumber camp where hoppers usually abound, they can be obtained in plentiful quantities by the Pentecost method. Let two men each hold the end of a ten-yard strip of mosquito netting and run into the wind with it. The netting bellies out like a seine, and the grasshoppers flying downwind are soon swarming in the net seine, which is held only a few inches above the ground. Then you flop the netting together and pick the hoppers out and put them in your hopper bottles. This method takes all the labor out of hopper catching.

Grubs, beetles of all kinds, hornet grubs, trout fins, chunks of liver from a partridge or duck are all emergency baits that will catch trout when you are in the bush and cannot get worms or hoppers.

Muddlers, or miller's thumbs, little flat-headed minnows that look like miniature catfish, are very killing baits for big trout. They live under rocks in fast water, and are very difficult to catch.

The usual method is to go after them with a small dip net or a fork fastened to a stick, and try to spear them or scoop them up as they shoot out when you turn the rocks over.

An unfortunate experience wherein I speared my big toe, mistaking it for a muddler in the rapids of the Black River, has prejudiced me against them.

All those baits will catch trout. If you are fishing with a light rod and a leader, the trout has exactly the same chance as though you were fly fishing. In addition you are at least giving the trout something for his money—if he gets away he has a good meal instead of just a memory of tinsel and feathers. And when you are fishing with grasshoppers you will find that unless you have a wrist that is two shades quicker than an otter trap, you will present the trout with a lot of free meals this summer.

Buying Commission Would Cut Out Waste

☆ THE TORONTO DAILY STAR
April 26, 1920

The present government system of purchasing supplies is comparable to having every engineer on the C.P.R. negotiate for the coal, water and oil for his own engine, said Ralph Connable today.

Mr. Connable, who heads the Woolworth Company in Canada, at the request of the War Purchasing Commission, made a thorough investigation of the system of buying supplies for the twenty or more departments of the Dominion Government with instructions to apply business methods and put the department on an efficient basis.

According to Mr. Connable, each department is now buying supplies in utter ignorance of what the others are doing. The Post Office Department, Customs Office Department, Departments of Justice and Militia all buy their own equipment without any knowledge of what the other is purchasing. This is as wasteful of money as though each section boss of a railway negotiated for his own rails and ties and each station agent bought his own oil, soap and brooms, printed his own timetables and built the particular type of station he most admired.

One of the disadvantages of the present system is that the departments generally do not get the benefit of the technical knowledge and experience acquired in each department. This and a number of other faults that aid in the operation of the patronage system, but that cost the public hundreds of thousands of dollars, would be done away with by centralization of the purchasing.

For example, the quantities of goods demanded by some of the departments are not sufficient to enable them to purchase at the lowest wholesale price. Centralizing would make all the goods be bought together and combining the purchases of the departments in one would make a sufficient quantity to get the rock-bottom wholesale price.

Now there is no uniform standard as to sizes and qualities for the different departments. Thus each may demand a certain size envelope or certain quality of form. Adoption of standard sizes alone would save enormously.

Departments bidding against each other for supplies have raised prices materially. Lack of standardized inspection has been another difficulty.

Mr. Connable advocates forming a Central Purchasing Staff such as that headed by Sir Hormidas Laporte, the late W.P. Gundy and Galt, of Winnipeg, during the war. This staff would handle all the purchasing stock from budgets made up by each department the first of the year. Thus they would be able to take advantage of market conditions as all big commercial houses do.

Each department should have a requisition clerk to look after the interests of the department, to handle emergency orders, and to act as a medium of quick communication between the department and the commission. Having him an employee of the commission would be a quick red-tape cutter.

Even if the men in charge of the purchasing commission were paid $10,000 to $25,000 a year salaries there would be a net gain of millions to the government by stopping the present wasteful system of uncontrolled buying. It is necessary to pay good salaries to get men above the influence of political pull and patronage.

An advisory board of such men as Harry McGee, R.Y. Eaton, H.J. Daly and J. Allen Ross should be appointed to serve without pay and give the new commission the benefit of their experience during the first two or three years of its life. Management of this kind would turn the purchasing department from the haphazard, muddling, wasteful squanderer of public money that it is today into a compact business organization that will get the public the best value for every dollar it spends.

Car Prestige

☆ THE TORONTO STAR WEEKLY
May 1, 1920

This deals with the Other Half. The Other Half, you know, is that stratum of society from which any of us have just now emerged. We have magazine articles on How the Other Half Lives, How the Other Half Eats. And so on. All the doings of the Half are chronicled by faithful observers. Anything the Half does is interesting.

Of course, most of us would never admit having emerged from anything. We all cherish a fond delusion that we have sunk to this present level.

Look at our grandfather! Or if by chance he should be living, look at our great-grandfather. There was a man for you. All great-grandfathers are enveloped in a mantle of romantic gentility.

If our great-grandfather isn't a great man, it is our own fault. We can go as far as we like with him. Nobody can prove us wrong.

Almost the first thing a newly minted millionaire acquires is a genealogy. This is expensive but it is bound in leather and titled "History of the Kale Family." No one ever reads it, of course, but it goes backward through a series of begats to some suitable and defenseless ancestor selected for the millionaire by the genealogist.

This is a fine thing for the millionaire, for it gives him the feeling common to all of us that he had a great-great-great-great-grandfather who was a greater man than he was. Thus the millionaire, whose father may have run a soap boiler, enjoys that feeling of having come down in the world and always thinks of himself as a decayed gentleman.

To the millionaire, we are all the Other Half. There are just two classes of people, he and others. To the rest of us, humanity is divided into a greater number of classes.

The present social scale seems to be dictated by the motorcar. All of Toronto is divided into those with and those without. To those with, those without are the Other Half. They have been much spoken of in various Other Half books.

First in the scale of the new feudal system comes the Fordowner. The Fordowner has just got under the wire in the race for social supremacy.

Every Fordowner has one ambition, to cease to be a Fordowner. This is not because he is dissatisfied with his car but because all Fordowners are looked upon as the Other Half by those who possess cars with a different type of gear shift.

Of course there is the case-hardened type of Fordowner who declares that the little car is good enough for him. She'll pull through anything and it doesn't bankrupt a man to buy a new casing once in a while. No big cars for him. But steal a glance at the look in his eye when a McSwizzle Light Four goes by.

As soon as a man leaves the Fordowner class he is lost. From then on it is a mad race until he achieves a Rice-Rolls or the grave. The most cautious bookmaker would lay thirty to one on the grave. But the ex-Fordowner is not daunted. He smashes into the race.

His easiest time is during his service in the medium-priced car class. There are a number of cars of about the same price and the man and his wife who own a Choochoolay feel themselves on terms of equality with the possessors of Overseas Darts and other cars of about the same voltage.

This time is one of comparative comfort. The Choochoolay owner refers affectionately to his car as "a good little wagon." He contemplates trading it in next year for another of the same make. He has a comfortable disdain for Fordowners and We Who Walk. Then the blow falls.

Jones across the street, who is not earning a cent more than he is, has a McSwizzle Light Six. Mrs. Jones tells his wife about it. All unsuspecting, he arrives home from the office in the good old Choochoolay only to be confronted by the fact that it is doomed. Jones has started the race. Perhaps it was Mrs. Jones who put him up to it, but at any rate no one in the Choochoolay set can be comfortable any longer. Jones has a McSwizzle.

Once out of the Choochoolay class there is no more peace before the achievement of a Rice-Rolls or Rose Hill. Buying a McSwizzle Light is like stepping into the rapids above Niagara. Once in, you must go the pace.

Of course he has moments of triumph, as when he first owns a Delusion-Demountable. But the Delusion-Demountable is three hundred dollars cheaper than a Complex Collapsible, and the Browns have just purchased a Complex. The Complex is a good car and it is a far cry to the first motor. He is a changed man, for a man changes with his cars. He is making much more money, too. He has to or face bankruptcy. In fact he is so successful that one night after dinner the Mrs. broaches the subject of a Pierced-Sparrow.

Going from even such a car as the Complex Collapsible to a Pierced-Sparrow is only comparable to the initial jump out of the Fordowner class. A Pierced-Sparrow is the insignia of success. In our modern system of civilization the Pierced-Sparrow takes the place of the heads that our ancestors used to dry in the smoke of their hut fires. In the Pierced-Sparrow are concentrated all the scalps of his business competitors. It is better than the accolade. He thinks that if he has a Pierced-Sparrow it will mean that he has arrived in the elect.

So he buys a Pierced-Sparrow, unhappy man! As soon as he has the Pierced-Sparrow he discovers that a great many other people have them too. Then one day at the club he overhears this conversation:

"What kind of a car has he?" asks the first gentleman.

"Pierced-Sparrow," replies the second, blowing a cloud of smoke.

"Upper Middle Class people, eh?" says the first comfortably.

It is the beginning of the end. The ex-Fordowner has achieved business success. He has raised a son who knows more than his father. He has a daughter who smokes cigarettes and has been a successful debutante for eight years. He has enough servants to make him uncomfortable. You would imagine that he would be happy. But he is not.

He makes one last desperate effort to escape from the Other Half. He buys a Rice-Rolls. He can't afford it, of course. But it is necessary for his self-respect. The Rice-Rolls is the ultimate.

Now if this were comedy we would leave him in happiness riding through life in his Rice-Rolls, having attained the true happiness of success. His chauffeur might even let him drive his Rice-Rolls sometimes. Nothing would be lacking. His son would know more every day and his daughter would learn to roll her own. But this is tragedy.

There is no peace for him this side of the sepulcher. We have reliable information from England that a super-car is being brought out which will cost at least four times as much as the Rice-Rolls. The curtain falls upon the tragedy of How the Other Half Lives.

Prizefight Women

☆ THE TORONTO STAR WEEKLY
May 15, 1920

Toronto women were present at prizefights for the first time last Saturday night. A press agent story said there would be four hundred boxes filled with members of society attending the bouts in evening clothes. There really were about a hundred women present.

They came ostensibly to see Georges Carpentier give a sparring exhibition. In reality they saw a series of gladiatorial combats and they smiled and applauded through it all. For the benefit of those Toronto women who do not attend prizefights, this is what they saw, and this is how they acted.

In the center of the floor of the Arena is a raised platform with a square of roped-off space. Rows of seats are banked on each side of the ring. A number of women were sprinkled among the men who occupied these ringside places. More women were scattered in the boxes along the side of the ring.

Two women sat just behind me at the ringside with their escorts.

"They wear gloves so they can't hurt each other," one of the men explained to his girl.

In the first bout a young stockily built Jewish boy in about a minute and a half clouted into insensibility a much smaller, weaker and inexperienced lad from Hamilton. The little kid never had a chance against his huskier opponent, who smashed him around the roped enclosure from the clang of the gong, and finally hit him hard enough so that he stayed on the floor. It was not a display of skill, of science nor of nerve. It was simply a case of a larger, stronger kid knocking a smaller and weaker kid unconscious. It was not a pretty sight.

"My, that one was over quickly!" said one of the women back of me, with obvious disappointment.

"I'll say it was," exulted her partner. "Young Lisner sure clouted that baby plenty."

The second so-called boxing bout was even shorter. A hard-faced, heavily muscled slugger with a reputation for cowardice was in one corner. A big, fat, lubberly chap, who looked as though he had never been in a ring before, occupied the other.

As the gong rang the craggy-faced slugger shot out of his corner. The dub made an awkward attempt to put up his hands. The slugger swung his right fist in a deadly semicircle to the dub's jaw, and the fight was over. The fat, untrained dub crashed on his face on the resined canvas. When his seconds pulled him over to his corner, the canvas had sandpapered most of the skin off one side of his face. The slugger had knocked out the set-up provided to get him back into the good graces of his hometown as a fighter.

He spat on the floor, assumed a "look what I've done to that guy" expression, and walked out of the ring and climbed down the platform.

Everyone applauded, including the ladies.

"He hit him pretty hard, didn't he?" said one of the women.

"I hope ta tell ya he did," answered her partner gleefully.

Over in his corner the dub's handlers were working over him, sponging the blood off his sandpapered face and bringing him back to his senses with cold water. It was not a pretty sight.

It was during the fourth bout between a hard-hitting, perfectly conditioned little Toronto fighting machine named Benny Gould and a willing, nervous youth from Buffalo who was proving himself a good bleeder that the women's attention was distracted from the ring. A box party of prominent Torontonians entered and settled themselves in the box. Every woman in the Arena eyed them in a quick attempt to identify the ladies of the party whose coming gave social sanction to their own presence.

Just then the willing bleeder from Buffalo landed his first blows of the fight, and there was a burst of applause. The slender kid with the badly smashed face was fighting back like a tiger and soon had young Gould's face bloody. But he was outclassed by the more experienced boxer, who continued to batter him till the end of the fight.

The society box party smiled and applauded all through the fight. But the hardened fans at the ringside, while they applauded the game fight the Buffalo kid was making, did not smile. For they could see the terrific punishment he was taking. They watched the way Gould kept smashing his left fist onto the kid's broken nose. They knew the way Gould's punches were weakening the kid. They admired his game fight but they did not smile. But the ladies in the box party smiled every minute.

In the old days at the Colosseum in Rome the ex-gladiators and their pals who sat at the side of the arena applauded the deadly thrusts. They clapped when a swing of the cestus bashed in a Cisalpine gladiator's face. They may have cheered when the man with the fishnet and the trident entangled his opponent with the short sword and they clapped when he finished him with a few well-placed thrusts of the spear. But they didn't laugh. They knew what it meant.

"He jests at scars who never felt a wound." And as on last Saturday night the laughter was reserved for the nobility.

Then the champion of Europe and the idol of France, with a name that is pronounced as many ways as Ypres used to be, danced through four rounds with his sparring partner. The sparring partner was evidently selected because of his startling facial likeness to a certain Mr. Jack Dempsey. His name is Laniers, pronounced Lanears by the referee and he lets M. Carpentier hit him about two hundred and fifty times during the course of the entertainment.

Carpentier showed the ladies present that he has a nice taste in dressing gowns, two hands that strike as fast as cobras, and a rather good-looking face. He got into the ring, stood at attention while the "Marseillaise" was played and then slapped, poked, jabbed, stabbed, jolted, hooked and biffed Lanaers around the ring for four short rounds. Then he left the ring and went home.

But did any of the ladies who had come only to see Georges Carpentier leave after he had made his exit? They did not. They stayed and cheered while chubby Bobby Eber of Hamilton clouted Toronto's gamest and toughest featherweight around the ring for six rounds. And the two ladies who sat back of me were several times distinctly heard yelling for a knockout.

Is it the magic name Arena that brings back to the alleged gentler sex their old Roman attributes? Lecky, the historian, says that the majority of the old gladiatorial crowds were women.

Madame Carpentier wasn't there though. Her husband is a fighter and she knows what it means. So she stayed home and waited for Georges.

Galloping Dominoes

☆ THE TORONTO STAR WEEKLY
May 22, 1920

Prancing Parchesi has invaded the realm of sport of Toronto's smart set. Formerly bridge was the only recognized method of coaxing money out of one pocket into another. Now Mississippi Marbles play the role of the great kale transferer. Galloping Dominoes have at last come into their own in the high life. In short, Toronto society is shooting craps.

The game may have been introduced by some member of the well-tailored staff who in the course of his activities as a conducting officer was brought into forced contact with the hoi polloi. He observed the manner of play with the cubes of certain of the rougher elements of the troops he conducted to England. On his return from the rigors of conducting, to show his familiarity with the lower classes, he introduced the game. It was a kind of slumming at first.

However the game was introduced, it is now firmly established. And now being able to seven easily and graciously on the initial roll is as much a social asset as the ability to negotiate a five-barred gate in good form.

Craps is defined in the dictionary as: "U.S. Local. A game of chance in which the object is to guess the numbers thrown on two dice."

That is what it may have been originally. Now it is international. Starting originally as a Negro game along the Mississippi waterfront, it has spread to every part of the world and is perhaps the most popular game of chance today.

Wherever the Yank has wandered, been sent, or fled to, he has taken the bones with him in the bottom of his tightest pocket. But they haven't remained there. They have come forth to the light and worked for him and spread their peculiar verbiage over most of two hemispheres.

For the benefit of those who are confronted with a succession of crap stories in the magazines, and whose knowledge of the game is only that it has something to do with seven and eleven, it might be explained. Since such highbrow writers as Joseph Hergesheimer have taken to writing crap stories such as his "Read Them and Weep" in a recent *Century Magazine*, it behooves the non-gambling reader to know something of the game purely for literary purposes.

The rudiments of Senegambian Polo are these:

The man rolling the dice decides what stake to put out. This is covered, or faded, by his opponent. The man with the dice then rolls.

He loses on the first roll of the two dice if the spots added together make two, three or twelve. This is called crapping out.

He wins on the initial roll if the numbers of the cubes add to seven or eleven.

If the shooter rolls any other number than those mentioned previously, he rolls again until he either wins by again rolling his first number or loses by rolling a seven.

That is all there is to craps on the surface. But the true crapshooter knows that it is a psychological study, a test of judgment, and that a knowledge of the law of averages is necessary to success. This is not a treatise on "how to shoot craps," but merely a statement of the remarkable way in which a game starting from such a lowly source has spread to such high places. The finer points of crap shooting will not be gone into. However, the dictionary was only half right. Craps is only to a limited extent a game of chance. If you don't believe this, try your luck against an experienced manipulator of the ivories. It shouldn't take him longer than about six passes to convince you that craps is a game of skill.

Toronto society can rest assured that it is not the only smart set that is playing Louisiana Lacrosse. While the gay blades kneel about the tea table and adjure Little Joe to come to father that baby may not be unclothed, they can be comfortable in the knowledge that they are quite *au fait*. For a certain Italian cavalry regiment whose officers rank socially with British Guards officers has been marked with the cloven hoof of the Yank and craps is the regimental passion.

An American consul tells of entering the barracks of the regiment and coming into the high-ceilinged dining hall, the walls lined with cases that contained the trophies of the regiment's glorious history.

Kneeling on the floor of the dining hall in a reverent attitude were three captains, a major and a lieutenant of the Imperial cavalry and a young American sublieutenant.

The colonel was juggling the bones in his hand and addressing them in words the meaning of which he did not know, but whose potency he had often witnessed.

"Leetle Fever! Come to ze Doctor," shouted the colonel, giving the cubes a Latin twist. A five appeared.

"You're faded," said the American, and he and the captain covered the bills that the colonel left on the floor.

The colonel rattled the dice in his hand and then shot them out onto the tiled floor. A ten showed. "Dieci!" said the captain joyfully.

"Beeg Deeck from Bawston!" The colonel caressed the cubes as he picked them up. He fondled them. He blew on them softly. "Reechard ze Lion 'Earted rally round. Wham!"

It was a ten and the consul tiptoed out of the room. He was homesick and he couldn't afford to lose.

Toronto society shouldn't worry, its dalliance with the joy cubes has plenty of precedent. But I hope for their own sake that in their manipulations of the gallopers they never run afoul of a certain colonel of Italian cavalry.

Photo Portraits

☆ THE TORONTO STAR WEEKLY
May 29, 1920

You can pay as much or as little as you wish for a photograph in Toronto and you can have it look as much or as little like you as you wish to.

Strange to say, the less accurate reproduction you want, the more it costs. For twenty-five cents on Yonge Street you can obtain a perfect rogue's gallery likeness while you wait. Every facial attribute will be as plain and distinct as in a life mask. It will be an exact reproduction. But we are not a beautiful race, the unfair sex at least, hence the existence of the artistic photographer.

The announced aim of the artistic photographer is to photograph personality. That is flattering. We observe the wonderful-looking men whose photograph personalities illuminate the windows of the artistic photographers and smile. Perhaps our personality when photographed will look like that.

But you cannot get your personality photographed for twenty-five cents. It costs nearer twenty-five dollars for three good-sized reproductions of a personality. But it is worth it if the photo really shows the true personality.

Showing a personality, as far as we are able to discover, consists in revealing with great clearness the features of people with attractive, good-looking faces and very kindly blurring the rather undesirable countenances of the rest of us. Our own personality is very unkindly concealed behind our face. We have always esteemed it a great privilege to be behind our face rather than in front of it. However, on viewing the wonderful-looking creatures in the window, we thought that perhaps the photographer could do something for us.

So we awaited the proofs with great expectations. There did not seem to be anything very mysterious about the way the photographer took the picture. We sat on a chair and turned when bidden. He arranged some screens for the lights and capped and uncapped the muzzle of the big camera. We were astounded at his consummate artistry. Personalities revealed with that simplicity of technique. It was astounding. We awaited the proofs. As we passed out we stole another glance at the man on the wall with the Eugene O'Brien "Chase me and I won't run" look in his eyes. Perhaps we might even look like that.

Then the proofs came. It was terrible. We have no personality. It was just the face. Blurred artistically to be sure, but the same old face. The same homely but honest countenance that has stared reproachfully at us out of a thousand shaving mirrors looked at us from the proofs.

"You can't get away from me," it seemed to say. "You can blur me all you want to. But I'm the same old face."

As we passed out with the proofs of our personality under our arm we gazed resentfully at the beautiful men on the walls. Evidently the photographer had something to work on there.

There is an innovation in photographing being introduced into Toronto now that holds out hope even for those with a countenance that defies the blurrers of art. The latest fad is miniatures which are painted from photographs and cost from two hundred to five hundred dollars.

In a miniature there is room for latitude. After the artist has blocked in a representation of the subject's facial troubles the subject should be allowed to make suggestions. If your nose is not to your liking, tell the artist so and have the type of Greco-Roman proboscis that you admire included in the miniature.

If you have big ears, suggest to the artist that he reduce the ears to half a column. Select your own type of mouth. In this way we will be able to get a picture of ourselves that really pleases us.

That is the trouble with photographs, even the blurry ones, they are too blamed accurate.

Fox Farming

☆ THE TORONTO STAR WEEKLY
May 29, 1920

Canadian silver fox ranching has been investigated and studied by the Japanese and United States Governments and is rapidly gaining a foothold in those countries. This gives a decided impetus to Dominion fox ranching, says the head of one of the largest fox ranches in Canada.

The United States Government report lists the various States where fox raising is practical and ranches have been started in localities as far separated as Idaho and Illinois. Thirty pairs of foxes were sold a few days ago in the States by one Prince Edward Island fox breeder. All were black foxes worth from $800 to $1,400 a pair. A number of fox-raising companies have been formed in Japan and about twenty-five pairs of silver foxes sent there.

Nearly all the silver fox ranches of Canada are in Prince Edward Island. The climate there is ideal for fur producing. The first ranch in Canada was started in 1902, but the industry was undeveloped until 1909, when a well-organized ranch was founded.

Silver fox farming as a get-rich scheme seized the public fancy and in 1912 and 1913 there was a flood of fake corporations formed to get the public's sheckels. These companies put the silver fox game into disrepute, but meanwhile the legitimate ranchers were going ahead with their fox breeding. The war killed off the fake companies and the present-day fox ranchers are anything but conductors of stock-floating enterprises. At the apex of the boom as much as $18,000 was paid for a pair of breeding foxes. Now the prices rarely run over $1,500.

At present, however, the foxes are really being bred instead of appearing largely in prospectuses. In Prince Edward Island there are about 400 ranches and there are a half-dozen companies that are incorporated at from a half to a quarter of a million dollars.

Silver foxes start as accidents, or casuals, in a litter of red foxes, but they breed true to form. For instance, a red fox may have a silver fox among her cubs, but all the cubs of a silver fox will be silvers.

Fox ranchers only kill the poorest foxes for furs. For in spite of the fabulous prices paid for silver fox furs, with the new scope given the fox-ranching industry the foxes are worth much more to sell for breeding. Furs are graded according to quality and length of hair and fullness of the brush and are shipped to the St. Louis and London fur markets.

Eggs and milk are the principal articles of diet for the young foxes. The older ones are fed fox biscuits and skimmed milk, apples, rabbits and chickens and inspected horse meat.

One of the big problems of the fox ranchers is to prevent stealing. A few years ago there were organized gangs who ranged over the Island and raided the fox ranches. With a fox worth $1,400 as easy to steal as a pullet it was a better business than bank robbing.

Now every ranch has its armed watchman and a pack of bloodhounds. Someone is on guard night and day. In addition, each fox rancher has some system of marking his foxes so that he can positively identify them. These marks are usually branded on the pads of the feet or else the teeth are marked.

An organization of fox ranchers called the Prince Edward Island Fox Breeders' Association is keeping the pedigrees of all silver foxes and standardizing the breeding. They also look after legislation that will help the ranchers.

Rum-Running

☆ THE TORONTO STAR WEEKLY
June 5, 1920

A man living in a small town in Iowa recently paid two hundred and fifty dollars a case for ten cases of Canadian whiskey. They were delivered by motortruck from Detroit. He has more ordered.

Canadian whiskey can be bought by the case from bootleggers in almost all of the Michigan border towns for one hundred and twenty dollars a case. Single quarts cost fifteen dollars. There is plenty of liquor and there are plenty of purchasers and the price seems to be no deterrent.

It is no wonder that the question that is most often asked of an American returning to the States from Canada is, "How long are they going to be able to ship grog out of Canada?"

There is both organized and unorganized rum-running across the border on an unbelievably large scale. Fortunes are being made by the bootleggers who have the liquor shipped to their carefully established residences at Windsor and nearby towns, and then run it across the river to the States. That short trip across the river is one of the most expensive in the world. A case of whiskey, which retails at forty-eight dollars in Windsor, is ferried over to the United States side in a skiff—but as soon as it touches the alien shore its minimum value is automatically one hundred and twenty dollars.

On the train from Toronto to Windsor, I talked with a man who was bringing twenty cases of whiskey to Windsor. He estimated that his profits on the liquor when it was deposited on the United States side would be fourteen hundred and fifty dollars.

"It's a little risk," he said. "We run it all at night in small boats. The revenue agents have motorboat patrols, but we keep out of their way pretty well."

According to this bootlegger the recent story about the electrical torpedo which was said to be shot from Canada to the United States filled with liquor is a pipe dream of some overworked newspaperman. "It is either a straight newspaper fake or else the revenue men started this yarn," declared this man, who ought to know. "There is so much booze coming into Detroit that the revenue gang have to have an alibi somewhere, so they may have framed the torpedo story."

Another bootlegger in Detroit quizzed me about the length of time the importation of liquor between the provinces would be allowed.

"I'm afraid of that referendum. The farmers are liable to cut us off. But if we can have six months more of this, even if I get pinched a couple of times, I'll be able to retire."

All the rum-running is not confined to the cities. You hear tales of lonely shacks along the rocky north shore of Lake Superior, where hundreds of cases of whiskey are stored. You hear of the trapper who invested the savings of a lifetime in liquor that he plans to smuggle into the States this summer. You hear stories of Mackinaw boats manned by Ojibway Indians from around the Garden River district, which stop in at Upper Peninsula [Michigan] ports after dark and are gone in the morning.

You hear of cities like Grand Marais in Upper Michigan, which have been dead for twenty years, that are now coming back to a furtive, silent existence since the passage of the Eighteenth Amendment.

In the cities you see the evidences that there is a liquor traffic between Canada and the States. I saw a slack-lipped, white-faced kid being supported on either side by two scared-looking boys of his own age in an alley outside a theater in Detroit. His face was pasty and his eyes stared unseeingly. He was deathly sick, his arms hanging loosely.

"Where'd he get it?" I asked one of the scared kids.

"Blew in his week's pay for a quart of Canuck bootlegged." The two boys hauled him up the alley. "Come on, we got to get him out of here before the cops see him."

If the people who talk about "good liquor" could see a kid drunk—but this isn't a sermon. It is merely a few facts on the way liquor is coming into the United States from Canada.

It is coming in in large quantities in as widely divergent places as New York City and Minneapolis. The other day in New York a schooner from Halifax successfully smuggled in enough liquor to make the owner a fortune. Twenty-five dollars a quart is the price for the cheapest whiskey in New York.

There is a long unguarded frontier between Canada and the States and as long as liquor is allowed to be shipped to border provinces that are supposed to be dry it will find its way into the States. What interests the people of the States, both bootleggers and the people who voted the States dry, is how long is the liquor going to come in? They are watching for the result of Ontario's referendum on prohibition.

The Hamilton Gag

☆ THE TORONTO STAR WEEKLY
June 12, 1920

If you are a regular attendant at the theaters of Toronto you always go to a musical show with a calm mind. You may not know the tunes. The lyrics may be new to you. It may be the first time that you have seen the principals. But your mind is calm and quiet. Sooner or later you know that you will hear it. Before the evening is over you are confident it will make its appearance. It always does.

It is the thousand-time perpetrated Toronto-Hamilton gag. Usually it comes out like this.

First Comedian: "Do you live in the city?"

Second Comedian, hitting him across the face with a sausage so the audience will not forget that he is a comedian: "No, I live in Hamilton!"

Always someone laughs heartily. Look at the laugher. Mark him well. He may be a distinguished visitor from foreign parts. One thing at least is certain: it is his first time at a musical show in Toronto.

Of course twenty years ago native Torontonians probably laughed when the jest was first pulled. It is their fault. For a tradition has evidently been established in the profession that to ensure success to their patter it should contain some reference to Toronto and Hamilton.

It may have been funny at first. There might be certain funny aspects of the seizure by infantile paralysis of a neighbor's child. But why refer to it year after year? There must be other local things that could be utilized as jokes instead of eternally inflicting the Hamiltonian tragedy on the theatergoer.

The essence of true comedy as observed at the shows that have appeared here this season seems to be to inflict severe physical suffering on one or both of the comedians. Any fat man falling down anywhere is good for a laugh. If a fat man falls into a tub of water, the applause is tremendous. The fatter the man and the larger the amount of water he falls into the greater the humor of the situation.

Working on that principle, if it could be arranged to have a really enormous fat man drowned in an ocean, the production staging the spectacle would be assured of success. It would be the comedy triumph of the age.

Any vaudeville team act in which the feminine half constantly slaps and smacks the masculine half in the face is a riot. In a recent act at a local vaudeville house neither the man nor girl could sing or dance well enough to earn even a ripple of applause. By dint of the girl's constant slappage of her partner's countenance, the house was soon in an uproar and the act was an immense hit.

Combining this principle of comic violence with some really snappy local dialogue, visiting comedians should be able to add the desired "hometown" stuff to their performance without employing the haggard old Hamilton wheeze.

These are offered as suggestions to any members of either voadveel or the legit who care to make use of them:

This would be very funny:

First Comedian: "Have you a mayor here?"

Second Comedian: "Ha, haw!"

First comedian then hits second comedian with a chair, knocking him over the footlights into the audience. Cheer after cheer rocks the house.

Or they might employ more subtle stuff like this:

First Comedian, shooting second in the back: "Did you hear about the new man working on the new Union Station?"

Second Comedian, knocking his teeth out with a blackjack: "Oh, the other man got lonesome!"

It is very easy. Anyone can do it with a little practice. There are two jokes. One will be good until a change of administration and the other until the station is finished. All comedians are quite welcome to them. By the time they are too old I will have thought of a couple more. But let us bury the Hamilton joke.

Camping Out

☆ THE TORONTO STAR WEEKLY
June 26, 1920

Thousands of people will go into the bush this summer to cut the high cost of living. A man who gets his two weeks salary while he is on vacation should be able to put those two weeks in fishing and camping and be able to save one week's salary clear. He ought to be able to sleep comfortably every night, to eat well every day and to return to the city rested and in good condition.

But if he goes into the woods with a frying pan, an ignorance of black flies and mosquitoes, and a great and abiding lack of knowledge about cookery, the chances are that his return will be very different. He will come back with enough mosquito bites to make the back of his neck look like a relief map of the Caucasus. His digestion will be wrecked after a valiant battle to assimilate half-cooked or charred grub. And he won't have had a decent night's sleep while he has been gone.

He will solemnly raise his right hand and inform you that he has joined the grand army of never-agains. The call of the wild may be all right, but it's a dog's life. He's heard the call of the tame with both ears. Waiter, bring him an order of milk toast.

In the first place he overlooked the insects. Black flies, no-see-ums, deer flies, gnats and mosquitoes were instituted by the devil to force people to live in cities where he could get at them better. If it weren't for them everybody would live in the bush and he would be out of work. It was a rather successful invention.

But there are lots of dopes that will counteract the pests. The simplest perhaps is oil of citronella. Two bits' worth of this purchased at any pharmacist's will be enough to last for two weeks in the worst fly- and mosquito-ridden country.

Rub a little on the back of your neck, your forehead and your wrists before you start fishing, and the blacks and skeeters will shun you. The odor of citronella is not offensive to people. It smells like gun oil. But the bugs do hate it.

Oil of pennyroyal and eucalyptol are also much hated by mosquitoes, and with citronella they form the basis for many proprietary preparations. But it is cheaper and better to buy the straight citronella. Put a little on the mosquito netting that covers the front of your pup tent or canoe tent at night, and you won't be bothered.

To be really rested and get any benefit out of a vacation a man must get a good night's sleep every night. The first requisite for this is to have plenty of cover. It is twice as cold as you expect it will be in the bush four nights out of five, and a good plan is to take just double the bedding that you think you will need. An old quilt that you can wrap up in is as warm as two blankets.

Nearly all outdoor writers rhapsodize over the browse bed. It is all right for the man who knows how to make one and has plenty of time. But in a succession of one-night camps on a canoe trip all you need is level ground for your tent floor and you will sleep all right if you have plenty of covers under you. Take twice as much cover as you think that you will need, and then put two-thirds of it under you. You will sleep warm and get your rest.

When it is clear weather you don't need to pitch your tent if you are only stopping for the night. Drive four stakes at the head of your made-up bed and drape your mosquito bar over that, then you can sleep like a log and laugh at the mosquitoes.

Outside of insects and bum sleeping, the rock that wrecks most camping trips is cooking. The average tyro's idea of cooking is to fry everything and fry it good and plenty. Now, a frying pan is a most necessary thing to any trip, but you also need the old stew kettle and the folding reflector baker.

A pan of fried trout can't be bettered and they don't cost any more than ever. But there is a good and bad way of frying them.

The beginner puts his trout and his bacon in and over a brightly burning fire the bacon curls up and dries into a dry tasteless cinder and the trout is burned outside while it is still raw inside. He eats them and it is all right if he is only out for the day and going home to a good meal at night. But if he is going to face more trout and bacon the next morning and other equally well-cooked dishes for the remainder of two weeks, he is on the pathway to nervous dyspepsia.

The proper way is to cook over coals. Have several cans of Crisco or Cotosuet or one of the vegetable shortenings along that are as good as lard and excellent for all kinds of shortening. Put the bacon in and when it is about half cooked lay the trout in the hot grease, dipping them in cornmeal first. Then put the bacon on top of the trout and it will baste them as it slowly cooks.

The coffee can be boiling at the same time and in a smaller skillet pancakes being made that are satisfying the other campers while they are waiting for the trout.

With the prepared pancake flours you take a cupful of pancake flour and add a cup of water. Mix the water and flour and as soon as the lumps are out it is ready for cooking. Have the skillet hot and keep it well greased. Drop the batter in and as soon as it is done on one side loosen it in the skillet and flip it over. Apple butter, syrup or cinnamon and sugar go well with the cakes.

While the crowd have taken the edge from their appetites with flapjacks, the trout have been cooked and they and the bacon are ready to serve. The trout are crisp outside and firm and pink inside and the bacon is well done—but not too done. If there is anything better than that combination the writer has yet to taste it in a lifetime devoted largely and studiously to eating.

The stew kettle will cook you dried apricots when they have resumed their predried plumpness after a night of soaking, it will serve to concoct a mulligan in, and it will cook macaroni. When you are not using it, it should be boiling water for the dishes.

In the baker, mere man comes into his own, for he can make a pie that to his bush appetite will have it all over the product that mother used to make, like a tent. Men have always believed that there was something mysterious and difficult about making a pie. Here is a great secret. There is nothing to it. We've been kidded for years. Any man of average office intelligence can make at least as good a pie as his wife.

All there is to a pie is a cup and a half of flour, one-half teaspoonful of salt, one-half cup of lard and cold water. That will make piecrust that will bring tears of joy into your camping partner's eyes.

Mix the salt with the flour, work the lard into the flour, make it up into a good workmanlike dough with cold water. Spread some flour on the back of a box or something flat, and pat the dough around a while. Then roll it out with whatever kind of round bottle you prefer. Put a little more lard on the surface of the sheet of dough and then slosh a little flour on and roll it up and then roll it out again with the bottle.

Cut out a piece of the rolled-out dough big enough to line a pie tin. I like the kind with holes in the bottom. Then put in your dried apples that have soaked all night and been sweetened, or your apricots, or your blueberries, and then take another sheet of the dough and drape it gracefully over the top, soldering it down at the edges with your fingers. Cut a couple of slits in the top dough sheet and prick it a few times with a fork in an artistic manner.

Put it in the baker with a good slow fire for forty-five minutes and then take it out, and if your pals are Frenchmen they will kiss you. The penalty for knowing how to cook is that the others will make you do all the cooking.

It is all right to talk about roughing it in the woods. But the real woodsman is the man who can be really comfortable in the bush.

Ted's Skeeters

☆ THE TORONTO STAR WEEKLY
August 7, 1920

He is one of the few wild animals that are not afraid of man. He scents him afar off and with a zooming cry attacks him and sucks his blood. He has driven men to madness and made whole sections of a continent uninhabitable. No, he is not a vampire bat, he is the mosquito.

This yarn is for the city dweller who can't get away for a vacation this summer. When he finishes it he will chortle with glee, think sadly of the poor people who have gone up into the bush and stride off to a movie with his heart full of love for Toronto. There are very few mosquitoes in Toronto.

We were up in the bush. Our camp was so far out in the tall and unsevered [bushes] that there wasn't even an echo. An echo would die of lonesomeness out there.

The first night was perfect. There was a wind from the north and it was cold and we slept like logs. There wasn't a mosquito around.

But the next night at dusk a warm south wind brought them up from the cedar swamp in clouds. If you have never seen a cloud of mosquitoes you cannot appreciate it. It is just like a cloud of dust. Only it is mosquitoes.

We retired into our tent and dropped the mosquito netting over the front. Pretty soon a mosquito bit me on the nose. I killed him and another took his place. Ted lit a candle and started to hunt down all the mosquitoes in the tent. We cleared the tent of them and lay down to sleep and then came that familiar zoom and another proboscis was inserted into my face.

The mosquitoes were coming through the netting as though it were the bars of a cage. By smearing ourselves with citronella oil we managed to get some sleep. About as much sleep as a man gets with a few thousand buzzing, biting, ungentlemanly insects settling down on his face as soon as it comes out of the blankets and satisfying their hunger by pushing their bills into his countenance.

The next night I came in soaked and tired from a day's fly fishing and as I emptied my creel I noted a hunted look on Ted's face.

"I lost the skeeter dope," he said.

"You what?" said I, paralyzed.

"I was trying to get the cork out and it stuck and I pushed it in and then I set the bottle down and it spilled."

Then I knew how Napoleon felt on St. Helena and what Caesar's feelings were when he observed Brutus sticking his jackknife in him, and how the "only one grain of corn, mother" bird felt when he found that there wasn't any corn.

We were out for two weeks. We were twenty-six miles from the nearest town. Our mosquito netting had meshes that would permit a mosquito to be as active as a Sinn Feiner, and Ted had lost the mosquito dope.

Just then a warm breeze commenced to blow from the south across the cedar swamp up toward the high ground of our camp and a keen observer could have seen what looked like a cloud of dust coming up from the swamp. Then I began to appreciate mosquitoes.

We built two smudges and sat between them. The mosquitoes stuck around and every once in a while made a dash through the smoke.

Then we built four smudges and sat inside of them. The mosquitoes came in through the cracks in the smoke. We began to feel like smoked hams. I suggested as much to Ted.

"We are," he said.

Then I started to cheer him up.

"Suppose," said I, "that mosquitoes were as big as crows? What chance would we have then?" He said nothing.

"Suppose they ate fish? There wouldn't be a fish in the stream." He didn't reply.

"We've got a lot to be thankful for," I said.

"Oh, shut up!" he said in a very unmannerly way.

We stuck it for two weeks. But sometimes we were pretty desperate.

Ted suggested that after we had eaten my cookery for a long enough time we would be poisonous to a mosquito.

I retorted that he was probably poisonous to them anyway.

He suggested that I had bought that mosquito netting.

I asked who lost the skeeter dope?

He threw a flapjack at me.

Finally, after a few days it commenced to blow from the north, and we didn't see another mosquito.

Ted remarked that I was a fine cook.

I said that he certainly cast a wicked fly.

The moral is that we should have had cheesecloth instead of the kind of mosquito netting they are selling this year. And you need two bottles of dope. Better make it three.

The Best Rainbow Trout Fishing

☆ THE TORONTO STAR WEEKLY
August 28, 1920

Rainbow trout fishing is as different from brook fishing as prizefighting is from boxing. The rainbow is called *Salmo iridescens* by those mysterious people who name the fish we catch and has recently been introduced into Canadian waters. At present the best rainbow trout fishing in the world is in the rapids of the Canadian Soo.

There the rainbow have been taken as large as fourteen pounds from canoes that are guided through the rapids and halted at the pools by Ojibway and Chippewa boatmen. It is a wild and nerve-frazzling sport and the odds are in favor of the big trout who tear off thirty or forty yards of line at a rush and then will sulk at the base of a big rock and refuse to be stirred into action by the pumping of a stout fly rod aided by a fluent monologue of Ojibwayian profanity. Sometimes it takes two hours to land a really big rainbow under those circumstances.

The Soo affords great fishing. But it is a wild nightmare kind of fishing that is second only in strenuousness to angling for tuna off Catalina Island. Most of the trout, too, take a spinner and refuse a fly, and to the ninety-nine percent pure fly fisherman, there are no one hundred percenters, that is a big drawback.

Of course the rainbow trout of the Soo will take a fly but it is rough handling them in that tremendous volume of water on the light tackle a fly fisherman loves. It is dangerous wading in the spots that can be waded too, for a misstep will take the angler over his head in the rapids. A canoe is a necessity to fish the very best water.

Altogether it is a rough, tough, mauling game, lacking in the meditative qualities of the Izaak Walton school of angling. What would make a fitting Valhalla for the good fisherman when he dies would be a regular trout river with plenty of rainbow trout in it jumping crazy for the fly.

There is such a one not forty miles from the Soo called the—well, called the river. It is about as wide as a river should be and a little deeper than a river ought to be and to get the proper picture you want to imagine in rapid succession the following fade-ins:

A high pine-covered bluff that rises steep up out of the shadows. A short sand slope down to the river and a quick elbow turn with a little flood wood jammed in the bend and then a pool.

A pool where the moselle-colored water sweeps into a dark swirl and expanse that is blue-brown with depth and fifty feet across.

There is the setting.

The action is supplied by two figures that slog into the picture up the trail along the riverbank with loads on their backs that would tire a packhorse. These loads are pitched over the heads onto the patch of ferns by the edge of the deep pool. That is incorrect. Really the figures lurch a little forward and the tump line loosens and the pack slumps onto the ground. Men don't pitch loads at the end of an eight-mile hike.

One of the figures looks up and notes the bluff is flattened on top and that there is a good place to put a tent. The other is lying on his back and looking straight up in the air. The first reaches over and picks up a grasshopper that is stiff with the fall of the evening dew and tosses him into the pool.

The hopper floats spraddle-legged on the water of the pool an instant, an eddy catches him and then there is a yard-long flash of flame, and a trout as long as your forearm has shot into the air and the hopper has disappeared.

"Did you see that?" gasped the man who had tossed in the grasshopper.

It was a useless question, for the other, who a moment before would have served as a model for a study entitled "Utter Fatigue," was jerking his fly rod out of the case and holding a leader in his mouth.

We decided on a McGinty and a Royal Coachman for the flies and at the second cast there was a swirl like the explosion of a depth bomb, the line went taut and the rainbow shot two feet out of water. He tore down the pool and the line went out until the core of the reel showed. He jumped, and each time he shot into the air we lowered the tip and prayed. Finally he jumped and the line went slack and Jacques reeled in. We thought he was gone and then he jumped right under our faces. He had shot upstream toward us so fast that it looked as though he were off.

When I finally netted him and rushed him up the bank and could feel his huge strength in the tremendous muscular jerks he made when I held him flat against the bank, it was almost dark. He measured twenty-six inches and weighed nine pounds and seven ounces.

That is rainbow trout fishing.

The rainbow takes the fly more willingly than he does bait. The McGinty, a fly that looks like a yellowjacket, is the best. It should be tied on a number eight or ten hook.

The smaller flies get more strikes but are too small to hold the really big fish. The rainbow trout will live in the same streams with brook trout but they are found in different kinds of places. Brook trout will be forced into the shady holes under the bank and where alders hang over the banks, and the rainbow will dominate the clear pools and the fast shallows.

Magazine writers and magazine covers to the contrary, the brook, or speckled, trout does not leap out of water after he has been hooked. Given plenty of line, he will fight a deep rushing fight. Of course if you hold the fish too tight he will be forced by the rush of the current to flop on top of the water.

But the rainbow always leaps on a slack or tight line. His leaps are not mere flops, either, but actual jumps out of and parallel with the water of from a foot to five feet. A five-foot jump by any fish sounds improbable, but it is true.

If you don't believe it, tie on to one in fast water and try and force him. Maybe if he is a five-pounder he will throw me down and only jump four feet eleven inches.

Canadians: Wild/Tame

☆ THE TORONTO STAR WEEKLY
October 9, 1920

Seeing ourselves as others see us is interesting but sometimes appalling. Remember the unexpected glimpse of your profile caught in one of those three-way mirrors at your tailor's?

This refers to men and nations—women see full face, profile and their back hair at least every day and therefore are not appalled.

William Stevens McNutt, in a recent issue of *Collier's Weekly*, told his version of what Canadians think of Americans.

Herein is the opinion and views of that average American, whom cub reporters delight to call the man in the street, on Canadians.

Just as a tip to budding journalists, there is no such thing as the man in the street in either the States or the Dominion. The phrase is French and is applicable enough there where nearly all human intercourse is carried on in or on the streets. But here the only time an American either north or south of the border is in the street is when he is busily going somewhere.

An average citizen should be called the man going hungry from the quick-lunch joint to the man standing in the streetcar or, even, the righteous man afraid of a policeman.

In the States the average unseated male in a public conveyance has a vague idea of Canada.

Canada is, for him, the North-West Mounted Police, winter sports, open snowy places replete with huskie dogs, Canadian whiskey, race reports from Windsor, the Woodbine and Blue Bonnets, and a firm and dominant passion that no one will slip him any Canadian silver.

He remembers that when Taft was president there was a big fuss about reciprocity—but he isn't quite sure how it all came out. He is sure to have heard of Sir Wilfrid Laurier and may have heard of ex-Premier Borden but is apt to confuse him with the milk manufacturer. That covers his knowledge of Canadian politics.

Surprising as it may be to many Canadians, the average American is tremendously proud of Canada's war record. An American who served with the Canadian forces, whether in the A.S.C. or originals, is a hero to his fellow countrymen.

A typical Canadian as pictured by the man in the pressed-while-you-wait shop in the States is of two types, wild and tame.

Wild Canadians mean Mackinaw blanket pants, fur caps, have rough bewhiskered but honest faces and are closely pursued by corporals of the Royal North-West Mounted Police.

Tame Canadians wear spats, small mustaches, are very intelligent looking, all have M.C.'s, and are politely bored.

Both wild and tame Canadians are in contrast with the average American man munching peanuts in the ballpark's conception of the British.

All inhabitants of Great Britain are divided into three classes, to wit, sanguinary Englishmen, cricket players and lords.

Sanguinary Englishmen are so considered because of their penchant for qualifying all remarks with the term sanguinary. They wear cloth caps and eat raw herrings.

Cricket players stalk in flannels through the best American fiction, and lords are dealt with by the comic supplements.

Then there is a type of Englishman created for American consumption by Mr. William Randolph Hearst, who is a combination of the Emperor Nero, the worst phases of the Corsican, George the Third, and whoever wouldn't give the Bay three grains of corn.

Jesting aside, there is a lamentable lack of sympathetic understanding between Canada and the United States. It is a fact that Canada is a closed book to the average Yank, a book with a highly colored jacket by Robert W. Service.

Americans admire and respect Canadians. There is not the slightest trace of anti-Canadian sentiment anywhere in the States. And among the roughneck element there is a positive love for Canada.

But you know what the average Canadian roughneck thinks of a Yank.

Maybe when Hearst dies and the war is a longer way off and exchange gets back to normal and there is an exchange system between Canadian and American universities and Americans lower their voices and Canadians lower their pride, or say there was a good war and we both went in at the same time, maybe we'd be pals.

Carpentier vs. Dempsey

☆ THE TORONTO STAR WEEKLY
October 30, 1920

Can Georges Carpentier beat Jack Dempsey in a fight for the heavyweight championship of the world? That is a question that is going to be in the minds of every man, woman and child in Canada, whether they are readers of the sporting page or not.

The answer is that Carpentier has a most excellent chance to defeat Dempsey. There is a greater interest being taken in this fight than any previous championship encounter has drawn.

People who wouldn't know a left hook from a referee read all the dope they can get in the hope that Carpentier may have a chance. Fight experts all over the States are unanimous in assuring these hopers that Dempsey will practically murder Carpentier.

If we are to believe the experts and some of the editorial writers in U.S. newspapers, it is practically suicide for Georges to climb into the same ring with Jack. Dempsey will hit him once and it will all be over. Dempsey is the greatest heavyweight of all time. It looks bad for Carpentier.

But let the layman who is reading his first boxing dope remember that these same experts picked Jess Willard to defeat Dempsey in their farcical encounter at Toledo a year ago in July. Willard was picked by most of the boxing writers and the odds were 6 to 5 on Willard.

Experts are all victims of "Championitis." Whoever happens to be the titleholder is the greatest fighter of all time. Thus they write reams about the wonderful superman that is Dempsey.

It is bunk and twaddle of the worst kind.

Jack Dempsey has an imposing list of knockouts over bums and tramps, who were nothing but big slow-moving, slow-thinking set-ups for him. He has never fought a real fighter.

He has been beaten by Willie Meehan, who is an acknowledged second-rater.

When Dempsey fought Willard the Kansas farmer was thirty-eight years old. Willard had been living a life of ease and sloth for several years and, according to report, drinking steadily of corn whiskey. Willard had never fought a good fight, and had won the title from Johnson in a contest that has always had the taint of crookedness about it.

Dempsey, young and powerful puncher, went into the ring that hot day at Toledo and waited till Willard stuck out his long, slow left hand at him. Then Dempsey swung from near the floor and caught the big, fat old set-up on the jaw with a regular haymaking swing.

Willard went to the floor and Dempsey stood over him. The referee did not hold Dempsey off until he counted over Willard, but walked around the ring nervously.

As soon as Willard's hands left the floor and he prepared to get to his feet, Dempsey crashed another swing against his unprotected jaw. Dempsey hit Willard while he was down, whenever he tried to get up, and then could not knock him into insensibility.

When the fight stopped at the end of the third round Dempsey was so tired that he was breathing drunkenly and his hands hung by his side! Willard seemed the fresher of the two, but his handlers knew that in a shorter bout he could not overcome the disadvantage of those earlier knockdowns and so tossed in the towel. In this way Jack Dempsey won the heavyweight championship of the world from a man who was never anything but a joke as champion.

Since winning the title Dempsey has appeared in only one fight. This was with one of his closest friends, who had been an invalid for over a year, all the time under a physician's care.

Billy Miske was regarded as a jest and could not have lasted ten rounds against any good fighter, but he was an old friend of Dempsey's and had been promised the first crack at the title and the accompanying $25,000. He looked ridiculous against Dempsey as he would have against any good fighter. But Dempsey took no chances with him. After he had knocked Miske down and had him dazed and blind he stood behind him, and as he got to his feet, before he had his hands up, smashed him on the jaw for the finish.

So because he beat an old whiskey-rotted set-up and knocked out a sick acquaintance Jack Dempsey is hailed as the greatest fighter of all time by the critics.

On the other hand the critics have dubbed Carpentier a flash in the pan, a grandstander, a false alarm, a morning glory, a night-blooming cereus, and a number of other things. Critics agree that Carpentier would have no chance with Dempsey.

Here is the cold dope:

Carpentier will weigh 176 pounds against Dempsey's 185, but Carpentier has beaten men that would have chased Dempsey out of the ring.

Let those critics of Carpentier who say that he will not last against Dempsey remember that Georges fought twenty rounds with Joe Jeannette when that great Negro fighter was at the top of his form. Carpentier, when he was 19 years old, fought Frank Klaus, who beat Stanley Ketchell, the man who knocked down Jack Johnson.

Carpentier has twice knocked out Bombardier Wells, who was one of the cleverest boxers and fastest punchers that ever lived.

In 1914 Gunboat Smith beat Jess Willard in twenty rounds out in California. Beat him so decisively that Willard was crying from the punishment he was taking.

Gunboat Smith then came over to London and was matched with Carpentier at the National Sporting Club. The Gunner at that time was one of the hardest hitters and most dangerous fighters in the game, and had just beaten the enormous Willard and most of the other white hopes. Carpentier knocked him down three or four times and had him in such bad shape that Smith, rather than be knocked out, fouled the Frenchman and lost the fight.

Carpentier then served through the war with honor and in his first big postwar fight, knocked out Joe Beckett, the champion of England, in a single round.

Recently he came to the States and fought a formerly good American heavyweight named Battling Levinsky. In the first round Carpentier was covered up and cautious. He felt out Levinsky and discovered that he had nothing to fear. Then he sailed in and, recognizing that he was up against a comparative tyro, he threw aside all thought of defense and punished Levinsky at will.

A layman would think that performance would satisfy his critics that he was a fighter as well as a matchless boxer.

But the cry of the critics is: He has no defense. He is just a swinger. Dempsey will murder him.

Wild West: Chicago

☆ THE TORONTO STAR WEEKLY
November 6, 1920

Canada never had a Wild West. Largely, perhaps, because as soon as anyone came over from across the border and started to Wild West around, the North-West Mounted Police very quietly and firmly put him away where he wouldn't harm any one.

Now the States had a Wild West. It was as good as the movies portray. It had faro, dice, wide-open towns, bad Injuns, red eye, gamblers in frock coats, Bill Hart bad men, discriminate and indiscriminate killings, and all the jolly features.

In place of the Redskins biting the dust it is now the commercial traveler that bites the dust.

Where the elk once roamed, the Elk now roams, but with him are the Mason and Odd Fellow. Thus, to coin a phrase, the old order passeth, giving way to the new.

But the Wild West hasn't disappeared. It has only moved. Just at present it is located at the southwestern end of Lake Michigan, and the range that the bad men ride is that enormous smoky jungle of buildings they call Chicago.

Every year some Congressman or Senator rises in the U.S. Congress and reports that during the past year thirty-two or twenty-seven American citizens have been killed in Mexico. All the Congressmen shudder as one Congressman. Mexico is obviously a bad place. "Something must be done about it. It can't go on any longer. Steps must be taken."

Yet in the city of Chicago during the present year from January to November there have been one hundred and fifty killings. One hundred and fifty murders in ten months means a murder every forty-eight hours.

Of course that record may not look so good against the score of some of the early Nevada mining towns where they boasted to kill a man for breakfast every morning. Some of the Nevada breakfasts, though, must have been furnished by sheriffs and marshals ushering out bad men.

In the Chicago figures, however, no count has been made of the killings by police. By including the police bag, it would be pretty safe to say they kill somebody every day in Chicago.

Chicago is supposed to be a dry town. But anybody willing to pay twenty dollars a quart for whiskey can get all they want. In the first days of the dry law enforcement much of this contraband whiskey was Canadian. The dealers feared to move the enormous stores of whiskey there are in the South.

Now most of the whiskey you buy has a Kentucky label. Canadian whiskey costs too much and there is too much American liquor on hand.

Gambling is flourishing again after a temporary retirement. Of course in every city there will always be certain types of gambling that can go on in spite of all the police can do. Those are the games that require no apparatus, but can be conducted anywhere. When the police raid a crap game, for instance, all that the gamblers must do is have the doors hold long enough for them to sweep the money into the buckskin bag that lies flat open on the billiard table, throw the dice out of the window, and the evidence is missing.

Roulette wheels in operation mean only one thing, police protection. For you can't hide a roulette wheel and you can't throw it out of the window. It is expensive, bulky and heavy. Before a gambling joint decides to put a wheel into operation they must know that they will not be raided without a proper warning to give them time to stow away their equipment.

At present it is common talk that there is in Chicago on the West Side a gambling house where roulette is played for as big stakes as obtain in Monte Carlo. So there is murder, drink and gambling in the new Wild West just as in the old.

Now the reason that Chicago is crime-ridden and Toronto is not lies in the police forces of the two cities. Toronto has a force that for organization, effectiveness and esprit de corps is excelled nowhere in the world. Crooks steer clear of Toronto because they know the reputation of that force. It has established the same reputation for a city that the North-West Mounted Police did for a Dominion.

Chicago's crime record is the best description of her police force. Even if you escape all the various brands of criminal homicide that Chicago offers, the nightgowny person with the scythe has another sickle up his wide-flowing sleeve. There have been to date four hundred and twenty people killed this year in Chicago by motor cars.

Newspapermen's Pockets

☆ THE TORONTO STAR WEEKLY
November 6, 1920

A manufacturer recently made a canvass of his employees and found that the average amount of currency that each carried in his pocket was $28.50. In commenting on this, an editorial writer asked us to realize that ten million men, each with only $20 in his pocket, will hold out of use $200,000,000 in currency, which could well be set to work.

Let the editorial writer stop worrying. Although the factory employees may have had $28.50 apiece in their pockets consider the rest of us. For basis of comparison a series of composite photographs of the contents of the pockets of a number of persons of the same occupation have been obtained at great labor and expense.

There are, for example, newspapermen. In the pocket of the average newspaperman (unmarried and hardened) there are the following articles:

One handsome leather wallet (a gift).

Three pencils.

Two complimentary tickets to any poor show.

A number of unredeemable mutuel tickets.

Three letters from his best girls (who are soon to marry somebody with enough money to support them).

A number of streetcar tickets.

$2.85 in cash.

Newspaper reporter (married):

A varying number of Please Remits.

A single mutuel ticket. He played a rank outsider who would have paid thirty to one for $5 on the chance of staving off the coal shortage. It was a poor chance.

A picture of the wife.

Lunch money.

A cub reporter's pockets contain:

One large collection of clippings. These are stories written by the reporter himself which have actually appeared in a real newspaper. They show his splendid ability to handle such vital stories as an unidentified Negro being struck by a motortruck while crossing Dundas Street. There is usually some short feature story by the reporter describing how the wind blows up and down King Street. This was inserted in the paper by the city editor one Monday when copy was short and because he was once a cub reporter himself.

When the police find a dead body with a pocket full of clippings they know it is either a cub reporter or an actor. As reporters never die, it is always an actor.

In addition to the clippings cub reporters' pockets contain a number of other things.

A collection of letters from his best girl who hasn't yet realized that she is going to marry somebody else.

A street directory.

A number of postage stamps, purchased in a moment of affluence and now stuck together.

A receipt from his tailor for ten dollars' payment on account.

A handsome cigarette case. The cub reporter thought this was silver once, but a pawnbroker disillusioned him.

An expense voucher which he plans to cash for supper.

The editorial writer shouldn't worry. As long as there are newspapermen, bond salesmen, automobile salesmen, bank employees and similar occupations, there will be a great enough lack of pocket money to balance the excess of the factory employees.

Indoor Fishing

☆ THE TORONTO STAR WEEKLY
November 20, 1920

Now when the old fly rod is hanging by its tip in the garret, and the flies that remain of the bright legion that opened the season are tattered feathered veterans and the patched waders are put away in the closet and the new net is lost, it looks as though the fishing season is over.

But it isn't. It is just under way. No, this doesn't mean that they are fishing for trout in New Zealand, or the Andes or Lago di Garda. This yarn deals with the opening of the great indoor fishing season.

More fish are caught in clubs at this time of year than ever were taken from the Nipigon. Bigger trout are taken around the tables in King Street cafeterias than win the prizes offered by the sporting magazines. And more fish get away within the confines of Toronto than are lost in all the trout streams of Christendom.

That's where indoor fishing has it on outdoor fishing. It is cheaper and the fish run bigger.

It's a peculiar thing that no man likes to hear another man talk about his golf game. Of course, most men spend the majority of their working hours talking about their golf game to other men. But do the other men enjoy it? They do not. They loathe it. They are merely listening in the hope that that blithering idiot will stop and give them a chance to talk about their own game.

For a man's golf game is self-contained within him. Outside influences haven't much to do with it. He is really just talking about himself.

Fishing is different. One fisherman loves to hear another fisherman tell about his fishing. For the fishing is something altogether outside of the fisherman. And while the one fisherman is listening he is mentally taking notes. Where did all this happen? How far is it from Toronto? Could he find the place? Are there any more as big up there? And so on.

We were fishing for the rainbow trout where a little river comes into a lake and cuts a channel alongside the bank. Into the mouth of this river and the bay it empties into, big schools of rainbow trout come out of the big lake. They chase the shiners and young herring and you can see their back fins coming out of the water like porpoises with a shower of minnows shooting up into the air. Every once in a while a big trout will jump clear of the water with a noise like somebody throwing a bathtub into the lake.

These monster trout won't touch a fly and we fish for them by casting out from the bank with minnows and letting them lie on the bottom of the channel. We use an Aberdeen number four hook, a six-foot leader and sixty-five yards of twenty-pound test line, a quadruple multiplying reel and a fly rod.

You cast your minnow out into the channel and let it sink to the bottom and there it waits until the trout grabs it. In the meantime you set the click on the reel and put a slab under the rod butt.

None of these lake rainbows run under four pounds and when one hits the minnow the reel buzzes, the rod tip jerks down and you grab the rod and strike and the fight is on. The point of this is that we have caught trout in this way over nine pounds in weight. We have never had one run out all the line and, while we have lost many leaders, we had never had a fish big enough to break the line.

One day in September I had just cast out the minnow into the channel, the rod was pointing up into the air and the click was set on the reel. I was about twenty-five yards down the shore getting some driftwood for the fire when the reel gave a shriek that mounted to about high C. Not the familiar bzzzzzzzzz but a steady shriek. The rod jerked down so hard that it was flattened straight out on the water.

I raced for the rod the instant I heard the reel start. Just as I reached it, the shriek of the reel stopped. There was a big wallowing explosion out in the lake, the line broke at the reel and the rod—the butt had been under a log and resting on another—shot up into the air. I jumped into the water but the line had vanished into the lake.

Don't ask me how big he was. But he was big enough to take out over forty yards of line in the time it takes me to cover sixty feet and he was big enough to break a brand-new twenty-three pound test line without an instant's strain. As soon as his weight hit the direct pull of the line it snapped.

The other one I didn't see. But one night Jock Pentecost came into camp wet to the skin, his rod broken at the second joint, his net gone and a story that made our eyes bug out.

It seems that he was fishing a particularly deep and difficult stretch of river when he hooked a trout that he claimed was as long as his arm. He went downriver with him through a pretty sizable rapids where he lost his net. Sometimes the fish would sulk at the foot of a big boulder and Jock would have to throw pebbles at him to start him moving. He was afraid to pump him too much with his rod for fear of parting the leader.

At other times the fish would rush and jump until Jock's heart would be somewhere in his gullet with each jump. Jock said that when the trout jumped he made a noise like a beaver diving into the river.

Of course it was a hopeless battle without a net and no other fishermen within two or three miles. Jock might have had a chance of beaching him if there had been any shallow places or patches of shingle. But the river runs waist deep and as fast as a millrace.

Jock claims that he fought the trout for an hour and a half and then the big fellow started downstream and something had to smash.

The enormous size of the fish and the length of time of the fight seemed unbelievable to us as it does to you. But Jock had the look of truth in his eyes.

Two weeks after, the fish commission men netted some trout out beyond a dam on the river and put them upstream. They were too big to use the fish ladder. One of them was a rainbow trout weighing twenty-one pounds.

And what is more, no one has caught him and he's still in the river.

Plain and Fancy Killings, $400 Up

☆ THE TORONTO STAR WEEKLY
December 11, 1920

Chicago.—Gunmen from the United States are being imported to do killings in Ireland. That is an established fact from Associated Press dispatches.

According to underworld gossip in New York and Chicago, every ship that leaves for England carries its one or two of these weasels of death bound for where the hunting is good. The underworld says that the gunmen are first shipped to England where they lose themselves in the waterfronts of cities like Liverpool and then slip over to Ireland.

In the Red Island they do their job of killing, collect their contract price and slip back to England. It is said that the price for a simple killing, such as a marked policeman or member of the "Black and Tans," is four hundred dollars. It may seem exorbitant when you remember that the old pre-war price in New York was one hundred dollars, but the gunman is a specialist and his prices, like those demanded by prizefighters, have advanced.

For killing a well-guarded magistrate or other official, as much as one thousand dollars is demanded. Such a price for even a fancy killing is ridiculous, according to an ex-gunman I talked with in Chicago.

"Some of those birds are sure grabbing off the soft dough in Ireland. It's mush to pull a job in that country but trust the boys to get theirs. One job means a trip to Paris."

It is a fact that there have been more American underworld characters in Paris this summer and fall than ever before. They say that if you throw a stone into a crowd in front of one of the mutuel booths at the famous Longchamps racecourse outside of Paris, you would hit an American gunman, pickpocket or strong-arm artist.

Most of the blood money from Ireland went to back some pony or other. For the gunman believes in taking a chance. He believes that if he can make enough of a stake he can settle down and quit the business. But it is hard for him to quit, for there are very few professions outside of prizefighting that pay so well.

The retired shuffler off of mortal coils who honors me with his acquaintance is about thirty-eight. Perhaps it were better not to describe him too closely, because he might run on to a Toronto paper. But he is about as handsome as a ferret, has fine hands, looks like a jockey a bit overweight.

He quit gunning when the quitting was good—when the country went dry and liquor running became the best-paying outdoor occupation.

After his principal customers discovered that it was altogether better and cheaper to ship whiskey up from the big warehouses in Kentucky than to take the chance of running it across the imaginary line that separates the U.S. and Canada, he retired.

Now he is a man-about-town and bond salesmen call on him. When I talked with him he kept steering the subject away from gunning and the Irish situation to ask my honest opinion on some Japanese government bonds that will pay eleven percent interest.

In the course of an afternoon I learned a number of things about the trade. Yes, there were American "bump-off" artists in Ireland. Yes, he knew some that were there personally. Well, he didn't know who was in the right in Ireland. No, it didn't matter to him. He understood it was all managed out of New York. Then you worked out of Liverpool. No, he wouldn't care particularly about killing Englishmen. But, then, they gotta die sometime.

He's heard that most of the guns were Wops—Dagoes, that is. Most gunman were Wops, anyway. A Wop made a good gun. They usually worked in pairs. In the U.S.A. they nearly always worked out of a motorcar, because that made the getaway much easier. That was the big thing about doing a job. The getaways. Anybody can do a job. It's the getaway that counts. A car made it much easier. But there was always the chauffeur.

Had I noticed, he went on, that most of the jobs that fell through were the fault of the chauffeur? The police traced the car and then got the chauffeur and he squealed. That was what was bad about a car, he said. "You can't trust any of them."

That's the type of mercenary that is doing the Irishmen's killings for them. He isn't a heroic or even a dramatic figure. He just sits hunched over his whiskey glass, worries about how to invest his money, lets his weasel mind run on and wishes the boys luck. The boys seem to be having it.

Trading Celebrities

☆ THE TORONTO STAR WEEKLY
February 19, 1921

Why not trade other public entertainers as the big leagues do ball players? At any time you can pick up a paper and read "Aleck to Redlegs?" or "Hornsby Traded—Rumor." By internationalizing the trading of public assets in personality, stories like this would occur:

TO SWAP CLEMMY

> Paris, France, Feb. 5.—A report is current that France is in the market for a couple of good statesmen to replace Georges Clemenceau. Although his legs have gone back on him, the Frenchman is thought to have several good years of statesmanship left and it is reported that a number of nations will put in a claim for him via the waiver route. He was at one time internationally known as the Tiger of France.

What a boon to a community like Toronto, which doesn't know what else to do but elect officials who will keep on running. As in this case:

CHURCH GOES OVER

> Toronto, Feb. 16.—Unnamed parties have completed negotiations between the Toronto City Council and the Hamburgervolks-parteiverein of Hamburg, Germany, for the exchange of Mayor Thomas Church in return for 20,000 tons of German shipping. Hamburg being in desperate need of civic and industrial re-establishment, it turned naturally to Church, whose remarkable success with Toronto is internationally recognized. Toronto, in turn, having acquired its power, light and now its street railway to public ownership, is anxious to add to its utilities by owning some ships to grace its new harbor. In an interview confirming the trade, Mayor Church said: "I regard this opportunity to

further Toronto's public ownership plans as a significant honor from my people."

What about those great cultural influences, the newspapers?

TELE FOR TIMES

London, England, Feb. 10.—In recognition of a mutual need, the municipal governments of London, England, and Toronto have agreed to exchange the *Toronto Telegram* for the *London Times.* The university professors who constitute a large percentage of Toronto's population are growing insistent in their demand for a local paper of the *Times*' intellectual status. As for London, it has long been in need of a thorough blowing up. And in the matter of Lord Mayors, this city has fallen into the habit of electing a fresh one every year. It is expected that the *Telegram* will correct this.

Novelists and literati in general would make excellent trading material:

SCRIBES MUST PACK

Washington, D.C., Jan. 30.—In the biggest literary deal of the decade, articles were signed yesterday transferring Anatole France, Jean Jacques Rousseau and Voltaire from France to the United States in exchange for Harold Bell Wright, Owen Johnson, Robert W. Chambers and $800,000 in gold. The trade is said to be due to the present low rate of exchange of the franc. Rousseau and Voltaire, whose first name could not be learned at a late hour, are dead.

Occasionally a trade might not be consummated—See this dispatch in the *N.Y. Tribune.*

CANADA SPURNS OUR JACK

Ottawa, Jan. 7.—Canada yesterday refused an offer of Jack Dempsey and $200,000 in exchange for the province of Manitoba. Jack Kearns, Dempsey's manager, in making the offer, said that Dempsey would be known as the Canadian champion and would at once become naturalized as a Canadian citizen. Manitoba is noted for wheat.

Visualize the nationwide rejoicing at an exchange of this sort—

SHAKESPEARE NEW YANK

Stratford-on-Avon, England, Feb. 22.—An impressive ceremony marked the celebration here yesterday of Shakespeare's American citizenship.

The little English town on the Avon was decked with American flags and all the buildings were placarded.

"We Wanted Bill and We Got Him" and "Yea Bill! You Brought Home the Bacon" were the legends on some of the placards. Floats were borne in a parade depicting Shakespeare wearing the clothes of a widely advertised American tailor and bearing this sign—"Big Bill Shakespeare—One Hundred Percent American."

An American whose name cannot be used, who was one of the big movers in obtaining Shakespeare's citizenship for the United States, when approached on the Bacon controversy, said, "If need be, we will buy Bacon's citizenship, too."

Or it would give the greatest couper of our age a workout—

ETNA TO SWEDEN IN BIG MATCH MERGER— D'ANNUNZIO COUP PLANNED

Rome, Italy, Feb. 24.—Articles were signed here yesterday for one of the biggest trades of the year. Sweden is to receive a ninety-nine-year lease to Mts. Etna and Vesuvius in exchange for the title to all Nobel Peace prizes for a period of twenty years. Sweden has been dickering for the mountains for some time to relieve the present shortage of sulphur in the Swedish match industry.

Naples, Italy, Feb. 24.—Special—Gabriele D'Annunzio has occupied both Mt. Etna and Mt. Vesuvius. In an ultimatum last night the poet-warrior said: "I hope to die on both of these glorious mountains if frozen Swedes ever touch one powdered fragment of their holy sulphurs."

Our Confidential Vacation Guide

☆ THE TORONTO STAR WEEKLY
May 21, 1921

Any steady reader of obituaries is familiar with the phrase "He had not taken a vacation in twenty years."

Of course there is no ironbound rule about the period. It may be that the dead man had not taken a vacation in ten years, in thirty years, during all the time he was mayor, or during his entire lifetime. It all points toward the same false moral. It seems obvious that if the poor chap had only accepted the vacation his employers kept forcing on him, he might be alive today.

This is very wrong. The trouble is that newspapers do not make a practice of printing as a cause of death this statement: "He spent every summer at Lake Milkitossup," or, "The deceased was in the habit of spending the month of August at Lake Wah Wah."

A few statements like these would clear up matters. Newspaper readers would then realize that the reason the first man lived twenty years was because he had carefully preserved his health through abstaining from vacations. The reason that the other splendid fellows had dropped like ripened grapefruit at the end of their thirty years, mayoralty terms or lifetimes was the fact that they had never visited such places as Lake Screaming Water or picturesque Bum View. Just a few seasons at Giggling Perch Inn or the New Nokomis, American plan, would have cut them off like flies in the pride of their young manhood.

If you must take a vacation, read this confidential guide on places to avoid. It has been compiled at great labor and is available here for the first time. It means a longer life and happier to stay away from the following:

POACHDALE INN, ONTARIO

How to reach Poachdale Inn—this is not important.

How to get away from Poachdale Inn—Bounce in a hurdling Ford through five miles of mud. Wait at the railway until the train comes. There is no train on Sunday. Try not to be hysterical when the train comes in sight.

BEAUTIFUL LAKE FLYBLOW

Beautiful Lake Flyblow nestles like a plague spot in the heart of the great north woods. All around it rise the majestic hills. Above it towers the majestic sky. On every side of it is the majestic shore. The shore is lined with majestic dead fish—dead of loneliness.

SMILING LAKE WAH WAH

Smiling Lake Wah Wah is always smiling. It is smiling at the people who stalk along its shores, grim and unsmiling. Smiling Wah Wah knows that the people are from Giggling Perch Inn. Wah Wah sees that the people are undernourished. She sees their gaunt faces and the feverish eager light in their eyes as they wave off the clouds of mosquitoes. Smiling Wah Wah knows what is in their minds as they walk along her shores. They are waiting for the two weeks to end.

BEAUTIFUL BOZO BEACH

Beautiful Bozo Beach nestles next to the largest inland body of fresh water on the American continent. Arm yourself with a boat hook and Bozo Beach is an ideal place for the little ones. They can play in the sands of Beautiful Bozo Beach to their little hearts' content. After their little hearts are contented they will rub the sand in their eyes and chase one another screaming into the largest inland body of fresh water on the American continent. You can usually bring the little ones back from the largest inland body of fresh water with the boat hooks.

PICTURESQUE BUM VIEW

Bum View is one of the quieter resorts in the States on Lake Erie, where you go for a good solid rest. That's the big thing about Bum View, the solid comfort and the quiet. It is run by S. A. Jarvis.

Every morning at 3 a.m. the Jarvis's rooster announces that it will soon be daylight. All the other roosters give him their endorsement. Then the Jarvis's rooster announces that it is daylight. Thousands of other roosters bear him out. There is a great clattering in the kitchen as the hired help start the day. The pump squeaks as Jim, the hired man, pumps the water. The Putnam twins are up early and their childish voices rise above the sound of the phonograph they start playing.

By this time the sun is shining so hotly on the wall of your room that it is becoming as hot as a bake oven. The rosin begins to melt in the knots in the hemlock boarding of the room walls. You had no sleep the first part of the night—mosquitoes. Your head begins to ache with the heat. You dress and come downstairs to breakfast. There is a pale green hard slice of melon on the plate. The eggs are brought in, fried to a cold rubbery consistency. There are white spots in the bacon. The toast is cold and rancid. The beautiful day is before you.

It is too hot at Bum View to do anything except read. The heat beats down and forces every one into the shade of the porch. That is all the shade there is. Facilities have been provided for reading. There are: a hammock—a large weak hammock which someone is occupying—and several uncomfortable chairs. A library of books including Hall Caine and Marie Corelli, an illustrated history of the Japanese-Russian War, the Canadian Almanac for 1919, a small red set of volumes of the world's best short stories arranged according to nationality and an illustrated book on the wild flowers of Palestine.

It is too hot in the house. It is too hot anywhere but on the porch. In the afternoon it is too hot on the porch. When it is too hot on the porch the guest goes to the back of the house where a shadow is beginning to start and lies down on the grass. In a short time he is asleep. Thousands of weird-shaped insects climb carefully down from the grass stems and up on the sleeper. He sleeps on. More insects abandon the grass stems to come and climb on him. He still sleeps. He will sleep all afternoon—then he will lie awake all night. Then the Jarvis's rooster will crow again and it will be another day. He has thirteen more to go till he gets back to his office.

Will he last it? Or will the vacation kill him?

Ballot Bullets

☆ THE TORONTO STAR WEEKLY
May 28, 1921

Chicago.—Anthony D'Andrea, pale and spectacled, defeated candidate for alderman in the 19th Ward, Chicago, stepped out of the closed car in front of his residence and, holding an automatic pistol in his hand, backed gingerly up the steps.

Reaching back with his left hand to press the door bell, he was blinded by two red jets of flame from the window of the next apartment, heard a terrific roar and felt himself clouted sickeningly in the body with the shock of the slugs from the sawed-off shotgun.

It was the end of the trail that had started with a white-faced boy studying for the priesthood in a little Sicilian town. It was the end of a trail that had wound from the sunlit hills of Sicily across the sea and into the homes of Chicago's nouveau riche. A trail that led through the penitentiary and out into the deadliest political fight Chicago has ever known.

But it was not quite the end. For the pale-faced D'Andrea, his body torn and huddled, his horn-rimmed spectacles broken, but hooked on, pulled himself to his knees and looking with his near-sighted eyes into the darkness jerked five shots out of his automatic pistol in the direction of the shotgun that had roared his death warrant.

For months D'Andrea had been entering his home, gun in hand, in the expectation of such a death. He knew he was doomed—but he wanted to protest the verdict. It is all part of the unfinished story of the gunmen's political war that is raging in Chicago at present.

Anthony D'Andrea, who is dead in Jefferson Park Hospital today with twelve slugs in his body, was educated at the University of Palermo. He renounced a career in the church and went to the States.

In Chicago he became a foreign-language teacher to some of the wealthiest families of the city, numbering among his pupils many of the newer members of society. D'Andrea became an American citizen in 1899, and in subsequent years embarked on various commercial enterprises. In a small way he was a real estate dealer, macaroni manufacturer and banker.

Secret service agents raided his home in 1902 on a tip that D'Andrea was the man who was flooding Chicago with spurious ten-cent pieces. Counterfeit coins were found by the government operatives at both D'Andrea's home and his macaroni factory. He was tried, pleaded guilty and sentenced to Joliet penitentiary. After serving thirteen months, he was pardoned by President Roosevelt.

After coming out of the penitentiary he became an Italian labor leader and shortly announced his intention of entering politics. His first venture in politics was in 1914, when he was defeated as candidate for city commissioner.

In 1916 he first contested the seat of Alderman John Powers, who has been the alderman from the 19th Ward for twenty-five years. Although D'Andrea proved he was not disfranchised due to his pardon by President Roosevelt, his past record defeated him.

His power over the Italians continued to grow, however, and the first of the murders that have marked the Powers-D'Andrea feud occurred when Frank Lombardi, a strong Powers adherent, was killed in his saloon.

This last election started off with the bombing of Alderman Powers' home. Then D'Andrea's headquarters were bombed while a meeting was in progress and many of his henchmen badly wounded.

Alderman Powers, who is known to the Italians as "Johnny de Pow," won the election of last November by about 400 votes. Immediately D'Andrea announced a contest—and a series of killings commenced.

Gaetano Esposito, a strong Powers worker, was tossed out of a speeding motorcar, in the heart of the city, his body riddled with bullets.

Paul A. Labriola, municipal court bailiff, who many believed was being groomed by Powers to take his place, was shot by five men who cornered him on his way to court. After he had fallen, one of his assassins bent over him and fired five times into his back.

The same day Harry Raimondi, a fellow Sicilian of D'Andrea's and another strong Powers worker, was shot while in his own grocery store.

Police were informed that twenty-five Powers workers were on a proscription list. All were marked for death. No Powers man in the ward has felt sure of his life. Then came the first threat of reprisal and vengeance.

"D'Andrea is a dying man," Alderman Powers is reported to have said. "I can no longer keep my men in check."

Everything quieted down—and then D'Andrea was shot on May 11.

But the war in the 19th Ward of Chicago is not yet over. There are hints, there are rumors, and there are whispers in the saloons and cafés and the question that is being whispered is "Who will be the next man to die?"

There are many answers.

Chicago Never Wetter Than Today

☆ THE TORONTO STAR WEEKLY
July 2, 1921

Chicago.—For a time after Prohibition set in there was a romantic aura about obtaining liquor in Chicago. The wily hooch-seeker was accustomed to make various cabalistic signs to the watchful bartender. Cults of the lifted finger and the thumbed ear flourished. There was a certain pride in being "known." That has all passed.

Anyone wanting a drink in Chicago now goes into a bar and gets it. Known or unknown, he will obtain it if he has seventy-five cents. It is safe to say that no one in Chicago is ever more than three blocks away from a saloon where whiskey and gin are sold openly over the bar.

Visitors from other parts of the States are astonished and amazed. It seems unbelievable. But the explanation is very simple.

In Chicago the city police take no part in enforcing the Eighteenth Amendment. Chicago always voted wet, and the Chicago police, with the splendid bovine mind of the American "Bull," still consider it wet.

There are eight federal Prohibition-enforcement officers in Chicago. Four of them are doing office work, the other four are guarding a warehouse. And the city is, except for the price of liquor, as it was before Prohibition became a reality over the rest of the country.

Then there is beer. St. Louis was the greatest brewery city in the States. When Prohibition came into effect, the St. Louis brewers believed that the end had come to the brewery business, and at once turned their big plants into soft-drink factories. Chicago saw the handwriting on the brewery wall, but didn't believe it for a moment. They shut down for a while and then commenced making beer again—real beer—with a greater percentage of alcohol than had been allowed for a long time before the Eighteenth Amendment.

Now we have the interesting spectacle of the St. Louis breweries fighting to have Prohibition enforced. For the tremendous flow of real beer from the Chicago breweries, that have been running full blast, is killing the demand for near beer.

When the breweries first started on their old pre-Prohibition schedule of production, there was a great deal of beer to be had in the city, but it cost fifty cents a stein. Then some bars and restaurants started cutting prices and now real beer can be had all over the city for thirty cents a stein —fifteen cents a glass or fifty dollars a barrel.

The other day in a Loop restaurant I saw three mounted policemen seated at a table with tall steins of beer before them. Their horses were hitched outside the restaurant. As we sat at our table the headwaiter came up and requested that we excuse him just a moment while he moved the table. We rose, the table was pushed to one side, and a trapdoor opened. Out from the trapdoor four white-uniformed bartenders rolled twelve barrels of beer. As they were rolled across the floor, past the policemen's table, the three looked lovingly at the big brown casks.

"It's the real old stuff, Bill," said one appreciatively, "the real good old stuff."

So much for police enforcement of Prohibition.

Of course there are shakedowns. Every bartender who runs openly has to pay his bit for police protection, and that keeps the price of liquor up. To combat this necessity for charging a high tariff for drinks the "Athletic Club" has appeared.

The Nowata Athletic Club is a type of this institution. Its reason for existence is to eliminate the weekly slush fund for police. So far it is highly successful.

Passing a lynx-eyed, derby-hatted, red-faced observer who stands with his hand toying with an electric bell at the entrance, you climb three flights of stairs to the clubrooms. Entrance is barred by a chain lock, and is only effected by presenting a blue card bearing your name and number, and the name of the club. After the card is scrutinized, you are admitted to the clubrooms.

Furnishings of the Nowata Club consist of a number of tables and chairs. As soon as you are seated a Negro waiter appears with a number of drinks equal to the number of men in the party. The charge is only fifty cents a drink and the whiskey is slightly older than that bought over the adjacent bars.

"Fred," the waiter is instructed, "there are some gentlemen here who want to become members of the club."

"Yassuh?" Fred is very dignified. "If they will be so kind as to write theah names on this slip of papah, I will be honohed to tendah them membeahship cahds."

In a short time the membership cards are brought to the members of the party and the Nowata Club's membership is again increased.

There never has been any record of anyone being blackballed at the Nowata Club. Its membership is well over a thousand now and it bids fair to be the largest club in Chicago.

Brokers, board of trade operators and men from the La Salle Street bond houses form the bulk of its membership.

Present conditions cannot last in Chicago. The government will send more Prohibition agents or there will be a less liberal administration, but it is a strange situation at present, a city legally bone-dry, in which liquor is one of the leading occupations.

Condensing the Classics

☆ THE TORONTO STAR WEEKLY
August 20, 1921

They have nearly finished with their job of condensing the classics. They are a little group of earnest condensers, said to be endowed by Andrew Carnegie, who have been laboring for the last five years at reducing the literature of the world into palatable morsels for the tired businessman's consumption.

Les Misérables has been cut to ten pages. *Don Quixote* is said to run to about a column and a half. Shakespeare's plays would be cut to eight hundred words each. The *Iliad* and the *Odyssey* might reduce to about a stick and a half apiece.

It is a splendid thing to bring the classics within range of the tired or retired businessman, even though it casts a stigma on the attempt of the colleges and universities to bring the businessman within range of the classics. But there is a quicker way to present the matter to those who must run while reading: reduce all literature to newspaper headlines, with a short news dispatch following, to give the gist of the matter.

Take *Don Quixote* for example:

CRAZED KNIGHT IN WEIRD TILT

Madrid, Spain (By Classic News Service) (Special).—War hysteria is blamed for the queer actions of "Don" Quixote, a local knight who was arrested early yesterday morning when engaged in the act of "tilting" with a windmill. Quixote could give no explanation of his actions.

William Blake would reduce well.

BIG CAT IN FLAMES

Heat-maddened brute terrorizes jungle

Rajputana, India, June 15 (By Classic News Service) (Special).—William Blake, widely known English poet, arrived here today in a state of nervous collapse after a series of nerve-racking adventures in the Rajputana jungle. Blake was lost without food or clothing for eleven days.

Blake, still delirious, cries, "Tiger, tiger, burning bright in the forest of the night."

Local hunters have gone out in search of the beast. The "forest of the night" is believed to refer to the Nite River, a stream near Rajputana.

Then there is Coleridge:

ALBATROSS-SLAYER FLAYS PROHIBITION

"Ancient" Mariner in bitter assault on bone-dry enforcement

Cardiff, Wales, June 21 (By Classic News Service) (Delayed).—"Water, water everywhere and not a drop to drink" is the way John J. (Ancient) Mariner characterized the present Prohibition regime in an address before the United Preparatory Schools here yesterday. Mariner was mobbed at the end of his address by a committee from the Ornithological Aid Society.

Operas are much too long—there's *Pagliacci*—it doesn't even merit a large headline.

RIOT IN SICILY, 2 DEAD, 12 WOUNDED

Palermo, Sicily, June 25 (By Classic News Service).—Two are dead and half a score wounded as the result of a brawl started in the local opera house here last night. Giuseppe Canio, a ringleader of the rioters, committed suicide.

Shakespeare was obviously verbose and his plots are too sensational. Here's the gist of *Othello*:

SLAYS HIS WHITE BRIDE

Society girl, wed to African war hero, found strangled in bed

Jealousy, fanned into fury by primitive jungle rage, is believed by the police to have caused the death of Mrs. Desdemona Othello of 2345 Ogden Avenue.

It was just a little over two years ago that Captain Frank Othello stepped off the transport at Hoboken. On his breast glittered the decorations bestowed by an admiring sovereign. His dark face gleamed with pleasure as he saw the lithe figure.

There would be more—much more—perhaps. Shakespeare wasn't so verbose after all. The Othello case would fill almost as much space in the newspapers as the Stillman case. Special articles, psychoanalysts' reports, discussions of intermarriage by women feature writers would flood the papers. Perhaps Shakespeare is pretty well condensed as he is.

Muscle Shoals: Cheap Nitrates

☆ THE TORONTO STAR WEEKLY
November 12, 1921

Muscle Shoals means Clam Shallows, but it did not mean even that to most Canadians or Americans until Henry Ford dragged the name out of the wartime morass where it had sunk in company with Hog Island and Eagle Boat and other great war hopes.

Mr. Ford brought Muscle Shoals, Alabama, back into public consciousness when he made an offer to the United States War Department, a few months ago, to buy or lease the great government nitrate plant there for a period of 100 years.

Muscle Shoals is a rocky, shallow place in the Tennessee River in North Central Alabama, where the United States government has built a great concrete-constructed plant for making death and life. It was designed as a death factory, and the largest dam in America was thrown across the river to furnish water power for the manufacture of ammonium nitrate, the base of high explosives. But when the armistice came, scientists set to work converting the grim war plant into an aid to life, and it is now a producer of commercial nitrogen, the element that must be given the soil in order to grow the crops that feed North America and the world.

For years engineers had advocated the construction of a dam across the Tennessee River at the shallows where Muscle Shoals' rocks prevent the passage of steamers up and down the stream.

The country adjacent to Muscle Shoals was surveyed, as a result of this agitation, several years ago. When the United States entered the war, and were at once in need of nitrate in large quantities for explosives, the advocates of Muscle Shoals as a power site pressed their claims to President Wilson and through him convinced the congressional board that the needed nitrate plant should be built at Sheffield, Alabama, three miles from the shoals. A dam was ordered built at the shoals to furnish power for the nitrate project, and at the same time render the river navigable.

After careful consideration the United States government finally decided to build their plant for the manufacture of ammonium nitrate by the cyanamide process and to operate it by steam-generated electrical power until the dam was completed. The nitrate plant was practically completed and in operation two months before the armistice was signed.

It was an interesting situation, a situation interesting to everyone who eats, that forced the United States into the building of the Muscle Shoals nitrate plant. Nitrogen is the base of all explosives, at the same time it is the absolutely indispensable fertilizing element for the growth of the world's great staple crops, corn, wheat, grains and grasses.

Twenty-three years ago Sir William Crookes, the British scientist, made the startling statement that the world was rapidly approaching starvation. Sir William laid this to the concentration of an increasing population into cities and the consequent multiplication of food demands upon each acre of tilled land. He pointed out that the grain-eating habit of mankind was rapidly robbing the soil of its nutrition, that there was not enough agricultural land to keep the race going for more than a few decades and that nothing could avert world famine except the development of new sources of nitrogen and the discovery of new methods to apply this gaseous element to the soil in new and usable forms.

Although Sir William's forecast was too pessimistic (he predicted general starvation by 1933), he served a valuable turn to the world by calling attention to the problem of supplying "fixed" nitrogen.

Before the war, the world's nitrate supply was found in the sodium mountain beds located in the arid, desert plateau of northern Chile and Peru. Germany saw that she was amply supplied with "Chile nitrates" before she made war. She valued the Chilean source so greatly, however, that she lost a part of her fleet off the Falkland Islands when Von Spee's patrolling squadron was wiped out by the British navy.

Confronted by the sudden need of commercial nitrates for the manufacture of ammunition in the United States, the government started the building of the Muscle Shoals plant, and, until it was completed, imported the Chilean product, releasing to the farmers only one-sixth of the 600,000 tons of imported nitrates they need annually.

The Wilson Dam, which is to furnish power for the operation of the nitrate plants, is still some months from completion. With the single exception of the Asswan Dam across the Nile in Upper Egypt, and perhaps the Vyrnwy Dam, in Wales, it will be the largest dam in the world.

Although many subprojects will undoubtedly develop out of the Muscle Shoals great water power, due to its great manufacturing situation, its fundamental purpose is the manufacture of nitrogens, and it is as such that Mr. Ford, and recently other agencies, have offered to take it over from the government. Pressure, however, has been brought to bear on the U.S. government to refuse to appropriate money to complete the Wilson Dam, which is the generative heart of the whole project.

The annual loss in depreciation and interest on the already half-constructed dam will be greater than the appropriation needed to complete it. At the rate at which work was being carried on, the entire dam will be completed in about twenty-two more months.

When completed, in whosever hands it may be, the Muscle Shoals plant will give all of North America what it vitally needs—a source of cheap nitrates for farm consumption. All these nitrates are imported from Chile at present, and their cost will be cut to the bone by American production. Cutting down the cost of nitrates will be a valuable step in reducing the cost of production of all grains and will be a shortcut to lowering the present price of bread.

It seems a long way from a wartime plant on the shallows of the Tennessee River to a reduction in the price of a loaf of bread on a Toronto table, but it is a straight way, if the Muscle Shoals plant is carried on and completed.

On Weddynge Gyftes

☆ THE TORONTO STAR WEEKLY
December 17, 1921

Three traveling clocks
Tick
On the mantelpiece
Comma
But the young man is starving.

That is the beginning of a poem in the best of late 1921 rhythms. The rest of it will never be finished. It is too tragic. It deals with a subject too tragic for this typewriter to chatter about. It is a poem about wedding gifts.

A day will come when I shall be able to hear the words "wedding gift" spoken without suffering the acute nervous sensation of a man who steps unconsciously upon the tail of a large and hitherto silent cat, at the same time thrusting his hand unknowingly into a mass of closely curled rattlesnakes. That day is not yet here.

It started with our rich friends. In common with most other poor people, we have a few rich friends. A rich friend is a wonderful potentiality. You always have a vague sort of feeling that when your very rich and very close friend decides to join his very rich ancestors in one of the more exclusive Elysian residential districts, he may do something very handsome for you in the way of a bequest. You also have a feeling that when you marry, your richest friends may do something very fitting about it all.

All our friends did. They all gave us traveling clocks. Now one traveling clock is a delight; two traveling clocks are a pleasure; three traveling clocks are unnecessary, and four traveling clocks are ridiculous. The traveling clock is evidently the dernier cri in wedding gifts. We have four of them. That ought to be the dernier shout.

There are a number of things we need badly, and a large assortment of things we could use. We need towels, spoons, to replace the tarnished ones that are constantly becoming rusty and scratching the mouths of careless guests, and we need a great deal of money.

When an assortment of checks came from old family friends, at first it seemed sad that the blue slips of paper should be the only reminders of their personalities. Later, when we discovered that large, blue, iridescent fruit bowls were to be the only reminders of the personalities of eighty percent of our friends, we changed our minds. Of course, I have a few friends who remind me of large, blue, iridescent punch bowls but their number is limited.

I once had a friend who reminded me of a large, blue, iridescent traveling brewery, but I recall no friend who reminds me of a suede leather traveling clock. And while I have had a number of friends who were perfect pictures, I have never had a friend who was a perfect picture frame. The gift as an expression of personality is a huge fallacy. What personalities are to be suggested to us by a handsome soup ladle or a Sheffield silver vegetable dish? Even the checks only suggest the personalities of the landlord, the milk man, the telephone company and the grocer.

This all may sound like a cold-blooded lack of appreciation, but while written in a personal way, it is an impersonal protest against wedding gifts as an institution. Some conference on limitation ought to restrict the giving of wedding gifts to the immediate parents of the bride and the immediate parents of the groom.

There are our stairs, for instance. Our landlord, a romanticist, when he rented the apartment, described it as a "third floor apt." That was taking a very romantic view of it. Our landlord would probably refer to a villa on the extreme top of Mount Vesuvius as "an ideal location, well heated, reached by a pleasant climb, only 28 minutes from the heart of Naples."

The first floor in the apartment is called an English Basement. The second floor, I believe, is a Mezzanine. After those two flights the floors proper begin. Ours is on the third floor proper.

Expressmen leave their packages at the English Basement. They do this to the accompaniment of a jovial shout of "One-eighty-nine!" That cabalistic cry means that you must pay the expressman one dollar and eighty-nine cents; a very considerable sum. Personally I have never seen a wedding gift that I would pay one dollar and eighty-nine cents for in cold blood. That, however, is a matter of opinion.

After you settle with the expressman, you stagger up five flights of stairs with the box. The box is always large and heavy. The first flight is comparatively easy; you take it in your stride and think of Alpine climbers, mountaineers and the nobility of toil. On the second flight you think of Mount Everest, the white man's burden and how heavy the box is. After the second flight you just climb.

When you finally open the box, with the aid of a kitchen knife, you find it to be full of excelsior. You make some joke about excelsior. The excelsior spills all over the rug. You plunge into the excelsior in search of the present. It is like going into the center of a haycock in search of an egg. Lifting out a jumble-shaped package, you open it and find a beautiful broken bowl. It represents Uncle George. You drop Uncle George gently into the ashcan and try to get in a little more work before the bell rings again.

Twenty-two boxes came yesterday, forwarded from a distant city collect. One of them contained two handsome towels. They were not broken nor packed in excelsior in an enormous wooden box. Every little while I go over and fondle them lovingly. I do not know whose personality they represent, but I am sure it must be a very lovely one.

Tourists Scarce at Swiss Resorts

☆ THE TORONTO DAILY STAR
February 4, 1922

Les Avants, Switzerland.—Because the Swiss franc is still worth approximately twenty cents, the country is rapidly becoming impoverished. Tourists were always the principal Swiss source of income, and now tourists look at the exchange rates, see that they can get only five francs for a dollar, and stay away from Switzerland. As a result, parts of the country that were jammed with a tourist population before the war now look like the deserted boomtowns of Nevada.

Hundreds of hotels are closed in Switzerland, and the tourists are coming into the country in mere trickles of the streams that poured in before the war. The hotelmen are desperate. Wealthy Swiss people, when they want a holiday, go into the Austrian Tyrol where their francs will buy a bushel basket full of kronen. French people are not coming to Switzerland at all.

"I wish the Swiss franc would drop to the same value as the French," the manager of a big hotel said to me today. "Then we might get our share of the flood of tourists coming to Europe now. Prices here are practically as low as similar resorts in the French Alps, but all the tourists want to get as many francs as they can for their dollars, so they stay away."

As a matter of fact, the tourist would do as well in Switzerland as he would in France, for the big hotels in France and Italy counteract the rate of exchange by raising their prices in proportion. Room and board in a good Swiss hotel cost the tourist fifteen to twenty-five francs or three to five dollars. In a French hotel of the same class the rate would be thirty-five to fifty-five francs in French money, or three to five dollars.

The thing for tourists to remember is that all European hotelkeepers that have any clientele among tourists from America or England watch the exchange rates like hawks and make their room rates correspond to the pre-war value in dollars. So Switzerland is as cheap as anywhere else. But the tourists do not know it and Switzerland is paying the price of neutrality in a quite unforeseen way.

Living on $1,000 a Year in Paris

☆ THE TORONTO STAR WEEKLY
February 4, 1922

Paris.—Paris in the winter is rainy, cold, beautiful and cheap. It is also noisy, jostling, crowded and cheap. It is anything you want—and cheap.

The dollar, either Canadian or American, is the key to Paris. With the U.S. dollar worth twelve and a half francs and the Canadian dollar quoted at something over eleven francs, it is a very effective key.

At the present rate of exchange, a Canadian with an income of one thousand dollars a year can live comfortably and enjoyably in Paris. If exchange were normal the same Canadian would starve to death. Exchange is a wonderful thing.

Two of us are living in a comfortable hotel in the Rue Jacob. It is just back of the Academy of the Beaux Arts and a few minutes' walk from the Tuileries. Our room costs twelve francs a day for two. It is clean, light, well heated, has hot and cold running water and a bathroom on the same floor. That makes a cost for rent of thirty dollars a month.

Breakfast costs us both two francs and a half. That totals seventy-five francs a month, or about six dollars and three or four cents. At the corner of the Rue Bonaparte and the Rue Jacob there is a splendid restaurant where the prices are à la carte. Soup costs sixty centimes and a fish is 1.20 francs. The meals are roast beef, veal cutlet, lamb, mutton and thick steaks served with potatoes prepared as only the French can cook them. These cost 2.40 francs an order. Brussels sprouts in butter, creamed spinach, beans, sifted peas, and cauliflower vary in price from forty to eighty-five centimes. Salad is sixty centimes. Desserts are seventy-five centimes and sometimes as much as a franc. Red wine is sixty centimes a bottle and beer is forty centimes a glass.

My wife and I have an excellent meal there, equal in cooking and quality of food to the best restaurants in America, for fifty cents apiece. After dinner you can go anywhere on the subway for four cents in American money or take a bus to the farthest part of the city for the same amount. It sounds unbelievable but it is simply a case of prices not having advanced in proportion to the increased value of the dollar.

All of Paris is not so cheap, however, for the big hotels located around the Opera and the Madeleine are more expensive than ever. We ran into two girls from New York the other day in the Luxembourg Gardens. All of us crossed on the same boat, and they had gone to one of the big, highly advertised hotels. Their rooms were costing them sixty francs a day apiece, and other charges in proportion. For two days and three nights at their hotel they received a bill for five hundred francs, or forty-two dollars. They are now located in a hotel on the left bank of the Seine, where five hundred francs will last two weeks instead of two days, and are as comfortable as they were at the tourist hotel.

It is from tourists who stop at the large hotels that the reports come that living in Paris is very high. The big hotelkeepers charge all they think the traffic can bear. But there are several hundred small hotels in all parts of Paris where an American or Canadian can live comfortably, eat at attractive restaurants and find amusement for a total expenditure of two and one half to three dollars a day.

Poincaré's Folly

☆ THE TORONTO DAILY STAR
February 4, 1922

Paris.—Canadian interest in European politics is as dead as a bucket of ashes. There are plenty of politics in Canada, and the good Canadian is sick of old-world tangles that are merely older and dirtier than the Dominion product. But all people who were in the war are interested in the inside reason for the turn of events that has cost France the sympathy of the world.

When the armistice came, France occupied the strongest moral position any country could hold. People spoke of "The soul of France." France was immaculate. And then came the peace conference of Versailles.

The world condoned the French attitude at the peace conference because the war was so recent and France had suffered so much that it seemed natural for her to make an unjust, conqueror's peace. It was Clemenceau's peace, his last tigerish move, for now Clemenceau is the deadest name in France. But it was an understandable peace, with the war so recent, and a forgivable peace.

Now the Versailles peace is a long time back, the war is over. Germany is making an earnest effort to build up her country to pay the money she owes the Allies and England is trying to help Germany that she may be able to pay. It is to France's interest to see that Germany has a chance to pay, and she must see that the economic recovery of Germany is necessary if Europe is ever to get back to normal. But France keeps an enormous standing army, rattles the saber against Germany, destroys the effect of the Washington limitation of armament conference by adopting a Prussian attitude about submarines and talks of the next war.

Nobody that had anything to do with this war wants to talk about another war. Least of all should France want there to be a "next war." The French people do not want any war. But, at present, the French people do not happen to be in control of the French government. That is the secret of the whole thing.

The present Chamber of Deputies, which corresponds to the Dominion Parliament, was elected in the year after the war, and the majority is held by the old reactionary party. They believe that they can get all the money they wish out of Germany if they only threaten her enough and cannot see that they will only produce utter bankruptcy and get nothing. They are the ones who want to go on and occupy the Ruhr basin, not realizing that the occupation would cost more money than she could get from the mines. They are too old to learn new things and they no longer represent the people who elected them.

Those old-line politicians were not satisfied with Premier Briand. He was too gentle, and he was fooling with that terrible thing, Russia. So they forced his resignation. Briand was not liberal enough for the Allies and the United States, but that made no difference. He was forced out and Poincaré made premier.

Now Poincaré and the blindest of the reactionaries are in the saddle and riding for all they are worth. But the ride will not be long, and it will be their last ride for a long time. It is the thin majority of the present chamber, coupled with the stupidest of the professional politicians that are giving the world the impression it is getting of France at present. It is a slim majority, and the next election will wipe it out; then France will resume her place as a nation with the good of herself and the world at heart, and cease to be a military power run by an irascible lot of old gentlemen.

For the French people have been thinking and working while their politicians have been talking. If they hadn't been working so hard (unemployment has almost vanished in France) they would have kicked the present Chamber of Deputies out long before this.

Tuna Fishing in Spain

☆ THE TORONTO STAR WEEKLY
February 18, 1922

Vigo, Spain.—Vigo is a pasteboard-looking village, cobble-streeted, white- and orange-plastered, set up on one side of a big, almost landlocked harbor that is large enough to hold the entire British navy. Sun-baked brown mountains slump down to the sea like tired old dinosaurs, and the color of the water is as blue as a chromo of the bay at Naples.

A gray pasteboard church with twin towers and a flat, sullen fort that tops the hill where the town is set up look out on the blue bay, where the good fishermen will go when snow drifts along the northern streams and trout lie nose to nose in deep pools under a scum of ice. For the bright, blue chromo of a bay is alive with fish.

It holds schools of strange, flat, rainbow-colored fish, hunting-packs of long, narrow Spanish mackerel, and big, heavy-shouldered sea bass with odd, soft-sounding names. But principally it holds the king of all fish, the ruler of the Valhalla of fishermen.

The fisherman goes out on the bay in a brown lateen-sailed boat that lists drunkenly and determinedly and sails with a skimming pull. He baits with a silvery sort of a mullet and lets his line out to troll. As the boat moves along, there is a silver splatter in the sea as though a bushel full of buckshot had been tossed in. It is a school of sardines jumping out of the water, forced out by the swell of a big tuna who breaks water with a boiling crash and shoots his entire length of six feet into the air. It is then that the fisherman's heart lodges against his palate, to sink to his heels when the tuna falls back into the water with the noise of a horse diving off a dock.

A big tuna is silver and slate-blue, and when he shoots up into the air from close beside the boat it is like a blinding fish of quicksilver. He may weigh 300 pounds and he jumps with the eagerness and ferocity of a mammoth rainbow trout. Sometimes five and six tuna will be in the air at once in Vigo Bay, shouldering out of the water like porpoises as they herd the sardines, then leaping in a towering jump that is as clean and beautiful as the first leap of a well-hooked rainbow.

The Spanish boatmen will take you out to fish for them for a dollar a day. There are plenty of tuna and they take the bait. It is a back-sickening, sinew-straining, man-sized job even with a rod that looks like a hoe handle. But if you land a big tuna after a six-hour fight, fight him man against fish until your muscles are nauseated with the unceasing strain, and finally bring him up alongside the boat, green-blue and silver in the lazy ocean, you will be purified and will be able to enter unabashed into the presence of the very elder gods and they will make you welcome.

Clemenceau Politically Dead

☆ THE TORONTO DAILY STAR
February 18, 1922

Paris.—There is nothing deader than a dead tiger and Georges Clemenceau was a very great tiger. Therefore Georges Clemenceau is very dead.

Coming from Canada, where an interview with Clemenceau still makes the front page of the newspapers, it is one of the big surprises to find that the one-time Tiger of France is as dead politically as that ex-president of France who lost his place through falling out of a moving Pullman car in his pajamas. No one quotes Clemenceau, no one in the government asks Clemenceau's opinion, when you say "Clemenceau" people merely smile, and finally M. Clemenceau has been forced to start a small newspaper to get his views before the public at all.

If you want an explanation of the atrophy of Clemenceau as a political figure you can go to two places to get it. You may interview politicians who will talk about Versailles, the reparations question, open diplomacy, Genoa, the Ruhr basin, and the Kemalists. Or you can go to the cafés and get the truth. For no politicians could keep a man out of the public eye if the people wanted him.

In the cafés the Frenchmen have nothing to gain or lose by the things they say, so they consequently say the things that they believe. Of course if they have been sitting in a café too long they sometimes say even more than they believe. But if you catch a Frenchman when he has been in the café just long enough to come to a boil, and before he has begun to boil over and spill on the stove, you will find out what he really thinks of Clemenceau or anything else. And if you catch enough Frenchmen in different parts of France, you will have the national opinion; the real national opinion, not the shadow of the national opinion that is reflected in elections and newspapers.

"The things Clemenceau says have turned sour in the mouths of the people. They do not taste like truth. They may have been true once, but they do not taste true now," one Frenchman told me.

"But has everyone forgotten what he did in the war?" I asked.

"The war is over and he was a very great tiger in the war, but he wanted to go on being a tiger after the war. After the war tigers are a handicap to a country. You need workhorses and mules, maybe, but not tigers. The people are tired of Monsieur Clemenceau, and he will have to wait until he is dead to be a great man again."

That is the result of the talk of many Frenchmen. It does not go into details, nor cite instances, but France wants a new type of statesman and needs him badly. She wants a builder instead of a fighter, a man who will think forward instead of backward, and because there is no fighting to be done, with the callousness of republics, she has dropped Clemenceau. He lived too long after his job was finished, and now, as the Frenchman in the café said, "he must wait until he is dead to be a great man again."

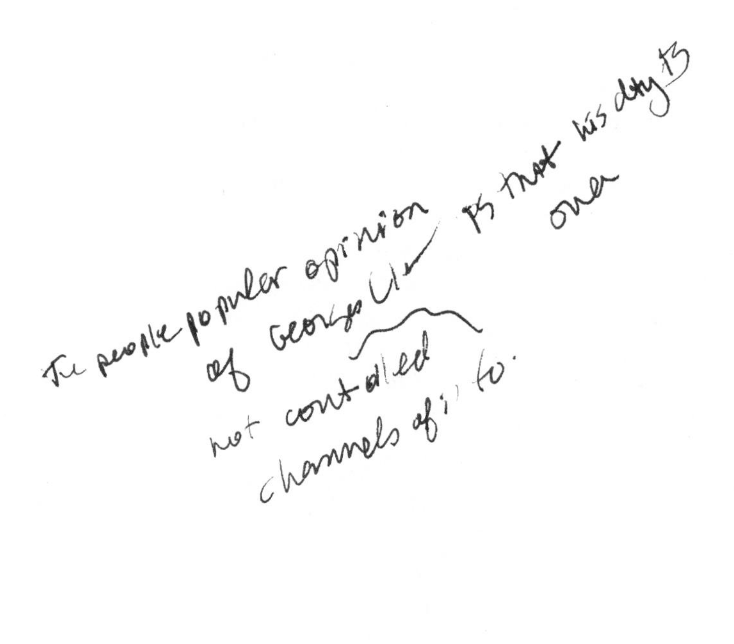

German Export Tax Hits Profiteers

☆ THE TORONTO STAR WEEKLY
February 25, 1922

Basel, Switzerland.—Germany has passed a law taxing exports that makes it impossible for foreigners to buy enormous quantities of German products and make four or five hundred percent profit on them through the low value of the German mark.

Now, when you enter Germany, you are required to furnish the German customs officials with a list of absolutely everything you take into the country. This includes pairs of socks, underclothing, shirts, and even handkerchiefs. No personal clothing is exempt. When you leave Germany, all your belongings are checked over and if you have one shirt more than when you entered the country, you pay a fat export tax on it that robs it of its value as a bargain.

As you go back into Switzerland from Germany you must present your German lists of belongings again and an import tax is levied on anything you have paid to bring out of the German republic. It is a wonderful example of getting them coming and going.

Both Germany and Switzerland have been forced to protect themselves in this manner because of the tremendous difference in value of their money. Before the export and import taxes went into effect, Germany was a happy hunting ground for Swiss exchange pirates. Anyone with a Swiss ten-franc note could buy a half basket full of German marks and it took the Swiss living along the German border about as long as it does a cat to smell fish to realize what they should do with those marks.

A German clothing store in one of the little German towns across the Swiss borderline would open for the day with a store full of goods priced in marks at prices comparable to the wages the Germans in the town were making. A couple of Swiss who had saved two or three weeks' wages in francs and bought all the marks they could carry would enter the store and buy out its entire contents. Then they would drive their wagonload of clothing back a mile or so to the Swiss border to enter their native land and start a clothing store of their own, with prices marked down to half what their own Swiss competitors charged.

These exchange pirates were ruining the market for Swiss products and the Germans in the border villages could get no clothing at all; it was all going to Switzerland. So the governments of both countries passed the present strict customs laws.

Of course there is still a big traffic in smuggled goods but it is nothing like the great days when the Swiss could buy out a clothing store and drive triumphantly home with it for the same expenditure that they would make for a pair of shoes in their own country.

Paris Is Full of Russians

☆ THE TORONTO DAILY STAR
February 25, 1922

Paris.—Paris is full of Russians at present. The Russian ex-aristocracy are scattered all over Europe, running restaurants in Rome, tearooms on Capri, working as hotel porters in Nice and Marseilles and as laborers along the Mediterranean shipping centers. But those Russians who managed to bring some money or possessions with them seem to have flocked to Paris.

They are drifting along in Paris in a childish sort of hopefulness that things will somehow be all right, which is quite charming when you first encounter it and rather maddening after a few months. No one knows just how they live except it is by selling off jewels and gold ornaments and family heirlooms that they brought with them to France when they fled before the revolution.

According to the manager of a great jewel house on the Rue de la Paix, pearls have come down in price because of the large numbers of beautiful pearls that have been sold to Parisian jewel buyers by the Russian refugees. It is true that many Russians are living fairly lavishly in Paris at present on the sale of jewels they have brought with them in their exile.

Just what the Russian colony in Paris will do when all the jewels are sold and all the valuables pawned is somewhat of a question. It is usually impossible for a large body of people to support themselves indefinitely by borrowing money, although a few people enjoy a great success at it for a time. Of course things may change in Russia, something wonderful might happen to aid the Russian colony. There is a café on the Boulevard Montparnasse where a great number of Russians gather every day for this something wonderful to happen and to recall the great old days of the Czar. But there is a great probability that nothing very wonderful nor unexpected will happen and then, eventually, like all the rest of the world, the Russians of Paris may have to go to work. It seems a pity, they are such a charming lot.

Papal Poll: Behind the Scenes

☆ THE TORONTO STAR WEEKLY
March 4, 1922

Paris.—Once a week Anglo-American newspaper correspondents resident in Paris meet to talk shop. If the world could have a Dictaphone in the room it would have such a backstage view of European politicians, conferences, coronations and world affairs that it would spin very fast for quite a time from the shock.

All week the correspondents have been mailing or cabling dispatches giving the news as they saw it as trained professional observers. For a couple of hours each Wednesday they talk it over as they saw it as human beings watching human beings instead of newspapermen with diplomas.

"They crowned the pope on a plain pine board throne, put together just for that," says one of the men who has spent twenty-one days in Rome covering the death of the pope [Benedict IV] and the coronation of the new pontiff [Pius XI] for one of the big wireservices.

"It reminded me of a fraternity initiation when I saw the throne and watched them getting the scenery out the day before."

"Afterwards Johnson and I" (the name isn't Johnson, but that of a correspondent of one of the great press syndicates) "were talking with Cardinal Gasparri about why they didn't wait for the American cardinals. Johnson was asking him why they hadn't waited.

" 'We do things very quickly here,' Gasparri said to Johnson.

" 'Perhaps you do them a little too quickly for Americans and Canadians, your eminence,' Johnson said to him.

" 'We have to be careful about you newspapermen,' the cardinal said to Johnson.

" 'Perhaps you wouldn't have to be if you took us more into your confidence, your eminence," Johnson answered.

" 'Who is that funny little fat man?' Gasparri asked one of his attendants.

" 'You have a lot of nerve to call me fat, your eminence,' Johnson said."

The dialogue between the Vatican and the press did not appear in any of the news dispatches. Neither did the news dispatches tell of the difficulties the correspondents had to get their news out of Rome.

All cables were sent from the post office, where there were three rooms for newspapermen. In one of those rooms one typewriter was permitted to be used. More than one typewriter was supposed to make too much noise for the Italian correspondents to be able to think. When the Americans and Britons unlimbered Coronas there was a fearful row.

Half the people in the telegraph office were betting on the result of the balloting for the new head of the church, and when an American correspondent would tear through the crowd from the phone to write on a cable blank, he would be hemmed in by excited shouters demanding in German, French and Italian to know his news.

A papal censorship had been established and all cables containing the names of certain cardinals were automatically held up at the sending office. In the end this censorship protected some correspondents who had learned from "absolutely reliable sources" of the election of a certain cardinal who did not become the new pope, and sent cables announcing his election.

Rome was jammed for the coronation of the pope but there were only about fifty newspapermen. This is accounted for by the speed with which the election of a new pope follows the death of the old; there is not time to get men over from abroad to cover the event. Prices were sky high and double and treble rates in force for Americans.

"I found the way to get through the crowds though," an American correspondent said. "The only people in Italy who wear silk hats are diplomats and so I bought a top hat, and whenever I wanted to get through anywhere I put it on, and it worked like a charm."

By dint of top hats, bribes, shoving, proxies, and Italians to translate the Italian newspapers, the correspondents got the news, and sometimes got it on the wire. To read the even paragraphs in the news dispatches, you would have no idea under what conditions they were written.

Try Bobsledding if You Want Thrills

☆ THE TORONTO DAILY STAR
March 4, 1922

Les Avants, Switzerland.—If you want a thrill of the sort that starts at the base of your spine in a shiver and ends with your nearly swallowing your heart, as it leaps with a jump into your mouth, try bobsledding on a mountain road at fifty miles an hour.

The bob holds two persons. There is a steering wheel about twice as big as a doughnut for the victim in front to hang on to and two steel brakes that jam into the road on either side of the rear of the sled to make arm holds for the victims in the rear. You sit down, someone shoves you, and the road starts slipping about six inches below where you are sitting. On a steep slope of icy road it takes a bobsled just about as long to get started into high as it does a gun to shoot after you pull the trigger.

You hang on to the wheel, watch the road and a mountain unreels alongside of you like a movie film. The bob is rushing along with a steely lisp from the runners and a rising dive like the galloping horse when you hit the uneven places in the road. It is picking up speed and you make a turn and the road drops down an even steeper shoot of road and the bob roars down over the ice. There is a great snowy valley on the left with huge saw-toothed bulks of mountains on the other side, but you only get rushing glimpses of it out of the corner of your eye as the bob shrieks around a turn.

You feel it is all you can do to hold the sled on to the road when the road swoops into a forest and you roar through it on the iciness of the road that is as hard as the way of the transgressor. Just then you hear a shout of "Garde" behind you and the braker looks around and sees through the trees a big eight-passenger bob just dropping down the slope into the forest stretch of the road. Everyone in the big bob screams at you and you pull over to the right of the road to let them pass. But the road is icier there and you pick up more speed while they are slowed by the newer snow at the left and fall back of you again. You go down the next slope abreast with the bob runners making a whispering rush on the ice and then at a wide turn they pass you with a roar and a slither of ice from the brakes.

The road is not so steep here and you slow to about twenty miles an hour and steer with one hand, wipe the wind tears out of your eyes and look back at the sunset that is turning the white shoulders of the mountain pink. It is just a glimpse, for the road dips into another stretch of timber and you roar down the last steep slope to the railway station. There are a crowd of people in snow clothes and four or five bobs waiting for the train to take them up the mountain and you stamp your feet warm and brush the snow and ice thrown up by the brakes from each other's backs. While you wait for the train, you munch at ham sandwiches that a little boy peddles from a basket to the bobsledders, watch the sun go down over the great sweep of snow-covered country and wonder why people go to Palm Beach or the Riviera in the wintertime.

The Hotels in Switzerland

☆ THE TORONTO STAR WEEKLY
March 4, 1922

Les Avants, Switzerland.—Switzerland is a small, steep country, much more up-and-down than sideways, and is all stuck over with large brown hotels built on the cuckoo-clock style of architecture. Every place that the land goes sufficiently sideways a hotel is planted, and all the hotels look as though they had been cut out by the same man with the same scroll saw.

You walk along a wild-looking road through a sweep of dark forest that spreads over the side of a mountain. There are deer tracks in the snow and a big raven teeters back and forth on the high branch of a pine tree, watching you examine the tracks. Down below there is a snow-softened valley that climbs into white, jagged peaks with more splashes of pine forest on their peaks. It is as wild as the Canadian Rockies. Then you round a bend in the road and see four monstrous hotels looking like mammoth children's playhouses of the iron-dog-on-the-front-lawn period of Canadian architecture squatting on the side of the mountain. It does something to you.

The fashionable hotels of Switzerland are scattered over the country, like billboards along the right of way of a railroad and in winter are filled with the utterly charming young men, with rolling white sweaters and smoothly brushed hair, who make a living playing bridge. These young men do not play bridge with each other, not in working hours at least. They are usually playing with women who are old enough to be their mothers and who deal with a flashing of platinum rings on plump fingers. I do not know just how it all is worked, but the young men look quite contented and the women can evidently afford to lose.

Then there are the French aristocracy. These are not the splendid aristocracy of toothless old women and white-mustached old men that are making a final stand in the Faubourg St. Honoré in Paris against ever-increasing prices. The French aristocracy that comes to Switzerland consists of very young men who wear very old names and very-tight-in-the-knees riding breeches with equal grace. They are the few that have the great names of France who, through some holdings or other in iron or coal, were enriched by the war and are able to stop at the same hotels with the men who sold blankets and wine to the army. When the young men with the old names come into a room full of profiteers, sitting with their pre-money wives and post-money daughters, it is like seeing a slim wolf walk into a pen of fat sheep. It seems to puncture the value of the profiteers' titles. No matter what their nationality, they have a heavy, ill-at-ease look.

Besides the bridge men who were the dancing men and will be again, and the old and the new aristocracy, the big hotels house ruddy English families who are out all day on the ski slopes and bobsled runs; pale-faced men who are living in the hotel because they know when they leave it they will be a long time in the sanitarium, elderly women who fill a loneliness with the movement of the hotel life, and a good sprinkling of Americans and Canadians who are traveling for pleasure.

The Swiss make no difference between Canadians and citizens of the United States. I wondered about this, and asked a hotelkeeper if he didn't notice any difference between the people from the two countries.

"Monsieur," he said, "Canadians speak English and always stay two days longer at any place than Americans do." So there you are.

Hotelkeepers, they say, are very wise. But all the Americans I have seen so far were very busy learning to talk English. Harvard was founded for that purpose, it is sometimes rumored, so if the people from the States ever slow up, the hotelkeepers may have to find some new tests.

Wives Buy Clothes for French Husbands

☆ THE TORONTO STAR WEEKLY
March 11, 1922

Paris.—At last the balloon-shaped, narrow-at-the-bottom trousers of the French workman are explained. People have wondered for years why the French workingman wanted to get himself up in the great billowy trousers that were so tight at the cuffs as to hardly be able to pull over his feet. Now it is out. He doesn't. His wife buys them for him.

Recently at the noon hour in French factories there has been a great trading of clothing by the men. They exchange coats, trousers, hats and shoes. It is a revolt against feminism. For the wife of a French workingman from time immemorial has bought all her husband's clothes, and now the Frenchman is beginning to protest against it.

Two Frenchmen who served in the same regiment together and had not seen each other since the demobilization aired their grievances in a bus the other day when they met.

"Your hair, Henri!" said one.

"My wife, old one, she cuts it. But your hair, also? It is not too chic!"

"My wife too. She cuts it also. She says barbers are dirty pigs, but at the finish I must give her the same tip as I would give the barber."

"Ah the hair is a small matter. Regard these shoes."

"My poor old friend! Such shoes. It is incredible."

"It is my wife's system. She goes into the shop and says, 'I want a pair of shoes for mon mari. Not expensive. Mon mari's feet are this much longer than mine, I believe, and about this much wider. That will do nicely. Wrap them up.' Old one, it is terrible!"

"But me also. I am clothed in bargains. What matter if they do not fit? They are bon marché. Still she is a wonderful cook. She is a cook beyond comparison. My old one, it would take one of your understanding to appreciate what a treasure among cooks she is."

"Mine also. A cook beyond all price. A jewel of the first water of cooks. What do clothes matter after all?"

"It is true. Truly it is true! They are a small matter."

So in spite of the trading which has been going on in the factories and sporadic outbreaks of protest, the reign of feminism will probably continue.

Tip the Postman Every Time?

☆ THE TORONTO STAR WEEKLY
March 11, 1922

Paris.—Tipping the postman is the only way to insure the arrival of your letters in certain parts of Spain.

The postman comes in sight down the street waving a letter. "A letter for the Señor," he shouts. He hands it to you.

"A splendid letter, is it not, Señor? I, the postman, brought it to you. Surely the good postman will be well rewarded for the delivery of such a splendid letter?"

You tip the postman. It is a little more than he had expected. He is quite overcome.

"Señor," says the postman, "I am an honest man. Your generosity has touched my heart. Here is another letter. I had intended to save it for tomorrow to insure another reward from the always generous Señor. But here it is. Let us hope it will be as splendid a letter as the first!"

The postman bows and departs. If you have been in Spain long enough you are able to hang on to your temper. It is the climate that does it, they say. The climate is so soft and gentle that it makes it seem not worthwhile to kill the postman. Life is mellow in Spain.

The conversation above actually occurred, and was brought back to Paris intact by an American who has been painting down in Majorca. All the American magazines that were sent to him had illustrations cut out. They were excised to brighten the walls of the local post office.

When the artist asked the postman about the magazines, he answered, "We have so little to read. It is such a dull town. Surely the Señor who has so much would not grudge us the mere pictures from his reviews?"

"And do you know," the artist said, "after a while I got so that it didn't bother me a bit. It's funny the way things get you down here."

It must certainly be the climate.

Poincaré's Election Promises

☆ THE TORONTO DAILY STAR
March 11, 1922

Paris.—No matter what your political views may be, it is impossible not to admire the way ex-President Raymond Poincaré, newly appointed prime minister of France, is administering his government.

M. Poincaré has a difficult task. It was made more difficult because for a long time before he came back into power he had been explaining from the outside just what he would do if he were in power. Then he was suddenly required to do all the things he had been suggesting as an onlooker. The situation presented difficulties.

It is easier to advise than execute and so far M. Poincaré has occupied no territory, nor sent French troops into any new territory. But he and his government have settled down to a study and administration of their various departments that is drawing much admiration. Meetings of the heads of various departments are held each week and the underheads confer constantly. This efficiency contrasts with the Briand government, which was greatly lacking in liaison between its different branches.

Financial affairs look better each day. The inflating of the paper currency has been stopped. Unemployment is daily less and French export trade is booming. Germany's meeting of her indemnity payments in the present revised schedule has been a stabilizing factor.

Of course the French budget is still a long way from balancing, and there are the national defense bonds, which run from three months to a year in length, to be paid. The official journal has recently announced that there will be no more of these bonds issued. That means that those outstanding, some 68 billion francs according to reports, will have to be paid inside of a year at the latest. The government may plan to convert them to long-term bonds, but the people who have bought them have tied up their money with the understanding that they are to get it back in a year. Being French people, there is a very great chance that at the end of the year, the six months or the three months, they will ask for their money in cash. That may start the paper-money presses going again.

Meanwhile the Poincaré ministry is going well. "France was quite sick," an American writer who has lived in France for many years said to me the other day, "and she tried all sorts of medicines. Finally, after she had tried doctors of all sorts, she took to Poincaré, who is a patent medicine." Now it appears that the patent medicine is making a cure.

Sparrow Hat on Paris Boulevards

☆ THE TORONTO STAR WEEKLY
March 18, 1922

Paris.—Parisian milliners have at last discovered a use for the English sparrow. The sparrow hat has made its appearance on the boulevards and the unpopular little bird has come into its own.

The new hat, of which milliners assure me they are having a big sale, is a brown, mushroom-shaped affair with a girdle of stuffed English sparrows. The sparrows look as though they were nestling against the band of the hat and there are about fifteen of them to a headpiece.

So far the milliners are pushing the sparrow creation strongly. Still, you never can tell, it took monkey fur a long time to catch on but the only thing that will ever end the monkey-fur rule now is for the monkeys to give out. The peculiar long-furred monkey has to be imported from Africa and South America and is becoming noticeably scarcer. There will not be that trouble with sparrows at any rate.

The Luge of Switzerland

☆ THE TORONTO STAR WEEKLY
March 18, 1922

Chamby sur Montreux, Switzerland.—The luge is the Swiss flivver. It is also the Swiss canoe, the Swiss horse-and-buggy, the Swiss pram and the Swiss combination riding horse and taxi. Luge is pronounced looge, and is a short, stout sled of hickory built on the pattern of little girls' sleds in Canada.

You realize the omnipotence of the luge when on a bright Sunday you see all of Switzerland, from old grandmothers to street children, coasting solemnly down the steep mountain roads, sitting on these little elevated pancakes with the same tense expression on all their faces. They steer with their feet stuck straight out in front and come down a twelve-mile run at a speed of from twelve to thirty miles an hour.

Swiss railroads run special trains for lugeurs between Montreux, at the edge of Lake Geneva, and the top of Col du Sonloup, a mountain 4,000 feet above sea level. Twelve trains a day are packed on Sunday, with families and their sleds. They put up their lunch, buy an all-day ticket, good for any number of rides on the winding, climbing, Bernese Oberland railway, and then spend the day sliding gloriously down the long, icy mountain road.

Steering a luge takes about as long to learn as riding a bicycle. You get on the sled, lean far back and the luge commences to move down the icy road. If it starts to sheer off to the right, you drop your left leg and if it goes too far to the left, you let your right foot drag. Your feet are sticking straight out before you. That is all there is to steering, but there is a great deal more to keeping your nerve.

You go down a long steep stretch of road flanked by a six-hundred-foot drop-off on the left and bordered by a line of trees on the right. The sled goes fast from the start and soon it is rushing faster than anything you have ever felt. You are sitting absolutely unsupported, only ten inches above the ice, and the road is feeding past you like a movie film. The sled you are sitting on is only just large enough to make a seat and is rushing at motor-car speed toward a sharp curve. If you lean your body away from the curve and drop the right foot, the luge will swing around the curve in a slither of ice and drop shooting down the next slope. If you upset on a turn, you are hurled into a snowbank or go shooting down the road, lugeing along on various plane surfaces of your anatomy.

Additional hazards are provided for the lugeurs by hay sleds and wood sleds. These have long, curved-up runners, and are used to haul the hay down from the mountain meadows where it was cut and cured in the summer, or to bring down great loads of firewood and faggots cut in the forests. They are big, slow-moving sledges and are pulled by their drivers, who haul them by the long curved-up runners and pull themselves up in front of their loads to coast down the steepest slopes.

Because there are many lugeurs, the men with the hay and wood sleds get tired of pulling their loads to one side when they hear a lugeur come shooting down, shouting for the right of way. A lugeur at thirty miles an hour, with no brakes but his feet, has the option of hitting the sleds ahead of him or shooting off the road. It is considered a very bad omen to hit a wood sled.

There is a British colony at Bellaria, near Vevey, in the canton of Vaud, on Lake Geneva. The two apartment buildings they live in are at the foot of the mountains and the British are nearly all quite rapid luguers. They can leave Bellaria, where there will be no snow and a mild, springlike breeze, and in half an hour by the train be up in the mountain where there are fast, frozen roads and thirty inches of snow on the level. Yet the air is so dry and the sun shines so brightly that while the Bellarians are waiting for a train at Chamby, halfway up the mountain to Sonloup, they have tea out of doors in the afternoon in perfect comfort clad in nothing heavier than sports clothes.

The road from Chamby to Montreux is very steep and fairly dangerous for lugeing. It is, however, one of the favorite runs of the Britons from Bellaria, who take it nightly on their way home to their comfortable apartment buildings just above the lake. This makes some very interesting pictures, as the road is only used by the most daring lugeurs.

One wonderful sight is to see the ex-military governor of Khartoum seated on a sled that looks about the size of a postage stamp, his feet stuck straight out at the sides, his hands in back of him, charging a smother of ice dust down the steep, high-walled road with his muffler straight out behind him in the wind and a cherubic smile on his face while all the street urchins of Montreux spread against the walls and cheer him wildly as he passes.

It is easy to understand how the British have such a great Empire after you have seen them luge.

Black Novel a Storm Center

☆ THE TORONTO STAR WEEKLY
March 25, 1922

Paris.—"Batouala," the novel by René Maran, a Negro, winner of the Goncourt Academy Prize of 5,000 francs for the best novel of the year by a young writer, is still the center of a swirl of condemnation, indignation and praise.

Maran, who was born in Martinique and educated in France, was bitterly attacked in the Chamber of Deputies the other day as a defamer of France, and biter of the hand that fed him. He has been much censured by certain Frenchmen for his indictment of French imperialism in its effects on the natives of the French colonies. Others have rallied to him and asked the politicians to take the novel as a work of art, except for the preface, which is the only bit of propaganda in the book.

Meanwhile, René Maran, black as Sam Langford [the boxer], is ignorant of the storm his book has caused. He is in the French government service in Central Africa, two days' march from Lake Tchad, and seventy days' travel from Paris. There are no telegraphs or cables at his post, and he does not even know his book has won the famous Goncourt Prize.

The preface of the novel describes how peaceful communities of 10,000 blacks in the heart of Africa have been reduced to 1,000 inhabitants under the French rule. It is not pleasant and it gives the facts by a man who has seen them, in a plain, unimpassioned statement.

Launched into the novel itself, the reader gets a picture of a native village seen by the big-whited eyes, felt by the pink palms, and the broad, flat, naked feet of the African native himself. You smell the smells of the village, you eat its food, you see the white man as the black man sees him, and after you have lived in the village you die there. That is all there is to the story, but when you have read it, you have seen Batouala, and that makes it a great novel.

It opens with Batouala, the chief of the village, waking up in his hut, roused by the cold of the early morning and the crumbling of the ground under his body where the ants are tunneling. He blows his dead fire into life and sits, hunched over, warming his chilled body and wondering whether he will go back to sleep or get up.

It closes with Batouala, old and with the stiffened joints of his age, cruelly torn by the leopard that his spear-thrust missed, lying on the earth floor of his hut. The village sorcerer has left him alone, there is a younger chief in the village, and Batouala lies there feverish and thirsty, dying, while his mangy dog licks at his wounds. And while he lies there, you feel the thirst and the fever and the rough, moist tongue of the dog.

There will probably be an English translation shortly. To be translated properly, however, there should be another Negro who has lived a life in the country two days' march from Lake Tchad and who knows English as René Maran knows French.

American Bohemians in Paris

☆ THE TORONTO STAR WEEKLY
March 25, 1922

Paris.—The scum of Greenwich Village, New York, has been skimmed off and deposited in large ladles on that section of Paris adjacent to the Café Rotonde. New scum, of course, has risen to take the place of the old, but the oldest scum, the thickest scum and the scummiest scum has come across the ocean, somehow, and with its afternoon and evening levees has made the Rotonde the leading Latin Quarter showplace for tourists in search of atmosphere.

It is a strange-acting and strange-looking breed that crowd the tables of the Café Rotonde. They have all striven so hard for a careless individuality of clothing that they have achieved a sort of uniformity of eccentricity. A first look into the smoky, high-ceilinged, table-crammed interior of the Rotonde gives you the same feeling that hits you as you step into the bird-house at the zoo. There seems to be a tremendous, raucous, many-pitched squawking going on, broken up by many waiters who fly around through the smoke like so many black and white magpies. The tables are full—they are always full—someone is moved down and crowded together, something is knocked over, more people come in at the swinging door, another black and white waiter pivots between tables toward the door and, having shouted your order at his disappearing back, you look around you at individual people.

You can only see a certain number of individuals at the Rotonde on one night. When you have reached your quota you are quite aware that you must go. There is a perfectly definite moment when you know you have seen enough of the Rotonde's inmates and must leave. If you want to know how definite it is, try and eat your way through a jug of soured molasses. To some people the feeling that you cannot go on will come at the first mouthful. Others are hardier. But there is a limit for all normal people. For the people who crowd together around the tables of the Café Rotonde do something very definite to that premier seat of the emotions, the stomach.

For the first dose of Rotonde individuals you might observe a short, dumpy woman with newly blond hair, cut Old-Dutch-Cleanser fashion, a face like a pink enameled ham and fat fingers that reach out of the long blue silk sleeves of a Chinese-looking smock. She is sitting hunched forward over the table, smoking a cigarette in a two-foot holder, and her flat face is absolutely devoid of any expression.

She is looking flatly at her masterpiece that is hung on the white plaster wall of the café, along with some 3,000 others, as part of the Rotonde's salon for customers only. Her masterpiece looks like a red mince pie descending the stairs, and the adoring, though expressionless, painter spends every afternoon and evening seated at the table before it in a devout attitude.

After you have finished looking at the painter and her work you can turn your head a little and see a big, light-haired woman sitting at a table with three young men. The big woman is wearing a picture hat of the "Merry Widow" period and is making jokes and laughing hysterically. The three young men laugh whenever she does. The waiter brings the bill, the big woman pays it, settles her hat on her head with slightly unsteady hands, and she and the three young men go out together. She is laughing again as she goes out of the door. Three years ago she came to Paris with her husband from a little town in Connecticut, where they had lived and he had painted with increasing success for ten years. Last year he went back to America alone.

Those are two of the twelve hundred people who jam the Rotonde. You can find anything you are looking for at the Rotonde—except serious artists. The trouble is that people who go on a tour of the Latin Quarter look in at the Rotonde and think they are seeing an assembly of the great artists of Paris. I want to correct that in a very public manner, for the artists of Paris who are turning out creditable work resent and loathe the Rotonde crowd.

The fact that there are twelve francs for a dollar brought over the Rotonders, along with a good many other people, and if the exchange ever gets back to normal they will all have to go back to America. They are nearly all loafers expending the energy that an artist puts into his creative work in talking about what they are going to do and condemning the work of all artists who have gained any degree of recognition. By talking about art they obtain the same satisfaction that the real artist does in his work. That is very pleasant, of course, but they insist upon posing as artists.

Since the good old days when Charles Baudelaire led a purple lobster on a leash through the same old Latin Quarter, there has not been much good poetry written in cafés. Even then I suspect that Baudelaire parked the lobster with the concierge down on the first floor, put the chloroform bottle corked on the washstand and sweated and carved at the *Fleurs du*

Mal alone with his ideas and his paper as all artists have worked before and since. But the gang that congregates at the corner of the Boulevard Montparnasse and the Boulevard Raspail have no time to work at anything else; they put in a full day at the Rotonde.

Wild Night Music of Paris

☆ THE TORONTO STAR WEEKLY
March 25, 1922

Paris.—After the cork has popped on the third bottle and the jazz band has brayed the American suit- and cloak-buyer into such a state of exaltation that he begins to sway slightly with the glory of it all, he is liable to remark thickly and profoundly: "So this is Paris!"

There is some truth in the remark. It is Paris. It is a Paris bounded by the buyer's hotel, the Folies Bergère and the Olympia, traversed by the Grands Boulevards, monumented with Maxim's and the So-Different, and thickly blotched with the nightlife resorts of Montmartre. It is an artificial and feverish Paris operated at great profit for the entertainment of the buyer and his like who are willing to pay any prices for anything after a few drinks.

The buyer demands "that Paris be a super-Sodom and a grander Gomorrah" and once alcohol loosens his strong racial grasp on his pocketbook he is willing to pay for his ideal. He does pay for it too, for the prices charged at the various Parisian resorts that begin to liven up around midnight are such that only a war profiteer, a Brazilian millionaire, or an American on a spree can pay.

Champagne, that can be bought anywhere in the afternoon for 18 francs a bottle, automatically increases in price after ten o'clock to 85 to 150 francs. Other prices are in proportion. An evening at a fashionable dancing café will cut into a foreigner's pocketbook to the extent of at least 800 francs. If the pleasure-seeker includes a supper in his program he will be lucky to get out without spending a thousand francs. And the people he is with will do it all so gracefully that he will, after the first bottle, consider it a privilege until the next morning when he contemplates the damaged bankroll.

From the taxi-driver who automatically cranks up five francs on his meter as soon as he picks up an American, either North or South, from in front of a fashionable hotel, to the last waiter in the last place he visits who has no change under five francs, the study of rooking the rich foreigner in search of pleasure has been reduced to a fine art. The trouble is that no matter how much he pays for it, the tourist is not seeing what he really wants.

He wants to see the nightlife of Paris and what he does see is a special performance by a number of bored but well-paid people of a drama that has run many thousands of nights and is entitled "Fooling the Tourist." While he is buying champagne and listening to a jazz band, around the corner somewhere there is a little Bal Musette where the apaches, the people he thinks he is seeing, hang out with their girls, sit at long benches in the little smoky room, and dance to the music of a man with an accordion who keeps time with the stamping of his boots.

On gala nights, there is a drummer at the Bal Musette, but the accordion player wears a string of bells around his ankle and these, with the stamping of his boots as he sits swaying on a dais above the dancing floor, give the accent to the rhythm. The people that go to the Bal Musette do not need to have the artificial stimulant of the jazz band to force them to dance. They dance for the fun of it and they occasionally hold someone up for the fun of it, and because it is easy and exciting and pays well. Because they are young and tough and enjoy life, without respecting it, they sometimes hit too hard, or shoot too quick, and then life becomes a very grim matter with an upright machine that casts a thin shadow and is called a guillotine at the end of it.

Occasionally the tourist does come in contact with the real nightlife. Walking down the quiet hill along some lonely street in a champagne haze about two o'clock in the morning, he sees a pair of hard-faced kids come out of an alley. They are nothing like the sleek people he has just left. The two kids look around down the street to see if there is a policeman in sight and then close in on the night-walking tourist. Their closing in and a sudden dreadful jar are all that he remembers.

It is a chop back of the ear with a piece of lead pipe wrapped in [*Le*] *Matin* that does the trick and the tourist has at last made contact with the real nightlife he has spent so much money in seeking.

"Two hundred francs? The pig!" Jean says in the darkness of the basement lit by the match which Georges struck to look at the contents of the wallet.

"The Red Mill holds him up worse than we did, not so, my old?"

"But yes. And he would have a headache tomorrow morning anyway," says Jean. "Come on back to the Bal."

The Mecca of Fakers

☆ THE TORONTO DAILY STAR
March 25, 1922

Paris.—Paris is the Mecca of the bluffers and fakers in every line of endeavor from music to prizefighting. You find more famous American dancers who have never been heard of in America; more renowned Russian dancers who are disclaimed by the Russians; and more champion prizefighters who were preliminary boys before they crossed the ocean, per square yard in Paris than anywhere else in the world.

This state of affairs exists because of the extreme provinciality of the French people, and because of the gullibility of the French press. Everyone in Canada knows the names of half a dozen French soldiers and statesmen, but no one in France could give you the name of a Canadian general or statesman or tell you who was the present head of the Canadian government. By no one I mean none of the ordinary people; shop keepers, hotel owners and general bourgeois class. For example, my *femme de ménage* was horrified yesterday when I told her there was a Prohibition in Canada and the States. "Why have we never heard of it?" she asked. "Has it just been a law? What then does a man drink?"

An American girl was recently billed at the Paris music halls as "America's best known and best loved dancer." None of the recent arrivals in Paris from the States had ever heard of her, but Parisians flocked to see the American "Star." Later it came out that she had a small part in a U.S. musical show some years ago.

Russians have inundated the city. They can get away with almost anything, because it is easy for a Russian to claim that he was anything he may want to say, in Russia; there is no way to check up on Russian reputations at present. So we have great Russian dancers, great Russian pianists, flutists, composers, and organists—all equally bad.

Jack Clifford, who styled himself the colored light-heavyweight champion of the United States and Canada, was a recent nine-days' wonder in France. He avoided meeting any fighters and demanded tremendous sums to box, but announced his willingness to meet Carpentier if a suitable purse was offered. No American had ever heard of him—but the Europeans swallowed him whole.

Clifford met his downfall in Vienna, where a third-rate Austrian pugilist, with an unpronounceable name, punished him so badly that the fight was halted in the third round to save the Negro from further punishment. Clifford had been on the floor most of the evening and did not show even an amateur's knowledge of fighting. The crowd, which had paid several baskets of kronen apiece to see the American black champion, attempted to lynch Clifford with the ropes cut from the ring, but the Negro was saved by the police and left Vienna that night.

At present a familiar figure to those Torontonians who attend boxing matches is basking in the pleasant spotlight of European publicity. It is none other than Soldier Jones. Jones is being hailed by the Paris papers as "the heavyweight champion of Canada, the man who has never been knocked off his feet, the winner of eighty-five fights by knockouts and the best fighter that Canada has ever produced."

Jones is at present in England, where he is being groomed for a fight with [Joe] Beckett, but his manager has sent press dope over to Paris, where it is being published by the English papers and avidly copied by the French.

Torontonians who recall what happened one night last year, when this same Soldier Jones abandoned caution so far as to enter the ring with Harry Greb, will be able to form their own opinions of how easy it is to become a "champion" abroad. The only rule seems to be that you must choose to be a champion of some very distant country and then stay away from that country. That is the way the fiddlers, fighters, painters and dancers are doing.

M. Deibler, A Much-Feared Man

☆ THE TORONTO DAILY STAR
April 1, 1922

Paris.—Monsieur Deibler is the most feared man in France. Deibler lives comfortably and respectively in a snug bourgeois suburb of Paris. He is a large, jovial-looking man and his neighbors know that he has some permanent position or other with the Ministry of Justice. They do not fear Deibler on the Avenue de Versailles, where he lives, because they do not know Deibler.

Every so often Deibler and three heavily built men go off on a mysterious trip. They are accompanied by a boxcar that carries the very grimmest load a French train has ever hauled. It is these trips that have earned Deibler his name of the most feared man in France, for in the boxcar is a guillotine.

Deibler is the permanent public executioner of France. He receives a fixed salary and fees for executions out of which he pays his three husky assistants. One of his assistants is his son-in-law, who, when business is light, runs a small café.

Deibler has two guillotines. One is a very large model, a replica of the grim framework that stood in the Place de la Concorde when the tumbrils jolted along the cobbled, narrow way of the Rue St. Honoré. The large guillotine is used for executions in Paris. The other guillotine is much smaller and is kept loaded in a special box ready to travel with Deibler and his three aides to any part of the provinces.

Under the French law a condemned prisoner is not told the time of his execution until an hour before it is to occur. Execution takes place at daybreak. The condemned man is aroused, signs certain papers, is given a cigarette and a drink of rum, the barber is called in to shave the back of the prisoner's neck and he is marched out to meet Monsieur Deibler. The guillotine is set up just outside the prison gate and troops keep any spectators a hundred yards away. It is the French law.

When it is all over, M. Deibler and his three muscular assistants take down the guillotine and go back to Paris, where the son-in-law totals up the receipts of his café and Monsieur Deibler returns to his family. The Avenue de Versailles is glad to see him back, he is a very jolly man, and his neighbors say: "Deibler's back. He's been away on another of his trips for the government. I wonder what this Deibler does, anyway?"

95,000 Wear the Legion of Honor

☆ THE TORONTO DAILY STAR
April 1, 1922

Paris.—Have you your cross of the Legion of Honor? If not, there is not much chance of getting it now for the boom days are past.

M. Raynaldy, of the French Chamber of Deputies, threw a handful of sand into the smooth-working distribution of decorations of the Legion of Honor when he placed some figures before a committee that was considering granting a number of honors on the occasion of the Molière tercentenary.

Since the armistice, M. Raynaldy's figures show, 95,000 decorations of the Legion of Honor have been granted. 72,000 of these decorations were exclusively military and 23,000 were awarded to civilians for work during the war. You cannot walk twenty yards on the Grands Boulevards without seeing the familiar red ribbon of the Legion in someone's buttonhole.

After seeing M. Raynaldy's figures, the committee unanimously rejected the proposal to grant any new decorations on the occasion of the Molière festival.

Active French Anti-Alcohol League

☆ THE TORONTO DAILY STAR
April 8, 1922

Paris.—Models of ravaged brains and livers, dramatic colored charts, posters showing father brandishing a drink in one hand and a black bottle in the other, while he kicks the children about the house, hold a crowd open-mouthed all day before a great window frontage on the Boulevard St. Germain.

Thirst-driven Americans see the exhibit and shudder. They are afraid it presages the beginning of the end of what they regard as the golden age of European culture; the present blissful time when the French bartender has at last learned to mix a good martini and a palate-soothing bronx. For the big window on the boulevard houses the exhibit of the Ligue Nationale Contre Alcoolisme, a name that needs no translating.

The league is not a prohibition measure. It is, strictly, a league against alcoholism and is receiving the support of a large faction of the French people. Already it is making itself felt in France; its posters are in all railway stations and public places, and its greatest practical achievement has been the banishment of absinthe from France.

Its posters read something like this:

1—Do you know that liqueurs are one of the greatest causes of tuberculosis?

2—Do you know that apéritifs are deadly poisons?

3—Do you know that the use of picons often leads to insanity?

At the bottom of the poster, however, in small type, is the announcement that the league does not want people to drink only water; but no, there are the wines of France, yes, and the beers. It describes some and tells of their good effects so attractively that the reader usually leaves the poster in search of a café. The Frenchman still believes that water is only useful for washing and to flow under bridges.

Just across from the offices of the league is the Deux Magots, one of the most famous of the Latin Quarter cafés. Here at tables you see students sipping the liqueurs that cause tuberculosis, quaffing the apéritifs that are deadly poisons, and swigging the picons that often lead to insanity. But occasionally they cast an eye toward the crowd in front of the league window, and as they walk up the boulevard, they have a worried look at the models that show the horrible state of the human liver and lights under alcohol. The window has a sort of fascination for them.

An educational campaign takes years, but I believe that it is the beginning of the end and that alcohol, except for wine, beer and the cider of the north, is doomed in France. The reason I think so is because of the look on the students' faces when they leave the league's window, the fact that absinthe has already gone, and because the anti-alcohol forces are organized while the consumers are not. It is only a question of time.

Canada's Recognition of Russia

☆ THE TORONTO DAILY STAR
April 10, 1922

Genoa.—"Canada's chief interest in the Genoa conference is the recognition of Russia," said Sir Charles Gordon on his arrival in Genoa. "Canada has much harvest machinery for Russian export and wants recognition of Russia to open the market."

Canada will act as a unit with the Empire delegation, Sir Charles said. This makes his statement extremely significant.

Tchitcherin Speaks at Genoa Conference

☆ THE TORONTO DAILY STAR
April 10, 1922

Genoa.—Genoa is crowded, a modern Babel with a corps of perspiring interpreters trying to bring the representatives of forty different countries together. The narrow streets flow with crowds kept orderly by thousands of Italian troops. The journalists, however, today deserted Genoa to see the Soviet delegation at Rapallo, a hot eighteen-mile ride, to interview [George] Tchitcherin. Tchitcherin, blond and wearing new Berlin clothes with a large red rectangular badge, looks like a businessman. He talks with a slight purr because of missing teeth.

He saw the flood of reporters in batches, speaking to them in their own languages. Hundreds of photographers tried to get past guards who examined their cameras for bombs.

Tchitcherin said to me, "Regarding all matters of debts, we come with our hands free, without committing ourselves. The rights of foreign capital will be perfectly secured but Russia will resist all attempts by consortiums to make Russia a colony."

Questioned about Soviet revolutionaries and moderate Socialists now on trial, Tchitcherin said: "The social revolutionaries are not being persecuted. They are being prosecuted for real offenses, such as the blowing up of banks, shooting at Lenin, blowing up ammunition dumps, and attempting to dynamite Trotsky's train. We are changing our penitentiary system to educate and reform criminals."

Questioned on the famine, Tchitcherin said: "Four years of blockade made the famine. The government is taxing all of Russia to aid the starving, and the transport system is working well."

The eighty members of the Soviet delegation sat at a common table. The delegation is guarded by circles of soldiers, carabinieri and volunteer guards of Italian Communists. The telephone service is horrible and the Soviets are dissatisfied with their quarters so distant from Genoa.

Italian Premier

☆ THE TORONTO DAILY STAR
April 10, 1922

Genoa.—"The spirit of the Washington arms conference must inspire this gathering," Premier Facta said in his opening address. "The cloud that hung over the Pacific already has disappeared as a result of the limitation of arms conference," the Italian statesman declared amid applause. "We at Genoa must now work for the peace of Europe in the same way."

Tchitcherin Wants Japan Excluded

☆ THE TORONTO DAILY STAR
April 11, 1922

Genoa.—The economic conference is proceeding amicably after the stormy scene at the opening session between Louis Barthou of France and Tchitcherin, head of the Russian Soviet delegation.

Tchitcherin caused another diversion today when he protested against the presence of Japan and Rumania. Count Ishii of the Japanese delegation retorted that Japan was here to stay, whether Tchitcherin liked it or not.

The commission appointed to consider the question of Russia consists of seven great powers and Switzerland, Sweden, Poland and Rumania. Ten delegates are to be elected to represent the balance of the states, including Canada.

Genoa Conference

☆ THE TORONTO DAILY STAR
April 13, 1922

Genoa.—Italy realizes the danger of inviting the Soviet delegation to the Genoa Conference, and has brought fifteen hundred picked military policemen from other parts of Italy into Genoa to crush any Red or anti-Red disturbance as soon as it starts.

This is a farsighted move, for the Italian government remembers the hundreds of fatal clashes between the Fascisti and the Reds in the past two years, and is anxious that there should be as little civil war as possible while the conference is in progress.

They face a very real danger. Sections of Italy, principally Tuscany and in the north, have seen bloody fighting, murders, reprisals and pitched battles in the last few months over communism. The Italian authorities accordingly fear the effect on the Reds of Genoa when they see the delegation of eighty representatives from Soviet Russia amicably received and treated with respect.

There is no doubt but that the Reds of Genoa—and they are about one-third of the population—when they see the Russian Reds, will be moved to tears, cheers, gesticulations, offers of wines, liqueurs, bad cigars, parades, vivas, proclamations to one another and the wide world and other kindred Italian symptoms of enthusiasm. There will also be kissings on both cheeks, gatherings in cafés, toasts to Lenin, shouts for Trotsky, attempts by three and four highly illuminated Reds to form a parade at intervals of two and three minutes, enormous quantities of chianti drunk and general shouts of "Death to the Fascisti!"

That is the way all Italian Red outbreaks start. Closing the cafés usually stops them. Uninspired by the vinous products of their native land, the Italian Communist cannot keep his enthusiasm up to the demonstration point for any length of time. The cafés close, the "Vivas" grow softer and less enthusiastic, the paraders put it off till another day and the Reds who reached the highest pitch of patriotism too soon roll under the tables of the cafés and sleep until the bartender opens up in the morning.

Some of the Reds going home in a gentle glow, chalk up on a wall in straggling letters, "VIVA LENIN! VIVA TROTSKY!" and the political crisis is over, unless of course they meet some Fascisti. If they happen to meet some Fascisti, things are very different again.

The Fascisti are a brood of dragons' teeth that were sown in 1920 when it looked as though Italy might go Bolshevik. The name means organization, a unit of Fascisti is a fascio, and they are young ex-veterans formed to protect the existing government of Italy against any sort of Bolshevik plot or aggression. In short, they are counterrevolutionists, and in 1920 they crushed the Red uprising with bombs, machine guns, knives and the liberal use of kerosene cans to set the Red meeting places afire, and heavy iron-bound clubs to hammer the Reds over the head when they came out.

The Fascisti served a very definite purpose and they crushed what looked like a coming revolution. They were under the tacit protection of the government, if not its active support, and there is no question but that they crushed the Reds. But they had a taste of unpenalized lawlessness, unpunished murder, and the right to riot when and where they pleased. So now they have become almost as great a danger to the peace of Italy as the Reds ever were.

When the Fascisti hear that there is a Red demonstration on, and I have tried to indicate the casual and childish nature of ninety-seven out of every hundred Red demonstrations in Italy, they feel in honor bound as the ex-preservers of their country in time of peril to go out and put the Reds to the sword. Now the North Italian Red is father of a family and a good workman six days out of seven; on the seventh he talks politics. His leaders have formally rejected Russian communism and he is Red as some Canadians are Liberal. He does not want to fight for it, or convert the world to it, he merely wants to talk about it, as he has from time immemorial.

The Fascisti make no distinction between Socialists, Communists, Republicans or members of cooperative societies. They are all Reds and dangerous. So the Fascisti hear of the Red meeting, put on their long, black, tasseled caps, strap on their trench knives, load up with bombs and ammunition at the fascio and march toward the Red meeting singing the Fascist hymn, "Youth" ["*Giovanezza*"]. The Fascisti are young, tough, ardent, intensely patriotic, generally good-looking with the youthful beauty of the southern races, and firmly convinced that they are in the right. They have an abundance of the valor and intolerance of youth.

Marching down the street, the Fascisti, marching as a platoon, come on three of the Reds chalking a manifesto on one of the high walls of the narrow street. Four of the young men in the black fezzes seize the Reds and in the scuffle one of the Fascisti gets stabbed. They kill the three prisoners and spread out in threes and fours through the streets looking for Reds.

A sobered Red snipes a Fascisto from an upper window. The Fascisti burn down the house.

You can read the reports in the papers every two or three weeks. The casualties given are usually from ten to fifteen Reds killed and twenty to fifty wounded. There are usually two or three Fascisti killed and wounded. It is a sort of desultory guerrilla warfare that has been going on in Italy for well over a year. The last big battle was in Florence some months ago, but there have been minor outbreaks since.

To prevent any Fascisti–Red rows happening in Genoa, the fifteen hundred military police have been brought in. They are none of them natives of Genoa, so they can shoot either side without fear or favor. Italy is determined on order during the conference, and the carabinieri, as the military police are called, wearing their three-cornered Napoleon hats, with carbines slung across their backs, with their fierce upturned mustaches and their record as the bravest troops and the best marksmen in the Italian army, stalk the streets in pairs, determined that there shall be order. And, as the Fascisti fear the carabinieri, when they have orders to shoot, as much as the Reds fear the Fascisti, there is a pretty good chance that order will be kept.

Objections to Allied Plan

☆ THE TORONTO DAILY STAR
April 13, 1922

Genoa.—The Allied proposals seek to reduce Russia to the level of Turkey, George Tchitcherin declared today.

The Russian leader announced objection to the Allied experts' plan which was submitted to the subdivisions of the conference as a basis for European rehabilitation, and asked twenty-four hours in which to prepare a formal negative reply.

The Genoa Conference was to get down to the bedrock of its work today, with four commissions—political, economic, financial and transportation—considering the experts' proposals which were laid before them in great detail at yesterday's sessions. The Russian refusal, anticipated by Allied leaders, presented an immediate snag at peaceful progress of the conclave.

The Allied proposals regarding Russia were more drastic than had been anticipated. They included Russian recognition of czarist and provisional government debts and guarantees for non-aggression and for safety of foreigners in Russia. This was expected. But a French proposal for establishment of foreign tribunals within the borders of Russia and a measure of supervision over Russian internal affairs also was included in the experts' plan. It was to this last suggestion that Tchitcherin indicated Russia never would agree. He declared his delegation was willing to give financial and other guarantees in the name of his government, but that it was impossible to grant special tribunals, infringing upon Russian sovereignty.

The Russian spokesman today prepared a list of counterproposals based on the following program:

1. That Russia be granted a loan of $500,000,000.
2. Russia will guarantee the safety of foreigners within her borders in exchange for similar guarantees by other countries.
3. Russia will agree to recognize czarist debts and those of the Kerenski regime, but will ask for a moratorium, and for payment of damage caused by attacks of Wrangel, Denikin, Kolchak and other commanders, backed by the Allies in futile attacks against the Soviets.

4. Russia will insist upon absolute sovereignty and will under no circumstances permit Allied supervision of her internal affairs.

Tchitcherin today said the Allied plan apparently contemplated a regime of capitulations on the part of Russia.

Germany also will object to the Allied experts' proposals regarding finance, it was understood. The German reply was to be submitted today.

Russian Claims

☆ THE TORONTO DAILY STAR
April 14, 1922

Genoa.—"No country intends to pay its war debts; France does not intend to pay the United States; to pay Allied claims would make Russia a slave state; Russia will not calmly agree to pay what four years of war could not force from her; we must find a common basis" was the Russian delegation statement today. Russian counterclaims make the first big snag in the conference. Russians will offer a counterclaim for each Allied demand.

Parisian Boorishness

☆ THE TORONTO STAR WEEKLY
April 15, 1922

Paris.—The days of Alphonse and Gaston are over. French politeness has gone the way of absinthe, pre-war prices and other legendary things. It has become so bad that French newspapers have carried columns of discussion on the question of how the French can regain the position they once held as the politest people in the world.

There is such pushing in the Paris subway, cheating women of their seats in the crowded buses, violent rows over prices, barefaced demands for tips in the once polite city that the person who knew Paris in the days before the war would turn away in horror. It is a very different Paris from the old days when the French people enjoyed a world reputation for pleasant gentleness, affability, and instinctive kind attention.

Cabdrivers, of course, always have been discourteous. They are so because they expect never to see their fares again, in a city of tens of thousands of drifting cabs, and have one object: to see how much they can get out of their trip.

It is a safe generalization that no non-French-speaking person ever paid the fare shown on the cab meter and supplemented it with a ten percent tip without having the cabby follow him into his destination cursing and raving that he has been cheated. It is simply a case of the cabdriver having found that there is as much money in doing that as in driving a cab.

The Paris buses provide the worst instances of the new rudeness. You rise in a bus to offer a lady your seat and a walrus-mustached Frenchman plops into it, leaving you and the lady standing. If you say anything to him, he will roar something like this at you: "Eject me if you dare. Try it! Lay just one finger on me and I will have you before the police!"

As a matter of fact, he is in a strongly entrenched position. No matter what the provocation, a foreigner must keep his temper in France. The French engage in some terrific battles with each other, but they are entirely verbal. Once you put a finger on a man, no matter how aggravating the circumstances, you are guilty of assault and go to jail for a term running upward from six months.

Next to the buses and subways, the minor government officials give the most offense to courtesy. These are the men in parks and museums, not the police; for the police, through the most trying times, have remained courteous, polite and obliging.

For instance, there is the reptile house in the Jardin des Plantes, the great Paris zoological gardens. People were coming out of the door of the reptile house when I went up to it. It was placarded as being open from eleven to three o'clock. It was twelve o'clock when I tried to enter.

"Is the reptile house closed?" I asked.

"Fermé!" the guard said.

"Why is it closed at this hour?" I asked.

"Fermé!" shouted the guard.

"Can you tell me when it will be open?" I queried, still polite.

The guard gave me a snarl and said nothing.

"Can you tell me when it will be open?" I asked again.

"What business is that of yours?" said the guard, and slammed the door.

Then there is the office where you go to get your passports stamped in order to leave Paris. There is a large sign on the wall saying employees are paid and that it is forbidden to tip them. The visa costs two francs forty centimes. I gave the clerk, back of the long board counter, five francs. He made no move to give me any change and when I stood there he sneered at me and said, "Oh, you want the change, do you?" and slammed it down on the counter angrily.

Those are all samples of the type of thing one encounters daily in Paris. Marcel Boulanger, writing in the *Figaro*, holds out hope for the future.

"But I believe that the soul of good society is still fine enough and at bottom—clear at the bottom, alas—sufficiently gracious," he says, after deploring the present state of politeness in France.

"Three centuries of civilization and of the spirit of the salon are not to be lost in four or five years. Nothing good is done without trouble. Observe the fashion in which, except in the homes of the newly rich, one introduces the son of a celebrity! One never says in a breath, 'Monsieur So and So, son of the illustrious Monsieur So and So,' as if the only reason the son had to exist were to carry the name of his famous father. On the contrary, one shades the introduction in spite of himself: 'Monsieur So and So,' says one. Then, after an instant, and smiling gently: 'Monsieur So and So is the son of the illustrious Monsieur So and So.' Thanks to the pause, the remark takes on the air of a courtesy between you, as if you were congratulating the father on having such a son.

"A thousand precautions of taste still are part of the current conversation and may be reinstated. They form a powerful arm which in ordinary times a man carries against wretchedness."

Woman Takes Crumbs

☆ THE TORONTO DAILY STAR
April 15, 1922

Genoa.—Women have little part in the Genoa Conference. There is not one on any of the thirty-four delegations as a responsible member. Mme. Alexandra Kollantay, leader of the feminist movement in Russia, objected because the secretary of the conference did not include a woman member, and the women leaders of Germany and the Central European countries at once drew attention to the slight they had suffered. However, several prominent women are included on the various staffs, and the clerical forces of nearly all the delegations consist largely of the gentler sex. Signora Oliva Rossetti Agresti is the chief interpreter employed in translating the Italian addresses into English at the important sessions. She is a granddaughter of the poet Dante Gabriel Rossetti, and has attracted particular attention owing to her unusual ability to remember long addresses and deliver them immediately in another language without the benefit of notes.

Signorina Italia Garibaldi, granddaughter of the famous Italian patriot, who attended the Washington Conference, with the Italian delegation, has been loaned to the Russian delegation by the Italian foreign office.

Signora Ungaretti is an important member of the Italian government's publicity staff, and is entrusted with the task of keeping the Japanese and American correspondents advised on news matters.

Russians Hold Up Progress

☆ THE TORONTO DAILY STAR
April 17, 1922

Genoa.—Progress at Genoa waits on Russia. The Bolshevik delegation's official reply to the Allied proposals is not expected before Thursday. Meantime the conference marks time.

Many delegates went home over the Easter holidays which, in Europe, include Easter Monday. Only two subcommissions of the parley met today.

The critical situation at Genoa today is that which concerns recognition by Russia of her debts, and recognition of Russia by the Allies. The political commission, of which the leading statesmen of the conference are members, has this matter in hand.

The Soviet delegation here, which seemed on the point of capitulating, has been granted time to confer with the Kremlin, seat of the Bolshevik government at Moscow. This is unfortunate for progress, because the Soviet leaders at home are far more intransigent than those who have come into contact with Allied and European delegates and viewpoints here.

The Russian difficulty is as follows:

1—Through the initiative of Lloyd George, Russia and the Allies have been brought to a point where they agree in principle upon the following: (a) Russia will recognize her pre-war (czarist) debts; (b) A method for adjusting war debts and counterclaims has been worked out; (c) The Allies agree that if these matters are arranged, recognition of Russia, with a wiping clean of the Bolshevik past, can follow.

2—The difficulty lies in the fact that Russia, when she had secured tentative agreement by the Allies as to the justice of the counterclaims by the Soviet for damage done by Denikin, Wrangel and others, made the bill so large that it outweighed the entire Russian war debt and left the Allies owing Russia money.

3—Besides this, the first consideration of the Soviet delegation is to secure a large loan, and this is frowned upon by the Allies.

There the Russian situation rests, with the next word due from the Soviet delegation. If that word constitutes a refusal to accept the Allied experts' proposals, the conference may have to deal firmly with its Russian guests.

Genoa.—Premier Facta of Italy, as president of the economic conference, issued a sudden summons this afternoon for a conference at 3 p.m., of the heads of the inviting powers now in Genoa. It is believed one reason for the calling of the conference was the announcement of the signing of the Russian-German treaty.

The announced object of the meeting was to adjust by consultation the attitude of the Allies toward the Russian question. The Japanese were included in the invitation.

German Machiavellianism

☆ THE TORONTO DAILY STAR
April 18, 1922

Genoa.—The conference is wabbling like a ship in a hurricane. The Russo-German treaty, which is really a political alliance, is regarded by the Allies as a return to German Machiavellianism.

German Blow—Disloyal?

☆ THE TORONTO DAILY STAR
April 18, 1922

Genoa.—*Corriere Mercantile*, the first Italian paper to comment on the new agreement, says:

"This is the most sinister blow Germany was able to deliver at the Allies. It constitutes the most striking act of disloyalty German diplomacy has ever accomplished. We express the most emphatic indignation against those abusing the Allies' confidence. They have compromised a situation founded upon a policy of peace."

The British delegation has not been far behind the French and Italians in expressing profound disapproval of the Russo-German treaty. Lloyd George was quoted as saying that Britain could only regard it as the first step toward a Russo-German alliance.

The German treachery, for as such it is universally regarded, has unquestionably imperiled the very existence of the conference, delegates of many smaller nations agreed. The Little Entente of Serbia, Czechoslovakia, Poland, and Rumania has joined in the chorus of disapproval.

Barthou Refuses Conference

☆ THE TORONTO DAILY STAR
April 18, 1922

Genoa.—France will take no further part in conferences at Genoa with either Russia or Germany, Louis Barthou, head of the French delegation, declared today, if the treaty signed at Rapallo by Tchitcherin and Rathenau is not immediately abrogated.

Allied leaders met at 11 o'clock. Other committee meetings were canceled in view of the importance of the decision to be taken regarding the Russo-German pact.

Well-informed observers declared the Allied leaders considered the Treaty of Rapallo jeopardizes success of the entire conference.

When the heads of the Allied delegations went into conference, Barthou was armed with instructions from his government declaring the agreement signed at Rapallo to be in direct violation of the Treaty of Versailles.

A statement from Lloyd George was eagerly awaited. The British premier promises France that existing treaties should not be abrogated by any action at Genoa. The French look to the British premier to call upon Germany and Russia to renounce the Treaty of Rapallo.

Italy, which hitherto has backed Lloyd George against the French, is openly opposed to permitting the Russo-German treaty.

Russian Girls at Genoa

☆ THE TORONTO DAILY STAR
April 24, 1922

Genoa, Italy.—The great hall of the Palazzo San Giorgio, where the sessions of the Genoa Conference are held, is about half the size of Massey Hall [Toronto] and is overlooked by a marble statue of Columbus sitting on a pale marble throne sunk deep into the wall.

Columbus, and the press gallery at the other end of the hall, look down on a rectangle of green-covered tables arranged in the familiar shape of tables at banquets, lodges, Y.M.C.A. dinners and college reunions. There is a white pad of paper at each table that, from the press gallery, looks like a tablecloth, and for two hours before the conference opened a woman in a salmon-covered hat arranged and rearranged the inkwells at the long rectangle of tables.

At the left of the statue of Columbus, a marble plaque twelve feet high is set into the wall bearing a quotation from Machiavelli's history, telling of the founding of the Banco San Giorgio, site of the present palace, the oldest bank in the world. Machiavelli, in his day, wrote a book that could be used as a textbook by all conferences, and from all results, is diligently studied.

To the left of the rather pompous marble Columbus is another plaque similar in size to the quotation from Machiavelli on which is carved two letters from Columbus to the Queen of Spain and the Commune of Genoa. Both letters are highly optimistic in tone.

Delegates began to come into the hall in groups. They cannot find their place at the table, and stand talking. The rows of camp chairs that are to hold the invited guests begin to be filled with the top-hatted, white-mustached senators and women in Paris hats and wonderful wealth-reeking fur coats. The fur coats are the most beautiful things in the hall.

There is an enormous chandelier, with globes as big as association footballs, hanging above the tables. It is made up of a tangled mass of griffons and unidentified beasts and when it switches on everyone in the press gallery is temporarily blinded. All around the wall of the hall are the pale marble effigies of the fine, swashbuckling pirates and traders that made Genoa a power in the old days when all the cities of Italy were at one another's throats.

The press gallery fills up and the British and American correspondents light cigarettes and identify for one another the various bowing delegates as they enter the hall at the far end. The Poles and Serbs are the first in; then they come in crowds carrying their eight-quart silk hats. Marcel Cachin, editor of *Humanité*, circulation 250,000, and leader of the French Communist party, comes in and sits behind me. He has a drooping face, frayed red mustache and his black tortoise-shell spectacles are constantly on the point of sliding off the tip of his nose. He has a very rich wife and can afford to be a Communist.

Next to him sits Max Eastman, editor of *The Masses*, who is doing a series of special articles for a New York paper and who looks like a big, jolly, middle-western college professor. He and Cachin converse with difficulty.

Movie men set up a camera under the nose of the niched-in Genoese heroes who look down at it with a frozen marble expression of disapproval. The Archbishop of Genoa in wine-colored robes and a red skullcap stands talking with an old Italian general with a withered apple of a face and five wound stripes. The old general is General Gonzaga, commander of the cavalry corps; he looks a sunken-faced, kind-eyed Attila with his sweeps of mustaches.

The hall is as noisy as a tea party. Journalists have filled the gallery, there is only room for 200 and there are 750 applicants and many late-comers sit on the floor.

When the hall is nearly full, the British delegation enters. They have come in motorcars through the troop-lined streets and enter with élan. They are the best-dressed delegation. Sir Charles Blair Gordon, head of the Canadian delegation, is blond, ruddy-faced and a little ill at ease. He is seated fourth from Lloyd George's left at the long table.

Walter Rathenau, with the baldest bald head at the conference and a scientist's face, comes in accompanied by Dr. Wirth, German chancellor, who looks like a tuba player in a German band. They are halfway down one of the long tables. Rathenau is another wealthy Socialist and considered the ablest man in Germany.

Prime Minister Facta of Italy takes the chair. So obscure has been his political career, until he came into light as a compromise premier when it looked as though Italy would be unable to form a cabinet, that biographies of him were issued to all the newspapermen by the Italian government.

Everyone is in the room but the Russians. The hall is crowded and sweltering and the four empty chairs of the Soviet delegation are the four emptiest-looking chairs I have ever seen. Everyone is wondering whether they will not appear. Finally they come through the door and start making their way through the crowd. Lloyd George looks at them intently, fingering his glasses.

Litvinoff with a big ham-like face is in the lead. He is wearing the rectangular red insignia. After him comes Tchitcherin with his indeterminate face, his indefinite beard and his nervous hands. They blink at the light from the chandelier. Krassin is next. He has a mean face and a carefully tailored Van Dyke beard and looks like a prosperous dentist. Joffe is last. He has a long, narrow, spade beard, and wears gold-rimmed glasses.

A mass of secretaries follow the Russian delegates, including two girls with fresh faces, hair bobbed in the fashion started by Irene Castle, and with modish tailored suits. They are far and away the best-looking girls in the conference hall.

The Russians are seated. Some one hisses for silence, and Signor Facta starts the dreary round of speeches that sends the conference under way.

Barthou Crosses Hissing Tchitcherin

☆ THE TORONTO DAILY STAR
April 24, 1922

Genoa.—There was a sensation at the opening of the Genoa Conference greater than Secretary Hughes' naval scrapping speech at Washington—but it came when the scheduled speeches had been droned through and most of the newspapermen had left the hall to put their cut-and-dried reports of the opening on to the cables.

Suddenly into the fatigue-charged air of a crowded roomful of people who had heard speeches for four hours came an instantaneous electric thrill. Tchitcherin, head of the Soviet delegation, looking like a country grocery storekeeper with a ragged indefinite beard and a hissing purr of a voice that was almost un-understandable in the press gallery, had just taken his seat at the green-covered rectangle of tables.

"Is there anyone else that would like to speak?" asked Signor Facta, president of the conference, in Italian.

"The president asks if there is anyone else that wants to speak," translated the English interpreter, a square-faced woman with a high, theatrical voice.

M. Barthou, heading the French delegation, rose to his feet and launched into a passionate torrent of words. Barthou looks like the left-hand one of the Smith Brothers and waddles when he walks but speaks with the impassioned vigor and earnestness of the French orator.

Suddenly the dull, sleepy atmosphere of the foul-aired conference hall was cut through as by a flash of summer lightning. The correspondents who had been sitting heavily in the press gallery began to take notes like mad. The delegates who had been leaning back in their chairs anticipating an adjournment of the conference, stiffened forward to attention, Tchitcherin's hand began to tremble on the table and Lloyd George began to draw meaningless designs on the pad of paper before him.

All the "wise" journalists had left the hall when Tchitcherin stopped speaking. Only a few remained who believed in seeing a game through until the last man is out in the ninth inning.

Barthou stopped speaking and the interpreter who has officiated at every conference since the first session of the League of Nations started his translation into English in a ringing voice. "If this question of disarmament is brought up, France will absolutely, categorically, and finally refuse to discuss it, either in plenary session or in any committee. In the name of France I make this definite protest—"

The interpreter went on with the speech. He finished.

Tchitcherin rose and, his hands shaking, spoke in French, in his queer, hissing accents, the result of an accident that knocked out half his teeth. The interpreter with the ringing voice translated. There was not a sound in the pauses except the clink of the mass of decorations on an Italian general's chest as he shifted from one foot to another. It is an actual fact. You could hear the faint metallic clink of the hanging decorations.

"In regard to disarmament," the interpreter said for Tchitcherin. "Russia took the attitude of France from M. Briand's Washington speech. In this speech he said France must stay armed because of the danger of Russia's great army. I, for Russia, want to remove this danger.

"In regard to a succession of conferences I am only quoting from Lloyd George's speech to the British parliament. Monsieur Poincaré has said that the aims of the Genoa Conference have not been clearly outlined. There are several questions up for discussion here that were not in the Cannes agenda. If it is the collective will of the conference that disarmament should not be discussed, I will bow to the will of the conference. But disarmament is a capital question with Russia."

The interpreter sat down and Lloyd George got up. The conference was in a turmoil. It looked as though the French might walk out at any moment. Lloyd George, the greatest compromiser politics has ever seen, talked against time. He urged Tchitcherin in his suave manner not to overload the ship of Genoa with too many matters for discussion.

"Unless the Genoa Conference leads to disarmament it will be a failure," he said. "But we must prepare first. We must first settle other questions. I ask Mr. Tchitcherin to be calm. Let us bring this ship into port first before we start any other voyages. I suggest we drop the question of a universal conference at present." And so he continued talking against time and attempting to save the conference.

"The agenda of the Genoa Conference was sent out in the two finest languages in the world—English and French!" he said in the course of his rambling and conciliatory speech, masterly in its soothing and soporific effect on most of the delegates, for at this slip the Italians looked black and all the effect of Lloyd George's careful compliments earlier in the day was destroyed.

In the end Signor Facta adjourned the meeting, cutting off both Barthou and Tchitcherin who attempted to speak. "It is over. You have spoken. We must adjourn!" And the conference was saved from blowing up on the first day.

Stambouliski of Bulgaria

☆ THE TORONTO DAILY STAR
April 25, 1922

Genoa.—In the rows of white faces gathered around the green baize tables at the sessions of the Genoa Conference, the weatherbeaten red face of [Aleksandr] Stambouliski, prime minister of Bulgaria, stood out like a ripe blackberry in a bunch of daisies.

Stambouliski is chunky, red-brown-faced, has a black mustache that turns up like a sergeant major's, understands not a word of any language except Bulgarian, once made a speech of fifteen hours' duration in that guttural tongue, and is the strongest premier in Europe—bar none.

For years as leader of the agrarian, or Farmers', party, Stambouliski fought to keep Bulgaria out of the various Balkan wars. He had one idea. Bulgaria was a farming country and her salvation lay in farming, not fighting. He opposed Bulgaria going into the European war on the side of Germany.

"This step will cost you your head," he shouted at King Ferdinand and Ferdinand had him put into prison. Twice, for his attitude during the war, he was condemned to death; but the government lacked the courage to carry out the sentences for Stambouliski is the idol of the sheepskin-coated, ragged, dirty, courageous and hard-working farmers that make up eighty-five percent of Bulgaria's population.

When the army started drifting back after the armistice with revolutionary committees at the head of the various regiments, and it looked as though Bulgaria was going down to bolshevism as fast as greased skids could carry her, King Ferdinand sent for Stambouliski to be brought to him.

"Can you hold things together if I make you premier?" Ferdinand asked the man who was under sentence of death.

"I can never work with you and never will!" Stambouliski roared. "There is only one thing for you to do—get out of the country!" Ferdinand being a keen judge of situations, very promptly got out.

Boris, his son, wanted to leave the country with his father. Stambouliski took him by the shoulder.

"If you atttempt to leave Bulgaria I will put you under arrest," he said. "You are the new king."

So now Boris, a polished, good-humored, cosmopolitan youth is king, and being king consists in interpreting for Stambouliski, who comes into Sofia often enough from his farm to see that the government is running all right. Sometimes he stays on the farm for two and three weeks at a time. There are no telephone connections and ambassadors wait those two or three weeks to see him. Then he comes in, calls in Boris to interpret, tells the ambassador what he wants and what he does not want, what he will do and what he will not do, and goes back to his farm.

There are no internal problems in Bulgaria, there are no troublesome minorities. The Farmers' party—and they are actually farmers, attending parliament in their sheep coats and mud-covered boots—have 150 representatives. The Communist party is next with 50 members. The only other members are the two bourgeois representatives who have the inalienable right of all minorities—that to endorse.

It was at a meeting of the Farmers' party that Stambouliski made his famous fifteen-hour speech. That speech broke the hearts of the Communists. It is no good opposing a man of few words who can talk for fifteen hours.

Bulgaria is much better off than Serbia, who has to maintain a large army to keep all her troublesome "New Serbs" in order, many of them having no desire to be Serbs at all. Bulgaria is well fed also, while Europe all around her is starving, because Stambouliski keeps her farming.

At the conference, Stambouliski sits forward in his chair, looks at the ceiling with his bull-like old face, and the light from the great chandelier glints on his shiny, blue serge suit. Occasionally a slightly less stolid expression comes over his face, it relaxes just the least bit, that is the nearest he ever comes to smiling. When that expression comes it means that Stambouliski is thinking that while the conference at Genoa is going on, back in Bulgaria men are farming.

Schober Every Inch a Chancellor

☆ THE TORONTO DAILY STAR
April 26, 1922

Genoa.—Chancellor Schober of Austria is a white-haired old aristocrat, who took the post of chancellor for the remains of the Hapsburg Empire, after Austria had been using up about one prime minister a month and premiers were as popular as the income tax collector. He did not want the job but public opinion forced him into it, and since he has taken hold, Austria has gained the firmest position she has held in Central Europe since the break-up after the armistice.

Chancellor Schober is the only man at the Genoa Conference, with the exception of Lloyd George, that looks the romantic conception of what a chancellor should look. He has a stately presence and carriage, a patrician face, and a high forehead with his head of white hair brushed back.

For forty years under Emperor Franz Joseph and his son Carl, just dead in exile in Madeira, Schober was head of the police department of that strange jumble of geography that was the Austrian Empire. And when the new Austrian Socialist republic finally got completely sick of political leaders and wanted an administrator to head the government, they chose Schober.

After Austria's revolution, which came at a time when all of Europe was going off into revolutions like a pack of firecrackers, Austria reformed her army. The Socialists were in power and so all the men who tried to enlist in the army who were not Socialists were declared by the examining surgeons to have flat feet, defective lumbar vertebrae, cauliflower ears or some such physical reason for keeping them out of the service. The result was that a ninety-nine percent Socialist army was formed. The one percent who turned out not to be Socialists were promptly weeded out on account of astigmatism, myasma, myopia, too many wisdom teeth or some such cause and replaced by some of the comrades.

This Socialist army was lodged in barracks that were like country clubs, had unlimited leisure and entertainments, was well fed and happy and incidentally gave the Socialists complete control of the country. It began to be very difficult not to be a Socialist with the army to back up all promulgations of the Socialist party. The country was near to going into a sort of guerrilla warfare between the Conservatives and the army when Schober brought order out of the whole mess by a very simple procedure.

Schober, with forty years of police work to back him up, formed a government police force with authority to arrest all lawbreakers regardless of their political beliefs. With his experience, he picked and trained this force of twelve thousand men until they attained a morale and esprit de corps like that of the Royal North-West Mounted Police. In a very short time there was order in Austria. If someone threw a brick as the Socialist army marched past, Schober's men arrested the brick thrower. If members of the Socialist army coerced or beat anyone, Schober's men arrested the Socialist soldiers. It worked wonderfully.

So when Austria sickened of a series of prime ministers who went galloping into office under their promises to obtain credits from the Allies, and came sneaking out of office as soon as it became very apparent there were to be no credits, the Republican government turned to Herr Schober, the old Monarchist.

The last premier had some vague plan for selling all the national art treasures, renting out the museums and mortgaging all the government property to get money. Schober stopped this as he stopped the Monarchist-Socialist fight and went down to business on getting credit for Austria. The result is that credits have been granted that have started Austria back on to her feet again, and for the first time the financial situation of the Austrian republic shows a ray of hope.

The Unworldly Russians

☆ THE TORONTO DAILY STAR
April 27, 1922

Genoa.—The Russian envoys at Genoa look, talk and act like businessmen and yet there is a strange, unworldly something about them.

Tchitcherin, the head of the delegation, has a weak, indefinite sort of face that gains no character from his thin beard, and while he talks in his hissing, purring voice he is not at all impressive. Yet when you read his speech later and analyze it, you see how the points are jabbed home with rapier-like clarity. Tchitcherin's mind, when he talks, seems to come down from some Marxian heaven that looks down through the mezzanine of H. G. Wells' heaven to the earth far beneath. The earth looks very small, but very clear to Tchitcherin.

Joffe, with his narrow sod-spade beard, Krassin of the immaculate Van Dyke, Litvinoff with his big, blond, smooth Russian face all have this air of detachment—but all have it in a less degree than Tchitcherin. It is the sort of look that you saw on the faces of men who had been in the war so long that it had ceased to exist, a sort of exaltation of personality above their daily world.

The exception to this impressiveness of the Russians is Rosenberg, a small, nervous, hysterical and suspicious man who is in charge of the Russian press service. Now I am not anti-French, anti-Semitic, or anti-any nationality as far as I know. Neither am I pro-Bolshevik, pro-Irish, pro-Italian or have any special pros. I am trying to write an impartially observed account of the conference, untinged by propaganda of any sort. And I say if the Russians lose or have lost the sympathy of public opinion that they gained when they offered disarmament of Russia on the first day, it will be because of the utter lack of judgment and the complete lack of any grasp of the situation of their relation with the press.

Newspapermen in crowds make the long, all-day trip out to Rapallo and Santa Marguerita. They either go in motorcars and are choked with dust or sit in a dirty train that goes through some thirty tunnels as it follows the ocean shore. When they get to the Russian headquarters at the Imperial Hotel at Santa Marguerita the chances are more than even that the Russians refuse to see them.

The other day I waited an hour, being eyed with intense suspicion by the guards and submitted to a cross-examination, until Rosenberg finally sent down word he would not receive us. It was all right with me. I will continue to report impartially, but some of the other correspondents said, "All right, we'll roast them tonight for that. They'll find out if that is the way to treat the press." And the trouble is that the opinion of the world is made by those same correspondents.

Correspondents of the Communist papers like the *Daily Herald* of London and *Humanité* of Paris have begged Rosenberg to adopt a different attitude, but he is a small, weak, frightened man, with a job too big for him, and as a result the Russians suffer. It is a very big bet that the Soviet government is overlooking, and the reason for its being overlooked is this unworldly detachment of the heads of the Soviet delegation.

German Delegation at Genoa

☆ THE TORONTO DAILY STAR
April 28, 1922

Genoa.—Germany's position at the Genoa Conference is a very difficult one. She did not want to come to Genoa as she believed that she had nothing to gain and everything to lose. She believed that M. Poincaré's flat statement that France would have nothing to do with the conference if the question of reparations was brought up, or the revision of the Versailles treaty raised, killed any good Germany might get from Genoa.

Dr. Chancellor Wirth's speech at the opening session was a masterpiece of tact and kindliness—but it did not say anything. It merely meant that the Germans had come to make a good impression by their behavior, to hope for the best and expect the worst, and perhaps through the aid of the neutral countries to try and obtain a reduction of reparations. France says she will leave the conference if the question is raised—so there you are.

It is very significant that there is no representative of Hugo Stinnes, the sinister peacetime kaiser of Republican Germany, on the commission. Walter Rathenau, who is an enemy and business rival of Stinnes, is one of the heads of the German delegation and his presence may explain the fact that Stinnes is absent.

Another explanation is that it would be very hard for the conference to put up with Stinnes. He so completely destroys the illusion that is being built up by the sentimentalists of Germany as a sweet, friendly long-suffering and forgiving country. It is very hard for that picture to hold together when Hugo Stinnes is around. He, the most powerful factor in Germany today, seems to spoil the picture somehow. It invariably embarrasses the present crop of Germanophiles when Stinnes' name is mentioned. They want to forget him.

Hugo Stinnes is the industrial dictator of Germany today. He has a Lord Northcliffe hold on the press also and when he snaps the whip the editors jump through the hoop. He is one of the richest men in the world and he is a valuable asset to France in that he is making Germany work—and if she works she can pay. But he is not kindly, forgiving, Christian or sentimental.

It was Stinnes who made the plan for the destruction of the industries of northern France and who advocated the creation of a zone of complete industrial devastation of the manufacturing part of France. With a complete attitude of detachment, or even with a pro-German view, it is not nice to picture what Stinnes would have done to France if Germany and not France had been the victor in the war.

So they are keeping Herr Hugo Stinnes with his black derby hat and his ready-tied neckties, his celluloid collar and the meanest face in Europe well out of the Genoa Conference. It seems the better plan.

Germany is represented by the kindly, south German Dr. Wirth and the coldly intellectual Rathenau with his polished billiard-ball head—but somehow the shadow of Stinnes passes over occasionally and gives you the same sensation as seeing the black eagle on the flag that hangs over the German consulate at Genoa.

A Hot Bath an Adventure in Genoa

☆ THE TORONTO DAILY STAR
May 2, 1922

Genoa.—Lloyd George says that conferences are cheaper and better than war, but, as far as I know, Lloyd George has never been blown up by an exploding Italian bathroom. I just have been. That is one of the numerous differences between us.

A bursting bathroom is a singularly annoying thing. You feel so completely exposed to the whole affair. I do not mind being blown up in the trenches so much; it has its good side, you leave the trench and go to a hospital, you convalesce, you even swank about a bit. But a bursting bathroom is bad. You are going to leave the bathroom anyway in a few moments, the wounds do not come as a relief, they are only an indignity—and the end of the whole business is that you have to go right on working.

I entered my bathroom with a warm feeling of anticipation and a kindly love of Italy and the Italians. I left it in a scald of realization, hating everything Italian from Garibaldi to D'Annunzio.

It was a warm deep bath and the gas roared merrily under the big copper tank-heater that projected from the wall. I lay back and soaped merrily. To improve the story, there should be a long line of preliminaries. But there were not. It is a short story.

Suddenly the heater began to hiss and sputter. Then there rushed out a great strangled whish of steam like the last rush of an incoming shell and without further formality, the heater exploded. The shock of the explosion lifted me out of the tub as though on a solid wave, and flung me against the door. A roaring cloud of steam filled the room, and in all the clothes one wears in the bathtub, I flattened myself against the door, like a starfish on a rock, and finally got the key to work.

In passing from the tub to the door on that solid shock wave, it seems I had been smashed through—or over—an enameled foot tub and a chair. The proof was furnished by an eight-inch gash in my right shin and a long, rapidly greening bruise on my left hip. My right wrist was sprained where it struck the door, when I was flattened against it, and most of the skin was gone from the palm of the hand. The bottom of the copper heater had blown out.

A porter dove into the steam and choked off the heater and some other minor functionary wrapped me in an enormous towel. The wave of the explosion had driven all the breath out of my lungs and I could not talk above a whisper. But I whispered as emphatically as possible.

The owner of the hotel arrived and I started whispering to him in Italian.

"Do you speak French?" he said.

"A little."

"Ah then, we will converse in English." He waved his hands. "Monsieur has been discommoded?"

"Do I look happy?" I whispered, putting on the bathrobe.

"But monsieur should be happy. He might have been killed. Monsieur is a fortunate man!" He beamed.

"In this hotel, is a guest who is not killed by the exploding bathrooms fortunate?" I whispered very bitterly.

"Yes, monsieur, you might have been killed. You are very fortunate." He shrugged his shoulders.

"And the leg?" I asked. "It too is fortunate?"

"Yes, yes, monsieur. It might be so much worse. I will send for some iodine." He was gone without my having seen him go.

Later the boots explained to me that the accident was quite unavoidable. "You see, signor," he explained smilingly, in Italian, "the boy who makes the baths placed a small cork, a very old cork, in the siccura, the safety valve. By this the water heats much more quickly. We do this always. The boy—is a very nice boy—simply forgot to take the cork out. The safety lever remained jammed." He smiled charmingly and finished, "As the signor sees, it was absolutely unavoidable."

Now I am waiting to see if the bottle of iodine that the proprietor ordered will appear on my bill.

Well-Guarded Russian Delegation

☆ THE TORONTO DAILY STAR
May 4, 1922

Genoa.—Regardless of what they have or have not accomplished, the hardest-working delegation at Genoa is the Russian.

Night after night after the regular sessions, "conversations," or committee meetings are over, and the delegates of other nations, in evening clothes, are sipping at their liqueurs or listening to the orchestras at their various hotels, the Russians gather around a round table in an upper room of the Hotel Imperial at Santa Marguerita discussing, studying, poring over masses of documents and figures until three or four o'clock in the morning.

There is always an air of mystery about the Soviet delegation. This was first created by the manners and methods of the Italian secret police who are charged with guarding the delegates. The Soviets had exacted strict guarantees from the Italian government before they consented to come to Genoa and after they came the Italians certainly saw that their safety was guarded. In fact, the guarding was so thorough, complete and uncompromising that the Russians wearied of it after about one day and would have given a good deal not to be so strictly hedged about.

Italy's first move to guard the Soviet representatives was to give them, as living quarters, the Imperial Hotel at Santa Marguerita. It has large, steeply walled grounds and the walls are so far from the hotel itself that it would take a Babe Ruth to chuck a bomb over. There is no doubt but that the Imperial is a fine safe place but it is located so far from Genoa that at least four hours a day are wasted going to and from the various meetings.

After the Italians had lodged the Russians out at Santa Marguerita, they put so many carabinieri (royal military police) around the hotel, gardens and entrances that a mouse couldn't get into the Imperial. Then, at the one entrance permitted at the foot of a steep winding drive they stationed a commissioner of secret police that would keep St. Peter outside of the pearly gates if there was a single flaw in his papers, and what is more, make him feel that he had no right in heaven at all and would be lucky if he escaped without being arrested.

The commissioner has the manners of a Congo overseer, sun-tanned, thinly bald head, the most sinister face I have ever seen and one stock remark delivered in Italian: "Those papers are no good!" Occasionally he will unbend and tell you that there is no one in the hotel, that he doesn't know when they will get back or where they have gone, that he can tell you nothing, that he has no idea when the trains run, and that there is no use waiting to see anyone. That is when he is cheerful. He usually simply tells you that your papers are no good and will you please stay outside the gate?

I finally got hold of the cheka, or Russian personal bodyguard, a dark, cheerful-faced young Russian with a disarming grin, who drifts through the rooms and the luxurious gardens of the Imperial, a normal-looking, handsome young shadow with a flat bulge in his trousers pocket where the cloth tightens over his automatic pistol.

"It is impossible to get past those Italian secret police to get at the news up here," I told him as he listened smiling. "I want some sort of a pass to admit me at the gate so that when I make the long trip out I won't have to stand down there for two or three hours and then be turned away. I want to tell Canadians the truth about you and your delegation. I'm not a propagandist and you should be willing to let me get at the truth. I don't want to guess at the truth from outside the walls and I am sure you don't want me to."

He smiled and went away. In a little while he was back with a blue card. It read, in Italian:

No. 11
Russian Delegation
at the Genoa Conference.

Testimony of personal recognition
free ingress to the Hotel Imperial,
seat of the Russian delegation in St. Margherita
is given to
ERNEST HEMINGWAY

---

journalist ____ for ____ permanent ____
St. Margherita ________________ 1922

signed
Head of the Internal Service
of the Delegation

That pass is going among my most prized trophies. One flash of that at the gate and I entered while motorcars loaded with dusty journalists waited outside. The pass is number 11. It was among the last issued, and there were some 700 newspapermen at the conference.

Once inside the empty, barnlike Hotel Imperial, it was easy to see anyone. You asked to speak to Tchitcherin, the mystic economist, who heads the delegation, and if he was in you spoke to him. If not, they sent someone else. Tchitcherin I have described before.

Litvinoff is one of the most interesting of the Russian leaders. He looks very much like Mischa Elman—Elman with his features slightly coarsened, pale, but healthy-looking, big, coarse-featured face, a little taller than the average man, rather plump, in a badly cut German-made suit, wearing a low, bat-wing collar and a gray four-in-hand tie that has been tied so many times that it is wrinkled below the knot. He has an impersonal, strong handshake.

Maxim Litvinoff only moves his lower lip when he talks. He speaks English with a German accent—it may be Russian for all I know—but all the members of the delegation have a different accent in their English. He was exiled from Russia when he was a student and became a printer in England. During the war he was employed in some minor government department where his knowledge of languages was used. For years he had been one of the revolutionary leaders, although he lived in England, and in 1918, after the Russian revolution, he was appointed Soviet ambassador to England by wire.

As soon as he was appointed ambassador he began talking very big and showing a tremendous lack of tact and in 1918, very shortly after his appointment, he was expelled from England. Now he sits at the same table with Lloyd George as an equal representative in the Conference of Nations.

That is the amazing thing about the Russian delegation. Four years ago they were hunted, fleeing men. Tchitcherin was in prison at Brixton jail as an agitator. The others were scattered in different places. Now they sit at the table with the representatives of every great power, except the United States. They sit there with baskets full of documents and the largest army in the world back of them and say, "Russia will do this. Russia will do that." They control Russia, these men, who four years ago could not set foot in Russia. And even though you hate the things they do and the system of government they represent, you must admire the way the light shone out from under the crack at the base of the door of their council room at three o'clock in the morning.

German Journalists a Strange Collection

☆ THE TORONTO DAILY STAR
May 8, 1922

Genoa.—If it is true that the funnier-looking a newspaperman is the better work he does, there were some world-beaters at the Genoa Conference.

Applying the same rule, the Germans must be the greatest newspaper people on earth. Continuing under the same assumption, there is one German journalist who must be so good that it is a shame for him to take the money. That man haunts me still. At that I would rather he haunted me still than made any noise about it.

In the Casa della Stampa, literally translated as House of the Press, where some 300 journalists and twice that many camp followers of the press pounded child-sized typewriters, stood up to the bar, looked over one another's shoulders, asked one another, "Whadja hear at the Hotel de Genes?" and argued and swore at the Italian telegraph operator as they breasted the long counter that looked much more like a bar than the bar did—this particular German stood out like Paderewski's head in a bunch of ostrich eggs.

He had red hair, as red as a burning hemlock tree, a pale, wan, drawn face and he wore knickerbockers. No matter what happened—whether it was the German-Russian treaty explosion that set the correspondents in rows in front of the telegraph counter like travelers at a quick-lunch station during a five-minute stop; or the Allies' reproof of Germany that nearly broke up the conference and started typewriters clicking like Helen of Troy launching ships—this cadaverous, flaming German stood wanly aloof. He was above the battle, above interest, above everything. I only heard him speak once—and his voice was exactly like a peacock's.

Whatever type of German journalism he represented, its extreme opposite was present in the person of Theodore Wolff, editor of the *Berliner Tageblatt*. Wolff, gray-haired, with protruding lips, a permanent scowl and a mustache that still turned up in spite of close cropping, scowled away at telegraph blanks all day long and wrote rapidly in a tiny, microscopic fist. Wolff's snarling efficiency though was offset by the receding-faced German correspondent and the bobbed-haired German correspondent.

The receding-faced German had a face that turned in like a pancake that has had a fist pushed into it. He wore steel-rimmed spectacles and peered around nearsightedly. As I was coming upstairs from the telegraph office with a copy of the Russian-German treaty in my pocket, he peered at me anxiously. "Well, what do you know?" he asked. "Nothing but the treaty," I answered.

"But the treaty is not given out till tomorrow," he said. "I can promise you that. It is direct from our delegation."

When I showed him the treaty, which had been given out in mimeographed form by the Russians and which the English correspondents had been busy analyzing and dissecting for two hours past, he said mournfully, "Just think of that. Our delegation is wrong again!"

The bobbed-haired German had bobbed hair. It was cut like Molla Bjurstedt's, with a bang in front, and he wandered fatly around, fat-cheeked, fat-bodied and fat-headed. No doubt he was harmless; but it was very hard on newspapermen who were concentrating on an article in the overcrowded, noisy press room of the Casa della Stampa to look up and suddenly see either the thin, flaming, obviously dying-on-his-feet German; the German with the beat-in face and the peering look, or the fat German with the bobbed hair, directly in front of their typewriters.

And they all wore knickerbockers. I used to like knickerbockers for the country; they were such a fine, comfortable wealthy-feeling way of clothing your legs. But somehow I feel differently now; they could never feel the same again.

New Betting Game: Tennis Tamburello

☆ THE TORONTO DAILY STAR
May 9, 1922

Genoa.—There is an old gambling adage that runs, "Never bet on anything that talks," and sooner or later that adage will penetrate into Italy, and Tennis Tamburello, the latest Italian gambling craze, will be ruined.

Meanwhile more money is changing hands in the Tennis Tamburello courts in the basements of Genoa than in the roulette and baccarat casinos along the Ligurian Riviera. But the worst of the shady racetracks of the American continent are paradises of justice and honor besides the Tennis Tamburello dives.

A large square canvas with twenty-five numbered squares hangs at one end of the room. At the other end is a rectangular bookmaker's stand where bets are accepted. Seven men in white duck trousers, white shirts, slightly soiled and varicolored sashes around their waists, sit around on chairs back of a curtain. A bell rings and they come out, one at a time, and very solemnly bat a tennis ball bounced at them by another man in soiled white ducks up against the canvas screen at the end of the room.

The batsman hits the ball with a tambourine and either lofts it in a slow loop, or hits it out on a line at the canvas screen. The score made by the batsman depends on which one of the numbered squares he hits. For instance number one comes out and slams the ball that is bounced at him against the canvas. It hits square number six. Batsman number one, a short, heavy-set little Italian who walks springily on his toes, now goes back behind the screen and number two comes out. He hits square number eighteen. So it goes.

Bets are made on any one of six batsmen. You may bet on a man to hit the highest number or the lowest number. The odds are six to one, any way you bet. But there are seven horses in the race and you can only bet on six of them. When the seventh batsman wins, the money belongs to the house.

Italian nightlife has gone mad over the game. It gives all the excitement of horse-race gambling without having to go out to a racetrack, and all the population of Genoa that begin their day when most people are finishing theirs crowd around the Tamburello court to back their favorites as they come out from behind the dusty curtain to exercise their tambourine arms. When the police want anyone they make a trip to one of the Tennis Tamburello dives, where they are pretty sure to find either the man they are after or all his intimate friends. The game attracts the same night-living part of a city that you find at the six-day bike races in New York and Paris after one o'clock in the morning until the sweep-out hour of 7 a.m.

It is the big-money-playing element, the men in evening clothes and champagne breaths who are out to see the town, that makes the harvest for the Tennis Tamburello; just as it is the regular five-lire bettors of the night-life who make up the game's regular supporters.

When there is any amount of big money being played on any one batter, there is a scarcely perceptible pause between the bell that calls the men to the post and closes the betting wickets, and the appearance of the first batter. That pause gives time for instructions, and it is something better than 100 to 1 that the batter who is being heavily backed will not win.

Number twenty-five, painted red, is in the center of the canvas and it is a pretty poor Tennis Tambulleer who could not drive his ball away from the center if he had whispered instructions not to win. The lower right-hand side is where the low numbers are, and night after night you can watch a heavily backed batsman drive the ball into the lower right-hand corner with the ease and grace of young Jack Schaeffer making a simple billiard shot. That is where the old adage comes in. That is also where the money goes out.

Lloyd George's Magic

☆ THE TORONTO DAILY STAR
May 13, 1922

Genoa.—Inside the cool, marble-vaulted entrance of the Royal palace, the magnificently uniformed carabinieri stiffened to a rigid attention, a big limousine slipped quietly into gear and rolled forward from the row of cars parked in the hot sun of the palace courtyard, three photographers squatted and aimed with their Graflexes and David Lloyd George, smiling, assured and beautiful with his fresh young face, his smooth-brushed white hair and his smile-wrinkled eyes, climbed into the car, leaned back, bowed, and the car slid down the driveway and into the street.

I stood and watched the rest of the delegations' heads come down the steps, get into their closed motorcars and, housed in glass, ride out into the street. Barthou, the Frenchman, looked like the left-hand one of the Smith Brothers of cough-drop fame. Beneš, the Czechoslovak premier, looks exactly like a barber—a cropped-headed, rather sullen barber. Stambouliski, of Bulgaria, is a great, thick-bodied, black-headed, fierce-mustached, scowling Buffalo Bill; Viscount Ishii, a small cold-faced Japanese in a morning coat and silk hat; Walter Rathenau, an egotistical, brilliant, perfectly dressed, hawk-faced, bald-headed scientist, contemptuous and confident.

It was a great show and after it was all over and the last limousine had turned into the hot, crowd-lined street and the carabinieri had settled back into the complete erect relaxation of professional soldiers, there was only one of all the statesmen who had come out and ridden away enclosed in glass who had brought any magic with him—and that was Lloyd George.

Yet the photographers that took his picture did not capture any of that magic because Lloyd George does not look like his pictures. It is a second-rate face that photographs best. If you want to prove this, get a close-up, in-the-flesh view of say one of fifty movie stars, or recall how often you have been disappointed in a photograph of your best girl. Lloyd George has no movie face. His charm, his fresh coloring—almost girlish—the complexion of a boy subaltern just out of Sandhurst, his tremendous assurance that makes him seem a tall man until you see him standing beside someone of average height; his kindly, twinkling eyes; none of these show in the photographs.

In public his staff refer to him as the prime minister or Mr. Lloyd George, but in private they speak of him as L.G. The tired, hard-working, serious, shabbily dressed group of British political writers that have been following the prime minister around Europe from conference to conference for the past four years call him George. It is the mark of the greenhorn to call Lloyd George anything but George.

"George has certainly got into a mess now. I don't see what he is going to do," said one of these earnest, tired men who has been chronicling the dawn of a new era at the Cannes, Spa, San Remo, Washington, Boulogne, and Genoa conferences. When the Russian-German treaty was signed, L.G. fooled him. He did nothing. After an exchange of acrid notes between the Allies and Germany when an impasse was obviously reached and one side or the other must yield, L.G. simply considered the incident closed—and it was closed. All the flames died down and the conference went on with its work.

I stood behind Lloyd George at the meeting of the press of all nations that he called when the German-Russian treaty was under discussion. There had been wild rumors about the meeting. Some had it that L.G. was to read the Russians and Germans out of the conference and was calling us all together for the grand breakup speech. As soon as he came into the room—the meeting was held in the same hall of the Palazzo San Giorgio where the conference was opened—it was apparent that the rumor was wrong. L.G. came smiling in his greatest role, that of conciliator, and for an hour and a half he answered written questions submitted to him by the 400 newspapermen that sat at the delegates' tables and stood massed around the center of the hall.

While the answers, delivered standing in his clear, oratorically modulated voice, were being translated into French and Italian, I watched him studying the pile of papers before him scrawled with questions handed to his table by the journalists. Facing L.G., his white hair carefully brushed back above his ears does not look long. He looks anything but effeminate. But standing close behind him you see that his hair is really as long as Paderewski's. Just above his collar it is a thick mane that, if it were mussed and not carefully brushed would make a terrific shock.

While I watched Lloyd George studying the questions he would answer—and he answered six out of a hundred or more submitted, and they were very carefully selected queries, such as, "What kind of people do not like this conference?" and, "Does the prime minister believe that the Russians and Germans are seeking to wreck the conference?"—a young Italian artist was sketching him. When he finished answering questions and came smiling through the crowd, the young artist held up the sketch for him to sign.

Lloyd George smiled, wrinkled up his mustache and the corners of his eyes, as he looked at the sketch and signed it with the boy artist's crayon.

"There. Will that do?" He handed the sketch pad back to the boy.

"Thank you very much, sir," said the artist.

I looked at the sketch. It wasn't bad. But it wasn't Lloyd George. The only thing that was alive in it was the sprawled-out signature, gallant, healthy, swashbuckling, careless and masterful, done in a moment and done for all time, it stood out among the dead lines of the sketch—it was Lloyd George.

Fishing the Rhône Canal

☆ THE TORONTO DAILY STAR
June 10, 1922

Geneva.—In the afternoon a breeze blows up the Rhone valley from Lake Geneva. Then you fish upstream with the breeze at your back, the sun on the back of your neck, the tall white mountains on both sides of the green valley and the fly dropping very fine and far off on the surface and under the edge of the banks of the little stream, called the Rhone canal, that is barely a yard wide, and flows swiftly and still.

Once I caught a trout that way. He must have been surprised at the strange fly and probably struck from bravado, but the hook set and he jumped into the air twice and zigged nobly back and forth and toward every patch of weed at the current bottom until I slid him up the side of the bank.

He was such a fine trout that I had to keep unwrapping him to take a look and finally the day got so hot that I sat under a pine tree on the bank of the stream and unwrapped the trout entirely and ate a paper-bag full of cherries I had and read the trout-dampened *Daily Mail*. It was a hot day, but I could look out across the green, slow valley past the line of trees that marked the course of the Rhone and watch a waterfall coming down the brown face of the mountain. The fall came out of a glacier that reached down toward a little town with four gray houses and three gray churches that was planted on the side of the mountain and looked solid, the waterfall, that is, until you saw it was moving. Then it looked cool and flickering, and I wondered who lived in the four houses and went to the three churches with the sharp stone spires.

Now if you wait until the sun gets down behind the big shoulder of the Savoie Alps where France joins on to Switzerland, the wind changes in the Rhone valley and a cool breeze comes down from the mountains and blows downstream toward the Lake of Geneva. When this breeze comes and the sun is going down, great shadows come out from the mountains, the cows with their many-pitched bells begin to be driven along the road, and you fish down the stream.

There are a few flies over the water and every little while some big trout rises and goes "plop" where a huge tree hangs over the water. You can hear the "plop" and look back of you up the stream and see the circles on the water where the fish jumped. Then is the time to rewrap the trout in Lord Northcliff's latest speech reported verbatim, the reported imminent demise of the coalition, the thrilling story of the joking earl and the serious widow, and, saving the [Horatio] Bottomley [fraud] case to read on the train going home, put the trout-filled paper in your jacket pocket. There are great trout in the Canal du Rhone, and it is when the sun has dropped back of the mountains and you can fish down the stream with the evening breeze that they can be taken.

Fishing slowly down the edge of the stream, avoiding the willow trees near the water and the pines that run along the upper edge of what was once the old canal bank with your back cast, you drop the fly onto the water at every likely looking spot. If you are lucky, sooner or later there will be a swirl or a double swirl where the trout strikes and misses and strikes again, and then the old, deathless thrill of the plunge of the rod and the irregular plunging, circling, cutting upstream and shooting into the air fight the big trout puts up, no matter what country he may be in. It is a clear stream and there is no excuse for losing him when he is once hooked, so you tire him by working him up against the current and then when he shows a flash of white belly, slide him up against the bank and snake him up with a hand on the leader.

It is a good walk in to Aigle. There are horse chestnut trees along the road with their flowers that look like wax candles and the air is warm from the heat the earth absorbed from the sun. The road is white and dusty, and I thought of Napoleon's Grand Army, marching along it through the white dust on the way to the St. Bernard Pass and Italy. Napoleon's batman may have gotten up at sunup before the camp and sneaked a trout or two out of the Rhone canal for the Little Corporal's breakfast. And before Napoleon, the Romans came along the valley and built this road and some Helvetian in the road gang probably used to sneak away from the camp in the evening to try for a big one in one of the pools under the willows. In the Roman days the trout perhaps weren't as shy.

So I went along the straight white road to Aigle through the evening and wondered about the Grand Army and the Romans and the Huns that traveled light and fast, and yet must have had time to try the stream along toward daylight, and very soon I was in Aigle, which is a very good place to be. I have never seen the town of Aigle; it straggles up the hillside, but there is a café across the station that has a galloping gold horse on top, a great wisteria vine as thick as a young tree that branches out and shades the porch with hanging bunches of purple flowers that bees go in and out of all day and that glisten after a rain, green tables with green chairs, seventeen percent dark beer. The beer goes foaming out in great glass mugs that hold a quart and cost forty centimes, and a barmaid smiles and asks about your luck.

Trains are always at least two hours apart in Aigle, and those waiting in the station buffet, this café with the golden horse and the wisteria-hung porch is a station buffet, mind you, wish they would never come.

Trout Fishing in the Rhone Valley

Fascisti Party Half-Million

☆ THE TORONTO DAILY STAR
June 24, 1922

Milan.—Benito Mussolini, head of the Fascisti movement, sits at his desk at the fuse of the great powder magazine that he has laid through all Northern and Central Italy and occasionally fondles the ears of a wolf-hound pup, looking like a short-eared jackrabbit, that plays with the papers on the floor beside the big desk. Mussolini is a big, brown-faced man with a high forehead, a slow smiling mouth, and large, expressive hands.

"The Fascisti are now half a million strong," he told me. "We are a political party organized as a military force."

Talking slowly in Italian and choosing his words in order that he might be sure that I understood everything he said, he went on to tell how the Fascisti have 250,000 troops organized into squads of *Camicie Nere*, or black shirts, as shock troops of the political party. "Garibaldi had red shirts," he smiled deprecatingly.

"We are not out to oppose any Italian government. We are not against the law," Mussolini explained in carefully accented words, leaning back in his editorial chair and emphasizing his points with his great brown hands. "But," he enunciated very slowly and carefully, "we have force enough to overthrow any government that might try to oppose or destroy us."

"How about the Guardia Regia?" I asked. (The Guardia Regia are the recently organized force of troops from the South of Italy formed by Ex-Premier Nitti to keep the peace in case of civil war.)

"The Guardia Regia will never fight us!" Mussolini said.

Now that situation needs a bit of examination and comparison. The Fascisti platform is one of extreme conservatism. Imagine the Conservative party of Canada with 250,000 men under arms, "a political party organized as a military force," with their leader declaring that they have force enough to overthrow any Liberal or other government that might oppose them. It makes quite a picture, doesn't it? At the same time imagine a special military police force having been created to prevent the Conservatives from battling in the streets with the Liberals, and you have a good angle of observation on the present Italian political situation. Mussolini was a great surprise. He is not the monster he has been pictured. His face is intellectual, it is the typical "Bersagliere" face, with its large, brown, oval shape, dark eyes and big, slow-speaking mouth. Mussolini is often described as a "renegade Socialist," but he seems to have had a very good reason for his renunciation of the party.

Born 37 years ago in the Romagna in a little town called Foli, he started life in a hotbed of revolution. It was near his birthplace that the revolution of 1913 occurred, the "red wig" revolt in which Malatesta, the famous Italian anarchist, attempted to establish a republic. Mussolini began his career as a schoolteacher when he was under twenty. He drifted into journalism and made his first prominent appearance in Trento as an associate of Cesare Battisti on the *Libertà*. Cesare Battisti was the Italian who was captured, wounded by the Austrians while he was an officer of Alpini, and hanged in the Castle of Trento because he was born in the part of Italy held by the Austrians.

When war broke out in 1914 Mussolini was editor of *Avanti*, the Socialist daily paper of Milan. He worked for Italy going into the war on the side of the Allies so strongly that the management of his paper dispensed with his services and Mussolini founded his own paper, the *Popolo d'Italia*, to set forth his views. He sank all his money in this enterprise and as soon as Italy entered the war enlisted in the crack "Bersagliere" corps as a private.

Severely wounded in the fighting on the Carso plateau and several times decorated for valor, Mussolini, a patriot above all things, saw what he regarded as the fruits of Italy's victory being swept away from her in 1919 by a wave of communism that covered all of Northern Italy and threatened all private property rights. As a protest against this he organized the Fascisti or anti-Communist shock troops. The history of their activities in the next two years has been told very often.

Now Mussolini stands at the head of an organization of 500,000 members. It comprises men of almost every trade in Italy, several hundreds of thousand workers disgusted with the communism, having turned to the Fascisti as an armed force who might do something for them. Fascism thus enters its third phase. First it was an organization of counterattackers against the Communist demonstrations, second it became a political party, and now it is a political and military party that is enlisting the workers of Italy and invading the field of labor organizations. It is dominating Italy from Rome to the Alps.

The question is now, what does Mussolini, sitting at his desk in the office of the *Popolo d'Italia* and fondling the ears of his wolfhound pup, intend to do with his "political party organized as a military force"?

Italy's Blackshirts

☆ THE TORONTO STAR WEEKLY
June 24, 1922

Milan.—The Fascisti, or extreme Nationalists, which means black-shirted, knife-carrying, club-swinging, quick-stepping, nineteen-year-old potshot patriots, have worn out their welcome in Italy. Banks and large commercial houses, who contributed the funds that launched the Fascist movement as a protective measure against a threatened Communist revolution, have withdrawn their support and the mass of the Italian press have turned solidly against the Fascisti. Meanwhile the Fascisti, solidly organized, are forming themselves into a political party and by a constant series of outrages, keeping Italy in a state of class war.

On June 1 the Fascisti, as a demonstration of their strength, decided to capture the city of Bologna. The excuse was that the Prefect of Bologna was too friendly to radicals. Benito Mussolini, the renegade Socialist, ex-editor of *Avanti*, the Socialist newspaper of Milan, duelist, war hero and present member of the Italian Chamber of Deputies, gave the order for the occupation of the city from Rome. 15,000 Fascisti, averaging twenty years of age, "took" the town, burned the telegraph and post offices, beat up any- and everyone that objected to their seizure of Bologna and then withdrew, announcing that the next time they gave a demonstration they would be 50,000 instead of 15,000, and that they would kill instead of beating up.

It is that sort of demonstration, repeated in hundreds of other Italian towns, that has cost the Fascisti their old-time popularity. Trouble stirred up by Fascisti, with the consequent lack of political stability, is what is keeping the lira at its present low rate. That hits the businessmen in their pocketbooks and they would willingly pay more than they subscribed to found the bourgeois shock troops in order to buy them off now. In many cases they are now paying them blackmail to keep them from making trouble.

Their continued lawless tactics cost the Fascists a very real popularity too. After the war it was impossible for the wife of a merchant, a manufacturer, or a professional man to go about in any public places in northern Italy without being liable to insults of various kinds, from having her hat torn off and her face scratched to being hissed as a "borghese." Anyone buying a first- or second-class seat in an Italian train was never sure that they would not be thrown out of it by some worker with his dinner pail who had decided that he would ride first class on a third-class ticket. Gangs of hoodlums would swarm into a train as it stopped in some northern Italian town and after throwing the "borghese" out of the first-class compartments would gaily enter and ride a few stations, cutting all the red plush out of the seats as souvenirs.

When Benito Mussolini organized the Fascisti as a sort of Ku Klux Klan against this sort of terrorism, he was enthusiastically supported. The Fascisti were formed from all the excitement-loving youths of the middle- and upper-class families and set about a counter-campaign of terrorism against the workers. Wearing their black silk shirts, open at the neck, their black puttees, army breeches and black fezzes, and armed with clubs and revolvers, they fought some very gay battles with the workers and did some very effective raiding. The workers realized that the millennium, when a man could ride first class on a third-class ticket, was still some distance off and settled down to work again. It looked as though the whole business was settled and that the Fascisti could go home and put their black silk shirts into mothballs.

A hitch came in the arrangements when the Fascisti refused to consider the matter settled. They had a taste of killing under police protection and they liked it. They enjoyed hunting live Communists much more than going to school or working in their fathers' offices—and they intended to keep right on. So the Fascisti have kept on fighting, burning, pillaging anything resembling communism they could find. And as all of northern Italy is tinged with communism in one shade or another, the Fascisti have taken on a lifetime job.

The Fascisti leaders, seeing their well-organized gang, have developed political ambitions and want to make a solid political party of their followers. The politicians of other parties fear this and would do anything to break up the movement. Meanwhile the Communists, tiring of the fact that the Fascisti make no closed season on them, have organized Arditi del Popolo, or People's Shock Troops. These are being put into red shirts to oppose the Fascisti black shirts and are being trained in street fighting. The businessmen are hoping by stopping their money supply to choke the Fascisti, and the government has formed a special corps called the Guardia Regia, made up of men from the mountains of Abruzzi and the South, to fight both sides in case of a civil war. The whole business has the quiet and peaceful look of a three-year-old child playing with a live Mills bomb.

A Veteran Visits the Old Front

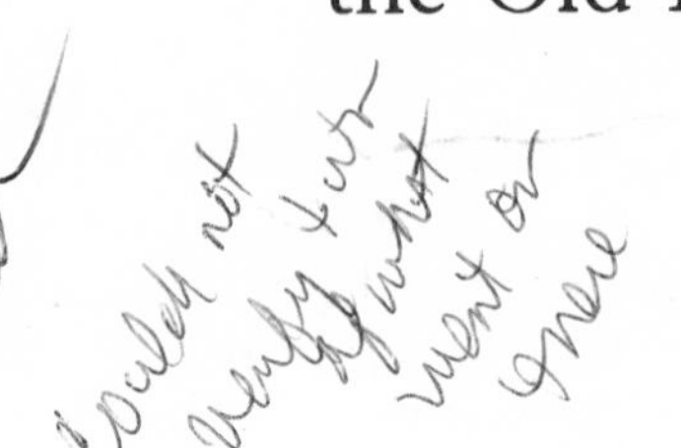

☆ THE TORONTO DAILY STAR
July 22, 1922

Paris.—Don't go back to visit the old front. If you have pictures in your head of something that happened in the night in the mud at Paschendaele or of the first wave working up the slope of Vimy, do not try and go back to verify them. It is no good. The front is as different from the way it used to be as your highly respectable shin, with a thin, white scar on it now, is from the leg that you sat and twisted a tourniquet around while the blood soaked your puttee and trickled into your boot, so that when you got up you limped with a "squidge" on your way to the dressing station.

Go to someone else's front, if you want to. There your imagination will help you out and you may be able to picture the things that happened. But don't go back to your own front, because the change in everything and the supreme, deadly, lonely dullness, the smooth green of the fields that were once torn up with shell holes and slashed with trenches and wire, will combine against you and make you believe that the places and happenings that had been the really great events to you were only fever dreams or lies you had told to yourself. It is like going into the empty gloom of a theater where the charwomen are scrubbing. I know because I have just been back to my own front.

Not only is it battlefields that have changed in quality and feeling and gone back into a green smugness with the shell holes filled up, the trenches filled in, the pillboxes blasted out and smoothed over and the wire all rolled up and rotting in a great heap somewhere. That was to be expected, and it was inevitable that the feelings in the battlefields would change when the dead that made them both holy and real were dug up and reburied in big, orderly cemeteries miles away from where they died. Towns where you were billeted, towns unscarred by war, are the ones where the changes hit you hardest. For there are many little towns that you love, and after all, no one but a staff officer could love a battlefield.

There may be towns back of the old Canadian front, towns with queer Flemish names and narrow, cobbled streets, that have kept their magic. There may be such towns. I have just come from Schio, though. Schio was the finest town I remember in the war, and I wouldn't have recognized it now—and I would give a lot not to have gone.

Schio was one of the finest places on earth. It was a little town in the Trentino under the shoulder of the Alps, and it contained all the good cheer, amusement and relaxation a man could desire. When we used to be in billets there, everyone was perfectly contented and we were always talking about what a wonderful place Schio would be to come and live after the war. I particularly recall a first-class hotel called the Due Spadi, where the food was superb and we used to call the factory where we were billeted the "Schio Country Club."

The other day Schio seemed to have shrunk. I walked up one side of the long, narrow main street looking in shop windows at the fly-speckled shirts, the cheap china dishes, the postcards showing about seven different varieties of a young man and a young girl looking into each other's eyes, the stiff, fly-speckled pastry, the big, round loaves of sour bread. At the end of the street were the mountains, but I had walked over the St. Bernard Pass the week before and the mountains, without snow caps, looked rain-furrowed and dull; not much more than hills. I looked at the mountains a long time, though, and then walked down the other side of the street to the principal bar. It was starting to rain a little and shopkeepers were lowering the shutters in front of their shops.

"The town is changed since the war," I said to the girl, she was red-cheeked and black-haired and discontented-looking, who sat on a stool, knitting behind the zinc-covered bar.

"Yes?" she said without missing a stitch.

"I was here during the war," I ventured.

"So were many others," she said under her breath, bitterly.

"Grazie, Signor," she said with mechanical, insolent courtesy as I paid for the drink and went out.

That was Schio. There was more, the way the Due Spadi had shrunk to a small inn, the factory where we used to be billeted now was humming, with our old entrance bricked up and a flow of black muck polluting the stream where we used to swim. All the kick had gone out of things. Early next morning I left in the rain after a bad night's sleep.

There was a garden in Schio with the wall matted with wisteria where we used to drink beer on hot nights with a bombing moon making all sorts of shadows from the big plane tree that spread above the table. After my walk in the afternoon I knew enough not to try and find that garden. Maybe there never was a garden.

Perhaps there never was any war around Schio at all. I remember lying in the squeaky bed in the hotel and trying to read by an electric light that hung high up from the center of the ceiling and then switching off the light and looking out the window down the road where the arc light was making a dim light through the rain. It was the same road that the battalions marched along through the white dust in 1916. They were the Brigata Ancona, the Brigata Como, the Brigata Tuscana and ten others brought down from the Carso to check the Austrian offensive that was breaking through the mountain wall of the Trentino and beginning to spill down the valleys that led to the Venetian and Lombardy plains. They were good troops in those days and they marched through the dust of the early summer, broke the offensive along the Galio-Asiago-Canoev line, and died in the mountain gullies, in the pine woods on the Trentino slopes, hunting cover on the desolate rocks and pitched out in the soft-melting early summer snow of the Pasubio.

It was the same old road that some of the same old brigades marched along through the dust of June of 1918, being rushed to the Piave to stop another offensive. Their best men were dead on the rocky Carso, in the fighting around Goritzia, on Mount San Gabrielle, on Grappa and in all the places where men died that nobody ever heard about. In 1918 they didn't march with the ardor that they did in 1916, some of the troops strung out so badly that, after the battalion was just a dust cloud way up the road, you would see poor old boys hoofing it along the side of the road to ease their bad feet, sweating along under their packs and rifles and the deadly Italian sun in a long, horrible, never-ending stagger after the battalion.

So we went down to Mestre, that was one of the great railheads for the Piave, traveling first class with an assorted carriageful of evil-smelling Italian profiteers going to Venice for vacations. In Mestre we hired a motorcar to drive out to the Piave and leaned back in the rear seat and studied the map and the country along the long road that is built through the poisonous green Adriatic marshes that flank all the coast near Venice.

Near Porto Grande, in the part of the lower Piave delta where Austrians and Italians attacked and counterattacked waist-deep in the swamp water, our car stopped in a desolate part of the road that ran like a causeway across the green marshy waste. It needed a long, grease-smearing job of adjustment on the gears and while the driver worked, and got a splinter of steel in his finger that my wife [Hadley] dug out with a needle from our rucksack, we baked in the hot sun. Then a wind blew the mist away from the Adriatic and we saw Venice way off across the swamp and the sea standing gray and yellow like a fairy city.

Finally the driver wiped the last of the grease off his hands into his over-luxuriant hair, the gears took hold when he let the clutch in and we went off along the road through the swampy plain. Fossalta, our objective, as I remembered it, was a shelled-to-pieces town that even rats couldn't live in. It had been within trench-mortar range of the Austrian lines for a year and in quiet times the Austrian had blown up anything in it that looked as though it ought to be blown up. During active sessions it had been one of the first footholds the Austrian had gained on the Venice side of the Piave, and one of the last places he was driven out of and hunted down in and very many men had died in its rubble- and debris-strewn streets and been smoked out of its cellars with *flammenwerfers* during the house-to-house work.

We stopped the car in Fossalta and got out to walk. All the shattered, tragic dignity of the wrecked town was gone. In its place was a new, smug, hideous collection of plaster houses, painted bright blues, reds and yellows. I had been in Fossalta perhaps fifty times and I would not have recognized it. The new plaster church was the worst-looking thing. The trees that had been splintered and gashed showed their scars if you looked for them and had a stunted appearance, but you could not have told in passing, unless you had known, how they had been torn. Everything was so abundantly green and prosperous-looking.

I climbed the grassy slope and above the sunken road where the dugouts had been to look at the Piave and looked down an even slope to the blue river. The Piave is as blue as the Danube is brown. Across the river were two new houses where the two rubble heaps had been just inside the Austrian lines.

I tried to find some trace of the old trenches to show my wife, but there was only the smooth green slope. In a thick prickly patch of hedge we found an old rusty piece of shell fragment. From the cast-iron look of the smoothly burst fragment I could tell it was an old bit of gas shell. That was all there was left of the front.

On our way back to the motorcar we talked about how jolly it is that Fossalta is all built up now and how fine it must be for all the families to have their homes back. We said how proud we were of the way the Italians had kept their mouths shut and rebuilt their devastated districts while some other nations were using their destroyed towns as showplaces and reparation appeals. We said all the things of that sort that as decent-thinking people we thought—and then we stopped talking. There was nothing more to say. It was so very sad.

For a reconstructed town is much sadder than a devastated town. The people haven't their homes back. They have new homes. The home they played in as children, the room where they made love with the lamp turned down, the hearth where they sat, the church they were married in, the room where their child died, these rooms are gone. A shattered village in the war always had a dignity, as though it had died for something. It had died for something and something better was to come. It was all part of the great sacrifice. Now there is just the new, ugly futility of it all. Everything is just as it was—except a little worse.

So we walked along the street where I saw my very good friend killed, past the ugly houses toward the motorcar, whose owner would never have had a motorcar if it had not been for the war, and it all seemed a very bad business. I had tried to recreate something for my wife and had failed utterly. The past was as dead as a busted Victrola record. Chasing yesterdays is a bum show—and if you have to prove it, go back to your old front.

Relat. to past

Sinclair Lewis's Horsebacking

☆ THE TORONTO STAR WEEKLY
August 5, 1922

They are telling a story in Paris on Sinclair Lewis, author of *Main Street*, that is unconfirmed by Mr. Lewis, but that has a strange ring of truth about it.

According to the story, Lewis on a recent visit to London, where he was working on a new novel to appear this fall, expressed a desire to ride in Rotten Row. He was astonished at the shortness of the Row and said as much to the groom that was accompanying him.

The groom, who had been eyeing Lewis's seat in a grieved and pained manner for some time, drew himself up in disgust.

"Well, sir," he said very haughtily over the top of his stock, "You cawn't expect the bloomin' prairies 'ere sir."

The Great "Apéritif" Scandal

☆ THE TORONTO STAR WEEKLY
August 12, 1922

Paris.—The great "apéritif" scandal that is agitating Paris has struck at the roots of one of the best-loved institutions of France.

Apéritifs, or appetizers, are those tall, bright red or yellow drinks that are poured from two or three bottles by hurried waiters during the hour before lunch and the hour before dinner, when all Paris gathers at the cafés to poison themselves to a cheerful pre-eating glow. The apéritifs are all patented mixtures, contain a high percentage of alcohol and bitters, have a basic taste like a brass doorknob, and go by such names as Amourette, Anis Delloso, Amer Picon, Byrrh, Tomyysette and twenty others. Now apéritifs blossom in Paris as new cigarettes do in Toronto. It is simply a matter of the number of persons anxious to try anything new.

The first scandal came when police discovered that absinthe, which was abolished six years ago, was being sold in great quantities under the name of Anis Delloso. Instead of producing a beautiful green color that minor poets have celebrated to the driest corners of the world, the absinthe manufacturers were turning it out in quantity production as a pale yellow syrup. It had the familiar licorice taste, however, and turned milky when water was added—and it had the slow, culminating wallop that made the boulevardier want to get up and jump on his new straw hat in ecstasy after the third Delloso.

One loud, glad cry was uttered on the boulevards and in a few days word-of-mouth advertising made Anis Delloso the most popular beverage in the city. It continued until the police suppressed the manufacture of absinthe.

Anis Delloso is still being manufactured. It still has the licorice flavor—but the boulevardier waits in vain for the feeling that makes him want to shinny rapidly up the side of the Eiffel Tower. For it is not absinthe any more.

Now the big scandal is concerned with the Fourteenth of July. Bastille Day is the great French holiday. This year it started on Wednesday night, the thirteenth of July, and continued unabated all Wednesday night, all day Thursday, all night Thursday, all day Friday, all night Friday, all day

Saturday, all night Saturday, all day Sunday, and all night Sunday. All big places of business, all department stores and banks were closed from Wednesday afternoon till noon on Monday. It would take about eight columns of closely set type to do justice in any way to that holiday.

Every two blocks there was a street ball where the people of that quarter danced. The street was decorated with colored lanterns and flags and music furnished by the municipality. That all sounds very tame and quiet, but it was not. Orders were given that neither buses nor taxicabs could go down a street where a ball was in progress. As a result there was no traffic.

The music for the ball in the street below our apartment consisted of an accordion, two drummers, a bagpiper and a cornettist. These four courageous and tireless men sat in a wagon box that was placed on four huge wine casks in the street and bowered with branches broken, I believe, from trees in the park. In this sylvan bower they sat, drank, ate, relayed one another on the instruments and played from 9 o'clock at night until 8 o'clock the next morning, while the crowd polkaed round and round!

This happened on four consecutive nights, while the inhabitants of the quarter had a little sleep in the daytime and the rest of the time jammed the street to dance. It was a wonderful thing to watch between twenty and thirty couples dancing hilariously in the street at eleven o'clock in the morning after having danced all night. These were not students or artists or such crazy people, mind you, but shop girls, butchers, bakers, laborers, tram conductors and laundresses, and bookmakers. It was a very great party—but it couldn't have occurred on water.

Enter the "apéritif" scandal. The government spent some millions of francs on the party. It was all considered wisely spent money in the cause of encouraging patriotism. French flags were everywhere, fireworks went off at all times, there was a great military review at Longchamps at eight o'clock in the morning, attended by thousands of people who had danced all night, and went to sleep on the grass. An unbalanced young Communist took a shot at a prefect of police by mistake for M. Poincaré and the patriotic crowd mobbed him. Every one agreed that M. Poincaré's life was undoubtedly saved by the Fourteenth of July because who could be expected to hit anyone they shot at after such a night as all Paris had just spent. It was a fine celebration.

The scandal consisted in the fact that above all the dancing places, over the heads of the musicians, where the government had placed the French flags and spent money for the music and decorations, were enormous banners advertising the different brands of apéritifs. Over the ball, flanked by the tricolor, would be a great sign "Drink Amourette." At another place the people of the quartier would be dancing in an ecstasy of patriotism under the legend "Vive Anis Delloso—the Finest Apéritif in the World."

No one seemed to notice the signs to any great extent during the evenings, but once the dancing was over a big inquiry was ordered to investigate why the government spent over a million francs to give the apéritif manufacturers about a million dollars worth of publicity. Several Paris newspapers have come out against there ever being such a July fourteenth again. There is a fearful scandal on and the inquiry about the apéritif signs still continues.

Did Poincaré Laugh in Verdun Cemetery?

☆ THE TORONTO DAILY STAR
August 12, 1922

Paris.—Did Premier Poincaré really laugh in the cemetery at Verdun when the United States government decorated the martyred city?

Whether M. Poincaré laughed or not, the pictures taken of him at the time caused the French Communist party to launch a bitter attack on the premier, brought forth a white-hot denial from M. Poincaré, caused a debate in the Chamber of Deputies, threw France into an uproar and also resulted in the country being flooded with postcards.

The picture published with this article was issued by the French Communist party in the form of a postcard, and first made its appearance at one of the Sunday Communist meetings held in the country outside of Paris. It shows M. Poincaré and United States Ambassador Herrick walking in the cemetery at Verdun and shows both M. Poincaré and the ambassador apparently laughing heartily. The Communists, who had always accused M. Poincaré of a great share in the responsibility for the war, issued the card with a flamboyant inscription, calling it "The Man Who Laughs" and saying that "Poincaré, like other murderers, returns to the scene of his crimes."

In a short time the Communist headquarters had sold over 100,000 of the postcards. The matter came to a head in the Chamber of Deputies when a young Communist deputy smiled at some remark of M. Poincaré's in regard to Communist propaganda in the French colonies in Northern Africa.

"You smile?" said M. Poincaré.

"Yes, I smile," said Vaillant-Coutourier, the young deputy who was one of the great war heroes of France, "but I do not laugh in the cemetery of Verdun!"

M. Poincaré went white with rage, and denounced the postcard as a fake and demanded that the entire matter be cleared up with an interpellation. That is, that the Communists accuse him publicly from the floor, and that he answer.

"I never laughed in the cemetery at Verdun," M. Poincaré said, denying the charge absolutely and categorically. "The explanation of the matter is that the sun got into my eyes and twisted my face so that it looked as though I were laughing."

M. Poincaré has stuck to this explanation through thick and thin.

An interesting Toronto angle to the story appears here in the fact that the *Star* on July 22, in their picture page, published, long before there was any controversy or before the Communists had issued their postcard, a picture of Ambassador Herrick and M. Poincaré, taken at the same ceremony as the picture that has caused the great trouble. The *Star*'s picture shows Ambassador Herrick obviously laughing but whether M. Poincaré is smiling must be left to the judgment of the reader.

According to the French papers, Ambassador Herrick gave two explanations of the affair. The papers first quote him as saying that of course he did not laugh, and after being shown the picture as saying, "Perhaps something I said to M. Poincaré made him laugh."

There are two divergent explanations already. M. Poincaré says he did not laugh. Ambassador Herrick says perhaps something he said to M. Poincaré made him laugh.

Now comes a third explanation. A movie photographer who was present on the occasion says that he was hurrying to get in front of Poincaré and Herrick and was running along with his tripod when he slipped and fell sprawling and both the French premier and the ambassador laughed heartily at his ridiculous plight.

Whatever the explanation, the incident, the debate in the Chamber of Deputies, and the postal card have raised a furor in France. Over 200,000 of the postcards have been sold and they are selling at present at the rate of 15,000 a day. Communists charge that those sent through the mail are being destroyed, but those familiar with the French policy of complete freedom of speech in politics doubt this. At any rate they have made their appearance in England.

"What if M. Poincaré did laugh at the cemetery?" many people will ask. "Anyone might have laughed accidentally. What is all the furor about anyway?"

To understand all that you must realize the French attitude toward the dead. It is safe to say that no living man in France today commands as much respect as any dead man does.

Marshal Foch, Anatole France, Henri Barbusse, M. Poincaré or the Pope could never, any one of them, receive the united respect of all the people they would meet if they drove two blocks down the Champs-Elysées. There are too many people with too many divergent political, religious and ethical views in France for any one person to be a complete national hero. But everyone in a motor bus, regardless of religion or politics, takes off their hats when the bus passes a hearse, even if it is a draggled black hearse with only one mourner walking behind. Even the caps of the motormen and chauffeurs come off when they pass a funeral.

It is that great spirit of respect for the dead, coupled with the significance of Verdun, that has given the question of whether M. Poincaré laughed or not the national prominence that it holds.

Rug Vendors in Paris

☆ THE TORONTO DAILY STAR
August 12, 1922

Paris.—No one can sit for twenty consecutive minutes in front of any Parisian café without becoming aware, aurally or nasally, of the fur rug vendor. Wearing a dirty red fez, a bundle of skins slung over his shoulder, a red morocco billfold in his hand, his brown face shining, the rug seller is as firm a feature of Paris life as the big green buses that snort and roar past, the little, old, red one-lung taxis that grind and beetle through the traffic or the sleek cat that suns herself in every concierge's window.

The rug seller comes by, smiles at each table, and spreads out one of his handsome fur rugs. If you assume such an expression as might fasten itself on the face of the Hon. Mr. Raney on the occasion of his receiving a delegation of the Young Men's Pari-Mutuel Association with a request for him to contribute some fitting sum toward cushions for the seats at the Woodbine [racetrack] and at the same time inform the rug vendor, with a dirty look, that you hate all rugs and have just come out of jail after having served twenty years for killing rug sellers on the slopes of Montparnasse, he may pass on to the next table.

Twenty to one, however, would be a good bet against his doing so. It is much more likely that he will fix you with a sad, brown stare and remark, "Monsieur jests about my beautiful rugs."

Now, if you, at this point, arise and kick the rug vendor with your strongest foot, at the same time hitting him heavily over the head with a café table and cry out in a loud clear voice: "Death to robbers and rug vendors!" there is a small chance that he will perceive that you are not in the market for rugs and move on to the next table. It is much more likely, however, that he will slip to his knees, grasp your foot in one hand, bow his head to the blow of the table and say, in a patient voice: "Monsieur kicks and hits me. It is on account of my beautiful rugs."

There is nothing for you to do after that but help him to his feet and ask: "How much?"

The rug vendor unslings something that looks like a royal Bengal tiger from his shoulder and spreads it out lovingly: "For you, Monsieur, two hundred francs."

You examine the royal Bengal tiger closely and perceive it is a beautifully patched and dyed goat skin.

"It is a goat," you say.

"Ah, no, Monsieur," says the rug vendor sadly. "It is a veritable tiger."

"It is a goat!" you grunt fiercely.

"Ah yes, Monsieur," the rug vendor puts his hand on his heart, "it is a veritable tiger. I swear by Allah."

"It is a goat," you repeat. "Stop this lying."

"Ah yes, Monsieur," the rug vendor bows his head. "It is a veritable goat."

"How much do you charge for this mean, ill-dyed, foul-smelling goat?"

"A gift to you, Monsieur, for one hundred francs."

"Forty francs. The last price," you say grimly.

The rug vendor puts the rug over his back and walks sadly away. "You jest, Monsieur, you jest about the beautiful skins. We cannot trade together."

You go back to your newspaper but in a moment there is a familiar aroma. You raise your eyes and there is the rug vendor. He is holding out the royal Bengal tiger. "A sacrifice. For Monsieur, because of his gentility, this beautiful tiger for fifty francs."

You pretend that the rug vendor is nonexistent. He goes off again but comes back. "Forty-five francs," he says brightly. "For Monsieur alone of all the world. Forty-five francs and Monsieur owns the very beautiful tiger."

"I have bought a thousand like it for forty francs," you answer, turning back to the newspaper.

"It is yours, Monsieur. You have bought it for forty francs. The beautiful tiger."

The beautiful tiger is laid across the back of your chair and at once commences his lifelong job of getting hair on your clothing. You give the rug vendor two twenty-franc notes and he bows low. He goes off a little way but you see him eyeing you. He comes back.

"Perhaps Monsieur would care for one of these lovely morocco pocketbooks," he says, smiling happily.

There is only one thing to do. Leave the café.

Several hundred rug vendors are employed by a syndicate that makes the rugs and pocketbooks and pays the salesmen five francs a day and everything they get over the minimum price. Rugs are usually priced at 200 francs to start, with a minimum price about 45 francs. Most of the salesmen are Arabs.

Many of the rugs are well made and very fine-looking and are good bargains at from 45 to 55 francs. Tourists buy them at from 75 to 150 francs and are invariably very satisfied with them—unless the goat develops atavistic tendencies in the hot weather. For that there is no remedy.

Old Order Changeth in Alsace-Lorraine

☆ THE TORONTO DAILY STAR
August 26, 1922

Strasbourg, France.—You have to watch your step in Alsace on the language question. When William E. Nash of the *Chicago Daily News* asked a chauffeur in Strasbourg if he spoke French and the chauffeur answered with a flawless Parisian accent, "But yes, Monsieur! And do you?" we all had the laugh on him.

"Don't you know that Alsace and Lorraine are French provinces?" we asked Nash and a good many other things of that sort. "What did you expect him to speak? Japanese?"

It was Nash's turn to laugh when I asked a cabby in French how to get to the Place Kléber.

"Say, how do you expect me to know French?" he answered in Rhenish German. "What do you think I am? A professor?"

It is a strange fact that the chauffeurs of the taxis all speak French and the drivers of the horse-drawn cabs speak and understand nothing but German. It is the new against the old regime.

Strasbourg is a lovely old town with streets of houses that look so much like old German prints that you keep looking up at the chimneys for stork's nests. Little rivers cut through it and there are picturesque quays where men sit fishing and women bend their backs to their laundering. It seems a very fine division of labor from the male standpoint but I think the women are revenged because I have never seen any of the men catch any fish and imagine it is the soapsuds that keep them from biting.

The great single spire of the cathedral is visible from nearly any part of the town and the cathedral itself is very fine. It is built of reddish stone and seems to get larger the longer you look at it. The best place to observe it from is the terrace of the café that faces it where you can lean back in a chair and sight it over the top of a tall beer. Strasbourg has the tallest and narrowest beers in the world.

I asked the waitress at the café why the beers were so tall and narrow and she said they had always been that way. Then I asked a keen-faced young priest at the next table about it and he smiled into his own beer and said perhaps it was the influence of the tall spire of the cathedral.

To the left of the cathedral is the Kammerzell, built in 1472 according to the tablet, that looks like the inn in a Grimm fairy tale. It is six stories high and has a restaurant on every floor. We ate on the first floor in a low wood-paneled room that seemed to reek of flagons of ale, poniards stuck in the table and quarreling Brandenburgers and women with the sort of headdresses that go way out to a point like a long slanted-back dunce's cap and have a veil draping down.

There was a roast chicken with tender green beans and a lettuce salad that came on after a fresh broiled brook trout from the Vosges and was followed by a fine sort of a cake and coffee. There was also a clear, dry Rhine wine in long, narrow bottles, much narrower than the beer glasses, and as tall as Indian clubs and obviously under the influence of the spire of the Strasbourg cathedral. Afterward there was a liqueur named quetch, a thimbleful made by distilling the big blue plums that grow in the orchards up in the hills. It tasted as plums look, but never taste.

We never bothered to find out what the restaurants on the six other floors were like.

At the grand hotel, called the Hotel de la Ville de Paris, where we were staying, there was a sentimental orchestra that sobbed out *Faust* and Puccini and worse half the night, swooning over the rests and generally making the night horrible, so we moved to a little old hotel with plastered walls that fronted on the square where the Lutheran church is. It was quiet there and we had a room twice as big as the grand hotel for about two-thirds of the price. But we made the mistake of dining there one night, having been encouraged by some wonderful rolls with fresh butter, good coffee and plump huckleberries in the morning, and found the food mediocre.

They advertised peach ice on the dinner and brought us instead soggy apple fritters and when Mrs. [Hadley] Hemingway spoke to the waiter, he answered us that there was no more peach ice to be had anywhere in the town, a statement that cost him half his tip when we saw some being served a few moments later at the next table. No, under the circumstances, even remembering the big room and the fine view on to the square and the excellent way our boots were done and the enormous big beds, it would be hardly the thing to recommend the hotel by name.

The cathedral has the largest and finest dramatic clock in the world. The twelve apostles come out at noon every day and walk around and around, a large cock crows and flaps his wings and things come off in general. We didn't see the spectacle. The Lutheran church, to put the cathedral in its place, has absolutely no clock at all.

As we left the town, at five o'clock in the morning, a couple of men were sitting on the damp stones at the side of one of the little rivers, fishing. They had probably gotten up early to get a start on the laundresses.

Homes on the Seine

☆ THE TORONTO DAILY STAR
August 26, 1922

Paris.—Instead of driving people back to the land, the Parisian apartment shortage is driving flat-dwellers on to the water.

A socially prominent Parisian, finding his rent tripled on the expiration of his lease, inaugurated the new movement by refusing to sign on at the advanced figure, buying an old canal barge, he remodeled it into a super-comfortable dwelling. The barge is large and roomy, the carpentry cost a fraction of the increased rent demanded, and the barge-dweller has a home he can moor in the Seine in the center of the most fashionable quarter. There are four bedrooms, a drawing room, kitchen, bathroom, dining room and billiard room in the floating flat and the owner is summering in it at present at Strasbourg, having crossed the width of France in a very enjoyable trip through the canal system of the Marne, Meuse and Moselle rivers.

Less pretentious "flat boats" are being launched at regular intervals and there is talk of a firm turning out standardized floating homes at popular prices for those Parisians who are desperate about the housing shortage.

The gravity of the housing situation was shown the other day by a rush on a Paris concierge who advertised a flat for rent through official channels. At nine o'clock in the morning the concierge informed the police that there was a flat vacant in the building at an annual rental of 1,800 francs. By five that afternoon the flat was rented.

In the next morning's official journal appeared the notice that the flat was for rent. By noon nearly four thousand people had gathered to see about the flat. It looked like a riot and the concierge called the police, who dispersed the crowd and helped the concierge letter a big sign announcing that the flat was already rented.

Germans Desperate over the Mark

☆ THE TORONTO DAILY STAR
September 1, 1922

Freiberg, Germany.—The German people, according to their temperaments, are watching the plunge to worthlessness of their currency with dogged sullenness or hysterical desperation.

Last November the Austrian crown stood where the German mark does today—at 800 to the dollar. Now it has dropped to 22,000 to the dollar. That is the reason the German newspapers publish the daily price of the mark in black type in the most important place on their front pages.

The debacle of the mark has made a significant change in the attitude of the Germans toward foreigners. A year ago, with the mark 130 to the dollar, British, Canadian and American correspondents were accorded all sorts of special facilities by the German foreign office. The Germans hated the French and tried to make things as hard for them as possible, but the other nations were regarded as Germany's possible friends in the future. Now there are no privileges for anyone. All foreigners are outlanders and enemies. For Germany is going to ruin and her only satisfaction is that she will probably take a nation or two, now supposedly in fairly sound financial shape, with her.

One of the strange results of the depreciation of German money is the money shortage. The more money is printed, the more is needed. As a result banks are frequently out of money since a factory owner with a weekly payroll to meet may come in and take out three bushels of marks. Every store has to have great packages of fifty- and hundred-mark notes for making change. The government, to meet the shortage, has printed five-hundred-mark "temporary" notes that are simply government I.O.U.'s printed on plain, white bank notepaper saying that in January, 1923, the holder of this note will receive a real five-hundred-mark note.

There is said to be wild spending because Germans have tired of seeing their money lose its purchasing power by half again and again and are buying jewels, fur coats, motor cars and other things that will have a certain amount of real value when the marks that bought them are being used for soap-wrappers.

These spending orgies, which you read about in the German papers but never encounter, are confined to Berlin, Hamburg and other places that were always more or less orgy centers. In a little town like Freiburg im Breisgau you run into a sort of dogged, blind resistance by the merchants to the fact that the mark is tobogganing, which keeps prices from going up in any sort of proportion to the fall of the currency.

Four of us stayed four days in a Freiburg hotel and the bill amounted to 2,200 marks, or about 20 cents a day apiece. The terrific taxes that you read so much about totaled less than 15 cents on the entire stay. Tips are included.

Freiberg seemed to be going on very well. Every room in every hotel in town was filled. There were strings of German hikers with rucksacks on their backs going through the town all day long, bound for the Black Forest. Streams of clear water flowed in the deep gutters on each side of the clean, scrubbed-looking streets. The red stone gothic spire of the red stone cathedral stuck up above the red-tiled roofs of the houses. The marketplace was jammed on Saturday morning with women with white handkerchiefs over their heads selling the fruit and vegetables they had brought in ox carts from the country. All the shops were open and prices were very low. It looked peaceful, happy and comfortable.

We saw a girl in a coffee shop eating a breakfast of ice cream and pretzels, sitting across the table from an officer in full uniform with an Iron Cross on his chest, his flat back even more impressive than his lean, white face, and we saw mothers feeding their rosy-cheeked children beer out of big half-liter steins.

We saw no evidence of panic, republicanism or malnutrition. Everyone looked well fed, no one seemed panicky, no one seemed happy, and there were pictures of Frederick, King of Baden, and his queen on the walls of every inn and pub.

The alarming part of the business, and the reason that Germany has so far defied all the economic laws that indicated a complete collapse, is the way the German merchants are selling their goods. They are selling goods now at retail prices that are less than half of what the goods would cost them to buy again wholesale.

"But what can we do?" a storekeeper said to me. "If we charged any higher prices, the people would not buy. We have to sell."

It is a solution to a problem that would set the average economist gibbering. He could have a good gibber at the problem and the German's solution of it would intensify his gibber into the finest product of the gibberer's art. If you have nothing else to do you might figure out what will happen to the German storekeepers when they have to replenish the stocks they are selling at half under future cost price.

The great national fire sale cannot last forever. While it is going on, however, the German storekeeper takes out his wrath on the foreigners who buy from him by acting as nastily as he can without forcing them out of the shop. He believes they are the cause of the fire, but he seems to feel he is in the position of a shopkeeper who is forced to sell goods at a fire sale to the men who set his shop on fire. That is his attitude, and he manages to be pretty nasty about it.

Fishing in Baden Perfect

☆ THE TORONTO DAILY STAR
September 2, 1922

Triberg-in-Baden, Germany.—If you want to go fishing in the Black Forest, you want to get up about four hours before the first Schwarzwald rooster begins to shift from one leg to the other and decide that it's time to crow. You need at least that much time to get through the various legal labyrinths in order to get on to the stream before dark.

In the first place the Black Forest is not the sweep of black forest that its name suggests. It is a chain of mountains cut up by railroads, valleys full of rank potato crops, pasture land, brown chalets and gravel-bottomed trout streams, broken out all over with enormous hotels run by Germanized Swiss who have mastered the art of making four beefsteaks grow where only one was cut by the butcher and where you waken up in the morning to find that the falling mark has cut your hotel bill to $3.75 a week and that the price of James E. Pepper Kentucky rye whiskey is 90 cents a bottle.

A Swiss hotelkeeper can raise prices with the easy grace of a Pullman car poker shark backing a pat full house, but the mark can fall faster than even a Swiss in good training can hoist the cost of living. A properly run race between a well-conditioned Swiss hotelkeeper and a fast-falling mark would provide an international financial spectacle that would bring the financial fans to their feet as one man, but my last kronen would go on the mark. In spite of it being the monetary medium that is in daily use in the Einsteinian household, the mark still seems affected by the laws of gravitation.

All of which and none of which has anything to do with the trout fishing in the Black Forest. Triberg consists of a single steep street lined by steep hotels. It is in a steep valley and a cool breeze is said to blow down the valley in wintertime. No one has ever been in Triberg in the wintertime to verify this legend but eight hundred sweltering tourists would gladly lay their right hands over where their hearts ought to be, if their hearts are in the right place, and swear there never has been a breeze of any kind in the summertime.

We landed in Triberg after a five-hour train ride from Freiberg. We had originally planned to walk across the Black Forest but we gave this up when we saw the crowd of German tourists touring in and out of all the roads leading to the woods. Our first disappointment was in finding that the Black Forest was no forest but just a lot of wooded hills and highly cultivated valleys, and our second was in discovering that you couldn't go fifteen yards along any of the wilder and more secluded roads without running into between six and eight Germans, their heads shaved, their knees bare, cock feathers in their hats, sauerkraut on their breath, the wanderlust in their eyes and a collection of aluminum cooking utensils clashing against their legs as they walked.

As I may have said, we landed in Triberg. It was the end of a five-hour ride with two changes and four hours of standing in the aisle while large and unhappy Germans and their large and marcelled wives pushed by us again and again with profuse apologies, and I don't know what aims.

"The proprietor will fix it up for you," said the head porter of the hotel. "He has a friend who has a fishing."

We went into the bar where the friend who had the fishing and six of his friends were sitting at a table and playing a game that looked like pinochle. The proprietor talked with the friend, who has one of the porcupine-quill haircuts that are all the rage this year, and the friend pounded the table with his fist while the rest of the table roared and laughed.

The proprietor came over to our table.

"They all make jokes," he said. "He says if you pay him two dollars you can fish all you want for the rest of your life."

Now we are all very familiar with the German when he starts making jokes about the dollar, and suggests that he be paid for such-and-such in dollars. It is a foul and nefarious habit. If it were allowed to go unchecked, it would soon force all Canadians and Americans back to Sarnia, Ontario, or Kokomo, Indiana. It is a habit that needs to be sat on with all severity.

There was a lot of dickering. The friend and his friends ceased laughing. We grew stern and strong and silent. The porter grew placatory. The atmosphere grew tense. We finally compromised by agreeing to pay 1,200 marks for the fishing unseen. We went to bed happy. We were the owner of a fishing in the Black Forest. We turned over in our thirty-seven-cents-a-night bed in the regal suite of the largest hotel in Triberg and kicked the eiderdown quilt onto the floor. After all, there seemed to be some justice in the world.

In the morning we got our tackle together and went down to breakfast. The porter, who is another Swiss passing as German, came up.

"I have news for you. It is not so easy. You must first obtain the permit of the police. You must get a fischkarte."

I pass over the next two days. They were spent in the offices of the

Kingdom of Baden, now doing business as a republic of sorts, and consisted of conversations like the following:

We enter an office where a number of clerks are sitting around while stern-looking soldiers scratch the small of their backs with the pommels of their swords, or is it only saddles that have pommels?

We, Mr. [William] Bird and myself, speak. "Vere ist der Burgomeister?"

The clerks eye us and go on writing. The soldiers look out of the window at the large stone monument to the war of 1870. Finally a clerk looks up and points to an inner door. There are a line of people outside. We are at the end of the line and finally get in.

Us, Mr. Bird, who is the European manager of the Consolidated Press, and myself speak: "Bitte, Herr Burgomeister. We wollen der fischkarten. We wollen to gefischen goen."

The Burgomeister looks at us and says, "Nix. Nein." That is the only understandable point of his discourse.

"Das fischenkarten," we explain sweetly.

"Nix," he says. "Nein," and points to the door.

We go out. This continues indefinitely.

When we finally, by tracing the person who owned it down at his factory where he makes lightning rods or hairbrushes, found where the fishing was located we were informed by another fine-looking burgomeister that we would have to give up our attempts at getting a fishing license in Triberg altogether and go to Nussbach. We didn't know where Nussbach was. It looked hopeless. We resolved to fish instead.

The stream was a beauty. The friend who owned it was evidently so busy making hair tonic or shoe buttons in his factory that he never fished himself and the trout bit as fast as you could wet a line. We took all we wanted and repeated the next day. On the third day my conscience bothered me.

"We ought to go to Nussbach and get that permit to fish," I suggested.

We went to Nussbach with the aid of a map. No one seemed to know where the burgomeister's office was. Finally we found him in a little shed across the street from the churchyard where a group of schoolboys were being given squad drill. We had been informed as to the dire penalties that were waiting for those who fished without a Badischer permit. Poaching was rigorously punished.

Mr. Bird, who answers to the name of Bill, can talk German. But he doesn't think he can. I, on the contrary, cannot talk German at all, but I think I can. Therefore, I usually dominate the conversation. Mr. Bird says that my system of talking German is to pronounce English with an Italian accent.

"Ve wishen der fischenkarten," I said, bowing low.

The Burgomeister looked at me over his steel-rimmed spectacles.

"Ja?" he said.

"Ve wishen der fischenkarten comme ça," I said very firmly, showing him the yellow card the friend had loaned us to locate the water.

"Ja," he said, examining the card. "Das ist gut wasser."

"Can ve gefischen in it?" I asked.

"Ja, ja," answered the Burgomeister.

"Come on, Bill," I said, "let's go."

We have been fishing the water ever since. No one has stopped us. Some day, doubtless, we will be arrested. I shall appeal to the Burgomeister of Nussbach. He is a splendid man. But I remember distinctly his having told us we could fish all the good water.

German Innkeepers

☆ THE TORONTO DAILY STAR
September 5, 1922

Oberprechtal-in-the-Black-Forest.—We came slipping and sliding down the steep, rocky trail through the shadowed light of the pine trees and out into the glaring clearing where a sawmill and a white plaster gasthaus baked in the sun.

A German police dog barked at us, a man stuck his head out of the door of the gasthaus and looked at us. We were not sure this was the place we had been sent to, so we walked a little way down the road that ran through the clearing to see if there was another inn in sight. There was nothing but the valley, the white road, the river and the steep wooded hills. We had been walking since early in the morning and we were hungry.

Inside the inn Bill Bird and I found the proprietor and his wife sitting at a table eating soup.

"Please can we get two double rooms?" Bill asked.

The proprietor's wife started to answer and the proprietor glared at her while onion soup dribbled through his mustache.

"You can't get rooms here today or tomorrow or any other time, Auslanders," he snarled.

"Herr Trinckler in Triberg recommended us to come here for the fishing," Bill said, trying to mollify him.

"Trinckler?" His lower lip reached up and swept a ration of onion soup out of his mustache. "Trinckler, eh? Trinckler is not the man who runs this place." He went back to the soup.

Bill and I each had a wife out in the clearing. Said wives had begun to be hungry about four miles back on the trail over the mountain. I, myself, was so hungry that my stomach was beginning to rumble and turn over on itself. Bill is built on the lean and graceful lines of an early Italian primitive. Any food he eats shows up on him at once like an ostrich swallowing a baseball. He looked leaner than ever. So we were very polite.

"We are very hungry," Bill said, and I can state he looked it. "How far is the next gasthaus?"

The proprietor pounded on the table. "You'll have to find that out for yourselves."

We found it at the end of four miles of hot, white road and it wasn't much to look at. Like most Schwarzwald inns it was named Gasthaus zum Roessle or Inn of the Pony. The pony is the favorite symbol of the Black Forest innkeeper but there are plenty of Adlers (Eagles) and Sonnes (Suns).

All these inns are white-plastered and clean-looking outside and uniformly neat and dirty inside. The sheets are short, the featherbeds are lumpy and the mattresses are bright red, the beer is good, the wine is bad, dinner is at noon, you have to select your piece of black bread carefully to make sure you are missing a sour one, the proprietor never understands what you say, his wife twists her apron strings and shakes her head, there are workmen with their suspenders over their undershirts eating hunks of black bread they carve off a loaf with a pocket knife and wash down with sour wine, the beams of the ceiling are dark and smoky, chickens scratch in the front yard and the manure pile smokes below the bedroom windows.

The particular pony inn we stopped at had all these attributes and a few more. It had a good meal of fried veal, potatoes, lettuce salad and apple pie, served by the proprietor who looked as stolid as an ox and sometimes stopped with a plate of soup in his hand to stare vacantly out of the window. His wife had a face like a camel. That particular lift of the head and look of utter stupidity that belongs only to the bactrian and the South German peasant woman.

It was a hot day outside but the inn was cool and dim and we ate a big dinner with our rucksacks piled in a corner. A table of Germans in the corner kept glancing over at us. When we were on the second bottle of beer and the last of the washbowl full of salad, a tall, dark-haired woman came over to our table and asked if we were not speaking English.

That was hard to answer and it developed that she was an American singer studying opera in Berlin. She looked about forty-five, but like all good singers she had at last discovered that all her life she had been on the wrong track, had been the victim of bad teachers and now she was at last on the right track. Elsa Sembry was teaching her and she was really teaching her. It was Sembry's great secret. Something about the glottis or epiglottis. I could not make out quite which. But it makes all the difference in the world. You depress one and elevate the other and that is all there is to it.

Mrs. Hemingway and Mrs. Bird went upstairs into one of the little whitewashed rooms to go to sleep on the squeaky beds after their fifteen-mile walk, Mrs. Hemingway's and Mrs. Bird's walk, not the bed's walk; and Bill and I went on down the road to find the town of Oberprechtal and try to get fishing licenses. We were sitting in front of the Gasthaus zur Sonne engaged in an intense conversation with the proprietor, which was proceeding very well as long as I kept my German out of it, when the singer appeared. She was carrying a notebook under her arm. She was in a confiding mood.

Her voice, it seemed—you understand she was telling us all this in the absolutely impersonal manner with which all singers discuss their voices—was a coloratura soprano that had been favorably compared with Melba's and Patti's.

"Gatti-Casazza said I needed just a little more seasoning," she explained. "That's why I'm here. But you ought to hear me trill"—she trilled softly and through her nose—"I never thought much of Galli-Curci. She's not really a singer, you know. Listen to this." She trilled again, a little louder and a little more through her nose. I was impressed. I had never heard anyone trill so softly through their nose or so loudly and clearly through their nose. It was an experience.

She then told us that Mary Garden could not sing, that Yvonne Gall was a bum, that Tetrazzini was a washout, that Mabel Garrison was a flat tire. After demolishing these imposters she again spoke in a cool impersonal manner of her own indistinguishability from Patti and Melba. We then went back up the road to our inn.

At dinner that night we ran into our second example of German nastiness—and there have only been two examples encountered in two weeks in the Black Forest. The trip isn't over yet but those are plenty.

Our table was set for five, the singer had joined us, and when we came into the dining room of the inn to sit down we found there were two blond-haired Germans sitting at the end of the table placed very close to ours. To avoid disturbing them, my wife walked all the way around the table. They then changed their seats and Mrs. Bird had to walk all the way around the other side of the table. While we were eating, they kept up a fire of comment in German on us Auslanders. Then they got up to go. They started to come past our end of the table and I stood up and moved my chair forward to let them by. The space was too narrow. There was a perfectly clear way for them to get out around the other end of the table. Instead, they grabbed my chair and pushed it. I stood up and let them through, and have regretted it ever since.

Early in married life I discovered that the secret of marital happiness did not lie in engaging in brawls in a public house.

"We are Germans," announced one of the two sneeringly.

"Du bist ein schweinhund," which was undoubtedly ungrammatical but seemed understandable. Bill grabbed a bottle by the neck. It looked like the beginning of an international incident.

They stood in the door a minute, but the odds evidently looked too even and workingmen at the next table seemed to be siding with us.

"Schieber!" one of them said, looking up at the two sport-clothed, round heads in the door. "Schieber" means profiteer.

The door closed. They went out.

"If only I could speak German," I lamented. It is bad to possess a fairly extensive vocabulary and to have a feeling to be dumb when someone is cursing you out.

"Do you know what you ought to have said to them?" said the singer in an instructive manner. "You ought to have asked them, 'Who won the war?' Or have said, 'Yes, it is easy to see that you are Germans.' I wish that I had thought to say the things I thought of."

That continued for some time. Then she began to trill. She trilled a great many operas while we sat in the smoky inn. However, that night we all went out walking up the road between the black pine hills with a thin fingernail paring of a moon in the sky, and the singer stepped in a puddle. The next morning the singer had a hoarse voice and she couldn't sing very well. But she did the best she could at demonstrating the use of glottis to Mrs. Bird and the rest of us all went fishing.

A Paris-to-Strasbourg Flight

☆ THE TORONTO DAILY STAR
September 9, 1922

Strasbourg, France.—We were sitting in the cheapest of all the cheap restaurants that cheapen that very cheap and noisy street, the Rue des Petits Champs in Paris.

We were Mrs. [Hadley] Hemingway, William E. Nash, Mr. Nash's little brother, and myself. Mr. Nash announced, somewhere between the lobster and the fried sole, that he was going to Munich the next day and was planning to fly from Paris to Strasbourg. Mrs. Hemingway pondered this until the appearance of the rognons sautés aux champignons, when she asked, "Why don't we ever fly anywhere? Why is everybody else always flying and we always staying home?"

This being one of those questions that cannot be answered by words, I went with Mr. Nash to the office of the Franco-Rumanian Aero Company and bought two tickets, half price for journalists, for 120 francs, good for one flight from Paris to Strasbourg. The trip is ten hours and a half by best express train, and takes two hours and a half by plane.

My natural gloom at the prospect of flying, having flown once, was deepened when I learned that we flew over the Vosges Mountains and would have to be at the office of the company, just off the Avenue de l'Opéra, at five o'clock in the morning. The name Rumanian in the title of the firm was not encouraging, but the clerk behind the counter assured me there were no Rumanian pilots.

At five o'clock the next morning we were at the office. We had to get up at four, pack and dress and wake up the proprietor of the only taxi in the neighborhood by pounding on his door in the dark, to make it. The proprietor augments his income by doubling at nights as an accordion player in a bal musette and it took a stiff pounding to wake him.

While he changed a tire we waited in the street and joked with the boy who runs the charcuterie at the corner and who had gotten up to meet the milkman. The grocery boy made us a couple of sandwiches, told us he had been a pilot during the war, and asked me about the first race at Enghien. The taxi driver asked us into his house to have a drink of coffee, being careful to inquire if we preferred white wine, and with the coffee warming us and munching the pâté sandwiches, we drove in state down the empty, gray, early-morning streets of Paris.

The Nashes were waiting at the office for us, having lugged two heavy suitcases a couple of miles on foot because they did not know any taxi drivers personally. The four of us rode out to Le Bourget, the ugliest ride in Paris, in a big limousine and had some more coffee in a shed there outside the flying field. A Frenchman in an oily jumper took our tickets, tore them in two and told us that we were going in two different planes. Out of the window of the shed we could see them standing, small, silver-painted, taut and shining in the early-morning sun in front of the airdrome. We were the only passengers.

Our suitcase was stowed aboard under a seat beside the pilot's place. We climbed up a couple of steps into a stuffy little cabin and the mechanic handed us some cotton for our ears and locked the door. The pilot climbed into his seat back of the enclosed cockpit where we sat, a mechanic pulled down on the propeller and the engine began to roar. I looked around at the pilot. He was a short little man, his cap backwards on his head, wearing an oil-stained sheepskin coat and big gloves. Then the plane began to move along the ground, bumping like a motorcycle, and then slowly rose into the air.

We headed almost straight east of Paris, rising in the air as though we were sitting inside a boat that was being lifted by some giant, and the ground began to flatten out beneath us. It looked out into brown squares, yellow squares, green squares and big flat blotches of green where there was a forest. I began to understand cubist painting.

Sometimes we came down quite low and could see bicyclists on the road looking like pennies rolling along a narrow white strip. At other times we would lift up and the whole landscape would contract. Always we were bounded by a smoky purple horizon that made all the earth look flat and uninteresting. And always there was the strong, plugged-out, roaring, the portholes to look out of, and back of us the open cockpit with the bridge of the pilot's broad nose and his sheepskin coat visible with his dirty glove moving the joystick from side to side or up and down.

We went over great forests, that looked as soft as velvet, passed over Bar le Duc and Nancy, gray red-roofed towns, over St. Mihiel and the front and in an open field I could see the old trenches zigzagging through a field pocked with shell holes. I shouted to Mrs. Hemingway to look out but she didn't seem to hear me. Her chin was sunk forward into the collar of her new fur coat that she had wanted to christen with a plane trip. She was sound asleep. Five o'clock had been too much.

Beyond the old 1918 front we ran into a storm that made the pilot fly close down to the ground and we followed a canal that we could see below us through the rain. Then after a long stretch of flat, dull-looking country we crossed the foothills of the Vosges that seemed to swell up to meet us and moved over the forest-covered mountains that looked as though they rose up and fell away under the plane in the misty rain.

The plane headed high out of the storm into the bright sunlight and we saw the flat, tree-lined, muddy ribbon of the Rhine off on our right. We climbed higher, made a long, left turn and a fine long swoop down that brought our hearts up into our mouths like falling in an elevator and then just as we were above the ground zoomed up again, then settled in another swoop and our wheels touched, bumped, and then we were roaring along the smooth flying field up to the hangar like any motorcycle.

There was a limousine to meet us to take us in to Strasbourg and we went into the passenger shed to wait for the other plane. The man at the bar asked us if we were going to Warsaw. It was all very casual and very pleasant. An annoying smell of castor oil from the engine had been the only drawback. Because the plane was small and fast and because we were flying in the early morning, there had been no airsickness.

"When did you have your last accident?" I asked the man back of the refreshment bar.

"The middle of last July," he said. "Three killed."

But that very morning in the south of France a slow-moving pilgrim train had slipped back from the top of a steep grade and telescoped itself on another train climbing the grade, making matchwood of two coaches and killing over thirty people. There had been a big falling off in business on the Paris–Strasbourg line after the July accident. But the same number of people seem to ride on railway trains.

German Inflation

☆ THE TORONTO DAILY STAR
September 19, 1922

Kehl, Germany.—The boy in a Strasbourg motor agency where we went to make some inquiries about crossing the frontier said, "Oh yes. It is easy to get over into Germany. All you have to do is go across the bridge."

"Don't you need any visa?" I said.

"No. Just a permit stamp to go from the French." He took his passport out of his pocket and showed the back covered with rubber stamps. "See? I live there now because it is so much cheaper. It's the way to make money."

It is all right.

It is a three-mile streetcar ride from the center of Strasbourg out to the Rhine and when you get to the end of the line the car stops and everyone piles out to herd into a long picket-fenced pen that leads to the bridge. A French soldier with a fixed bayonet loafs back and forth across the road and watches the girls in the passport pen from under his steel-blue helmet. There is an ugly brick customhouse at the left of the bridge and a wooden shed at the right where the French official sits behind a counter and stamps passports.

The Rhine is swift, yellow and muddy, runs between low, green banks, and swirls and sucks at the concrete abutments of the long, iron bridge. At the other end of the bridge you see the ugly little town of Kehl looking like some dreary section of Dundas [Toronto].

If you are a French citizen with a French passport, the man back of the counter simply stamps your passport "sortie Pont de Kehl" and you go across the bridge into occupied Germany. If you are a citizen of some other of the Allied countries, the official looks at you suspiciously, asks you where you are from, what you are going to Kehl for, how long you are going to stay, and then stamps your passport with the same sortie. If you should happen to be a citizen of Kehl who has been in Strasbourg on business and is returning to dinner—and as Kehl's interests are bound up in Strasbourg's as all suburbs are to the city they are attached to, you would be bound to have to go to Strasbourg on business if you had any kind of business at all—you are held in line for fifteen to twenty minutes, your name is looked up in a card index to see if you have ever spoken against the French regime, your pedigree taken, questions put to you and finally you are given the same old sortie. Everyone can cross the bridge but the French make it very nasty for the Germans.

Once across the muddy Rhine you are in Germany, and the end of the bridge is guarded by a couple of the meekest and most discouraged-looking German soldiers you have ever seen. Two French soldiers with fixed bayonets walk up and down and the two German soldiers, unarmed, lean against a wall and look on. The French soldiers are in full equipment and steel helmets, but the Germans wear the old loose tunics and high-peaked, peacetime caps.

I asked a Frenchman the functions and duties of the German guard.

"They stand there," he said.

There were no marks to be had in Strasbourg, the mounting exchange had cleaned the bankers out days ago, so we changed some French money in the railway station at Kehl. For ten francs I received 670 marks. Ten francs amounted to about ninety cents in Canadian money. That ninety cents lasted Mrs. Hemingway and me for a day of heavy spending and at the end of the day we had one hundred and twenty marks left!

Our first purchase was from a fruit stand beside the main street of Kehl where an old woman was selling apples, peaches and plums. We picked out five very good-looking apples and gave the old woman a fifty-mark note. She gave us back thirty-eight marks in change. A very nice-looking, white-bearded old gentleman saw us buy the apples and raised his hat.

"Pardon me, sir," he said, rather timidly, in German, "how much were the apples?"

I counted the change and told him twelve marks.

He smiled and shook his head. "I can't pay it. It is too much."

He went up the street walking very much as white-bearded old gentlemen of the old regime walk in all countries, but he had looked very longingly at the apples. I wish I had offered him some. Twelve marks, on that day, amounted to a little under two cents. The old man, whose life savings were probably, as most of the non-profiteer classes are, invested in German pre-war and war bonds, could not afford a twelve-mark expenditure. He is the type of people whose income does not increase with the falling purchasing value of the mark and the krone.

With marks at 800 to the dollar, or 8 to a cent, we priced articles in the windows of the different Kehl shops. Peas were 18 marks a pound, beans 16 marks a pound, a pound of Kaiser coffee—there are still many "Kaiser" brands in the German republic—could be had for 34 marks. Gersten coffee, which is not coffee at all but roasted grain, sold for 14 marks a pound. Fly paper was 150 marks a package. A scythe blade cost 150 marks, too, or 18¾ cents! Beer was 10 marks a stein, or 1¼ cents.

Kehl's best hotel, which is a very well-turned-out place, served a five-course table d'hôte meal for 120 marks, which amounts to 15 cents in our money. The same meal could not be duplicated in Strasbourg, three miles away, for a dollar.

Because of the customs regulations, which are very strict on persons returning to Germany, the French cannot come over to Kehl and buy up all the cheap goods they would like to. But they can come over and eat. It is a sight every afternoon to see the mob that storms the German pastry shops and tea places. The Germans make very good pastries, wonderful pastries, in fact, that, at the present tumbling mark rate, the French of Strasbourg can buy for a less amount than the smallest French coin, the one-sou piece. This miracle of exchange makes a swinish spectacle where the youth of the town of Strasbourg crowd into the German pastry shop to eat itself sick and gorged on fluffy, cream-filled slices of German cake at five marks the slice. The contents of a pastry shop are swept clean in half an hour.

In a pastry shop we visited, a man in an apron, wearing blue glasses, appeared to be the proprietor. He was assisted by a typical "boche"-looking German with close-cropped head. The place was jammed with French people of all ages and descriptions, all gorging cakes, while a young girl in a pink dress, silk stockings, a pretty, weak face and pearl earrings in her ears took as many of their orders for fruit and vanilla ices as she could fill.

She didn't seem to care very much whether she filled the orders or not. There were soldiers in town and she kept going over to look out the window.

The proprietor and his helper were surly and didn't seem particularly happy when all the cakes were sold. The mark was falling faster than they could bake.

Meanwhile out in the street a funny little train jolted by, carrying the workmen with their dinner pails home to the outskirts of the town, profiteers' motorcars tore by raising a cloud of dust that settled over the trees and the fronts of all the buildings, and inside the pastry shop young French hoodlums swallowed their last cake and French mothers wiped the sticky mouths of their children. It gave you a new aspect on exchange.

As the last of the afternoon tea-ers and pastry eaters went Strasbourg-ward across the bridge, the first of the exchange pirates coming over to raid Kehl for cheap dinners began to arrive. The two streams passed each other on the bridge and the two disconsolate-looking German soldiers looked on. As the boy in the motor agency said, "It's the way to make money."

British Can Save Constantinople

☆ THE TORONTO DAILY STAR
September 30, 1922

Constantinople.—Constantinople is noisy, hot, hilly, dirty and beautiful. It is packed with uniforms and rumors.

British troops have now arrived in sufficient numbers to prevent any Kemalist invasion.

Foreigners are nervous, however, remembering the fate of Smyrna, and have booked outgoing trains for weeks ahead.

Everything awaits the answer of the Angora National Assembly to the Allied peace terms. The assembly is now debating the Paris proposals, and their decision is expected next Wednesday.

Hubby Dines First, Wifie Gets Crumbs!

☆ THE TORONTO DAILY STAR
September 30, 1922

Cologne.—Traveling in Germany now is as exactly as much fun as strap-hanging in an Avenue Road car during the crest of the rush hour.

The railways lose money with every train they run, and as a result the minimum of cars hold the maximum of passengers jammed in the corridors like nails in a keg. Yesterday in Frankfurt at six o'clock in the morning there was a crowd of people big enough to fill any ordinary train strung out along the track waiting for the Amsterdam express which was switching in the yards. When the express pulled in, the passengers debarked, and the crowd was allowed to board the train, the corridors were still packed and every seat taken. But they all jammed in somehow or other.

No matter what your views on the reparations problem may be, nor how much you may see the necessity for allowing Germany to recover into a prosperous nation in order to secure the stability of Europe, you cannot admire the way German men treat their wives. In order not to indict a whole people for the acts of a few, that sentence is amended to read: "the German men I have seen in the last four weeks in various parts of Germany."

Here is an example. The kellner comes through the train announcing the third service in the dining car. A German gentleman in the compartment rises, hands the illustrated papers he has been reading to his wife and disappears toward the dining car. He returns an hour and a half later bearing a very beery breath and parts of rolls stuffed with bits of cheese. These he hands to his wife, who munches them avidly. German gentleman resumes the illustrated papers. The family has dined.

There was the other German gentleman who reached for his rucksack. The rucksack fell from the luggage rack striking his wife on the head. Tears came into the wife's eyes. The German gentleman looked annoyed. "You're not hurt," he said to the wife. Probably he was afraid that if he didn't check that sort of thing right at the start the wife might get to feeling there was something the matter with her and be unable to carry the rucksack.

Then, of course, there was the other German gentleman who was determined to obtain a seat in a fully occupied first-class compartment. There are three places on each side of a first-class compartment. This distinguishes it from the second-class, which has four, the third-class, with six, and the fourth-class which seats eight on a side.

In this particular case all the places were occupied, but an old lady who sat next to the window was standing up and looking out. We were stalled. Part of the train had run off the track. The German gentleman entered, followed by his wife, and sat down in the old lady's place. The old lady next sat down and being very nearsighted and not knowing that someone had appropriated her place, sat down on the German gentleman's lap.

His face never moved. He just sat there. The old lady jumped up and looked at him in terror. The German gentleman's wife blushed and went out of the compartment. He just sat there, his face as stolid as a ham, and the old lady looked out of the window, her lips trembling.

I thought of the Niagara of words a Frenchwoman would have turned loose, the way she would have torn into the big sulky-looking beast. But there was no outbreak. The old lady was simply frightened. She had evidently been through this sort of thing before.

In the present state of things in Germany foreigners do not start rows. They spend most of their time swallowing insults in order to avoid being mobbed. My own theory had been that if the Germans had no scruples about killing [Walther] Rathenau they would have no scruples about killing me—and I have trod very softly. But things in the compartment had reached the point where I was wondering what sort of weapon a tennis racket in its frame would really make and rehearsing the eleven variations of the one best way to cripple a man.

Of course the obvious way to bring on the trouble was to get up and give the old lady my seat. That is always regarded as a *casus belli* by every seated male in a German streetcar. Just then the wife opened the compartment door and said that she had found him a seat further up the train. The German gentleman remained seated a few minutes longer, just to show that he could if he wished, and then went out. The old lady sat down very thankfully.

German home life is supposed to be a very fine and perfect thing. It has such beautiful features as the mother and father and little children all gathering to drink beer together, and the little children are allowed such touching and rare intimacies as fetching father's slippers, lighting father's pipe, etc. But the part of it that appears in public conveyances has somehow lost its charm.

German Riots

☆ THE TORONTO STAR WEEKLY
September 30, 1922

Cologne.—British officers back from Silesia tell how British troops had to escort the French troops out of the country after the plebiscite in order to prevent attacks that would have brought on bloody fighting.

The British guard over the departing French troops prevented an outbreak, but the Germans' hatred of the French was so great that they exacted reprisals on their own people who had been overfriendly with the occupying army. German women who had been seen in public with French officers were seized, their heads were shaved and they were hooted around the streets. Other German girls known to have had closer relationship with French officers had their clothes torn off, their heads shaved, and were driven out of their towns.

The enormous equestrian statue of William Hohenzollern, that stands at the Cologne side of the beautiful Hohenzollern bridge across the Rhine, bears all the marks of another recent occasion when the German showed what he is still capable of being. Both spurs on William's giant iron boots were broken off and the blade of his sword is gone. These were smashed off in an attempt by some of the Cologne citizenry to overthrow the big statue in a brawl that started out as a revolution and ended as a small-sized riot.

During the attack on the statue, a policeman appeared and tried to quiet the mob. The mob threw the policeman into the river. In the cold, swift swirl of the Rhine against the base of the bridge, the policeman hung on to one of the abutments and shouted up that he knew who was in the mob and would see that they were all punished. So the mob swarmed down and tried to push the policeman loose into the current. It meant drowning for the policeman to let go—and he hung on. Then the mob chopped his fingers loose from the stone with the hatchet with which they had been attacking the statue.

It was a German policeman and a German mob. And all over Germany conflict goes on between German police and German mobs. In the north there are riots against the high cost of living, that are quelled by the police with machine guns. In the south there are riotous demonstrations in favor of Hindenburg, Ludendorff and a return to the monarchy in Munich at which the police quell the dissenting Republicans with clubs.

Meantime, in order that the profiteers on both sides shall not allow any of the money being spent to get out of their hands, Herr Stinnes and a group of French contractors have concluded an agreement that all material supplied by Germany to France for reconstruction shall come through Herr Hugo Stinnes.

Stinnes is to receive six percent by agreement on everything that passes through his hands. It is the final refinement of the whole profiteering business, whereby the profiteers of both countries get together and form a profiteers' trust, so that nothing can get away from them at either end. And the great reconstructed-devastated regions scandal, which is beginning to be talked about under their breath by many people, as a coming blowup that will make the Panama Canal scandal and the Marconi scandal pale into nothing, gets nearer and nearer.

British Planes

☆ THE TORONTO DAILY STAR
September 30, 1922

Constantinople.—The arrival of several thousand additional British troops has encouraged the Greeks and the Armenians here to discard their Turkish fezzes and resume conventional western headgear. At the beginning of the present crisis every Greek and Armenian provided himself with a fez, which he wore continuously until he thought the danger of Turkish occupation was past. British airplanes flew over the capital today, causing a flurry of excitement in Stamboul. The aerial maneuvers gave the population another evidence of Great Britain's preparedness to meet eventualities.

The continued arrival of British war units has lessened the danger of an uprising within the city and checked the panicky flight of Christians to neighboring countries.

British Order Kemal to Quit Chanak

☆ THE TORONTO DAILY STAR
September 30, 1922

Constantinople.—With British and Turks on the verge of war in the neutral zone, General Harington, British commander-in-chief, dispatched a new demand to Mustapha Kemal today that he evacuate the Chanak area.

It was understood that no time limit was set.

The dispatch of the fresh ultimatum followed the receipt of an ultimatum from Kemal, in which he demanded that the British evacuate the Asiatic side of the straits.

Kemal's note was considered decidedly hostile.

One high British official stated that the note had closed the door to peace.

Harington Won't Demand Evacuation

☆ THE TORONTO DAILY STAR
October 2, 1922

Constantinople.—British general headquarters here today issued a denial of a report originating in England that General Harington would demand the evacuation of the shores of the Dardanelles by Turkish troops within twenty-four hours. That question, it was stated, would be discussed at Mudania.

The Allied generals will leave for Mudania tonight. They are General Harington for Great Britain, General Sharpi for France and General Membelli for Italy.

Turk Red Crescent Propaganda Agency

☆ THE TORONTO DAILY STAR
October 4, 1922

Constantinople.—The Mudania Conference will determine the question of peace or war. General Harington has shown a steadily increasing desire for peace, but the Turk concentration of troops between the straits and Constantinople gives them a strong position to talk from. However, it is believed that Harington's good sense and the Franco-Turk accord will bring about an amicable settlement.

Thrace, an unproductive barren country, is the key to the present situation. To the reorganized Greek government, Thrace is another Marne, where a stand must be made or the end of greater Greece admitted.

Turkish Red Crescent (equivalent to the Red Cross) reports on Greek atrocities in Thrace must be discounted as the leader of the Red Crescent is Kemal's head in Constantinople and Red Crescent official reports are used as propaganda to force immediate occupation of Thrace by the Turks.

The Turks want Adrianople, their ancient capital, for sentimental reasons, and Thrace to give them a strong foothold in Europe. Eliminating the Greeks from Thrace will unite Bulgaria and Turkey, making a dangerous wedge of pro-Soviet countries thrust into the center of the Balkans.

Hamid Bey

☆ THE TORONTO DAILY STAR
October 9, 1922

Constantinople.—Bismarck said all men in the Balkans who tuck their shirts into their trousers are crooks. The shirts of the peasants, of course, hang outside. At any rate, when I found Hamid Bey—next to Kemal, perhaps the most powerful man in the Angora government—in his Stamboul office where he directs the Kemalist government in Europe, while drawing a large salary as administrator of the Imperial Ottoman Bank, a French-capitalized concern—his shirt was tucked in, for he was dressed in a gray business suit.

Hamid Bey's office is at the top of a steep hill beyond an old seraglio and houses the Red Crescent—equivalent to our Red Cross—of which Hamid Bey is one of the leaders and where attendants in Red Crescent khaki carry out the orders of the Angora government.

"Canada is anxious about the possibility of a massacre of Christians when Kemal enters Constantinople," I said.

Hamid Bey, big and bulky, with gray mustaches, wing-collared and with a porcupine haircut, looked over his glasses and spoke French.

"What have the Christians to fear?" he asked. "They are armed and the Turks have been disarmed. There will be no massacre. It is the Greek Christians who are massacring the Turks now in Thrace. That's why we must occupy Thrace to protect our people."

That is the only guarantee of protection Constantinople Christians have, except the Allied police force, while toughs from the Crimea to Cairo are gathered in Constantinople hoping that the patriotic orgy of Kemal's triumphant entry will bring a chance to start a fire in the tinder-dry, wooden tenements and begin killing and looting. The Allied police force is compact and efficient, but Constantinople is a great sprawling city of a million and a half, crowded with a desperate element.

The man who raises a thirst somewhere east of Suez is going to be unable to slake it in Constantinople once Kemal enters the city. A member of the Anatolian government tells me that Constantinople will be as dry as Asiatic Turkey, where alcohol is not allowed to be imported, manufactured or sold. Kemal has also forbidden cardplaying and backgammon and the cafés of Brusa are dark at eight o'clock.

This devotion to the laws of the prophet does not prevent Kemal himself and his staff from liking their liquor, as the American, who went to Smyrna to protect American tobacco, found when his eight bottles of cognac made him the most popular man in Asia Minor at Kemalist headquarters.

Kemal's edict will halt the great importation of American raw alcohol shipped to Constantinople in drums and marked "medicinal." This is made into an absinthe-like drink and is sipped by the Turks as they sit in the coffee shops, puffing their bubble-bubble pipes.

Turks Near Constantinople

☆ THE TORONTO DAILY STAR
October 9, 1922

Constantinople.—Turkish forces today withdrew from Ismed in the neutral zone, it was announced here.

The above dispatch should probably read that the Turks have withdrawn from the Ismed neutral zone. In the following dispatch it is said that General Harington had warned Ismet Pasha that a withdrawal must be made.

Constantinople.—Kemalist forces were within a day's march of Constantinople, on the Asiatic side of the Bosporus, as the Allied general met Ismet Pasha at Mudania in a renewed effort to untangle the Near Eastern problem today.

Turkish cavalry have reached Shileh and Yarmise, both places far within the neutral zone near the Bosporus at the right of the Sea of Marmora. Yarmise is within a day's march of Constantinople. The cavalry is also nearing Karayakobi, which is in the same area.

It was reported during the night that Turkish irregulars had appeared yesterday afternoon a short distance from Beikos, in the hills on the Asiatic side of the Bosporus. Beikos is a suburb of Constantinople. The British are entrenching around Beikos.

Turkish irregulars and small bands of guerrillas and bandits, which frequently form the advance guard of a Turkish army, have appeared in small villages east of Constantinople. These villages include Tashkeupsu, Tavshanjik, Omarli, Afga and Armudli, all within the suburban limits of Constantinople on the Asiatic side.

The British yesterday made final preparations for defense, blowing up bridges and crossroads.

A British destroyer anchored Sunday at Shileh on the Black Sea coast. The commander went ashore, met the Nationalist officer there and requested him to withdraw his forces. The Turk replied that he has orders to remain, whereupon the British commander declared he also would remain, and kept to his anchorage close in shore.

It is reported that an entire Turkish division has entered the neutral zone and General Harington is said to have warned Ismet Pasha that unless the Kemalists withdraw he may be obliged to make a military demonstration on the Turkish flanks. The Kemalist representative is said to have promised that the advance shall cease, and that the incident will not be repeated.

As a measure of protection for Constantinople, General Harington ordered suspension of ferry service across the Bosporus and the Sea of Marmora. There are said to be 12,500 Christians now in the Ismid zone outside the British lines, while many thousands more are within the lines, having been removed to a camp at Moda, directly across from Constantinople.

The Turk concentration in the neutral zone in the vicinity of Chanak is also continuing. In this area, infantry have replaced cavalry, which is taken to mean that the Turks intend to dig in to hold their positions.

Balkans: A Picture of Peace, Not War

☆ THE TORONTO DAILY STAR
October 16, 1922

Sofia, Bulgaria.—There was only twenty minutes to catch the Simplon-Orient Express leaving the Gare de Lyon, at the other end of Paris, for Constantinople—and only one taxi to be had.

One taxi was plenty. But this taxi had a drawback. The driver was drunk.

As we lurched, swung and tore through the jammed, congested seven o'clock Paris traffic, I hung on to the side of the taxi, fixed my gaze on the back of the driver's red neck and prayed that we wouldn't hit anything.

Coming into the big square in front of the gare, the driver, with alcoholic accuracy, picked a hole in the stream of juggernauting green buses and honking taxis and we skidded up to the curb.

"Voilà!" the driver shouted, and craving more dramatic gestures, picked my big suitcase up from the seat beside him and flung it down on to the sidewalk.

I knew what the fictioneers mean by "dumb with horror."

For in the suitcase was my typewriter, and a journalist cares only a little more for his typewriter than a mother does for her child, a Ford owner for his car, or a ball player for his right arm.

"Drunkard! My machine d'écrire is in there," I said with all the futility of rage.

The driver's heroic mood had passed, leaving him mellow. He tried to shake me by the hand.

"Monsieur can call me a thousand camels or pigs. I deserve it. But I was exalted!"

There was nothing to do but catch the train. I followed a porter into the long, dirty station with the driver still shouting, "I was not drunk. I was exalted!"

The results were the same. The typewriter carriage is bent; stuck tight, and will have to be freed in Constantinople.

So this is being scrawled in pencil while the long, brown Orient Express crawls its way across Europe, over imaginary borders, through mountains and across the level harvest fields toward Constantinople and Scutari, where a short, bronzed-faced, blond Turk with a seasoned army of 300,000 men and a united nation at his back dictates terms to the Allies who two years ago hunted him as a bandit.

Sharing my compartment is a young Serbian, who has been to school in Boston. His conversation runs about like this:

"Say. Wattaya think I paid for this coat in Paris? Hundertnfiftey francs. Pretty good? Huh? Wanta see picture my girl? Some girl? Huh? I got a better-looking girl but her picture's in my trunk. Say look at that Italian officer. Don't he look just like a woman? I bet he wears corsets. Don't tell me a guy dresses like that can fight. Say ain't he a scream?"

I note that the Italian officer, who wears a monocle, has three wound stripes and, in addition to decorations of his own country, a British M.C. [Military Cross].

"Say they ought to take birds like that out and shoot them," says the Serb.

I reflect that is very nearly what they have done.

We pass through the flat, rich, green and brown plain of Lombardy. It is sentineled by Lombardy poplars and cut up by thick mulberry hedges. Off beyond the rice fields and dry riverbeds with pebbles as big and white as hen's eggs, the clear, white shaft of a companile catches the sun. Oxen move along the dusty road and a lizard scuttles across the top of a wall as the train passes.

All of Europe is green and golden and ripe. The part of Serbia we are passing through looks like the Niagara peninsula. There is a blue, late-September haze over the fields and since we crossed the Croatian frontier early this morning we have been moving through country that looks like Eastern Ontario. It is hard to believe that this rich, pleasant farming country is the bleak-sounding Balkans. It is, though, and as you ride through it you can see how the love of the land can make men fight wars. It is a matter of land, of fields of corn and yellowing tobacco, of flocks of sheep and herds of cattle, of heaps of yellow pumpkins in the shocked corn, of beech groves and peat smoke from chimneys, a matter of mine and thine that is the cause of all just wars—and there can never be peace in the Balkans as long as one people holds the lands of another people—no matter what the political excuse may be.

Christians Leave Thrace to Turks

☆ THE TORONTO DAILY STAR
October 16, 1922

Constantinople.—Thousands of Christians, many hungry and with all their earthly belongings packed on their backs, trudged out of Thrace today as the cross made way for the crescent. Aged men and women, many carrying children, walked toward the Balkan peninsula, leaving forever the homes that they have occupied for years.

Some loaded their household goods in ox carts. Others left everything behind and fled in order to be out of Thrace in fifteen days, the time limit set by the Allied generals and Turkish representatives at the Mudania Conference.

Most of the trains in Thrace have been commandeered by the Greek government to carry soldiers, who will be loaded on transports when they reach the ports. The civilian population had to depend on the rickety carts or walk.

Rodosto, on the Balkan peninsula, was choked with refugees. The suffering and foodless Greeks and Armenians awaited some means to carry them into Greece.

Little relief, it is believed, will greet the refugees when they arrive in Greece. The food supplies there are very inadequate because of the thousands of refugees that are already dependent on the government and charitable agencies for food.

Four British and three French battalions were entering Thrace today on the heels of the departing Greeks.

Constantinople, Dirty White, Not Glistening and Sinister

☆ THE TORONTO DAILY STAR
October 18, 1922

Constantinople.—Constantinople doesn't look like the movies. It does not look like the pictures, or the paintings, or anything.

First your train comes winding like a snake down the sun-baked, treeless, rolling plain to the sea. It rocks along the shore where kids are bathing and out across the blue water you see a big brown island and faintly beyond it bulks the brown coast of Asia. Then it roars in between high stone walls and when you come out you are passing crazy, ramshackle, wooden tenements.

"Stamboul," the Frenchman who is standing looking out of the window with you, says.

From all I had ever seen in the movies Stamboul ought to have been white and glistening and sinister. Instead the houses look like Heath Robinson drawings, dry as tinder, the color of old weatherbeaten fence rails, and filled with little windows. Scattered through the town rise minarets. They look like dirty, white candles sticking up for no apparent reason.

The train passes the old, reddish Byzantine wall and goes into a culvert again. It comes out and you get flashes of squatting, mushroom-like mosques always with their dirty-white minarets rising from the corners. Everything white in Constantinople is dirty white. When you see the color a white shirt gets in twelve hours you appreciate the color a white minaret gets in four hundred years.

In the station are a jam of porters, hotel runners, and Anglo-Levantine gentlemen in slightly soiled collars, badly soiled white trousers, garlicized breaths and hopeful manners who hope to be hired as interpreters. There is a little something wrong with their passports, just enough to keep them from leaving Constantinople, and they turn their cuffs, clean their white shoes and hope that soon there will be tourists coming to town again. Meantime they will do anything for a price, and their price is very low.

I called a porter, gave him my bags, and told him, "Hotel de Londres," a hotel the Frenchman had recommended. We started for the cab and the white-trousered one came up. He was contorted with a smile.

"Ah. You are going to the Hôtel de Londres. I am from there. I will ride up with you and take care of your baggage."

"Get in," I said.

We drove in a mass of traffic onto a long bridge. White Pants gave the Turkish gendarme a dirty, crumpled note, and we crossed a tangle of shipping on both sides. You can only see patches of the water because of the way the boats were packed.

"What's that? The Golden Horn?" I asked. It looked more like the Chicago River.

"Yes," White Pants answered. "Those boats on the left go to the Bosporus and the Black Sea, and those on the right are excursion boats for the Isle of Princes."

We clattered up a steep street, past shop windows, banks, restaurants, saloons with their signs printed in four languages, scraped by jangling tramcars, were honked at by motorcars filled with British officers, were nearly run down by motors filled with French officers, passed a constant stream of men in business clothes, wearing either fezzes or straw hats, and climbed all the time.

We passed the square building of the American Embassy, looking like a Carnegie library, the square yellow building of the Allied police commission, also looking like a Carnegie library, and the square yellow building of the British Embassy, looking even more like a Carnegie library than the other. We were now in Pera.

Pera is the European quarter. It is higher on the hill than Galata, the business quarter, and is all strung along one narrow, dirty, steep, cobbled, tramcar-filled street. All the public buildings of Pera are uniform in their resemblance to the square, packing-case-shaped Carnegie library, and would make anybody from the States feel at home instantly as they are exact reproductions of the type of post office U.S. small-town congressmen get for their native city in order to assure their perpetual re-election.

The Rumanian and Armenian consulates can be distinguished from the others, however, by the long lines of their citizens, stretched out like the ticket line waiting to get into a big hockey match at the Arena, who are trying to get passports or visas. The Armenian Jews and Rumanians are clearing out of Constantinople. They are selling their property at any sacrifice and getting out. The government issues statements urging them not to be foolish, assuring them that all measures of protection for the inhabitants will be taken, that patrols are being reinforced, that there is no danger. But the Armenians and Jews and the Jewish Rumanians have heard all that before. It is probably all true, they reason, but we aren't going to take chances. Sooner or later the Kemal troops are going to enter Constantinople, or else there is going to be war and the Armenians, Jews and Greeks cannot forget Smyrna. So they go. With a history of a thousand years of massacre behind them, it is hard for the racial fear to be quieted, no matter who makes the promises.

The Greeks are in a different position. They have a guilty national conscience. It is an uncontested fact that the Greek army in its retreat across Anatolia laid waste and burned the Turkish villages, burnt the crops in the fields, the grain on the threshing floors and committed atrocities. These facts are testified to by American relief workers and Christians who were in the country before, during and after the Greek retreat.

I will take up the question of Greek atrocities later when I have the evidence and testimony of both Christians and Turks and will try and give a complete presentation of the matter to the *Star* readers. That is not the point now. The fact is that atrocities are always followed by counter-atrocities in these countries and have been since the siege of Troy. And it is the innocent who suffer. The victim of the revenge is rarely the perpetrator of the original outrage. It is this that is emptying Constantinople of Greeks.

I stood on the dusty, rubbish-strewn hillside of Pera, after I had cleaned up at the hotel, and looked down at the harbor, forested with masts and grimy with smoky funnels and across at the dust-colored hills on the other side where the Turkish town sprawled in square mud-colored houses, ramshackle tenements with the dirty-white fingers of the minarets rising like gray-white, slim lighthouses out of the muddled houses. With my glasses I could see an Italian steamer leaving the port, crowded to the rails with Greek refugees seen curiously clearly through the powerful lenses.

It all looked unreal and impossible. But it was very real to the people who were looking back at the city where they were leaving their homes and businesses, all their associations and their livelihoods, because they were afraid to wait and see what would happen when the brown-faced men in fezzes, their carbines strapped on their backs, riding their shaggy, short, mountain horses should come ashore from the ferry from Scutari just across the narrow harbor.

Waiting for an Orgy

☆ THE TORONTO DAILY STAR
October 19, 1922

Constantinople.—There is a tight-drawn, electric tension in Constantinople such as only people who live in a city that has never been invaded can imagine.

Take the tension that comes when the pitcher steps into the box before the packed stands at the first game of the world series, multiply it by the tension that comes when the barrier snaps up, the gong clangs and they're off at the King's Plate at the Woodbine [Toronto racetrack], add to it the tension in your mind when you walk the floor downstairs as you wait frightened and cold for someone you love, while a doctor and a nurse are doing something in a room above that you cannot help in any way, and you have something comparable to the feeling in Constantinople now.

It is we correspondents who have nothing at stake that get the selfish world series thrill. Even at that, I never lay awake all night in October before a world series because it was too hot to sleep, nor fought mosquitoes and bedbugs in the best New York or Chicago hotels.

It is the collection of cutthroats, robbers, bandits, thugs and Levantine pirates who have gathered here from Batum to Bagdad, and from Singapore to Sicily, that are getting the Woodbine thrill. They are waiting for the looting to begin. And they are ready to begin it on their own account as soon as the triumphal entry of Mustapha Kemal Pasha's troops starts the riotous orgy of celebration that will permit them to fire the wooden tenement quarter which will burn like a gasoline-soaked matchbox.

If the Allied and Turkish police prevent the orgy that has been planned for the celebration of the Kemal entry it will be one of the finest achievements in the world, because the tough element of all the Near East, of the Balkans, and of the Mediterranean are gathered in Constantinople like jackals waiting for the lion to make his kill.

The people who are getting the sickening, cold, crawling fear-thrill are the Armenians, Greeks and Macedonians, who cannot get away or who have elected to stay. Those who stay are arming themselves and talking desperately.

The landlord of my hotel is a Greek. He has bought the place with his life's savings. Everything he has in the world is invested in it. I am now the only guest.

"I tell you, sir," he said last night. "I'm going to fight. We are armed and there are plenty of Christians armed too. I am not going to leave all my life's work here just because the French force the Allies to give Constantinople to that bandit Kemal. Why do they do it? Greece fought for the Allies in the war and now they desert us. We cannot understand it."

There are many Greeks talking that way. And all those who are staying are arming. That, of course, increases the danger of trouble still further, because if some Greek in a nervous hysteria takes a potshot at some Turkish celebrators the whole pot will boil over in an instant.

Russian refugees are still another class that are tremendously affected by the coming entry of the Kemalist army. Up till now Constantinople has been the great place of refuge for those of the old regime in Russia who fled from the Soviets.

Many of them have death sentences pending which will be executed if they are handed over to the Soviet government. Kemal is hand in glove with the Soviets and his entry will wipe out the greatest Russian sanctuary.

Fully a fourth of the uniforms you see on the streets are Russian, either the old Imperial army or the troops of Wrangel, Denikin and Yudenitch. Their wearers fled to Constantinople or were evacuated with the remnants of the counterrevolutionary forces, and have not had enough money since to buy any other clothes. Just how Kemal, and his allies of the cheka, will dispose of these men in the high-booted, loosely bloused, worn old Russian uniforms who have been fighting against the Soviets and cannot disguise the fact, is not a pleasant problem.

I would hate to be Kemal with all the dangerous prestige of a great victory behind me and these problems ahead. All the East says that Mustapha Kemal Pasha is a great man. At least he is a successful man, but his entry into Constantinople will be the first indication of whether his fame is to be merely the bubble of military reputation, always burst by the first defeat, or the greatness of a man who can deal with the problems his victory has brought him.

The cards look stacked against him in Constantinople, but if he can accomplish a peaceful entry, keep his troops in hand, and see there is no reign of terror, it will be of greater permanent value to Turkey than many victories in Thrace.

A Silent, Ghastly Procession

☆ THE TORONTO DAILY STAR
October 20, 1922

Adrianople.—In a never-ending, staggering march, the Christian population of Eastern Thrace is jamming the roads toward Macedonia. The main column crossing the Maritza River at Adrianople is twenty miles long. Twenty miles of carts drawn by cows, bullocks and muddy-flanked water buffalo, with exhausted, staggering men, women and children, blankets over their heads, walking blindly along in the rain beside their worldly goods.

This main stream is being swelled from the back country. They don't know where they are going. They left their farms, villages and ripe, brown fields and joined the main stream of refugees when they heard the Turk was coming. Now they can only keep their places in the ghastly procession while mud-splashed Greek cavalry herd them along like cow-punchers driving steers.

It is a silent procession. Nobody even grunts. It is all they can do to keep moving. Their brilliant peasant costumes are soaked and draggled. Chickens dangle by their feet from the carts. Calves nuzzle at the draught cattle wherever a jam halts the stream. An old man marches under a young pig, a scythe and a gun, with a chicken tied to his scythe. A husband spreads a blanket over a woman in labor in one of the carts to keep off the driving rain. She is the only person making a sound. Her little daughter looks at her in horror and begins to cry. And the procession keeps moving.

At Adrianople where the main stream moves through, there is no Near East Relief at all. They are doing very good work at Rodosto on the coast, but can only touch the fringe.

There are 250,000 Christian refugees to be evacuated from Eastern Thrace alone. The Bulgarian frontier is shut against them. There is only Macedonia and Western Thrace to receive the fruit of the Turk's return to Europe. Nearly half a million refugees are in Macedonia now. How they are to be fed nobody knows, but in the next month all the Christian world will hear the cry: "Come over into Macedonia and help us!"

Russia Spoiling the French Game

☆ THE TORONTO DAILY STAR
October 23, 1922

Constantinople.—At Mudania, a hot, dusty, badly battered, second-rate seaport on the Sea of Marmora, the West met the East. In spite of the towering deadliness of the *Iron Duke*, the British flagship, that brought the Allied generals to confer with Ismid Pasha, the West was coming to ask for peace—not to demand it nor to dictate terms.

There were no newspapermen allowed to see the meeting because of the attitude of a certain lieutenant colonel in charge of the press, who still believes that what the army decides as to the fate of the world is none of the world's business. But even if no one was ever allowed to mention the meeting, if no one ever admitted that the West had come to the East to ask for peace, still the meeting would have the same significance, for it marks the beginning of the end of European domination in Asia.

Just now the Turkish Nationalists, who are the same thing as the Kemalists, are under French influence. This came about in a perfectly simple way. About two years ago Mustapha Kemal Pasha was denounced by the Earl of Balfour as a common bandit. He was, speaking in the broadest sense, for sale to the highest bidder. The French bought him. They supplied him with arms, ammunition and money. In return, it is rumored they received certain oil concessions in Asia Minor.

The British wanted control in Asia Minor but Kemal did not look like a good buy to them. So they backed the Greeks. The Greeks looked an excellent bet. But, as several people have remarked in the House of Commons, Mr. Lloyd George backed the wrong horse.

Kemal whipped the Greeks, as everyone knows. But when you realize that he was fighting a conscript army whose soldiers hated the barren country they were fighting to gain, who had been mobilized for nine years, who had no desire as men to conquer Asia Minor, and who were thoroughly fed up and becoming conscious that they were going into battle to die doing a cat's-paw job, it was not the magnificent military achievement that it is made out to be. Especially is that shown when you realize that Kemal's troops were fanatical patriots, anxious to drive the invaders out of their country.

The ratio of effectiveness of well-trained, well-armed, high fanatical patriots fighting in their own country against half-hearted, poorly officered, homesick conscript invaders is somewhere about ten to one. However, when Britain backed the Greeks she did not know that state of efficiency the Kemalists were going to reach.

Now, in the victorious Kemalist troops, French influence is at its height. I think it has reached the crest and will be on the downgrade from now on because of Kemal's affiliations with Soviet Russia. It is that which will sooner or later bring him into difficulties with France, and it is that which, next to the conflict between Islam and Christianity, makes the greatest danger to the peace of the world.

If Russia is the next dominant influence in Turkey, and every sign points to the fact that she will be, there will be a great curving horn of pro-Soviet countries with the Soviet Republic of Georgia and South Russia at the base curving along the Black Sea, crossing the straits and extending up into the heart of the Balkans with Bulgaria at its point, driving a wedge between Yugoslavia and Rumania.

That of course is only about as dangerous to the peace of the Balkans, which has managed to pretty consistently mean the peace of Europe, as going to bed with a percussion-capped stick of dynamite between the mattress and the springs. It may not go off, of course, for some time. Still it is not oversecure.

The next danger is the straits. The straits between the Black Sea and the Aegean are Russia's natural outlet. Constantinople, as you remember, was promised to Russia during the last war. There was once a war, of which no one remembers much except the charge of a certain British cavalry regiment and the work of a certain woman nurse, fought on the same question. There is not much difference, however, between Russia dominating the straits and Russia dominating Kemal who dominates the straits.

Sooner or later, under these circumstances, no matter how many statements Kemal may make saying he recognizes the principle of the freedom of the straits, unless England controls the straits she is going to find them shut against her. Then we can fight Gallipoli over again.

Turks Distrust Kemal Pasha

☆ THE TORONTO DAILY STAR
October 24, 1922

Constantinople.—Mustapha Kemal Pasha a few months ago was regarded as a new Saladin by the Moslem world. He was to lead Islam into battle against Christianity and to spread a holy war through all the East. Now the East is beginning to distrust him. Mohammedans I have talked to say: "Kemal has betrayed us." There is no talk now of the holy war.

This has happened because Kemal, the conquering general, has shown himself to be Kemal the businessman. He is now in something of the position Arthur Griffith and Michael Collins occupied in Ireland just before their death. That is, he is taking the tangible gains offered him, making what appear to the Pan-Islamites to be humiliating compromises, and trying to salt down his winnings—always planning to try for more when these are consolidated.

As yet his de Valera has not appeared. But if he continues to play a waiting game, there will be a de Valera sooner or later. And this possibility of a split in the Turkish forces may be the saving of the western power in the Orient.

One thing that may bring it about is the report that is current that the heads of the Turkish nationalist movement, which it should always be remembered is the Kemalist party, are many of them atheists and French Freemasons rather than good Mohammedans. That is the report you get as gossip when the Mohammedans talk politics and it is bringing about a distrust that is growing up in regard to Kemal in the minds of those people who had regarded him as a conquering Messiah for the Mohammedan peoples.

The Jews claim that Kemal is a Jew. His thin, intense, rigid face does look Jewish. But the Jews also claim Gabriele D'Annunzio and Christopher Columbus and a thousand years or so from now may even be claiming Henry Ford. At any rate that rumor about Kemal is doing him no harm and gaining very little credence; the charge of atheism is much more dangerous, for that is the one crime that any Turk is prepared to believe any other Turk is guilty of but there is no blacker crime in the Mohammedan world.

The Kemalists have a treaty and an alliance with Bolshevist Russia. They also have a treaty and something very like an alliance with France. As I explained in my last article, one of these alliances must go. Whichever alliance Turkey drops clears the air very little, because the one big aim of the Kemalists, the aim for which they are being criticized now in their own circles for not having fulfilled, the aim which does not appear in any published pacts but that everyone in the country understands is the possession of Mesopotamia. [Editor's note: A cable dispatch received yesterday says it is understood the Turks will claim Mesopotamia at the peace conference.] Turkey is bound to have Mesopotamia. If France is her ally when she goes after it or if, having broken with France, she is backed by Russia, the situation is equally dangerous. If there is war in Mesopotamia between Great Britain and Turkey, and I give Mustapha Kemal twenty months to consolidate his present gains before he provokes such a war, it may be the blaze that will start the holy war that the Pan-Islamites are praying for to destroy all western domination in the east. France, if she is Kemal's ally at that time, will probably remain neutral. Russia might not remain neutral.

It is oil that Kemal and company want Mesopotamia for, and it is oil that Great Britain wants to keep Mesopotamia for, so the East that is disappointed in Kemal the Saladin because he shows no inclination to plunge into a fanatical holy war may yet get their war from Kemal the businessman.

Near East Censor Too "Thorough"

☆ THE TORONTO DAILY STAR
October 25, 1922

Constantinople.—A censorship as rigid as it is unintelligent for all cable dispatches touching on any phase of the Near East situation is the reason the public at home has been so inaccurately and unreliably informed on the true state of Near East affairs.

It is very easy for the government to issue an appeal to the dominions to send troops to meet a certain crisis, but it is very hard for the dominions to know what the crisis is about when nothing but official communiqués on the situation are allowed to reach them.

Constantinople is a very simple place for the censor to control. There is only one cable company, and it has only one office where cables can be sent. The censor was naturally posted there. We all expected it, and no one worried over the matter when a notice was glued up that from September 20 a censor would be on duty in the office of the cable company for the convenience of correspondents who would continue to hand their messages in over the counter in the usual manner. It all sounded very simple and sweet.

The first break came when someone discovered that the censor was absent for periods of three and four hours at a time during the day, and that no relief man was taking his place. During his absence cables sent "urgent" at a cost of two and three hundred dollars would accumulate on his desk.

Four hours may not be much in the life of a censor but it is an eternity to a daily newspaper or a news service. Especially is it an eternity if the censor has passed the dispatch of a rival paper or news service immediately before going out to tea. A united protest of correspondents finally brought on a relief censor.

It was the haphazard manner of chopping up dispatches, a method without visible plan or purpose, except to censor everything by a system that everything ought to have something cut out of it, that made the most trouble. We had no way of knowing, for several days, what was being done to our dispatches. They were handed in over the counter and that was the last we saw of them.

One morning a correspondent of a New York paper found a note saying that his cablegram of the afternoon before had been held by the censor. He found that his references to the "level-headedness of Sir Charles Harington" had been deleted as an unjustified discussion of a military figure. On the same day all that was left of a dispatch of mine to the *Star* was a mention of the "good sense of General Harington." I was outlining the strong position the Turks had gained prior to the conference of Mudania by their peaceful penetration of the neutral zones which enabled them to mass over one hundred thousand troops between the straits and Constantinople. With those troops in position it was impossible for the Allies to dictate to them as they would have been able to if they occupied the most advantageous positions. The censor cut it all out.

I fought it out with him and was finally allowed to send a dispatch mentioning that the Turkish concentration of troops between the straits and Constantinople had given them a good position to talk from. The only difference between the blue-penciled dispatch and the one sent was that the first was accurate and exact, while the second contained the same information in an awkward form.

The maddening part was the way one of the censors would pass the dispatch of one correspondent while the next man on duty would cut out entirely the dispatch of another correspondent containing precisely the same information.

Another example of the thoroughness of the ban on information was at the time of the Mudania Conference. A dispatch stated: "War and peace hang in the balance today at Mudania, a town of six thousand inhabitants, forty-seven miles from Constantinople." All was cut, though what damaging effect the information that Mudania has six thousand inhabitants and is forty-seven miles from Constantinople could have on the British or any other public, I am unaware. At another point the dispatch mentioned that "Kemal had driven the invaders out of the country." All that was cut too, though every paper in the world had been publishing that information for weeks.

Personally I have never met nicer chaps than the two officers who were on censor duty at the telegraph office. We were always on the best of terms. I like them both tremendously. But I would rather have an unattractive, ugly, crabbed, sour-faced, dyspeptic, moss-covered paralytic censor my dispatches and have him know his business than to pass them through the hands of the most charming amateur on earth.

"Old Constan"

☆ THE TORONTO DAILY STAR
October 28, 1922

Constantinople.—In the morning when you wake and see a mist over the Golden Horn with the minarets rising out of it slim and clean toward the sun and the muezzin calling the faithful to prayer in a voice that soars and dips like an aria from a Russian opera, you have the magic of the East.

When you look from the window into the mirror and discover your face is covered with a mass of minute red speckles from the latest insect that discovered you last night, you have the East.

There may be a happy medium between the East of Pierre Loti's stories and the East of everyday life, but it could only be found by a man who always looked with his eyes half-shut, didn't care what he ate, and was immune to the bites of insects.

No one knows how many people there are in Constan. Old-timers always call it Constan, just as you are a tenderfoot if you call Gibraltar anything but Gib. There has never been a census. Estimates of the population give a million and a half inhabitants. This does not include hundreds of battered Fords, forty thousand Russian refugees in every uniform of the Czar's army in all stages of dilapidation, and about an equal number of Kemalist troops in civilian clothes who have filtered into the city in order to make sure that Constantinople will go to Kemal no matter how the peace negotiations come out. All these have entered since the last estimate.

If it doesn't rain in Constan the dust is so thick that a dog trotting along the road that parallels the Pera hillside kicks up a puff like a bullet striking every time his paws hit the ground. It is almost ankle-deep on a man and the wind swirls it in clouds.

If it rains this is all mud. The sidewalks are so narrow that everyone has to walk in the street and the streets are like rivers. There are no traffic rules and motorcars, streetcars, horse cabs and porters with enormous loads on their backs all jam up together. There are only two main streets and the others are alleys. The main streets are not much better than alleys.

Turkey is the national dish in Turkey. These birds live a strenuous life chasing grasshoppers over the sun-baked hills of Asia Minor and are about as tough as a racehorse.

All the beef is bad because the Turk has practically no cattle. A sirloin steak may be either the last appearance of one of the black, muddy, sad-eyed buffalo with the turned-back horns who sidle along the streets drawing carts or the last charge of Kemal's cavalry. My jaw muscles are beginning to bulge like a bulldog's from chewing, or chawing, Turkish meat.

The fish is good, but fish is a brain food and anyone taking about three good doses of a brain food would leave Constan at once—even if he had to swim to do it.

There are one hundred and sixty-eight legal holidays in Constan. Every Friday is a Mohammedan holiday, every Saturday is a Jewish holiday, and every Sunday is a Christian holiday. In addition there are Catholic, Mohammedan and Greek holidays during the week, not to mention Yom Kippur and other Jewish holidays. As a result, every young Constaner's life ambition is to go to work for a bank.

No one who makes any pretense of conforming to custom dines in Constantinople before nine o'clock at night. The theaters open at ten. The nightclubs open at two—the more respectable nightclubs, that is. The disreputable nightclubs open at four in the morning.

All night hot sausage, fried potato and roast chestnut stands run their charcoal braziers on the sidewalk to cater to the long lines of cabmen who stay up all night to solicit fares from the revelers. Constantinople is doing a sort of dance of death before the entry of Kemal Pasha, who has sworn to stop all booze, gambling, dancing and nightclubs.

Galata, halfway up the hill from the port, has a district that is more unspeakably horrible than the foulest heyday of the old Barbary Coast. It festers there, trapping the soldiers and sailors of all the Allies and of all nations.

Turks sit in front of the little coffeehouses in the narrow blind-alley streets at all hours, puffing on their bubble-bubble pipes and drinking deusico, the tremendously poisonous, stomach-rotting drink that has a greater kick than absinthe and is so strong that it is never consumed except with a hors d'oeuvre of some sort.

Before the sun rises in the morning you can walk through the black, smooth-worn streets of Constan and rats will scuttle out of your way, a few stray dogs nose at the garbage in the gutters, and a bar of light comes through the rack in a shutter letting out a streak of light and the sound of drunken laughing. That drunken laughing is the contrast to the muezzin's beautiful, minor, soaring, swaying call to prayer, and the black, slippery, smelly, offal-strewn streets of Constantinople in the early morning are the reality of the Magic of the East.

Afghans: Trouble for Britain

☆ THE TORONTO DAILY STAR
October 31, 1922

Constantinople.—Afghanistan is another weapon that is being forged against the British Empire by Kemal and his Pan-Eastern friends. For over a year Kemalist officers have been training Afghan troops, getting them ready for the moment to strike. Now they are ready.

I happen to know something about the inside history of contemporary Afghanistan with its aims and hatreds. It came to me from Shere Mohamet Khan, who lived in Rome for a while and is now Afghan minister for war.

Shere Mohamet—the Khan is the Afghan suffix meaning prince—was tall, dark-haired, hawk-faced, as straight as a lance, with the bird-of-prey eyes and the hooked nose that mark the Afghan. He looked like a man out of the Renaissance, though his breed are the original Semites and go back as an unconquered people to the days of the Medes and Persians.

The old Amir of Afghanistan was Abderahman Khan. All his life he hated the English, who were using Afghanistan as a buffer state between India and Russia, and who forbade them to have diplomatic relations with any country except England, runs Shere Mohamet's story.

He was a great man, was Abderahman, a hard man, a farseeing man and an Afghan. He spent his life consolidating Afghanistan into a strong nation, and in training his son. His son was to carry on his work, to make war on the English.

The old man died. The son, Habibullah Khan, became Amir. The English invited him to come down to India, on a state visit, and he went to see what manner of people these English were. There the English got him. First they entertained him royally. They showed him many delights and they taught him to drink. I do not say he was not an apt learner. He was no longer a man and an Afghan.

He came back to Kabul, that was just after the armistice in 1918, and the Afghans killed him. He was assassinated. It was really an execution. Then there was a meeting of the Great Council in Kabul and Nasirullah Khan, the oldest grandson of the old Amir, was questioned.

"Will you defend Afghanistan if you are chosen king?" they asked him.

"I will defend Afghanistan," he answered.

"Will you make war on the English?"

"I will try," he answered.

They let him go out of the council room.

Aminullah, the next grandson, was brought in.

"What will you do if you are chosen king?" they asked him.

"I will do two things," Aminullah answered. "I will defend Afghanistan and I will make war on the English."

So they chose him king, and a few weeks later he led his troops over the pass into India.

That is Shere Mohamet's story.

Very few people even remember that there was an Afghan war, just after the armistice. It was the Royal Air Force that won it by bombing out the Afghan cities back of the lines and destroying the mud forts where the hill men, having had no experience with planes before, congregated. At any rate it was a British victory and so announced.

But when they signed the treaty of peace, Great Britain gave up every right that she had always fought for in Afghanistan. Other countries were permitted by treaty to have diplomatic and consular representatives in Afghanistan, arms were permitted to be imported, arms were even permitted to be imported through India. The war may have been a British victory but the peace was certainly an Afghan victory. The Afghans had always hated England but now they felt contempt for her.

So now there are Soviet Russian consulates in all the Afghan cities, the Afghans are armed with modern arms and are trained by Kemalist officers. Aminullah, "my great king," Shere Mohamet calls him, has not forsworn his oath to make war on the English—and he has not gone down to the fleshpots of India.

When Kemal attacks Mesopotamia, and sooner or later he will, there will be a well-equipped, well-trained Afghan army come down the Khyber Pass that will not be the ill-equipped, unschooled band of hill men that were defeated in 1919. They have an alliance with Mustapha Kemal now. They are elated over the Kemalist successes and even their existence is a perpetual threat against the British rule in India that prevents her from drawing a single regiment from there in case of trouble elsewhere.

The Afghans will fight. It is their métier. Shere Mohamet has a story that illustrates the Afghan spirit.

"When I came home to my house in Kabul from the council that decided on the last war, my wife and my daughter had my pistols and my sword and all my kit laid out for me.

" 'What is this?' I said.

"'Your things for the war. There is going to be a war, is there not?' said my wife.

"'Yes. But I am the minister of war. I do not go to this war. The minister of war does not go to the war itself.'

"My wife shook her head. 'I do not understand it,' she said very haughtily. 'If you are this minister of war who cannot go to war, you must resign. That is all. We would be disgraced if you did not go.'"

That is the spirit the Kemalists trained, and armed by the Russians it makes another Eastern problem that does not look easy of solution.

The Greek Revolt

☆ THE TORONTO DAILY STAR
November 3, 1922

Muradli, Eastern Thrace.—As I write, the Greek troops are commencing their evacuation of Eastern Thrace. In their ill-fitting U.S. uniforms, they are trekking across the country, cavalry patrols out ahead, the soldiers marching sullenly but occasionally grinning at us as we pass their strung-out, straggling columns. They have cut all the telegraph wires behind them; you see them dangling from the poles like Maypole ribbons. They have abandoned their thatched huts, their camouflaged gun positions, their machine-gun nests, and all the heavily wired, strung-out, fortified ridges where they had planned to make a last stand against the Turks.

Heavy wheeled baggage carts drawn by muddy-flanked buffalo with slanted-back horns drag along the dusty road. Some soldiers lie on top of the mounds of baggage, while others goad the buffalo along. Ahead and behind the baggage carts are strung out the troops. This is the end of the great Greek military adventure.

Might-have-beens are a sad business and the end of Greek military power is sad enough as it is, but there is no blame for it to be given to the Greek common soldier. Even in the evacuation the Greek soldiers looked like good troops. There was a sturdy doggedness about them that would have meant a hard time for the Turk if Kemal's army would have had to fight for Thrace instead of having it handed to them as a gift at Mudania.

Captain Wittal of the Indian cavalry, who was attached to the Greek army in Anatolia as an observer during the Greek war with Kemal, told me the inside story of the intrigue that led to the breakdown of the Greek army in Asia Minor.

"The Greek soldiers were first-class fighting men," Captain Wittal said. "They were well officered by men who had served with the British and French at Salonika and they outclassed the Kemalist army. I believe they would have captured Angora and ended the war if they had not been betrayed.

"When Constantine came into power all the officers of the army in the field were suddenly scrapped, from the commander-in-chief down to platoon commanders. These officers had many of them been promoted from the ranks, were good soldiers and splendid leaders. They were removed and their places filled with new officers of the Tino [Constantine] party, most of whom had spent the war in Switzerland or Germany and had never heard a shot fired. That caused a complete breakdown of the army and was responsible for the Greek defeat."

Captain Wittal told me how artillery officers who had no experience at all took over the command of batteries and massacred their own infantry. He told about infantry officers who used powder, face powder not gunpowder, and rouge, and about staff work which was criminal in its ignorance and negligence.

"In one show in Anatolia," Wittal said, "the Greek infantry were doing an absolutely magnificent attack and their artillery was doing them in. Major Johnson [the other British observer who later acted as liaison officer with the press at Constantinople] is a gunner, you know. He's a fine gunner too. Well, Major Johnson cried at what those gunners were doing to their infantry. He was wild to take over the artillery. But he couldn't do a thing. We had orders to preserve strict neutrality—and he couldn't do a thing."

That is the story of the Greek army's betrayal by King Constantine. And that is the reason the revolution in Athens was not just a fake as many people have claimed. It was the rising of an army that had been betrayed against the man who had betrayed it.

The old Venizelist officers came back after the revolution and reorganized the army in Eastern Thrace. Greece looked on Thrace as a Marne where she must fight and make a final stand or perish. Troops were rushed in. Everybody was at a white heat. Then the Allies at Mudania handed Eastern Thrace over to the Turk and gave the Greek army three days to start getting out.

The army waited, not believing that their government would sign the Mudania convention, but it did, and the army, being soldiers, are getting out.

All day I have been passing them, dirty, tired, unshaven, wind-bitten soldiers hiking along the trails across the brown, rolling, barren Thracian countryside. No bands, no relief organizations, no leave areas, nothing but lice, dirty blankets, and mosquitoes at night. They are the last of the glory that was Greece. This is the end of their second siege of Troy.

Kemal's One Submarine

☆ THE TORONTO DAILY STAR
November 10, 1922

Constantinople.—Before the British fleet steamed into the Sea of Marmora, Constantinople was in a state of panic, the Turkish pound rocketing and falling, the European population panic-stricken, and ugly talk of massacres was blowing about everywhere.

Then the great, gray fleet came in one day and the town settled back in relief. There was no more massacre talk, for it was made known to Hamid Bey, Kemal's Constantinople representative, that if there was any massacre of Christians started, Stamboul would be razed to the ground. It may have been a bluff but the Turks believed it.

Perhaps it is because of the navy's treatment of war correspondents that it so effectively remains the Silent Service. It has a way with war correspondents, a most definite way. It divides them into friends and enemies.

Enemies receive the treatment the *Daily Mail* man got after Northcliffe's attack on Admiral Jellicoe, the idol of the Navy. He shared every hardship with his men and was loved like a father. The *Daily Mail* came out with an attack on him and shortly after the man who wrote it was assigned to the Grand Fleet. The journalist arrived armed with a letter from the admiralty ordering the commanders of all ships to give him transportation wherever he desired to go. He presented himself to a certain admiral.

"You can't come on board," said the admiral.

The *Daily Mail* man produced his letter. The admiral read it.

"Good," he growled. "This is a definite order. Where do you wish to go and when?"

The *Daily Mail* man told him.

"Good," said the admiral. "Send for Lieutenant Wilson."

Lieutenant Wilson arrived and saluted.

"This man has a letter from the admiralty ordering us to give him transportation. It is a definite order. But it says nothing about comfort, aid or anything else. You will take this man where he wishes to go on your destroyer but do not allow him off the deck or in the wardroom."

Lieutenant Wilson saluted again.

When the journalist went aboard no one spoke to him except the destroyer commander. "Oh, by the way, Paddock, [that is not his name] "this letter doesn't say anything about food. If you want to eat you'd better dig yourself up some grub ashore and bring it aboard."

That is the way the navy has with enemies. Its friends it entertains so amply, completely, thoroughly and enthusiastically that they retain only a vague and idyllic picture of the visit.

Kemal's only submarine was the principal problem and joy of the fleet at Constantinople. This submarine was given to Mustapha Kemal by Soviet Russia and sent out from Odessa. The captain was not enthusiastic about going and the Bolshevists told him he would be hanged if he came back to Odessa without having sunk a British warship.

British naval intelligence officers were advised of the undersea boat's departure and orders were given to sink it on sight with no questions asked or answered as soon as it crossed an imaginary line drawn across the Black Sea entrance to the Bosporus. Destroyer commanders were also instructed that this line was to be fairly elastic and subject to a little stretching.

As soon as the submarine was sighted, two destroyers were to put out into the Black Sea and get behind him so he couldn't go back. Four others were to proceed along the narrow channel of the Bosporus dropping depth charges at regular intervals.

Destroyers sighted the submarine on six different occasions, but he was always too far at sea for them to go after him, even allowing for extreme stretching of the imaginary deadline. Then the submarine disappeared.

He next turned up off Trebizond as a full-fledged pirate, halting ships, searching the passengers and crew and doing a very good business. He is still under the "Jolly Roger" and the captain is laying away plunder enough to enable him to retire if he escapes the gallows that are waiting for him at Odessa and the six lean gray destroyers cruise up and down the Bosporus waiting for him to appear.

The destroyer patrols have exciting times in the Bosporus. At one time, during the Mudania Conference, a destroyer was running a night patrol along the Asiatic side of the straits. No one knew whether there was going to be peace or war, and the destroyer had been picking up small boats with armed Turks in them who were making their way across to Constantinople.

Their searchlight showed something suspicious-looking in a cove near Belcos, not twelve miles from Constantinople, and a boat put ashore to investigate.

As the boat neared the beach, it was fired upon. It kept on going and after the first ragged volley there was no shooting. As the boat landed on the beach a horseman rode out of the black shadow at the side of the searchlight beam and spoke in French.

"We are a squadron of Kemalist cavalry," he said, and the officer in charge of the boat could see the horses huddled back of the little hill. "We have come here to show we could if we want to. Now we are going back."

There was nothing for the British officer to do. The cavalry were some thirty miles inside the neutral zone—but all the British army and navy's efforts in those days were directed to avoiding war instead of accepting provocations for making it. The officer went back with his boat to his destroyer.

Another night a destroyer patrol near the suburb of Bebek stopped a boatload of Turkish women who were crossing from Asia Minor after the ferries were stopped. On being searched for arms or contraband it turned out all the women were men. They were all armed—and later proved to be Kemalist officers sent over to organize the Turkish population in the suburbs in case of an attack on Constantinople.

But whether they were checking the infiltration of Kemalist troops, seizing Russian gold rubles and propaganda tracts that were being brought up the straits in crazy old fishing smacks from Batum, or simply seeing that the Turkish boats kept their riding lights lit, the destroyer flotilla remained a part of the Silent Service. Now with the censorship off, this is the first account of their activities or of the sad career of Kemal's Bolshevik submarine.

Refugees from Thrace

☆ THE TORONTO DAILY STAR
November 14, 1922

Sofia, Bulgaria.—In a comfortable train with the horror of the Thracian evacuation behind me, it is already beginning to seem unreal. That is the boon of our memories.

I have described that evacuation in a cable to the *Star* from Adrianople. It does no good to go over it again. The evacuation still keeps up. No matter how long it takes this letter to get to Toronto, as you read this in the *Star* you may be sure that the same ghastly, shambling procession of people being driven from their homes is filing in unbroken line along the muddy road to Macedonia. A quarter of a million people take a long time to move.

Adrianople itself is not a pleasant place. Dropping off the train at 11 o'clock at night, I found the station a mud hole crowded with soldiers, bundles, bedsprings, bedding, sewing machines, babies, broken carts, all in the mud and the drizzling rain. Kerosene flares lit up the scene. The stationmaster told me he had shipped fifty-seven cars of retreating troops to Western Thrace that day. The telegraph wires were all out. There were more troops piling up and no means to evacuate them.

Madame Marie's, the stationmaster said, was the only place in town where a man could sleep. A soldier guided me to Madame Marie's down the dark side streets. We walked through mud puddles and waded around sloughs that were too deep to go through. Madame Marie's was dark.

I banged on the door and a Frenchman in bare feet and trousers opened it. He had no room but I could sleep on the floor if I had my own blankets. It looked bad.

Then a car rolled up outside, and two moving picture operators, with their chauffeur, came in. They had three cots and asked me to spread my blankets on one. The chauffeur slept in the car. We all turned in on the cots and the taller of the movie men, who was called "Shorty," told me they had had an awful trip coming up from Rodosto on the Sea of Marmora.

"Got some swell shots of a burning village today." Shorty pulled off the other boot. "Shoot it from two or three directions and it looks like a regular town on fire. Gee I'm tired. This refugee business is hell all right. Man sure sees awful things in this country." In two minutes he was snoring.

I woke up about one o'clock with a bad chill, part of my Constantinople-acquired malaria, killed mosquitoes who had supped too heavily to fly away from my face, waited out the chill, took a big dose of aspirin and quinine and went back to sleep. Repeated the process along toward morning. Then Shorty woke me.

"Say, boy, look at the film box." I looked at it. It was crawling with lice. "Sure are hungry. Going after my film. Sure are hungry little fellows."

The cots were alive with them. I have been lousy during the war, but I have never seen anything like Thrace. If you looked at any article of furniture, or any spade on the wall steadily for a moment you saw it crawl, not literally crawl, but move in greasy, minute specks.

"They wouldn't hurt a man," Shorty said. "They're just little fellows."

"These fellows are nothing. You ought to see the real grown-up variety at Lule Burgas."

Madame Marie, a big, slovenly Croatian woman, gave us some coffee and sour black bread in the bare room that served as dining room, salon, hotel office and parlor.

"Our room was lousy, Madame," I said cheerfully to make table talk.

She spread out her hands. "It is better than sleeping in the road? Eh, Monsieur? It is better than that?"

I agreed that it was, and we went out with Madame standing looking after us.

Outside it was drizzling. At the end of the muddy side street we were on I could see the eternal procession of humanity moving slowly along the great stone road that runs from Adrianople across the Maritza valley to Karagatch and then divides into other roads that cross the rolling country into Western Thrace and Macedonia.

Shorty and Company were going a stretch along the stone road in their motorcar en route back to Rodosto and Constantinople and gave me a lift along the stone road past the procession of refugees into Adrianople. All the stream of slow big-wheeled bullock and buffalo carts, bobbing camel trains and sodden, fleeing peasantry were moving west on the road, but there was a thin counterstream of empty carts driven by Turks in ragged, rain-soaked clothes and dirty fezzes which was working back against the main current. Each Turk cart had a Greek soldier in it, sitting behind the driver with his rifle between his knees and his cape up around his neck to keep the rain out. These carts had been commandeered by the Greeks to go back country in Thrace, load up with the goods of refugees and help the evacuation. The Turks looked sullen and very frightened. They had reason to be.

At the fork of the stone road in Adrianople all the traffic was being routed to the left by a lone Greek cavalryman who sat on his horse with his carbine slung over his back and accomplished the routing by slashing dispassionately across the face with his quirt any horse or bullock that turned toward the right. He motioned one of the empty carts driven by a Turk to turn off to the right. The Turk turned his cart and prodded his bullocks into a shamble. This awoke the Greek soldier guard riding with him, and seeing the Turk turning off the main road, he stood up and smashed him in the small of the back with his rifle butt.

The Turk, he was a ragged, hungry-looking Turk farmer, fell out of the cart on to his face, picked himself up in terror and ran down the road like a rabbit. A Greek cavalryman saw him running, kicked spurs into his horse and rode the Turk down. Two Greek soldiers and the cavalryman picked him up, smashed him in the face a couple of times, he shouting at the top of his voice all the time, and he was led, bloody-faced and wild-eyed, back to his cart and told to drive on. Nobody in the line of march paid any attention to the incident.

I walked five miles with the refugee procession along the road, dodging camels, that swayed and grunted along, past flat-wheeled ox carts piled high with bedding, mirrors, furniture, pigs tied flat, mothers huddled under blankets with their babies, old men and women leaning on the back of the buffalo carts and just keeping their feet moving, their eyes on the road and their heads sunken, ammunition mules, mules loaded with stacks of rifles, tied together like wheat sheaves, and an occasional Ford car with Greek staff officers, red eyes grubby from lack of sleep, and always the slow, rain-soaked, shambling, trudging Thracian peasantry, plodding along in the rain, leaving their homes behind.

When I had crossed the bridge over the Maritza, running a brick-red quarter-mile-wide flood, where yesterday had been a dry riverbed covered with refugee carts, I turned off to the right and cut up side roads to Madame Marie's to write a cable to the *Star*. All the wires were cut and I finally got an Italian colonel, who was returning to Constantinople with an Allied commission, to promise to file it for me at the telegraph office there the next day.

The fever was going strong and Madame Marie brought me a bottle of sickly sweet Thracian wine to take my quinine with.

"I won't care when the Turks come," Madame Marie said, sitting her great bulk down at the table and scratching her chin.

"Why not?"

"They're all the same. The Greeks and Turks and the Bulgars. They're all the same." She accepted a glass of the wine. "I've seen them all. They've all had Karagatch."

"Who are the best?" I asked.

"Nobody. They're all the same. The Greek officers sleep here and then will come the Turk officers. Someday the Greeks will come back again. They all pay me." I filled up her glass.

"But the poor people who are out there in the road." I couldn't get the horror of that twenty-mile-long procession out of my mind, and I had seen some dreadful things that day.

"Oh well." Madame Marie shrugged. "It is always that way with the people. *Toujours la même chose.* The Turk has a proverb, you know. He has many good proverbs. 'It is not only the fault of the axe but of the tree as well.' That is his proverb."

That is his proverb all right.

"I'm sorry about the lice, Monsieur." Madame Marie had forgiven me under the influence of the bottle. "But what do you expect? This is not Paris." She stood up, big and slovenly, and wise as people get wisdom in the Balkans. "Good-bye, Monsieur. Yes, I know 100 drachmas is too much for the bill. But I have the only hotel here. It is better than the street? Eh?"

Mussolini, Europe's Prize Bluffer

☆ THE TORONTO DAILY STAR
January 27, 1923

Lausanne, Switzerland.—In the Château de Ouchy, which is so ugly that it makes the Odd Fellows' Hall of Petoskey, Michigan, look like the Parthenon, are held the sessions of the Lausanne Conference.

Ouchy is pronounced Ooshy, not Ouchy, and about sixty years ago was a little fishing village of weather-stained houses, a white-painted, pleasant inn with a shady front porch where Byron used to sit resting his bad leg on a chair while he looked out across the blue of Lake Geneva and waited for the supper bell to ring, and an old ruined tower that rose out of the reeds at the edge of the lake.

The Swiss have torn down the fishing buildings, nailed up a tablet on the inn front porch, hustled Byron's chair into a museum, filled in the reedy shore with dirt from the excavations for the enormous, empty hotels that cover the slope up the hill to Lausanne, and built the ugliest building in Europe around the old tower. This building, of pressed gray stone, resembles one of the love nests that sauerkraut kings used to build along the Rhine before the war as dream-homes for their sauerkraut queens and embodies all the worst phases of the iron-dog-on-the-lawn school of architecture. A steep hill runs up from the lakeside to the town of Lausanne itself on the hill.

You can tell when the conference is in session by the rows of limousines parked along the chateau facing the lake. These limousines each bear the flag of their delegation. The Bulgarian and Russian flags are missing. Premier Stambouliski, of Bulgaria, bulks out of the swinging doors of the chateau, looks suspiciously at the two helmeted Swiss policemen, scowls at the crowd and walks off up the hill to his hotel. Stambouliski cannot afford to ride in a limousine, even if he had the money. It would be reported to Sofia and his peasant government would demand an explanation. A few weeks ago he made an impassioned defense in the Bulgarian assembly to a charge by a group of his sheepskin-coated electors that he had been wearing silk socks, not getting up until 9 o'clock in the morning, drinking wine, and becoming corrupted by the slothful life of the city.

The Russian delegation never know when they are going to be invited to the conference and when excluded, and decided early, in one of their midnight family councils at the Hotel Savoy, that to keep a limousine all the time would be too expensive. A taxi comes up to the door and Arrens, the Cheka man and Bolshevist press agent, comes out, his heavy, dark facing sneering and his one roving eye shooting away out of control. He is followed by Rakovsky and Tchitcherin. Rakovsky, the Ukrainian, has the pale face, wonderfully modeled features, hawk-nosed and tight-lipped, of an old Florentine nobleman.

Tchitcherin is not as he was at Genoa when he seemed to blink at the world as a man who has come out of darkness into too-strong sunlight. He is more confident now, has a new overcoat, and a better-groomed look, he has been living well in Berlin, and his face is fuller, although he looks the same as ever in profile with his wispy red beard and mustache and his furtive old-clothes-man slouch.

Everyone wants to see Ismet Pasha but once they have seen him they have no desire to see him again. He is a little dark man, absolutely without magnetism, looking as small and uninteresting as a man can look. He looks more like an Armenian lace seller than a Turkish general. There is something mouse-like about him. He seems to have a genius for being unrecognized. Mustapha Kemal has a face that no one can forget, and Ismet has a face no one can remember.

I think the solution is that Ismet has a good movie face. I have seen him, in pictures, look stern, commanding, forceful and, in a way, handsome. Anyone who has seen in real life the weak, petulant face of any one of a dozen movie stars who look beautiful on the screen, knows what I mean. Ismet's face is not weak or petulant, it is simply plain and characterless. I remember seeing Ismet in the first days of the conference come into the Hotel Savoy as a crowd of newspaper correspondents was coming out from one of Tchitcherin's famous "mass interviews." Ismet, waiting for the lift, stood in the midst of this crowd of men who had been trying to get appointments to speak with him for days, and not one of them recognized him. He was too unobtrusive.

It was too good to spoil, but I slipped up and greeted him.

"It is very funny, this, Excellency," I said as a couple of correspondents crowded him away from the door of the lift.

He smiled like a schoolgirl, shrugged his shoulders and raised his hands to his face in a mock gesture of shame. He giggled.

"Get an appointment to come and talk with me," he said, shook hands, stepped into the lift and grinned at me. The interview was over.

When I did interview him we got along very well, as we both spoke such bad French. Ismet concedes his bad knowledge of French, which is a disgrace to an educated Turk, as in Turkey a knowledge of French is as much a social necessity as it is in Russia, by pretending to be deaf. He appreciates a joke, Ismet does, and he smiles delightedly to himself as he curls back in his chair and has the remarks of the great shouted into his ear in Turkish by his secretary.

The next time I saw Ismet, after I had interviewed him, he was sitting at a table in a jazz dancing palace in Montreux smiling delightedly at the dancers, a pair of large, gray-haired Turks sitting at his table with him looking morosely on while he ate quantities of cakes, drank three cups of tea and made countless jokes in bad French with the waitress who brought the tea. The waitress seemed delighted with Ismet and Ismet with her; they were having a wonderful time. Not a soul in the place had recognized him.

In contrast to Ismet there was Mussolini. Mussolini is the biggest bluff in Europe. If Mussolini would have me taken out and shot tomorrow morning I would still regard him as a bluff. The shooting would be a bluff. Get hold of a good photo of Signor Mussolini sometime and study it. You will see the weakness in his mouth which forces him to scowl the famous Mussolini scowl that is imitated by every 19-year-old Fascisto in Italy. Study his past record. Study the coalition that Fascismo is between capital and labor and consider the history of past coalitions. Study his genius for clothing small ideas in big words. Study his propensity for dueling. Really brave men do not have to fight duels, and many cowards duel constantly to make themselves believe they are brave. And then look at his black shirt and his white spats. There is something wrong, even histrionically, with a man who wears white spats with a black shirt.

There is not space here to go into the question of Mussolini as a bluff or as a great and lasting force. Mussolini may last fifteen years or he may be overthrown next spring by Gabriele D'Annunzio, who hates him. But let me give two true pictures of Mussolini at Lausanne.

The Fascist dictator had announced he would receive the press. Everybody came. We all crowded into the room. Mussolini sat at his desk reading a book. His face was contorted into the famous frown. He was registering Dictator. Being an ex-newspaperman himself he knew how many readers would be reached by the accounts the men in the room would write of the interview he was about to give. And he remained absorbed in his book. Mentally he was already reading the lines of the two thousand papers served by the two hundred correspondents. "As we entered the room the Black Shirt Dictator did not look up from the book he was reading, so intense was his concentration, etc."

I tiptoed over behind him to see what the book was he was reading with such avid interest. It was a French-English dictionary—held upside down.

The other picture of Mussolini as Dictator was on the same day when a group of Italian women living in Lausanne came to the suite of rooms at the Beau Rivage Hotel to present him with a bouquet of roses. There were six women of the peasant class, wives of workmen living in Lausanne, and they stood outside the door waiting to do honor to Italy's new national hero who was their hero. Mussolini came out of the door in his frock coat, his gray trousers and his white spats. One of the women stepped forward and commenced her speech. Mussolini scowled at her, sneered, let his big-whited African eyes roll over the other five women and went back into the room. The unattractive peasant women in their Sunday clothes were left holding their roses. Mussolini had registered Dictator.

Half an hour later he met Clare Sheridan, who has smiled her way into many interviews, and had time for half an hour's talk with her.

Of course the newspaper correspondents of Napoleon's time may have seen the same things in Napoleon, and the men who worked on the *Giornale d'Italia* in Caesar's day may have found the same discrepancies in Julius, but after an intimate study of the subject there seems to be a good deal more of Bottomley, an enormous, warlike, duel-fighting, successful Italian Horatio Bottomley, in Mussolini than there does of Napoleon.

It isn't really Bottomley though. Bottomley was a great fool. Mussolini isn't a fool and he is a great organizer. But it is a very dangerous thing to organize the patriotism of a nation if you are not sincere, especially when you work its patriotism to such a pitch that it offers to loan money to the government without interest. Once the Latin has sunk his money in a business, he wants results and he is going to show Signor Mussolini that it is much easier to be the opposition to a government than to run the government yourself.

A new opposition will rise, it is forming already, and it will be led by that old, bald-headed, perhaps a little insane but thoroughly sincere, divinely brave swashbuckler, Gabriele D'Annunzio.

Russian Uniforms

☆ THE TORONTO DAILY STAR
February 10, 1923

Lausanne, Switzerland.—George Tchitcherin comes from a noble Russian family. He has a wispy red beard and mustache, big eyes, a high forehead and walks with a slouch like an old clothes man. He has plump, cold hands that lie in yours like a dead man's and he talks both English and French with the same accent in a hissing, grating whisper.

Tchitcherin was an old Czarist diplomat and if Lenin is the Napoleon that made a dictatorship out of the Russian Revolution, Tchitcherin is his Talleyrand. Their careers are both very similar. Both Tchitcherin and Talleyrand were diplomats under the monarchy that preceded their revolution, both were sent abroad as ambassadors under the revolution, both were refused by the countries they were sent to, both were in exile and both became the director of foreign affairs of the dictatorship that followed their revolution.

"We came to Lausanne with one program," Tchitcherin said to me one afternoon. "And we will leave it with the same program. The straits, both the Dardanelles and the Bosporus, must be closed to warships."

He spoke with the tired intensity of a man who is saying a thing for the hundredth time, who believes it and is as impassioned about it as the first time, but has become wearied from not being understood.

"As long as the straits are open to warships," he went on, "Russia is at the mercy of any nation that sends a fleet into the Black Sea. We can have no safety, no freedom to develop, no security from invasion as long as battleships and dreadnoughts can enter the Black Sea. There is only one thing for Russia to do if warships are allowed to enter, and that is to arm. She must build battleships in order to have a great fleet in the Black Sea. That means the crippling of her productive powers by diverting it to building a great navy. But she must do it."

"How about naval disarmament?" I asked.

"Russia was not invited to the Washington Conference," Tchitcherin shrugged his shoulders. "And what has come of that conference? How near are we to naval disarmament now? We are dealing with facts, with conditions as they exist. Russia would be the first to accept an invitation to a naval disarmament conference, but until we have complete naval disarmament, we can only keep warships out of the Black Sea in one way. That way is to have the straits closed to all warships and fortified by the Turks so they can enforce the closing."

Tchitcherin was on his best ground now. He is an old Russian diplomat and he is soundest when he is fighting for the national aims of Russia. He sees that the problems of Soviet Russia, the territorial and national problems, are the same as they were under the Russian empire. The world revolution did not come off and Russia faces the same problems she always faced. Tchitcherin knows those problems. He knows the rivalry between Russia and Great Britain in the east and he knows that as long as Russia is a nation, no matter who governs, and as long as there is a British empire, their interests will conflict. Now he is trying to gain by treaties advantages and securities that later would have to be gained or lost by wars.

Tchitcherin knows that a Russian invasion of India through Afghanistan would be impossible as long as the Crimea was open to a counter-invasion by the British fleet. Lord Curzon knows that too. Tchitcherin knows that the Black Sea coast is the great thousand-mile Achilles tendon of Russia. Lord Curzon knows that too.

It was this daily, bitter struggle between the British empire and the future Russian empire with Curzon, a tall, cold, icicle of a man holding the whip hand with the British fleet, and Tchitcherin fighting, fighting, with arguments, historical instances, facts, statistics and impassioned pleas and finally, seeing it was hopeless, simply talking for history, registering his objections for future generations to read, that made the Lausanne conference so interesting. It is this same unreconcilable difference between Russia and Great Britain that will run like a crack through the Near East treaty that is made in Lausanne and keep it from having permanence.

With his cold hands and his cold brain and his red wispy beard, his inhuman capacity for work, his dislike and distrust of women, his indifference to publicity, public opinion, money or anything except his work and Russia, Tchitcherin looked like a man without a weakness. Then came the pictures that accompany this article.

Tchitcherin, you must know, has never been a soldier. He is timid, personally. He does not fear assassination, but he would turn pale if you shook your fist under his nose. Until he was twelve years old his mother kept him in dresses. He is all brain and he simply feeds his body because it is a supporting part of his brain.

Several of us knew all this about him. Then one Sunday morning as the churches were emptying in Lausanne and the mountain goers were hiking down the streets with their skis and packs to catch the train to Aigle or the Diablerets, a group of correspondents stopped in front of a photographer's window. It was displaying the photographs you see here.

"They're faked," one man said. "Why he's never had a uniform on in his life."

We all looked closely at the photographs.

"Nope. They're not faked," someone said. "I can tell. They're not faked. Let's go and ask Slocombe."

We found George Slocombe, the correspondent of the *London Daily Herald*, who is Tchitcherin's very good friend and sometimes his mouthpiece. George was sitting in the pressroom of the Lausanne Palace Hotel, his big black sombrero back on his head, his curling red beard sticking out at an angle, his pipe in his mouth.

"Yes," he said, looking at the picture I showed him, "aren't they awful? I couldn't believe it when I saw them. He had them taken himself, and now the photographer is selling them."

"But where does he get that awful uniform, George?" I asked. "He looks like a combination of the head keeper at Sing Sing and the concierge at the Crillon."

"Isn't it horrible?" George sucked his pipe. "All the commissars are automatically generals in the Red Army, and Tchitcherin is commissar for foreign affairs, you know. He got that uniform in Berlin. He took it off the hanger last night in the closet in his room and showed it to me. He is dreadfully proud of it. You ought to see him in it."

So that is Tchitcherin's weakness. The boy who was kept in dresses until he was twelve years old always wanted to be a soldier. And soldiers make empires and empires make wars.

The Franco-German Situation

☆ THE TORONTO DAILY STAR
April 14, 1923

Paris.—To write about Germany you must begin by writing about France. There is a magic in the name France. It is a magic like the smell of the sea or the sight of blue hills or of soldiers marching by. It is a very old magic.

France is a broad and lovely country. The loveliest country that I know. It is impossible to write impartially about a country when you love it. But it is possible to write impartially about the government of that country. France refused in 1917 to make a peace without victory. Now she finds that she has a victory without peace. To understand why this is so we must take a look at the French government.

France at present is governed by a Chamber of Deputies elected in 1919. It was called the "horizon blue" parliament and is dominated by the famous "bloc national," or wartime coalition. This government has two more years to run.

The Liberals, who were the strongest group in France, were disgraced when Clemenceau destroyed their government in 1917 on the charge that they were negotiating for peace without victory from the Germans. Caillaux, admitted the best financier in France, the Liberal premier, was thrown into prison. There were almost-daily executions by firing squads of which no report appeared in the papers. Very many enemies of Clemenceau found themselves standing blindfolded against a stone wall at Versailles in the cold of the early morning while a young lieutenant nervously moistened his lips before he could give the command.

This Liberal group is practically unrepresented in the Chamber of Deputies. It is the great, unformed, unled opposition to the "bloc national" and it will be crystallized into form at the next election in 1924. You cannot live in France any length of time without having various people tell you in the strictest confidence that Caillaux will be prime minister again in 1924. If the occupation of the Ruhr fails he has a very good chance to be. There will be the inevitable reaction against the present government. The chance is that it will swing even further to the left and pass over Caillaux entirely to exalt Marcel Cachin, the Communist leader.

The present opposition to the "bloc national" in the Chamber of Deputies is furnished by the left. When you read of the right and the left in continental politics it refers to the way the members are seated in parliament. The conservatives are on the right, the monarchists are on the extreme right of the floor. The radicals are on the left. The Communists are on the extreme left. The extreme Communists are on the outside seats of the extreme left.

The French Communist party has 12 seats in the chamber out of 600. Marcel Cachin, editor of *L'Humanité*, with a circulation of 200,000, is the leader of the party. Vaillant Coutourier, a young subaltern of Chasseurs who was one of the most decorated men in France, is his lieutenant. The Communists led the opposition to M. Poincaré. They charge him with having brought on the war, with having desired the war; they always refer to him as "Poincaré la guerre." They charge him with being under the domination of Léon Daudet and the Royalists. They charge him with being under the domination of the iron kings, the coal kings; they charge him with many things, some of them very ridiculous.

M. Poincaré sits in the chamber with his little hands and little feet and his little white beard and when the Communists insult him too far, spits back at them like an angry cat. When it looks as though the Communists had uncovered any real dirt and members of the government begin to look doubtfully at M. Poincaré, René Viviani makes a speech. M. Viviani is the greatest orator of our times. You have only to hear M. Viviani pronounce the words "la gloire de France" to want to rush out and get into uniform. The next day after he has made his speech you find it posted up on posters all over the city.

Moscow has recently "purified" the French Communist party. According to the Russian Communists the French party was mawkishly patriotic and weak-willed. All members who refused to place themselves directly under orders from the central party in Moscow were asked to turn in their membership cards. A number did. The rest are now considered purified. But I doubt if they remain for long. The Frenchman is not a good internationalist.

The "bloc national" is made up of honest patriots, and representatives of the great steel trust, the coal trust, the wine industry, other smaller profiteers, ex-army officers, professional politicians, careerists, and the Royalists.

While it may seem fantastic to think of France having a king again, the Royalist party is extremely well organized, is very strong in certain parts of the south of France, controls several newspapers, including *L'Action Française*, and has organized a sort of Fascisti called the Camelots du Roi. It has a hand in everything in the government and was the greatest advocate of the advance into the Ruhr and the further occupation of Germany.

There, briefly, are the political parties in France and the way they line up. Now we must see the causes that forced France into the Ruhr.

France has spent eighty billion francs on reparations. Forty-five billion francs have been spent on reconstructing the devastated regions. There is a very great scandal talked in France about how that forty-five billions were spent. Deputy Inghies of the Department of the Nord, said the other day in the Chamber of Deputies that twenty-five billions of it went for graft. He offered to present the facts at any time the chamber would consent to hear him. He was hushed up. At any rate forty-five billions were spent wildly and rapidly and there are very many new "devastated region millionaires" in the Chamber of Deputies. The deputies asked for as much money as they wanted for their own districts and got it and a good part of the regions are still devastated.

The point is that the eighty billions have been spent and are charged up as collectible from Germany. They stand on the credit side of the ledger.

If at any time the French government admits that any part of those eighty billion francs are not collectible they must be moved over to the bad side of the ledger and listed as a loss rather than an asset. There are only thirty billions of paper francs in circulation today. If France admits that any part of the money spent and charged to Germany is uncollectible she must issue paper francs to pay the bonds she floated to raise the money she has spent. That means inflation in her currency, resulting in starting the franc on the greased skids the Austrian kronen and German mark traveled down.

When Aristide Briand, former prime minister, who looks like a bandit, and is the natural son of a French dancer and a café keeper of St. Nazaire, agreed at the Cannes Conference to a reduction in reparations in return for Lloyd George's defense pact, his ministry was overthrown almost before he could catch the train back to Paris. The weasel-eyed M. Arago, leader of the "bloc national," and Monsieur Barthou, who looks like the left-hand Smith Brother, were at Cannes watching every move of Briand and when they saw he was leaning toward a reduction of reparations they prepared to skid him out and get Poincaré in—and accomplished the coup before Briand knew what was happening to him. The "bloc national" cannot afford to have anyone cutting down on reparations because it does not want any inquiry as to how the money was spent. The memory of the Panama Canal scandal is still fresh.

Poincaré came into office pledged to collect every sou possible from Germany. The story of how he was led to refuse the offer of the German industrialists to take over the payment of reparations if it was reduced to a reasonable figure, and the sinister tale that is unfolding day by day in the

French Chamber of Deputies about how Poincaré was forced into the Ruhr against his own will and judgment, the strange story of the rise of Royalists in France and their influence on the present government will be told in the next article.

French Royalist Party

☆ THE TORONTO DAILY STAR
April 18, 1923

Paris.—Raymond Poincaré is a changed man. Until a few months ago the little white-bearded Lorraine lawyer in his patent-leather shoes and his gray gloves dominated the French Chamber of Deputies with his methodical accountant's mind and his spitfire temper. Now he sits quietly and forlornly while fat, white-faced Léon Daudet shakes his finger at him and says "France will do this, France will do that."

Léon Daudet, son of old Alphonse Daudet, the novelist, is the leader of the Royalist party. He is also editor of *L'Action Française*, the Royalist paper, and author of *L'Entremetteuse*, or *The Procuress*, a novel whose plot could not even be outlined in any newspaper printed in English.

The Royalist party is perhaps the most solidly organized in France today. That is a surprising statement to those who think of France as a republic with no thought of ever being anything else. The Royalist headquarters are in Nîmes in the south of France and Provence is almost solidly Royalist. The Royalists have the solid support of the Catholic church. It being an easily understood fact that the church of Rome thrives better under European monarchies than under the French republic.

Philippe, the Duke of Orleans, is the Royalist's candidate for king. Philippe lives in England, is a big, good-looking man and rides very well to hounds. He is not allowed by law to enter France.

There is a Royalist Fascisti called the Camelots du Roi. They carry black loaded canes with salmon-colored handles and at twilight you can see them in Montmartre swaggering along the streets with their canes, a little way ahead and behind a newsboy who is crying *L'Action Française* in the radical quarter of the old Butte. Newsboys who carry *L'Action Française* into radical districts without the protecting guard of Camelots are badly beaten up by the Communists and Socialists.

In the past year the Royalists have received a tremendous impetus in some mysterious way. It has come on so rapidly and suddenly that from being more or less of a joke they are now spoken of as one of the very strongest parties. In fact Daudet is marked for assassination by the extreme radicals and men are not assassinated until they are considered dangerous. An attempt on his life was made by an anarchist a month or so ago. The girl assassin killed his assistant, Marius Plateau, by mistake.

General [Charles] Mangin, the famous commander of attack troops, nicknamed "The Butcher," is a Royalist. He was the only great French general who was not made a marshal. He can always be seen in the Chamber of Deputies when Léon Daudet is to speak. It is the only time he comes.

Now the Royalist party wants no reparations from Germany. Nothing would frighten them more than if Germany should be able to pay in full tomorrow. For that would mean that Germany was becoming strong. What they want is a weak Germany, dismembered if possible, a return to the military glories and conquests of France, the return of the Catholic church, and the return of the king. But being patriotic as all Frenchmen, they first want to obtain security by weakening Germany permanently. Their plan to accomplish this is to have the reparations kept at such a figure that will be unpayable and then seize German territory to be held "only until reparations are paid."

The very sinister mystery is how they obtained the hold over M. Poincaré to force him to fall in with their plan and refuse to even discuss the German industrialists' proposal to take over the payment of reparations if they were reduced to a reasonable figure. The German industrialists have money, have been making money ever since the armistice, have profited by the fall of the mark to sell in pounds and dollars and pay their workers in worthless marks, and have most of their pounds and dollars salted away. But they did not have enough money to pay the reparations as they were listed, and they wanted to make some sort of a final settlement with the French.

Now, we must get back to the little white-whiskered Raymond Poincaré, who has the smallest hands and feet of any man I have ever seen, sitting in the chair at the Chamber of Deputies, while the fat, white-faced Léon Daudet, who wrote the obscene novel and leads the Royalists and is marked for assassination, shakes his finger at him and says, "France will do this. France will do that."

To understand what is going on we must remember that French politics is unlike any other. It is a very intimate politics, a politics of scandal. Remember the duels of Clemenceau, the Calmette killing, the figure of the last president of the French republic [Deschanel] standing in a fountain at the Bois and saying: "Oh, don't let them get me. Don't let them get me."

A few days ago M. André Berthon stood up in the Chamber of Deputies and said: "Poincaré, you are the prisoner of Léon Daudet. I demand to know by what blackmail he holds you. I do not understand why the government of M. Poincaré submits to the dictatorship of Léon Daudet, the Royalist."

"Tout d'une pièce," all in one piece, as the *Matin* described it, Poincaré jumped up and said: "You are an abominable *gredin*, Monsieur." Now you cannot call a man anything worse than a *gredin*, although it means nothing particularly bad in English. The chamber rocked with shouts and catcalls. It looked like the free fight in the cigarette factory when Geraldine Farrar first began to play Carmen. Finally it quieted down sufficiently for M. Poincaré, trembling and gray with rage, to say: "The man who stands in the Tribune dares to say that there exist against me or mine abominable dossiers which I fear to have made public. I deny it."

M. Berthon said very sweetly: "I have not mentioned any dossiers." Dossiers are literally bundles of papers. It is the technical name for the French system of keeping all the documents on the case in a big manila folder. To have a dossier against you is to have all the official papers proving a charge held by someone with the power to use them.

In the end M. Berthon was asked to apologize. "I apologize for any outrageous words I may have used." He did so very sweetly. It took this form: "I only say, Monsieur le Président, that Monsieur Léon Daudet exercises a sort of pressure on your politics."

This apology was accepted. Poincaré, goaded out of his depression to deny the existence of papers that had not been mentioned, is back in his forlornness. You cannot make charges in France unless you hold the papers in your hands and those that do hold dossiers know how to use them.

Last July in a confidential conversation with a number of British and American newspaper correspondents Poincaré, discussing the Ruhr situation, said: "Occupation would be futile and absurd. Obviously Germany can only pay now in goods and labor." He was a more cheerful Poincaré in those days.

Meantime the French government has spent 160 million francs (official) on the occupation and Ruhr coal is costing France $200 a ton.

Government Pays for News

☆ THE TORONTO DAILY STAR
April 21, 1923

Paris.—What do the French people think about the Ruhr and the whole German question? You will not find out by reading the French press.

French newspapers sell their news columns just as they do their advertising space. It is quite open and understood. As a matter of fact it is not considered very chic to advertise in the small advertising section of a French daily. The news item is supposed to be the only real way of advertising.

So the government pays the newspapers a certain amount to print government news. It is considered government advertising and every big French daily like *Le Matin, Petit Parisien, Echo de Paris, L'Intransigeant, Le Temps* receives a regular amount in subsidy for printing government news. Thus the government is the newspapers' biggest advertising client. But that is all the news on anything the government is doing that the readers of the paper get.

When the government has any special news, as it has at such a time as the occupation of the Ruhr, it pays the papers extra. If any of these enormously circulated daily papers refuse to print the government news or criticize the government standpoint, the government withdraws its subsidy—and the paper loses its biggest advertiser. Consequently the big Paris dailies are always for the government, any government that happens to be in.

When one of them refuses to print the news furnished by the government and begins attacking its policy you may be sure of one thing. That it has not accepted the loss of its subsidy without receiving the promise of a new one and a substantial advance from some government that it is absolutely sure will get into power shortly. And it has to be awfully sure it is coming off before it turns down its greatest client. Consequently when one of these papers whose circulation mounts into millions starts an attack on the government it is time for the politicians in power to get out their overshoes and put up the storm windows.

All of these things are well-known and accepted facts. The government's attitude is that the newspapers are not in business for their health and that they must pay for the news they get like any other advertiser. The newspapers have confirmed the government in this attitude.

Le Temps is always spoken of as "semi-official." That means that the first column on the front page is written in the foreign office at the Quai d'Orsay, the rest of the columns are at the disposal of the various governments of Europe. A sliding scale of rates handles them. Unimportant governments can get space cheap. Big governments come high. All European governments have a special fund for newspaper publicity that does not have to be accounted for.

This sometimes leads to amusing incidents as a year ago, when the facts were published showing how *Le Temps* was receiving subsidies for running propaganda for two different Balkan governments who were at loggerheads and printing the dispatches as their own special correspondence on alternate days. No matter how idealistic European politics may be, a trusting idealist is about as safe in its machinery as a blind man stumbling about in a sawmill. One of my best friends was in charge of getting British propaganda printed in the Paris press at the close of the war. He is as sincere and idealistic a man as one could know—but he certainly knows where the buzz saws are located and how the furnace is stoked.

In spite of the fact that the great Paris dailies, which are so widely quoted in the States and Canada as organs of public opinion, say that the people of France are solidly backing the occupation of the Ruhr, it is nevertheless true. France always backs the government in anything it does against a foreign foe once the government has started. It is that really wonderful patriotism of the French. All Frenchmen are patriotic—and nearly all Frenchmen are politicians. But the absolute backing of the government only lasts a certain length of time. Then after the white heat has cooled, the Frenchman looks the situation over, the facts begin to circulate around, he discovers that the occupation is not a success—and overthrows the government. The Frenchman feels he must be absolutely loyal to his government but he can overthrow it and get a new government to be loyal to at any time.

Marshal Foch, for example, was opposed to the Ruhr occupation. He washed his hands of it absolutely. But once it was launched, he did not come out against it. He sent General [Maxime] Weygand, his chief of staff, to oversee it and do the best he could. But he does not want to be associated with it in any way.

Similarly Loucheur, the former minister of the liberated regions, and one of the ablest men in France, opposed the occupation. Loucheur is a man who does not mince words. During the period when France was pouring out money for reconstruction with seemingly no regard as to how it was spent or for what, Loucheur did all he could to control it. It was

Loucheur who told the mayor of Rheims: "Monsieur, you are asking exactly six times the cost of this reconstruction."

A few days ago M. Loucheur said to me in conversation, "I was always opposed to the occupation. It is impossible to get any money that way. But now that they have gone in, now that the flag of France is unfurled, we are all Frenchmen and we must loyally support the occupation."

M. André Tardieu, who headed the French mission to the United States during the war and is Clemenceau's lieutenant, opposed the advance into the Ruhr in his paper, the *Echo National*, up until the day it started. Now he is denouncing it as ill-run, badly managed, wishy-washy and not strong enough. M. Tardieu, who looks like a bookmaker, foresees the failure of the present government with the failure of the occupation but he wants to be in a position to catch the reaction in the bud and say: "Give us a chance at it. Let us show that, properly handled, it can be a success." For M. Tardieu is a very astute politician and that is very nearly his only chance of getting back into power for some time.

Edouard Herriot, mayor of Lyons, a member of the cabinet during the war, and dark-horse candidate for next premier of France, after supporting the occupation in the same way that Loucheur is doing, has now sponsored a resolution in the Lyons city council protesting the occupation and demanding consideration of a financial and economic entente with Germany. This demand of Herriot may be the first puff of the wind that is bound to rise and blow the Poincaré government out of power.

Now why are these, and many other intelligent Frenchmen, opposed to the occupation although they want to get every cent possible from Germany? It is simply because of the way it is going. It is losing France money instead of making it and from the start it was seen by the long-headed financiers that it would only cripple Germany's ability to pay further reparations, unite her as a country and reflame her hatred against France—and cost more money than it would ever get out.

Before the occupation a train of twelve or more cars of coal or coke left the Ruhr for France every twenty-eight minutes. Now there are only two trains a day. A train of twelve cars is now split up into four trains to pad the figures and make the occupation look successful.

When there is a shipment of coal to be gotten out, four or five tanks, a battalion of infantry, and fifty workmen go to do the job. The soldiers are to prevent the inhabitants beating up the workmen. The official figures on the amount of coal and coke that has been exported from the Ruhr and the money that has already been given by the Chamber of Deputies for the first months of the occupation show that the coal France was receiving as her reparations account is now costing her a little over $200 a ton. And she isn't getting the coal.

At the start of the occupation certain correspondents wrote that it would be easy for France to run the Ruhr profitably, all she would have to do would be to bring in cheap labor—Italian or Polish labor is always cheap—and just get the stuff out. The other day I saw some of this cheap labor locked in a car at the Gare du Nord bound for Essen. They were a miserable lot of grimy unfit-looking men, the sort that could not get work in France, or anywhere else. They were all drunk, some shouting, some asleep on the floor of the car, some sick. They looked more like a shanghaied ship's crew than anything else. And they were all going to be paid double wages and work halftime under military protection. No workmen will go into the Ruhr for less than double wages—and it has been almost impossible to get workmen for that. The Poles and Italians will not touch the job. If you want any further information on the way it works out economically, ask any businessman or any street railway head who has ever had a strike how much money his corporation made during the time it was employing strikebreakers.

Now that we have seen in a quick glance the forces that are at work in France in this war after the war, the situation of France, and the views of her people, we can next look at Germany.

The "Battle" of Offenburg

☆ THE TORONTO DAILY STAR
April 25, 1923

Offenburg, Baden.—Offenburg is the southern limit of the French occupation of Germany. It is a clean, neat little town with the hills of the Black Forest rising on one side and the Rhine plain stretching off on the other.

The French seized Offenburg in order to keep the great international railway line open. The line runs straight north from Basel in Switzerland through

Freiburg,
Offenburg,
Karlsruhe,
Cologne,
Düsseldorf

to Holland. It was the main artery of communication and commerce in Germany.

According to the French their occupation was to insure the safe passage of coal trains on the main line between the Ruhr and Italy. They feared the Germans might shunt the cars off at Offenburg and ship them on a branch line up into the Black Forest, and eventually back into the industrial district of what the French papers refer to as "unoccupied Germany."

Germany denounced the occupation of Offenburg, located in the Duchy of Baden in the far south of Germany, some hundreds of miles from the Ruhr, as a breach of the Treaty of Versailles. The French replied by expelling the burgomaster and some two hundred citizens who had signed the protest from the town. The Germans then informed the French that no more trains would run through Offenburg on the great main Rhineland railway.

For almost two months now not a train has run through Offenburg. I stool on the bridge over the right-of-way and looked at the four wide-gauge tracks stretching to Switzerland in one direction and Holland in the other, red with rust. Trains stop three miles each way from Offenburg, north and south. Passengers get out with their baggage, and if they are Germans, can ride into Offenburg in a motorbus and get another bus to take them the three miles the other side of the town where they can continue their journey. If they are French, they are allowed to walk, carrying their baggage.

No coal has gone through since the town was seized. Now the French face the problem—if they want to control the Rhine railway—of occupying every town along the whole length of it at an expenditure of at least four hundred thousand men, and then running the trains themselves. Otherwise the Germans say they will run trains to just outside the limit of the French occupation, and then stop them. It is their answer to the strategists who put their fingers on the map and said, "It is very simple. We will take this town here and that will control this country. It will take only a few men, etc."

The Franco-German commercial war has settled down to a question of which government goes absolutely broke first. All the Germans I have talked to say, "We could not do anything without our government. The government pays all the people who lose their jobs through the occupation. It pays all those who are expelled from the town. It pays the unemployed."

The German government is now using up the gold to stabilize the mark that it normally paid over to the reparations commission. It is using these marks that it buys at the fixed rate of 20,800 marks to the dollar to fight the occupation. It is also already using a good portion of its hoarded gold. When through the crippling of German industries and the exhaustion of the gold supply the German government is no longer able to fight the occupation by putting the government resources back of the individuals who suffer by the occupation, and making good their losses with government money, the French will have won the struggle of attrition. But Germany's gold will have been used up before she quits, her industries ruined, and she will be as profitable to the French as a squeezed lemon.

On the day before I left Paris M. Poincaré asked the Chamber of Deputies for 192,000,000 francs for the expenses of the first four months' occupation of the Ruhr. Four months more of that, and if the German government goes under, the French government will have won a commercial victory at the cost of biting off its own nose to spite Germany's face.

From Offenburg to Ortenberg, where there was a train, I rode in a motortruck. The driver was a short, blond German with sunken cheeks and faded blue eyes. He had been badly gassed at the Somme. We were riding along a white dusty road through green fields forested with hop poles, their tangled wires flopping. We crossed a wide, swift, clearly pebbled stream with a flock of geese resting on a gravel island. A manure spreader was busily clicking in the field. In the distance were the blue Schwarzwald hills.

"My brother," said the driver, guiding the big wheel with one arm half wrapped around it, "he had hard luck."

"So?"

"Ja. He never had no luck, my brother."

"What was he doing?"

"He was signalman on the railway from Kehl. The French put him out. All the signalmen. The day they came to Offenburg, they gave them all twenty-four hours."

"But the government pays him, doesn't it?"

"Oh yes. They pay him. But he can't live on it."

"What's the matter?"

"Well, he's got seven kids."

I pondered this. The driver went on in his drawling south German. "They pay him what he got, but the prices are up and where he was signalman he had a little garden. A nice garden. It makes a difference when you got a garden."

"What's he do now?" I asked.

"He tried working in a sawmill at Hausach, but he can't work good inside. He's got the gas like me. Ja. He's got no luck, my brother."

We passed another lovely clear stream that curved alongside the road. It had clear, gravel-bottomed ripples, and then deep holes along the bank.

"Trout?" I asked.

"Not anymore," the driver laughed. "When we had the revolution, nobody knew what to do. It was in the papers and it was posted up. They sang in the streets and said 'Down with the kaiser' and 'Hoch the republic,' and there was nothing more to do. But they had to do something, so because it was always trouble to get fischkarten [fishing licenses], they went out to the stream with hand grenades and killed the trout and everybody had trout to eat. Then the police came and put some in jail and the revolution was over."

"Herr Canada," said the driver, "how long do you think the French will stay in Offenburg?"

"Three or four months maybe. Who knows?"

The driver looked ahead up the white road that we were turning to dust behind us. "There will be trouble then. Bad trouble. The working people will make trouble. Already the factories are shutting down all around here."

"It won't be like the other revolution?" I asked.

The driver laughed, a hollow-cheeked, skin drum-tight, hollow-eyed laugh. "No, they won't throw any grenades at the trout then." The thought amused him very much. He laughed again.

The Belgian Lady and the German Hater

☆ THE TORONTO DAILY STAR
April 28, 1923

Frankfurt-on-Main.—On the frontier between Baden and Württemberg I found my first Hater. It was all the fault of the Belgian lady who would insist on speaking French. In the roaring dark of going through a tunnel the Belgian lady had shouted something at me. I didn't understand and she repeated, this time in French: "Please close the door."

When we came out of the tunnel the Belgian lady beamed an enormous beam and began talking French. She talked French rapidly and interestingly for the next eight hours in a country where to say one French word is to invite an attack.

During those eight hours we changed trains six times. Sometimes we stood on a platform at a little junction like Schiltach with a crowd of at least six hundred people waiting for the train to come. There would be four places vacant in the train. We always got two of them. That was the Belgian lady.

"You wait with the baggage," the Belgian lady would say as the train came in sight down the track. "I will go in ahead of these boche and get two places. I will open the window and you throw the bags through. We will be comfortable.

That was exactly the way it happened. The train stopped. The Belgian lady would go through "these boche" like the widely advertised Mr. Lionel Conacher through the line of scrimmage. Four hundred perspiring and worthy Germans would be assaulting the door. A window would fly open. The smiling face of the Belgian lady would emerge triumphantly shouting "Voici Monsieur! The baggage. Quick!"

Some way or other I would get aboard a platform of the train and in half an hour of apologetic threading my way, get through the sardine-packed aisles of the cars to where the Belgian lady was saving my "platz."

"Where have you been, Monsieur?" she would ask anxiously and loudly in French. Everyone in the car would look at us blackly. I would tell her I had been making my way through the crowd.

The Belgian lady would snort a terrific Belgian snort.

"Where would you be if you did not have me to take care of you, I ask you? Where would you be? Never mind. I am here and I will look after you."

So guided and guarded by the brave Belgian lady I crossed Baden, Württemberg and the Rhenish provinces in safety.

As we crossed the frontier into Württemberg a tall, distinguished-looking man with gray mustaches came into the car.

"Good day," he said and looked around keenly. Then asked politely but severely: "Is there an Auslander in this car?"

I thought my time had come. There are at least four special visas that no one ever bothers to get in Germany, for the lack of which you can be thrown into jail and fined anything up to a million marks. It is much better to have these visas, but if you take the time to get them you will spend eight out of every twenty-four hours in police and passport control offices, and these officials will discover that you lack nine other special and highly necessary visas that you have never heard of and throw you into the jug on general principles.

The gray-mustached man took my passport and luckily opened it to a page covered with Turkish, Bulgarian, Croatian, Greek, and other incomprehensible official stampings. It was simply too much of a mess for him. He was too much of a gentleman to go into that sort of thing. He folded the passport and handed it back with a courtly gesture, first carefully identifying the brave Belgian lady, from the picture of Mrs. Hemingway in the back of the passport, as my wife.

The lady whose picture appears in the passport has bobbed hair and has just finished a very successful season of tennis on the Riviera. I will not attempt to describe her, being prejudiced. The brave Belgian lady weighs perhaps 180 pounds, has a face like a composite Rodin's group of the Burghers of Calais waiting to be hanged, and sets this face off by a series of accordion-type double chins. This evidence is offered in the case of The People vs. Passports.

It was just after the passage of the knightly official that the Hater got into action. The Hater sat directly opposite us. He had been listening to our conversation in French, and some time back had begun to mutter. He was a small man, the Hater, with his head shaved, rosy cheeks, a big face culminating in a toothbrush mustache. The strain of his rapidly increasing hate was telling on him. It was obvious he could not hold out much longer. Then he burst.

It was just like the time a bath heater blew up on me at Genoa. I could not catch the first eight hundred words. They came too fast. The Hater's little blue eyes were just like a wild boar's. When my ears got tuned to his sending speed the conversation was going something like this:

"Dirty French swine. Rotten French change hyenas. Baby killers. Filthy attackers of defenseless populations. War swine. Swine hounds, etc."

The brave Belgian lady leaned forward into the zone of the Hater's fire and placed one of her twelve-pound fists on the Hater's knee.

"The Herr is not a Frenchman," she shouted at the Hater in German, "I am not French. We talk French because it is the language of civilized people. Why don't you learn to talk French? You can't even talk German. All you can talk is profanity. Shut up!"

It seemed as though we ought to have been mobbed. But nothing happened. The Hater shut up. He muttered for a time like a subsiding geyser, but he gradually shut up and sat there hating the brave Belgian lady. Once more he broke out as he got up to leave the train at Karlsruhe. He was always too fast for me and I didn't get it.

"*Qu'est-ce que c'est, ça?*" I asked the brave Belgian lady.

She snorted, her most devastating Belgian snort. "He makes some charge against France. But it is not important."

The B. B. lady was traveling through Germany without a passport. She avowed that she didn't need a passport anywhere. She and her "mari" were on the same passport and he was in Switzerland on business. If anyone demanded a passport she could always tell them that she was going to meet her husband at Mannheim.

"My husband is a Jew," she said, "but he is *très gentil.* One time in Frankfurt they would not let us stop the night at a hotel because he was a Jew. I showed them. We stayed there a week."

We talked finance for a long time. The B. B. lady wanted me to tell her confidentially whether the dollar was going to rise or fall in France. She said it would be extremely important if her husband could know that, and she wanted me to tell her so she could tell her husband. I did my best. Luckily she hadn't my address if I am wrong.

Then we talked about the war. I asked the B. B. lady if she had been in Belgium under the occupation.

"Yes," she said.

"How was it? Pretty bad?" I asked.

The B. B. lady snorted, her most powerful Belgian snort. "I did not suffer at all."

I believe her. In fact, having traveled with the brave Belgian lady, I am greatly surprised and unable to understand how the Germans ever got into Belgium at all.

Getting into Germany

☆ THE TORONTO DAILY STAR
May 2, 1923

Offenburg, Baden.—In Paris they said it was very difficult to get into Germany. No tourists allowed. No newspapermen wanted. The German consulate will not visa a passport without a letter from a consulate or chamber of commerce in Germany saying, under seal, it is necessary for the traveler to come to Germany for a definite business transaction. The day I called at the consulate it had been instructed to amend the rules to permit invalids to enter for the "cure" if they produced a certificate from the doctor of the health resort they were to visit showing the nature of their ailment.

"We must preserve the utmost strictness," said the German consul and reluctantly and suspiciously after much consultation of files gave me a visa good for three weeks.

"How do we know you will not write lies about Germany?" he said before he handed me back the passport.

"Oh, cheer up," I said.

To get the visa I had given him a letter from our embassy, printed on stiff crackling paper and bearing an enormous red seal which informed "whom it may concern" that Mr. Hemingway, the bearer, was well and favorably known to the embassy and had been directed by his newspaper, the *Toronto Star*, to proceed to Germany and report on the situation there. These letters do not take long to get, commit the embassy to nothing, and are as good as diplomatic passports.

The very gloomy German consular attaché was folding the letter and putting it away.

"But you cannot have the letter. It must be retained to show cause why the visa was given."

"But I must have the letter."

"You cannot have the letter."

A small gift was given and received.

The German, slightly less gloomy but still not happy: "But tell me why was it you wanted the letter so?"

Me, ticket in pocket, passport in pocket, baggage packed, train not leaving until midnight, some articles mailed, generally elated. "It is a letter of introduction from Sarah Bernhardt, whose funeral you perhaps witnessed today, to the Pope. I value it."

German, sadly and slightly confused: "But the Pope is not in Germany."

Me, mysteriously, going out the door: "One can never tell."

In the cold, gray, street-washing, milk-delivering, shutters-coming-off-the shops early morning, the midnight train from Paris arrived in Strasbourg. There was no train from Strasbourg into Germany. The Munich Express, the Orient Express, the Direct for Prague? They had all gone. According to the porter I might get a tram across Strasbourg to the Rhine and then walk across into Germany and there at Kehl get a military train for Offenburg. There would be a train for Kehl sooner or later, no one quite knew, but the tram was much better.

On the front platform of the streetcar, with a little ticket window opening into the car through which the conductor accepted a franc for myself and two bags, we clanged along through the winding streets of Strasbourg and the early morning. There were sharp-peaked plastered houses criss-crossed with great wooden beams, the river wound and rewound through the town and each time we crossed it there were fishermen on the banks, there was the wide modern street with German shops with big glass show windows and new French names over their doors, butchers were unshuttering their shops and with their assistants hanging the big carcasses of beeves and horses outside the doors, a long stream of carts were coming in to market from the country, streets were being flushed and washed. I caught a glimpse down a side street of the great red stone cathedral. There was a sign in French and another in German forbidding anyone to talk to the motorman and the motorman chatted in French and German to his friends who got on the car as he swung his levers and checked or speeded our progress along the narrow streets and out of the town.

In the stretch of country that lies between Strasbourg and the Rhine the tram track runs along a canal and a big blunt-nosed barge with *lusitania* painted on its stern was being dragged smoothly along by two horses ridden by the bargeman's two children while breakfast smoke came out of the galley chimney and the bargeman leaned against the sweep. It was a nice morning.

At the ugly iron bridge that runs across the Rhine into Germany the tram stopped. We all piled out. Where last July at every tram there had formed a line like the queue outside an Arena hockey match, there were only four of us. A gendarme looked at the passports. He did not even open mine. A dozen or so French gendarmes were loafing about. One of these came up to me as I started to carry my bags across the long bridge over the yellow, flooded, ugly, swirling Rhine and asked: "How much money have you?"

I told him one hundred and twenty-five dollars "Americain" and in the neighborhood of one hundred francs.

"Let me see your pocketbook."

He looked in it, grunted and handed it back. The twenty-five five-dollar bills I had obtained in Paris for mark-buying made an impressive roll.

"No gold money?"

"Mais non, monsieur."

He grunted again and I walked, with the two bags, across the barbed-wire entanglement with its two French sentries in their blue tin hats and their long needle bayonets, into Germany.

Germany did not look very cheerful. A herd of beef cattle were being loaded into a boxcar on the track that ran down to the bridge. They were entering reluctantly with much tail-twisting and whacking of their legs. A long wooden customs shed with two entrances, one marked "Nach Frankreich" and one "Nach Deutschland," stood next to the track. A German soldier was sitting on an empty gasoline tin smoking a cigarette. A woman in an enormous black hat with plumes and an appalling collection of hatboxes, parcels and bags was stalled opposite the cattle-loading process. I carried three of the bundles for her into the shed marked "toward Germany."

"You are going to Munich, too?" she asked, powdering her nose.

"No. Only Offenburg."

"Oh, what a pity. There is no place like Munich. You have never been there?"

"No, not yet."

"Let me tell you. Do not go anywhere else. Anywhere else in Germany is a waste of time. There is only Munich."

A gray-headed German customs inspector asked me where I was going, whether I had anything dutiable, and waved my passport away.

"You go down the road to the regular station."

The regular station had been the important customs junction on the direct line between Paris and Munich. It was deserted. All the ticket windows closed. Everything covered with dust. I wandered through it to the track and found four French soldiers of the 170th Infantry Regiment, with full kit and fixed bayonets.

One of them told me there would be a train at 11:15 for Offenburg, a military train: it was about half an hour to Offenburg, but this droll train would get there about two o'clock. He grinned. Monsieur was from Paris? What did Monsieur think about the match Criqui-Zjawnny Kilbane? Ah. He had thought very much the same. He had always had the idea that he was no fool, this Kilbane. The military service? Well, it was all the same. It made no difference where one did it. In two months now he would be through. It was a shame he was not free, perhaps we could have a talk together. Monsieur had seen this Kilbane box? The new wine was not bad at the buffet. But after all he was on guard. The buffet is straight down the corridor. If Monsieur leaves the baggage it will be all right.

In the buffet was a sad-looking waiter in a dirty shirt and soup- and beer-stained evening clothes, a long bar and two forty-year-old French second lieutenants sitting at a table in the corner. I bowed as I entered and they both saluted.

"No," the waiter said. "There is no milk. You can have black coffee, but it is ersatz coffee. The beer is good."

The waiter sat down at the table. "No, there is no one here now," he said. "All the people you say you saw in July cannot come now. The French will not give them passports to come into Germany."

"All the people that came over here to eat don't come now?" I asked.

"Nobody. The merchants and restaurant keepers in Strasbourg got angry and went to the police because everybody was coming over here to eat so much cheaper and now nobody in Strasbourg can get passports to come here."

"How about all the Germans who worked in Strasbourg?" Kehl was a suburb of Strasbourg before the peace treaty, and all their interests and industries were the same.

"That is all finished. Now no Germans can get passports to go across the river. They could work cheaper than the French, so that is what happened to them. All our factories here are shut down. No coal. No trains. This was one of the biggest and busiest stations in Germany. Now nix. No trains, except the military trains, and they run when they please."

Four *poilus* came in and stood up to the bar. The waiter greeted them cheerfully in French. He poured out their new wine, cloudy and golden in their glasses, and came back and sat down.

"How do they get along with the French here in town?"

"No trouble. They are good people. Just like us. Some of them are nasty sometimes, but they are good people. Nobody hates, except profiteers. They had something to lose. We haven't had any fun since 1914. If you made any money it gets no good, and there is only to spend it. That is what we do. Some day it will be over. I don't know how. Last year I had enough money saved up to buy a gasthaus in Hernberg; now that money wouldn't buy four bottles of champagne."

I looked up at the wall where the prices were:

Beer,	350 marks a glass.
Red wine,	500 marks a glass.
Sandwich,	900 marks.
Lunch,	3,500 marks.
Champagne,	38,000 marks.

I remembered that last July I stayed at a deluxe hotel with Mrs. [Hadley] Hemingway for 600 marks a day.

"Sure," the waiter went on. "I read the French papers. Germany debases her money to cheat the Allies. But what do I get out of it?"

There was a shrill peep of a whistle outside. I paid and shook hands with the waiter, saluted the two forty-year-old second lieutenants, who were now playing checkers at their table, and went out to take the military train to Offenburg.

It's Easy to Spend a Million Marks

☆ THE TORONTO DAILY STAR
May 5, 1923

Mainz-Kastel.—One hundred and twenty-five dollars in Germany today buys two million and a half marks.

A year ago it would have taken a motor lorry to haul this amount of money. Twenty thousand marks, then made into packets of ten of the thick, heavy hundred-mark notes, filled your overcoat pockets and part of a suitcase. Now the two million and a half fits easily into your pocketbook as twenty-five slim, crisp 100,000-mark bills.

When I was a small boy I remember being very curious about millionaires and being finally told, to shut me up, that there was no such thing as a million dollars, there wouldn't be a room big enough to hold it, and that, even if there was, a person counting them a dollar at a time would die before he finished. All of that I accepted as final.

The difficulty of spending a million dollars was further brought home to me by seeing a play in which a certain Brewster, if he spent a million dollars foolishly, was to receive six million from the will of some splendid uncle or other. Brewster, as I recall it, after insurmountable difficulties, finally conceived the idea of falling in love, at which the million disappeared almost at once only for poor Brewster to discover that his uncle was quite penniless, having died at the foundling's home or something of the sort, whereupon Brewster, realizing it was all for the best, went to work and eventually became president of the local chamber of commerce.

Such bulwarks of my early education have been shattered by the fact that in ten days in Germany, for living expenses alone, I have spent, with practically no effort at all, something over a million marks.

During this time, I have only once stopped at a deluxe hotel. After a week in fourth-class railway coaches, village inns, country and small-town gasthofs, finishing with a seven-hour ride standing up in the packed corridor of a second-class railway car, I decided that I would investigate how the profiteers lived.

On the great glass door of the Frankfurter Hof was a black-lettered sign, "French and Belgians Not Admitted." At the desk the clerk told me a single room would be 51,000 marks "with taxes, of course, added." In the Oriental lobby, out of big chairs, I could see heavy Jewish faces looking at me through blue cigar smoke. I registered as from Paris.

"We don't enforce that anti-French rule, of course," said the clerk very pleasantly.

Up in the room there was a list of the taxes. First, there was a forty percent town tax, then twenty percent for service, then a charge of 8,000 marks for heating, then an announcement that the visitors who did not eat breakfast in the hotel would be charged 6,000 marks extra. There were some other charges. I stayed that night and half the next day. The bill was 145,000 marks.

In a little railway junction in Baden a girl porter put my two very heavy bags onto the train. I wanted to help her with them. She laughed at me. She had a tanned face, smooth, blond hair and shoulders like an ox.

"How much?" I asked her.

"Fifty marks," she said.

At Mannheim a porter carried my bags from one track to another in the station. When I asked him how much, he demanded a thousand marks. The last porter I had seen had been the girl in Baden, so I protested.

"A bottle of beer costs fifteen hundred marks here," he replied, "a glass of schnapps, twelve hundred."

That is the way the prices fluctuate all over Germany. It all depends whether the prices went up to the top when the mark had its terrific fall last winter to around 70,000 to the dollar. If the prices went up they never came down. In the big cities, of course, they went up. A full meal in the country costs 2,000 marks. On the train a ham sandwich costs 3,000 marks.

Last week, investigating the actual living conditions, I talked to, among others, a small-factory owner, several workmen, a hotelkeeper and a high school professor.

The factory owner said: "We have enough coal and coke for a few weeks longer, but are short on all raw materials. We cannot pay the prices they ask now. We sold to exporters. They got the dollar prices. We didn't. We can buy coal from Czechoslavakia, where they have German mines they got under the peace treaty, but they want pay in Czech money, which is at par and we can't afford to pay. We are starting to lay off workmen, and as they have nothing saved there is liable to be trouble."

A workman said: "I cannot keep my family on the money that I am making now. I have mortgaged my house to the bank and the bank charges me forty percent interest on the loan. You see workmen who have plenty of money to spend, but they are the young men who are living at home. They get their board and room free and their laundry. Maybe they pay a little something on their board. They are the men you see around the wine and bierstubes. Maybe their father has some property in the country, a farm, then they are all right. All the farmers have money."

The hotelkeeper said: "All summer the hotel was full. We had a good season. I worked all summer in the high season from six o'clock in the morning until midnight. Every room was crowded. We had people sleeping in the billiard room on cots. It was the best year we ever had. In October the mark started to fall, and in December all the money we had taken in all summer was not enough to buy our preserves and jelly for next season. I have a little capital in Switzerland, otherwise we would have had to close. Every other summer hotel in this town has closed for good. The proprietor of the big hotel on the hill there committed suicide last week."

The high school professor said: "I get 200,000 marks a month. That sounds like a good salary. But there is no way I can increase it. One egg costs 4,000 marks. A shirt costs 85,000 marks. We are living now, our family of four, on two meals a day. I owe the bank money.

"People here in town cannot change their marks into dollars and Swiss francs so as to have them when the mark falls again, as it will as soon as they settle this Ruhr affair. The banks will not give out any dollars or Swiss or Dutch money. They hang on to all they can get. The people can't do anything.

"The merchants have no confidence in the money, and will not bring their prices down. The wealthy people are the farmers who got the high prices for their crops, which were marketed just after the mark fell last fall, and the big manufacturers. The big manufacturers sell abroad for foreign money, and pay their labor in marks. And the banks. The banks are always wealthy. The banks are like the government. They get good money for bad, and hang on to the good money."

The schoolteacher was a tall, thin man with thin, nervous hands. For pleasure he played the flute. I had heard him playing as I came to his door. His two children did not look undernourished, but he and his frayed-looking wife did.

"But how will it come out?" I asked him.

"We can only trust in God," he said. Then he smiled. "We used to trust in God and the government, we Germans. Now I no longer trust the government."

"I heard you playing very beautifully when I came to the door," I said, rising to go.

"You know the flute? You like the flute? I will play for you."

"If it would not be asking too much."

So we sat in the dusk in the ugly little parlor and the schoolteacher played very beautifully on the flute. Outside people were going by in the main street of the town. The children came in silently and sat down. After a time the schoolmaster stopped and stood up very embarrassedly.

"It is a very nice instrument, the flute," he said.

Starvers Out of Sight

☆ THE TORONTO DAILY STAR
May 9, 1923

Cologne.—Traveling on fast trains, stopping at the hotels chosen for him by the Messrs. Cook, usually speaking no language but his own, the tourist sees no suffering in Europe.

If he comes to Germany, even traveling quite extensively, he will see no suffering. There are no beggars. No horrible examples on view. No visible famine sufferers nor hungry children that besiege the railway stations.

The tourist leaves Germany wondering what all this starving business is about. The country looks prosperous. On the contrary in Naples he has seen crowds of ragged, filthy beggars, sore-eyed children, a hungry-looking horde. Tourists see the professional beggars, but they do not see the amateur starvers.

For every ten professional beggars in Italy there are a hundred amateur starvers in Germany. An amateur starver does not starve in public.

On the contrary no one knows the amateur is starving until they find him. They usually find him in bed. A very hungry person does not walk the streets after a certain length of time. It sharpens that feeling that is dulled by bed. In writing of amateur starvers no reference is meant to the inhabitants of breadlines, soup kitchens or rescue missions. They have violated their strictly amateur standing.

A few case histories of amateur starvers are appended.

No. 1—Frau B. is the widow of the owner of an apothecary shop, who died before the war. She has a yearly income of 26,400 marks, the interest on mortgages. Before the war this yielded her $100 a week. Her 29-year-old daughter is suffering from lung trouble and cannot work. Her 21-year-old son passed the final examination of the grammar school, but cannot go to the university, and is earning his living as a miner. Another 13-year-old boy is in school. The family was formerly very well-to-do. Today their income for one year is the minimum for the existence of a family of four persons for a period of two weeks.

No. 2—The married couple P., 64 years old, who have been blind for the last ten years, receive from their capital, which they earned by hard work, an income of 3,400 marks a year. They were formerly able to live comfortably on this income. Today it represents half a week's wages of an unskilled laborer.

No. 3—Frau B., widow of an architect, is obliged to live with her two children of 9 and 6 years on a yearly income of 2,400 marks. This represents less than two days' earnings of a laborer.

No. 4—The married couple K. receive 500 marks a month from rent of their house. The husband, formerly a farmer, is suffering from heart trouble. A short time ago he was in bed a number of weeks as a result of poisoning. For six months the wife has been almost completely paralyzed. The medicines necessary to their illness cost more than their income. In normal times the income derived from the rent would have afforded these people a comfortable existence.

No. 5—The widow H., 48 years old, has four children, three of whom still attend school. She has a capital of 100,000 marks. This gives her 15,000 marks yearly. On this the family can live for one week.

These cases are not exceptional. They are typical of the situation of the middle class in Germany who are dependent on a fixed income from savings. Neither are they German propaganda cases. All are taken from an appeal for the starving of Cologne signed by Mr. J. I. Piggott, commissioner, the Inter-Allied Rhineland High Commission, and Mr. D. W. P. Thurston, C.M.C., H.M. (His Majesty's) consul general, Cologne.

Cologne itself looks prosperous. The shop windows are brilliant. Streets are clean. British officers and men move smartly along through the crowds. The green-uniformed German police salute the British officers rigidly.

In the evening the brilliant red or the dark blue of the officer's formal mess kit that is compulsory for those officers who live in Cologne colors the drab civilian crowds. Outside in the street German children dance on the pavement to the music that comes from the windows of the officer's club.

Coming down the broad floor of the Rhine on a freight boat from Weisbaden through the gloomy brown hills with their ruined castles that look exactly like the castles in goldfish bowls, in fourteen hours on the river we only passed fifteen loaded coal barges. All were flying the French flag.

Last September, in an express passenger boat, we passed an endless succession of them moving up the river toward the canal mouth that would take them, by a network of quiet waterways, to feed the Lorraine furnaces. Then France was getting the hundreds of barges of coal as part of German reparation payment. Now the fifteen barges we passed were part of the thin stream of coal that trickles out of the Ruhr through the mazes of arrested industry and military occupation.

Hate in the Ruhr Is Real

☆ THE TORONTO DAILY STAR
May 12, 1923

Düsseldorf.—You feel the hate in the Ruhr as an actual concrete thing. It is as definite as the unswept, cinder-covered sidewalks of Düsseldorf or the long rows of grimy brick cottages, each one exactly like the next, where the workmen of Essen live.

It is not only the French that the Germans hate. They look away when they pass the French sentries in front of the post office, the town hall and the Hotel Kaiserhof in Essen, and look straight ahead when they pass *poilus* (French soldiers) in the street. But when Nationalists and workers meet, they look each other in the face or look at each other's clothes with a hatred as cold and final as the towering slag heaps back of Frau Bertha Krupp's foundries.

Most of the workers of the Ruhr district are Communists. The Ruhr has always been the Reddest part of Germany. It was so Red, in fact, that before the war troops were never garrisoned here, both because the government did not trust the temper of the population and feared that the troops would become contaminated with the Communist atmosphere. Consequently when the French moved in they had no barracks to occupy, and had a very difficult time billeting.

At the start of the occupation all of the Ruhr united solidly to back the government against the French. The night of the demonstration when [August] Thyssen came home from his trial at Mayence, a German newspaperman told me he identified over a hundred men in the mob, singing patriotic songs and shouting for the government, who had been officers or non-coms in the Red Army during the Ruhr rebellion. It was a great revival of national feeling that molded the country into a whole in its opposition to France.

"It was most uplifting," an old German woman told me. "You should have been here. Never have I been so uplifted since the great days of the victories. Oh, how they sang. Ach, it was wonderful."

That is finished now. The leaders of the workers are saying that the government has no policy, except passive resistance, and they are sick of passive resistance. Their newspapers are demanding that the German government start negotiations with the French. The French have seized millions of marks of unemployment doles, and as soon as the unemployment pay doesn't come in the workers begin grumbling.

It was beginning to look as though the workers would not hold out in the passive resistance, and the industrialists were extremely anxious to provoke an incident between the workmen and the troops. Something to stir up a little trouble and revive the old patriotic fervor. They ordered sirens blown to summon the workers for a passive resistance demonstration whenever. French troops appeared for requisitionings.

On the Saturday before Easter the incident occurred. It cost the lives of thirteen workmen. It would not have happened, perhaps, if the young officer in charge of the platoon that came to requisition motor trucks had not been nervous. But it did happen.

I have heard at least fifteen different accounts of what actually happened. At least twelve of them sounded like lies. The crowd was very thick and pressed tight around the soldiers. It was in a big courtyard. Those that were in the front rank of the crowd were killed or wounded. You are not allowed to talk to the wounded. The troops are not giving interviews. In fact, they were sent a very long way away very soon after the last ambulance-load of wounded had gone. Hearsay evidence is worthless, and there are plenty of wild stories.

Two things stand out. The French had no reason to make bloodshed and wanted none. On the contrary, they had every reason to avoid any sort of conflict, as they were making every effort to win over the workers from their employers. The industrialists, on the other hand, had been provoking incidents and advising the men to resist.

Twenty different workmen swore to me that there were Nationalist agitators, former German "Green police," in the crowd. The workmen say these men egged on the workers and told them they could swarm over the French, disarm them, and kick them out of the courtyard.

All the workmen said the crowd ran at the first volley, which was fired over their heads. They had all served in the army and had no desire to attack armed troops unarmed once they saw they meant business and would really shoot. It is there that the question arises whether or not the lieutenant proceeded to fire unnecessarily. I do not know. All the men I have talked to swear they were running after the first volley and did not see anything. After the first volley the troops fired independently.

The funeral at Essen was delayed the last time because the French and German doctors could not agree on the nature of the bullet wounds. The Germans claimed eleven of the workmen were shot in the back. The French surgeon claims that five were shot in the front, five bullets entered from the side and two in the back. I do not know the claims on the two men who died since the argument started.

At present the Ruhr workmen are feeling decidedly unpatriotic. They believe that sooner or later negotiations will start, their steadily dwindling unemployment pay will stop, the mark will plunge down again, and that they will not be able to work full-time, due to various sabotages and the general disorganization. None of them have any illusions that the government will be able to pay them unemployment pay indefinitely and they are demanding that the government start something.

The French seem to run the administration of the occupation admirably. The troops are kept out of sight as much as possible, and there is a minimum of interference with Germans going through from unoccupied to occupied Germany. They are all required to have red-card passes, but the examination of these passes is purely perfunctory. A non-com sees the red card, says, "bon," and the line of Germans passes through the barrier.

They run the military end smoothly but are only able to move six trains of the hundred and thirty-three from Essen each day. In three months of occupation France has obtained the same amount of coal she had been getting each day from Germany for nothing, before the Ruhr seizure.

M. Loucheur, millionaire ex-minister of the devastated regions under Briand, went to London and felt out public opinion on his own hook, although he told [Raymond] Poincaré he was going, and reported to him on his return. Poincaré was reported furious at Loucheur's trip, which he regarded as a first step in a Loucheur drive for the premiership when the Chamber of Deputies again sits in May. Loucheur suffers in France from being called the French Winston Churchill, and has a record for brilliant performances and brilliant failure. His very sound credentials for the premiership will be that he has always opposed the Ruhr venture.

Aristide Briand is now working on a speech that he hopes will return him to power. He is planning to attack Poincaré by stating the number of millions Briand got out of the Germans in reparations while he was prime minister and compare them with the money Poincaré has lost since he came into office.

The Caillaux Liberal camp have started a new paper in Paris. Léon Daudet says the first thing he will ask the chamber when it reopens is why M. Loucheur was allowed to go to England as an alleged representative of the government against the wishes of the government, etc.

André Tardieu has announced an attack on the Ruhr policy as it has been carried out. Things are beginning to boil.

The end of the Ruhr venture looks very near. It has weakened Germany, and so has pleased M. Daudet and M. Poincaré. It has stirred up new hates and revived old hates. It has caused many people to suffer. But has it strengthened France?

French Speed with Movies on the Job

☆ THE TORONTO DAILY STAR
May 16, 1923

Düsseldorf.—Hiking along the road that runs through the dreary brick outskirts of Düsseldorf out into the pleasant open country that rolls in green swells patched with timber between the smoky towns of the Ruhr, you pass slow-moving French ammunition carts, the horses led by short, blue-uniformed, quiet-faced Chinamen, their tin hats on the back of their heads, their carbines slung over their head. French cavalry patrols ride by. Two broad-faced Westphalian iron puddlers who are sitting under a tree and drawing their unemployment pay, watch the cavalry out of sight around a bend in the road.

I borrowed a match from one of the iron puddlers. They are Westphalians, hardheaded, hard-muscled, uncivil and friendly. They want to go snipe-shooting. The snipe have just come with the spring, but they haven't any shotguns. They laugh at the little Indo-Chinamen with their ridiculous big blue helmets on the back of their heads and they applaud one little Annamite who has gotten way behind the column and is trotting along to catch up, holding his horse's bridle with sweat running down his face, his helmet joggling down over his eyes. The little Annamite smiles happily.

Then at forty miles an hour in a sucking swirl of dust a French staff car goes by. Beside the hunched-down driver is a French officer. In the rear I get a glimpse of two civilians holding their hats on in the wind and another French officer. It is one of the personally conducted tours of the Ruhr. The two civilians are American ministers who have come to "investigate" the Ruhr occupation. The French are showing them around.

Personally conducted tours are a great feature of the Ruhr. The two gentlemen in the car are typical of the way it is done. They obtained a letter of introduction to General Degoutte from Paris. They wanted to make a full and impartial investigation of the Ruhr occupation in order that they might return to America and give their churches the facts. It is true they hadn't thought of this when they came to Europe, but the Ruhr was the big headline news and to be an authority on Europe when you returned to America you must have seen the Ruhr. If the Genoa Conference had been on they would have gone to Genoa and so on.

They are at Düsseldorf speaking a very little French and no German. The French were delightful to them. A staff car and two officers were placed at their disposal and they were told they could go anywhere they wanted. They didn't know much where they wanted to go so the French took them. At forty miles an hour they did the Ruhr in an afternoon. They saw towering mountains of coke, they saw great factories, they ascended the water tower and looked out over the valley.

"There," pointed a French officer, "are the steel works of Stinnes, there are those of Thyssen. Beyond you see the works of Krupp."

That night one of them said to me: "We've seen it all and I want to tell you right now that France is absolutely in the right. I tell you I never saw anything like it in my life before. I never saw such mines and factories in all my life. France did absolutely and un-ee-quivocally right to seize them. And let me tell you this thing is running like clockwork."

Next in point of amusement to the personally conducted tours in the Ruhr are the rival French and German press bureaus at the Hotel Kaiserhof in Essen. The French press officer is a large blond man who looks like the living picture of the conventional caricature of the German. On the other hand the German press officer who arrived at the Kaiserhof to give his thirty minutes of propaganda immediately after the French press officer had functioned, looked exactly like the caricatured Frenchman. Small, dark, concentrated-looking. Both sides freely distorted facts and furnished false news.

Sir Percival Phillips, of the *Daily Mail*, after he had been badly let down by a piece of French news he used which proved false the next day, said he would use no more of either press bureau's news without labeling it as from the press bureau. "My paper is pro-French," he said, "but it might not always be my paper, and I have a reputation as a journalist to sustain."

The French have a genius for love, war, making wine, farming, painting, writing and cooking. None of these accomplishments is particularly applicable to the Ruhr, except making war. The military end of the occupation has been carried out admirably. But to run this industrial heart of Germany, which has been pinched out and cut off by the military, requires business genius. Business genius is required to run it at all.

At the customs cordon which was designed to separate occupied from unoccupied Germany and yield tremendous revenue on taxes and duties, you see this spectacle: A long column of trucks on the occupied side of the imaginary line chained together, piled high with packages and goods, covered with tarpaulins, some of which had blown off. They have been standing there for weeks. The five *douaniers* or customs men have been too busy intercepting all goods to have time to search those they have held up. At the railroad siding there is a huge warehouse jammed to the rafters with held-up merchandise.

A fat movie operator comes up in a motorcar, taking propaganda pictures to show the people of France how well the occupation is going. He gets out of the car, sets up his camera and shouts instructions to the *douaniers* who have been sitting against the side of the shed smoking their pipes. They stir into action. The movie man shoots a long line of trucks, then the five *douaniers* each climb up the side of a truck and begin to pull packages out, rip them open, haul out the contents, put a chalk mark on the package and jam it back into the truck.

When he has enough footage the operator makes a note in his book, "Our Douaniers At Work In The Ruhr," shoves the book into his pocket, gets into the car, waves adieu to the long-suffering *douaniers*, who relapse back with their pipes against the wall of the shed.

I watched movies taken of coal being loaded. The same fat operator. An enormous pile of coal. Six workmen tore into the pile of coal. "Get a move on," said the operator. "Show some action. You're not on strike. You're working." They worked at top speed.

"*C'est fini*," said the operator, stopping cranking.

The workmen straightened up. The movie man moved off. One workman looked up at the enormous mountain of coal.

"He's a pig. That's what he is, that cinema thing." His pal agreed.

Reaching down the first workman pulled out of his musette a bottle of good red French wine. They had a long drink.

The movie man was writing in his notebook, "Our Workers Loading Coal In The Ruhr."

King Business in Europe

☆ THE TORONTO STAR WEEKLY
September 15, 1923

The other day in Paris I ran into my old pal Shorty. Shorty is a film service movie operator. He takes the news films you see at the movies. Shorty was just back from Greece.

"Say," said Shorty, "that George is a fine kid."

"What George?" I asked.

"Why, the king," said Shorty. "Didn't you meet him? You know who I mean. The new one."

"I never met him," I said.

"Oh, he's a white man," Shorty said, signaling the waiter. "He's a prince, this boy. Look at this."

I looked at it. It was a sheet of notepaper embossed with the royal arms of Greece, and written in English.

> *The King would be very pleased if Mr. Wornall would call either in the morning or in the afternoon. He will be expected all day. If he will be so good as to answer by the bearer, a carriage will be sent to bring him to the royal palace.*
>
> —(Signed) *George.*

"Oh, he's a wonderful kid," said Shorty, folding the letter carefully and putting it back into his wallet.

"Why, you know I went out there in the afternoon with my camera. We drove into the palace grounds past a lot of these big tall babies in ballet skirts with their rifles held at the salute. I got out and he came walking down the drive and shook hands and said: 'Hello. How have you been, Mr. Wornall?'

"We went for a walk around the grounds and there was the queen clipping a rosebush. 'This is the queen,' said George. 'How do you do?' she said."

"How long did you stay?" I asked.

"Oh, a couple of hours," Shorty said. "The king was glad to have somebody to talk to. We had whiskey and soda at a table under a big tree. The king said it was no fun being shut up there. They hadn't given him any money since the revolution, and wouldn't let any of the Greek aristocracy visit him. They wouldn't let him go outside the grounds.

" 'It's frightfully dull, you know,' he said. '[Prince] Andrew was the lucky one. They banished him, you know, and now he can live in London or Paris or wherever he wants.' "

"What language do you talk with him?" I said.

"English, of course," Shorty answered. "That's what all the Greek royal family speak. Mrs. W. B. Leeds, you know. I ran off a lot of film of him and the queen all around the palace and out in the field. He wanted me to take him with an old binder they had out in one of the big fields inside the walls. 'This will look fine in America, won't it?' he said."

"What's the queen like?" I said.

"Oh, I didn't get to know her very well," Shorty answered. "I only stayed a couple of hours. I never like to stick around with them too long. Some Americans just about abuse them. They get an invitation out to the palace and then the king can't get rid of them. But the queen's nice, all right. When I left the king said: 'Well, maybe we'll meet in the States sometime.' Like all the Greeks, he wants to get over to the States."

George of Greece is the newest king in Europe, and probably the most uncomfortable. As Shorty says, he is a very nice boy, and he isn't having any fun at all. He was put into the job by a revolutionary committee last fall, and he stays in just as long as they let him.

George is married to a Rumanian princess, daughter of Queen Marie and King Ferdinand of Rumania, and just now his mother-in-law is making a tour of the capitals of Europe to get George recognized—and, incidentally, her daughter recognized as queen.

Which brings us to Rumania, where the king business isn't flourishing so well either.

King Ferdinand looks as worried as any man who hides his true expression behind a crop of choice Upper Danube whiskers can look. Rumania is the one country that no one in Europe takes seriously. When the statesmen and their friends were living in the best hotels of Paris during the year 1919 and making the treaty that was designed to Europeanize the Balkans, and succeeded in Balkanizing Europe, the Rumanians had a choice collection of rapid talkers and historical-precedent-quoters manned for action.

When these talkers had finished and the treaties were signed it developed that Rumania had been given all the land of her neighbors in any direction that any Rumanian had mentioned. The treaty-makers probably considered this a cheap price to pay to free themselves from the presence of the ardent Rumanian patriots. At any rate, Rumania now has to maintain one of the largest standing armies in Europe to keep down revolts of her new Rumanians whose one desire is to cease to be Rumanians.

Sooner or later large chunks of Rumania are going to break off and drift away like an ice floe when it hits the Gulf Stream. Queen Marie, who is a first-class bridge player, a second-rate poetess, a very high-grade puller of European political strings, and who uses more makeup than all the rest of the European royal families combined, is making every effort to form such European alliances that this coming disintegration will be stopped. On the other side, Prince Carol, who is a most charming, oh, most charming young man and president of the Prince Carol Film Company, which had the exclusive filming of the especially staged Rumanian coronation, does not appear to be gravely interested.

Meanwhile the officers of the Rumanian army, which will bear the brunt of Hungarian and Russian attacks sometime within the next ten years, use lipstick, rouge their faces, and wear corsets. This is no exaggeration. I have, with my own eyes, seen Rumanian officers, infantry officers, using lipsticks in a café. I have seen cavalry officers rouged like chorus men. I would not swear to the corsets. Appearances may be deceptive.

Working back from Rumania, we enter the realm of King Boris of Bulgaria. Boris is the son of Ferdinand the Fox. When the Near Eastern front crumbled in 1918, and the Bulgarian troops came home with revolutionary committees at their heads, they released a large, rough, foul-mouthed ex-farmer named Stambouliski from the jail where he had been ever since he had tried to get Bulgaria into the war on the side of the Allies. Stambouliski came out of jail like a bull coming out from his dark pen into the bright glare of the bullring. His first charge was toward King Ferdinand. Ferdinand left the country. Boris, his son, wished to go, too. "If you attempt to leave the country I'll have you shot," Stambouliski roared.

Boris stayed. Stambouliski used to keep him in an anteroom and call him in when he wanted an interpreter to talk to people he wished to be especially polite to. Newspaper correspondents, for example.

Boris is blond, pleasant and talkative. He heartily dislikes Bulgaria and wants to live in Paris. Now Stambouliski has been overthrown by the old pro-German army officers, grafters, intriguing politicians and Balkan intellectuals, which means in Bulgaria people who have absorbed sufficient learning as to be no longer honest, and killed like an escaping convict by the people who ruined the country he has been trying to save. Boris is still the king, but he is now controlled by the will of his father Ferdinand and the old fox's advisers.

I have not seen him for over a year, but they say he is still as blond, but not as pleasant nor talkative. He is not married, but Queen Marie, the matchmaker, is grooming a daughter.

Next in line is Alexander of Yugoslavia, or as the Yugoslavs insist it is, the Kingdom of the Serbs, Croats and Slovenes. Alexander is the son of King Peter of Serbia. He is no relation to the Croats and Slovenes. I saw him one night in a Montmartre resort in Paris, where he had come incognito for a last visit to the capital before his marriage. There were a number of Serbs and several Frenchmen with him, all in evening dress. Various girls were at the table. It was a big night for the wine growers. Alexander was quite drunk and very happy.

Shortly after this trip the marriage was postponed, but eventually took place.

Victor Emmanuel of Italy is a very short, serious little man with a gray, goatlike beard and tiny hands and feet. His legs looked as thin but as sturdy as a jockey's when he used to wear roll puttees with his uniform. His queen is almost a head taller than himself. The Italian king's lack of stature is a characteristic of the ancient House of Savoy, the greatest of whose long heritage of rulers have been little taller than bantamweight boxers.

Just at present the king of Italy is probably the most popular king in Europe. He has handed over his kingdom, his army and his navy to Mussolini. Mussolini handed them politely back with many protestations of loyalty to the House of Savoy. Then he decided to keep the army and navy himself. When he will ask for the kingdom no one knows.

I have talked to many Fascisti, the old original nucleus of the party, who have all sworn that they are Republicans. "But we trust Mussolini," they said. "Mussolini will know when the time is ripe."

There is a chance, of course, that Mussolini will renounce his old republicanism just as Garibaldi did. He has done so temporarily, and he has a genius for making something that he is doing temporarily appear to be permanent.

But the Fascisti party to exist must have action. It is getting a little satisfaction now out of Corfu and the Adriatic. If it needed a republic to hold it together, it would get a republic.

As a man and a human being there is probably no finer father or more democratic ruler on the continent than Victor Emmanuel.

The King of Spain has been king ever since he can remember. He was born king, and you can trace the evolution of his familiarly photographed under-jaw on the five-peseta pieces since 1886. It's no treat for him to be king. He's never been anything else. He was much handsomer as a baby, if the peseta pieces are accurate, but then we all were.

Alfonso is another king whose throne rests on a volcano. But it doesn't seem to worry him much. He is an excellent polo player and the best amateur motorcar driver in Spain.

Recently the king drove his car from Santander, a summer watering place in the north of Spain, to Madrid, over mountains, hills, and along precipices at an average speed of sixty miles an hour. There was a good deal of criticism in many of the Spanish papers. "If we have responsibilities to a king does not a king have responsibilities to us to keep himself intact, etc." The trip was not well received. But two weeks later the king opened the new motor racing track at San Sebastian by turning off two laps himself at well over one hundred kilometers an hour. His time was only four kilometers an hour behind the winner of the Grand Prix.

The day of the Grand Prix at San Sebastian there was another Spanish military disaster in Morocco in which the Spanish lost over 500 killed, there was a revolt in the barracks at Málaga, and two regiments of troops mutinied, refusing to leave Spain for the Moorish front. The desultory guerrilla warfare that has been going on in Barcelona between the labor men and the government, and which has resulted in over two hundred assassinations in less than a year, continues. But there are no attempts on the life of the king. The people don't take Alfonso too seriously. They have had him for a long time.

In the north live the respectable kings—Haakon of Norway, Gustaf of Sweden and Christian of Denmark. They are so well situated that no one ever hears much about them. Except the king of Sweden, who is an ardent and very good tennis player and plays regularly with Suzanne Lenglen as his partner every winter at Cannes.

Albert of Belgium and his wife everyone knows.

John II of Liechtenstein is a ruler who has had little publicity. Prince John has ruled over the Principality of Liechtenstein since 1858. He is eighty-three years old this year.

I have always thought of Liechtenstein as a manager of prizefighters that used to live in Chicago, but it seems there is a very prosperous country of that name ruled over by John the Second. John the First was his father. They've kept the country very much in the family for over a hundred years. Liechtenstein is all of sixty-five square miles and lies on the border between Switzerland and Austria. It had been a dependency of Austria but announced its independence on November 7, 1918. Two years ago the gallant Liechtensteiners made a treaty with the Swiss to run their post and telegraph system for them. All of the 10,876 inhabitants were doing well at the last report except Prince John, who is having a little trouble with his teeth.

So far I have only mentioned the European kings who are still holding down their jobs. Ex-kings would take an article in themselves. I have never seen the kaiser nor Harry K. Thaw nor Landru. A good many of my best friends, though, have climbed up the wall of the garden at Doorn or attempted to gain admission disguised as bales of hay, cases of lager beer or Bavarian diplomats. Even when they have seen the kaiser, however, they report the result as unsatisfactory.

Search for Sudbury Coal

☆ THE TORONTO DAILY STAR
September 25, 1923

Sudbury, Ontario.—Is there coal in the Sudbury district?

This is no new question. For twenty-six years competent geologists have admitted that there was something very like coal in the Sudbury basin, but that the quantity was small and the coaly matter was so mixed with impurities that it made a very poor grade of fuel. The geologists decided to call the coaly stuff anthraxolite.

Last year, C. W. Knight, associate provincial geologist, said that if a great amount of the pure anthraxolite, giving an output of say six million tons, was ever found, it would be an event of great importance. But after examining the field he made an official report that he believed there were at most only a few thousand tons of coaly material in sight. He said, however, that the occurrence of the anthraxolite was more widespread than originally supposed.

The British Colonial Coal Mines, Limited, of Toronto, are drilling for coal in the Sudbury basin, a short distance from Larchwood, Ontario. They have sunk four diamond drill holes. According to Stewart Hood, president of the company, they hope and expect to find a great bed of coal. "But," said Mr. Hood, "it is a gamble. The only way we can get anywhere is by drilling to find the coal. All the people interested in the company have been told it is a gamble or speculation. But we hope and expect to find a great coal bed that will free Ontario from the necessity of depending on the United States for its anthracite coal."

I arrived in Sudbury at night. In the dark it was impossible to tell much about the town except there were plenty of red-brick buildings, plenty of streetlights, plenty of Chinese restaurants, and many girls on the streets. There was a movie showing Ben Turpin, French Canadian spoken in the bars, and real beer being sold on draft. I saw only three men drunk. In Cobalt there had been two men drunk at one bar before eleven o'clock in the morning.

In the morning the streets of Sudbury looked very much like the night before except there were no streetlights, no girls, and nobody loafing around.

In the office of the Ontario Diamond Drilling Company here, I found Mr. T. H. Hale, the secretary-treasurer, and Mr. Frank Pickard, who was in town from the diamond-drilling job the Ontario company was doing for the Toronto company, which has been drilling for coal near the Larchwood outcropping.

Mr. Pickard was going back to the job out near Larchwood, and we started out together in a car, with a fat French-Canadian chauffeur, who almost completely filled the front seat. Going west up and out of Sudbury, the road runs through the weirdest country I have ever seen. It is a jumble of great rolling hills—of absolutely bald purple black rock, sulphur-stained, and looking like a lava-scorched volcanic slope immediately after an eruption. Occasionally, thin, black-charred stumps stood in a dip in the bare burnt rock hills. But mostly there was no sign of vegetation.

Pickard said it had formerly been a timber country, but all vegetation had been destroyed by the sulphur smoke from the roasting beds. In these roasting beds the nickel ore was spread on beds of logs and chunk wood. Coal oil was poured over these huge beds of ore and wood, and the whole thing set on fire. After a while the ore burned of itself in the heat until all the sulphur was out of it. During the process the rolling clouds of sulphur smoke killed everything within miles right down through the grass roots to the bare rock.

Driving through it was like going through some desolate early illustration of *Pilgrim's Progress*. I thought I might see a lion on the way almost anywhere. Then we came up out of the valley, passed the big gray buildings of the Murray Mine on our right, and the tall stacks of smelters way off on our left and dipped down a hill into an open, flat, green farming country. It was the Sudbury basin, a clear tract of farming country, flat as Illinois or Holland, and held in by a horseshoe of blue mountains, the Nickel Range, that bound it in a dull, gray, irregular line all around the horizon.

Where the farming country began to bunch into foothills again toward the far side of the basin, the motorcar stopped at the bunkhouse and office of the drillers. Just down the road was the Larchwood station of the C.P.R. [Canadian Pacific Railway] and across the fields to the left the log farmhouse of Mrs. Davey, where I found Thomas Watson. Thomas Watson is a tall Scotsman with a yellow mustache, a slight stoop, and a low country burr in his talk. He is in charge of operations in the field for the British Colonial Coal Mines, Limited.

Thomas Watson was sitting down settling his dinner for a little while, and when the dinner was settled we got into the car and drove back down the road, and turned down a grass road toward where the drill was working on the company's hole number four.

At the end of a green slope of field stood the tripod with a plume of steam rising from the boiler shed. A diamond drill works like this. There is a steam-run sort of super brace and bit that whirls round and round a piece of steel pipe that has diamonds set in the end. This diamond-studded pipe end bores slowly into the rocks. Water is running into the drill and around it to hold down the temperature. The drill eats into the rock and everything it eats goes straight up inside it as a core. When the ten-foot segment of the pipe just back of the drill, called the core bottle, is full of the solid rock, the operator stops the drill whirring, hauls up the lengths of pipe. He stacks them in sheafs ready to go down again, and empties out the core bottle.

The core that comes out of the pipe is knocked out by whacking the pipe with a wooden block and is then placed in the grooves of a core box. This is a sort of narrow five-foot coffin for the cores which lie in it like leads for giant Eversharp pencils. The cores are all kept in stacks of core boxes, and these boxes numbered so that the man in charge of operations knows just what piece of core came from what hole, and just what depth.

After watching the drill work, and seeing a core of pure slate knocked out and packed away, we walked about three-quarters of a mile through a low-lying patch of bush to the outcropping of coal—anthracite, anthraxolite or whatever you want to call it.

This outcropping lies in a gash in the slate rocks at the top of a ridge. It looks to a non-geologist like a pocket of much-broken-up coal mixed with a foreign substance lying in a zigzag cleft in the rocks. It looks, feels and has every appearance of coal, but it is mixed with all sorts of quartz, iron pyrites, and other minerals. We climbed to the top of the ridge, and looked out over the low country where white surveyors' rods show the direct line the three holes have been bored in.

Then we went down and inspected a shaft that had been driven sixty feet into the base of the ridge below the outcropping of coal. Thomas Watson went ahead with a candle, and I followed him walking on boards over a waterhole to the end of the shaft, where was found the same sort of coal as had appeared in the outcropping. It looked like the same bed.

Farther down the ridge beside the original diamond-drill hole reported on in 1896 by Dr. A. P. Coleman, Mr. Watson had supervised the sinking of a diamond drill. "At 342 feet we struck eighteen inches of slate, and four and a half feet of coal," Mr. Watson said. "We went on down to 398 feet but there was no more coal except streaks in the rock at 378 feet."

The coal cores from the hole number one had been sent away to Toronto to the directors and officers, Mr. Watson said, except one box. I examined this and found some chunks of core that looked like very pure coal, then would come a streak of quartz, and silicate with chunks of iron pyrites and slate.

"We drilled hole number two here," Mr. Watson said. "At 1,398 feet we found seventeen inches of coal similar to the outcrop, but cleaner. Altogether we put the drill down 1,431½ feet."

We walked back through the bush toward the ridge, and stopped at a tramped-down piece with a large muddy area with a mud cone in the center. "Here we drilled number three hole," Mr. Watson pointed. "It has a total depth of 1,236 feet and at 1,141 feet we hit eighteen inches of coal. At from 248 to 258 feet there was a coal position. The coal at 1,141 feet was too soft for the drill, and the water washed it away and we have only the sludge. But it was coal all right."

"How about number four hole?" I asked.

"We had better wait till we get over there, and we'll look at the core boxes then," Mr. Watson said.

Of the cores from the first three holes, I had examined about sixteen inches of the first core, which I have described. The second was sludged, that is, the coal was too soft for the drill, and all there was to show for the coal core was a mixture of ground coal, shale and water. Of the core of number three hole, I saw several long rods. It was very black, and hard looking, streaked with quartz, shining iron pyrites, and slate.

We hiked back through the woods to where the drill was working on hole number four. On our way we crossed MacKenzie Creek, where there was a small outcropping of the same coal I had seen in the big outcropping on the ridge. We watched the drill a little while, and then went into a log shack, where the core boxes were stacked.

"I sent away some of this to Toronto, the other day," Mr. Watson said. "I'd best unscrew these two boxes."

I sat on the floor of the cabin with my notes and a pencil, and Thomas Watson worked over the boxes with a screwdriver. "Now give me the figures on this hole, Mr. Watson," I suggested. "At 148 feet to 168 feet, the position is twenty feet. I'd say roughly there is perhaps ten feet of coal core shown. Here—you look at it."

I looked at the black core. It had a coaly sheen and was mixed with quartz, and a new pure white quartz I had not seen before. There were also thick streaks of slate, and a good deal of iron pyrites. The coaly material was broken up and looked very hard, with a peculiar, slippery shine.

We were sitting on the floor of the cabin with the open core boxes before us, and Thomas Watson was lighting his pipe. Outside the drill was whirring and chunking. Coming over through the bush we had been talking about Mr. Lloyd George and the "standard of murrallity" in different countries, and from that to honor among newspapermen.

"Has this been analyzed?" I asked.

"I told them to get it analyzed. It looks like coal to me. But the eyes can be deceived. That's their business. I'm here on the practical side," Thomas Watson was saying. He leaned over the box.

"Mr. Watson, tell me is that stuff really coal?" I asked.

Thomas Watson said: "It's no coal. They write me that people that know all about it say it's coal. But it's no coal, I know. The outcropping is coal. What we hit in number one and number two holes is coal. I'd stake my life on it. But this ten feet in number three and this twenty feet is no coal."

"But how do you know it's not coal?" I said.

"How do I know, man? How do I know anything about coal mining? I've been doing it for forty years. The stuff here in the ten feet number three and the twenty feet in number four is exactly what we had in Newlands Colliery; it was called 'humph' coal. It was of absolutely no value."

"Where did you say the mine was?" I asked.

"Newlands Mine, ten miles out of Glasgow and roughly two miles north. It looked like coal, too, but it was of no value whatsoever, but there were two seams of good coal right alongside of it."

"But the first, the good coal. You think the vein runs down from the outcropping to where you picked it up at number one and number two holes at those depths?" I said.

"Surely, and I know there's coal there. But I won't say this other is coal, because it isn't."

Which settles the matter as far as Thomas Watson, British certified mining engineer, is concerned.

A prominent Ontario geologist who himself has examined the Larchwood coal beds told the *Star* that the anthraxolite occurs in veins, rather than in beds. According to this geologist, the outcropping near Larchwood is simply a niche in the rock filled with coaly matter.

There is no doubt but what the rocks are too old in the Sudbury basin to have a real coal bed, this geologist told the *Star*. The anthraxolite in its present form is so impure that it would have to be crushed, washed to get the impurities out, then in the form of a powder it would have to be briquetted. To be of real commercial value there would need to be millions of tons. However, no one really knows how much of this anthraxolite exists, and if people want to put their money into hunting for it in commercial quantities, it is a good way for them to gamble. The big question is, how much of the anthraxolite is there? If there is enough, it is, of course, really important.

The *Star* checked Mr. Watson's figures over with Mr. Stewart Hood and Mr. J. H. Henderson, who is also connected with the British Colonial Coal Mines, Limited.

"We have every confidence in Mr. Watson and in his reports," Mr. Hood said.

"Just how would you define a coal position, Mr. Henderson?" the *Star* asked.

"Well, you've asked a layman," Mr. Henderson answered. He hesitated for some time. "I have had it explained to me several times—" Mr. Hood demonstrated with two pieces of paper. "You go through certain formations and locate coal, then you find other formations, and strike off into another set entirely. When you get to the same formation, you leave off and you know you have the same position."

Mr. Henderson suggested that it was very hard for a layman to use geological or engineering terms.

The reporter asked Mr. Hood if the coal from number three and number four holes had been analyzed.

"No," said Mr. Hood.

"It has been burnt," Mr. Henderson said.

Mr. Hood said he had not been out to the field since the drill was started on number two hole. Consequently he had not seen either number three hole or number four hole. The company only has the drill logs for number one and number two holes, he said. "But," said Mr. Hood, "we have Mr. Thomas Watson's report and we are drilling, trying to trace the main seam back into the basin where we believe it lies."

Professor A. P. Coleman, spoken of with respect and affection as "The Old Man" by generations of Canadian geologists that have been uncovering the mineral wealth of the north country, read a proof of the *Star*'s investigation trip to the Sudbury "coal fields," presented herewith, in his office in the Royal Ontario Museum today.

"Everything reported here bears out our information and reports that there are small seams of anthraxolite near Larchwood, Ontario," Professor Coleman said, "but the thing to remember is that coal always occurs as beds. Anthraxolite is never found in beds. It is found in fissures."

Dr. Coleman examined specimens from two different outcroppings on the British Colonial Coal Mines, Limited, property brought to Toronto by a reporter for the *Star*.

"Yes. That is the same anthraxolite," he said.

The reporter showed him a piece of the "coal" from the drill hole of the company's number one hole. "We have a good many purer specimens of anthraxolite than that in the university," Professor Coleman said. "That is mixed with slate and other minerals."

"This is the great difference," Professor Coleman continued. "Coal is due to plant growth and always lies in distinctive beds. Anthraxolite always lies in a fissure. Anthraxolite was originally bitumen. It was a bituminous substance that could flow and occupy the fissures. It has a totally different origin than coal.

"The bitumen has lost its volatile constituents and the fixed carbon is left. That is why you get more carbon than in anthracite."

Professor Coleman paused. "The report is very vivid and seems to me to be very accurate," he said. "I would use the word silicon rather than silicates. That is the only thing I see to change. I see nothing in the drilling operations to indicate that conditions are in any way changed since we made our report in 1896. The three drill holes have all picked up the same fissure of anthraxolite that runs down from the outcropping. The only new thing is that there are more outcroppings. But these were bound to be found as the country was opened up."

"What is the significance of these new outcrops?" asked the reporter.

"These have no new significance," Professor Coleman said. "For the way in which it occurs proves it is not coal. As it is not coal, the whole series of inferences that you make for a coal bed disappears."

"Just what would you call a coal position, Dr. Coleman?" asked the reporter.

"In coal beds," Dr. Coleman explained, "if you know the stripe and the dip of the coal, you can work out roughly the amount. But when you have irregular fissures, such as anthraxolite, you can't predict what you'll find. Anthraxolite occurs in a very irregular crack or fissure that is constantly varying and full of big masses of rocks."

Dr. Coleman considered a moment. "You may be perfectly sure that if the material was of any use they would have used it in Sudbury," he said. "Hard coal is a good deal more expensive in Sudbury than in Toronto. I suppose that Mr. Watson is keeping a careful record of what the drill encounters and I hope that it will be at the disposal of the Bureau of Mines. We would be very interested in the different materials the drills encounter. For example, if they hit any amount of quartz and what quantity."

Japanese Earthquake

☆ THE TORONTO DAILY STAR
September 25, 1923

There are no names in this story.

The characters in it are a reporter, a girl reporter, a quite beautiful daughter in a Japanese kimono, and a mother. There is a small chorus of friends who spend some time talking in the next room, and get up as the reporter and the girl reporter go through the room and out of the door.

At four o'clock in the afternoon the reporter and the girl reporter stood on the front porch. The front doorbell had just rung.

"They'll never let us in," said the girl reporter.

Inside the house they heard someone moving around and then a voice said, "I'll go down. I'll attend to them, Mother."

The door opened one narrow crack. The crack ran from the top of the door to the bottom, and about halfway up it was a very dark, very beautiful face, the hair soft and parted in the middle.

"She is beautiful, after all," thought the reporter. He had been sent on so many assignments in which beautiful girls figured, and so few of the girls had ever turned out to be beautiful.

"Who do you want?" said the girl at the door.

"We're from the *Star*," the reporter said. "This is Miss So-and-So."

"We don't want to have anything to do with you. You can't come in," the girl said.

"But—"said the reporter and commenced to talk. He had a very strong feeling that if he stopped talking at any time, the door would slam. So he kept on talking. Finally the girl opened the door. "Well, I'll let you in," she said. "I'll go upstairs and ask my mother."

She went upstairs, quick and lithe, wearing a Japanese kimono. It ought to have some other name. Kimono has a messy, early-morning sound. There was nothing kimonoey about this kimono. The colors were vivid and the stuff had body to it, and it was cut. It looked almost as though it might be worn with two swords to the belt.

The girl reporter and the reporter sat on a couch in the parlor. "I'm sorry to have done all the talking," whispered the reporter.

"No. Go on. Keep it up. I never thought we'd get in at all," said the girl reporter. "She is good-looking, isn't she?" The reporter had thought she was beautiful. "And didn't she know what she was doing when she got that kimono!"

"Sh—. Here they come."

Down the stairs came the girl in the Japanese kimono. With her was her mother. Her mother's face was very firm.

"What I want to know," she said, "is where you got those pictures?"

"They were lovely pictures, weren't they?" said the girl reporter.

Both the girl reporter and the reporter denied any knowledge of the pictures. They didn't know. Really, they didn't know. It was a fact. Eventually they were believed.

"We won't say anything. We don't want to be in the newspapers. We've had too much already. There are plenty of people that suffered much worse than we did in the earthquake. We don't want to talk about it at all."

"But I let them in, Mother," said the daughter. She turned to the reporter. "Just exactly what is it you want to know from us?"

"We just want you to tell us as you remember it just what happened," the reporter said.

"If we talk to you and tell you what you want to know will you promise that you won't use our names?" asked the daughter.

"Why not just use the names," suggested the reporter.

"We don't say a word unless you promise not to use the names," said the daughter.

"Oh, you know newspaper reporters," the mother said. "They'll promise it and then they'll use them anyway." It looked as though there wasn't going to be any story. The remark had made the reporter violently angry. It is the one unmerited insult. There are enough merited ones.

"Mrs. So-and-So," he said, "the president of the United States tells reporters things in confidence which if known would cost him his job. Every week in Paris the prime minister of France tells fifteen newspaper reporters facts that if they were quoted again would overthrow the French government. I'm talking about newspaper reporters, not cheap news tipsters."

"All right," said the mother. "Yes, I guess it's true about newspaper reporters."

The daughter began the story and the mother took it up.

"The boat [the Canadian Pacific's *Empress of Australia*] was all ready to sail," said the daughter. "If Mother and Father hadn't been down at the dock, I don't believe they would have escaped!"

"The *Empress* boats always sail at noon on Saturday," said the mother.

"Just before twelve o'clock, there was a great rumbling sound and then everything commenced to rock back and forth. The dock rolled and bucked. My brother and I were on board the boat leaning against the rail. Everybody had been throwing streamers. It only lasted about thirty seconds," said the daughter.

"We were thrown flat on the dock," said the mother. "It was a big concrete dock and it rolled back and forth. My husband and I hung on to each other and were thrown around by it. Many people were thrown off. I remember seeing a rickshaw driver clambering back up out of the water. Cars and everything else went in, except our car. It stayed on the dock right alongside the Prince de Bearn's, the French consul's car, until the fire came."

"What did you do when the shock was over?" asked the reporter.

"We went ashore. We had to climb. The dock was crumbled in places and great chunks of concrete broken off. We started off up the Bund along the shore and could see that the big go-downs, the storage houses, were all caved in. You know the Bund. The driveway straight along the waterfront. We got as far as the British consulate and it was all caved in. Just fallen in on itself like a funnel. Just crumbled. All the walls were down and we could look through the front of the building to the open compound at the back. Then there was another shock and we knew it wasn't any use going on or trying to get up to our house. My husband heard that the people had been out of the office and there was nothing you could do about the men who had been working in the go-downs. There was a big cloud of dust all over everything from the buildings that had caved in. You couldn't hardly see through it, and fires were breaking out all over."

"What were the people doing? How were they acting?" asked the reporter.

"There wasn't any panic. That was the strange thing. I didn't see anyone even hysterical. There was one woman at the Russian consulate though. It stood right next to the British consulate and it hadn't fallen in yet but was badly shaken. She came out to the front gate crying and there were a bunch of coolies sitting against the iron fence in front of the consulate yard. She begged them to help her get her daughter out of the building. "She's just a little fellow," she said in Japanese. But they just sat there. They wouldn't move. It seemed as though they couldn't move. Of course nobody was going around helping anybody else then. Everybody had themselves to look after."

"How did you get back to the boat?" asked the girl reporter.

"There were some sampans, native boats, and finally my husband found one and we started back. But the fire was going so badly then and the wind was offshore. There was an awful wind for a while. We got to the dock finally and, of course, they couldn't get a gangplank out, but they put out a rope for us and we got on board."

The mother didn't need any prompting or questions now. That day and the following days and nights in Yokohama harbor had her in their grip again. Now the reporter saw why she didn't want to be interviewed and why no one had any right to interview her and stir it all up afresh. Her hands were very quietly nervous.

"The Prince's boy [son of the Prince de Bearn, French consul] was left in their house. He had been sick. They had just come down to the dock to see the boat off. The foreign quarter is up on a bluff where we all lived, and the bluff just slid down into town. The Prince got ashore and made his way up to the wreck of his house. They got the boy out but his back was hurt. They worked hours getting him out. But they couldn't get the French butler out. They had to go away and leave him in there because the fire got too close."

"They had to leave him in there alive with the fire coming on?" asked the girl reporter.

"Yes, they had to leave the French butler in there," said the mother. "He was married to the housemaid so they had to tell her they had gotten him out."

The mother went on in a dull, tired voice.

"There was a woman on the [liner] *Jefferson* coming home that had lost her husband. I didn't recognize her. There was a young couple, too, that had been only out a short time. They'd just been married. His wife was down in the town shopping when it happened. He couldn't get to where she was on account of the fire. They got the head doctor out all right from the American Hospital. They couldn't get out the assistant doctor and his wife though. The fire came so quick. The whole town was solid fire.

"We were on the boat of course. Part of the time you couldn't see the shore on account of the smoke. When it was bad was when the submarine oil tanks burst and the oil caught on fire. It moved down the harbor and toward the dock. When it got to the dock we wondered if we'd been saved on board the *Empress* just to get burned. The captain had all the boats launched on the far side away from the fire and was all ready to put us into them. We couldn't go on the side toward the fire of course. It was too hot. They were playing the hoses on it to drive it away. It kept coming on though.

"All the time they were working to cut through the anchor chain that had fouled in the propeller. Just to cut it away from the boat. Finally they got the *Empress* away from the dock. It was wonderful the way they got her away without any tug. It was something you wouldn't have believed it was possible to do in Yokohama harbor. It was wonderful.

"Of course they were bringing wounded people and refugees on all day and all night. They came out in sampans or anything. They took them all on. We slept on the deck.

"My husband said he was relieved when we'd got outside the breakwater," the mother said. "There're supposed to be two old craters in the harbor itself, and he was worried that something was going to happen from them."

"Was there no tidal wave?" asked the reporter.

"No. There wasn't any at all. When we were on our way to Kobe, after we had left Yokohama finally, there were three or four small shocks that you could feel in the boat. But there weren't any tidal waves."

Her mind was going back to Yokohama harbor. "Some of the people that had stood up all night in the water were very tired," she offered.

"Oh, the people that had stood up all night in the water," said the reporter softly.

"Yes, to keep out of the fire. There was one old woman who must have been seventy-six years old. She was in the water all night. There were lots of people in the canals, too. Yokohama's all cut up with canals, you know."

"Didn't that make it more confused in the earthquake?" asked the girl reporter.

"Oh, no. They were very good things to have in a fire," said the mother quite serenely.

"What did you think when it started?" asked the reporter.

"Oh, we knew it was an earthquake," said the mother. "It was just that nobody knew it was going to be so bad. There's been lots of earthquakes there. Once, nine years ago, we'd had five shocks in one day. We just wanted to get into the town to see if everything was all right. But when we saw it was so bad, we knew then it didn't matter about things. I hadn't intended to come home. Just my daughter and son were sailing. My husband is still in Kobe. He has a lot of work to do now reorganizing."

Just then the telephone rang. "My mother is busy just now interviewing the reporters," the daughter said in the next room. She was talking with some friends that had come in. It was something about music. The reporter listened with his odd ear for a moment to see if it was anything about the earthquake. But it wasn't.

The mother was very tired. The girl reporter stood up. The reporter got up.

"You understand. No names," said the mother.

"You're sure? They wouldn't do any harm, you know."

"You said you wouldn't use the names," the mother said wearily. The reporters went out. The friends stood up as they went through the room.

The reporter took a look at the Japanese kimono as the door was shut.

"Who's going to write the story. You or me?" asked the girl reporter.

"I don't know," said the reporter.

Lord Birkenhead

☆ THE TORONTO DAILY STAR
October 4, 1923

Lord Birkenhead, the austere, unapproachable, super-cynical and supercilious Earl of Birkenhead is a myth.

On the Woolsack as Lord High Chancellor in a wax-white wig he had the profile of a pharaoh and the grave and graven immobility of a sphinx.

When the *Star* saw him at the breakfast table in his private car at the Union Station, he wore a madonna or cigar-blue sweater coat and a Roman punch or Roman stripe tie. These were tennis togs and he was keener for postprandial tennis than for postprandial oratory.

He is supposed to have a personality that bristles with thorns of mordant wit. He has been called a stream of lava, a political scorpion, a douche of vitriol and other things that indicate verbal asperity. Above all he was said to have a dislike of interviews.

However that may be, his Canadian tour has put him in excellent humor. Toronto smiled on him with a warm October sun and he smiled back at Toronto, even though the only indication of a civic welcome was a great pile of milk cans—empties—on the platform alongside his car.

He was cheerful, affable, chatty, but of course not too politically or personally communicative. The *Star* was equipped with a formidable list of questions as if he were the Encyclopaedia Britannica. But he has disclaimed that distinction. He has won many honors but that is not one of them.

"Do you care to say anything about the League of Nations or your estimate of Woodrow Wilson?" asked the *Star*. "I have said my say on that," he replied. "I retract nothing, but there is no point in stirring the matter up again."

He was not discussing those high problems during his trip. "Oh dear, no," he said. "I am just giving my reminiscences of twenty years of public life, the celebrities I have met and so forth."

On the question of Prohibition he did not mince matters but he was judicial rather than vitriolic. "You cannot say that Prohibition in the States has been a failure. You cannot say it has been a success. For myself I do not like it."

"Then it is not true," remarked the *Star*, "that you have made a wager of $5,000 that you would be a Prohibitionist for two years."

It was not true. His views on this matter were not undergoing any conversion into specie. Neither was it true that he had given up smoking for health reasons. The long after-breakfast cigar in his mouth, the tan on his face and his general appearance of health and vigor belied that rumor. In fact, in his flannels and striped tie, he looked not unlike one of the Leander rowing men, except, for course, for a slight discrepancy at the waist.

"Is there any English opinion on the matter of rum-running?" asked the *Star*, pursuing the Prohibition topic. "Not that I am aware of," said he. "We feel no obligation to help in the enforcement of American sumptuary laws. That is their own internal question. It is not for us to interfere."

He did not wish to pose as a political prophet but he saw no signs of England going dry. England's humidity would last his time. After him the drought, perhaps, but it was a very great perhaps.

"Then Lady Astor's broom is not really sweeping England?" He shrugged his shoulders and smiled. "England will never tolerate," he went on, "a condition of things under which wealthy men have special liquor privileges. Our people would rebel against inequalities in this matter. Prohibition has, of course, certain things to its credit. It has another thing to its debit, the infringement of personal liberty, and social and legal inequalities."

Lord Birkenhead, as F. E. Smith, which some after his phenomenal success at the bar called "Fee" Smith, won all the prizes Balliol had to offer. The talk turned on Oxford and the good port at the high tables and the exceedingly bad port at the undergraduate tables. Here Lord Birkenhead indulged in a legal jest. "*Lex non curat de minimis*," said he. That is to say the Dons do not worry about undergraduate stomachs. After all even England has inequalities in the matter of liquor.

Asked if he approved of the Canadian appeal to the Privy Council, he gave a cautious opinion which he has given before. "We are pleased to act," said he, "as your supreme court of judicature. We assign to it our best judges. It is for you to say when that system shall cease." But while it lasted, English judges were proud to devote their talents to the elucidation of Canadian legal mysteries. But it was a labor of love and glory, not of profit, for it imposed extra and unpaid burdens.

"Some people here," said the reporter, "complain of the expense."

"We cannot be expected to provide litigants with transportation," laughed the earl. "If that were so all our legal roads would lead to London."

Lighter questions seemed more appropriate to the breakfast table. "When is the prince going to get married?" asked the *Star*.

"How should I know," laughed Lord Birkenhead. When he passed through Alberta the other day, the prince had not summoned him to communicate any matrimonial secret.

But what about the girl in green? Did he know anything about the girl in green? Again Lord Birkenhead laughed. He had been keeper of the Great Seal. He was not his prince's keeper.

The reporter left the girl in green and asked: "What of the movies? What do you think of the movies?"

The ex-lord high chancellor did not frown on this frivolous inquiry. "You should ask my daughter," said he with a laugh. "She is our family authority on the moving pictures."

Unfortunately Lady Eleanor is not with him. She has remained behind in New York, where movies are at their best. But was it true as rumored that she was going to appear on the screen?

The thought of his daughter becoming a moving picture actress did not appear to disturb Lord Birkenhead in the least. He who is so modern in every detail is also a modern father. "She will no doubt do as she pleases," he replied indulgently. But it was not at all likely that she would please.

Still, with all his modernity Lord Birkenhead did not seem quite to appreciate the function of women in modern journalism. A woman reporter from the *Star* dropped in in quest of the absent Lady Eleanor. "I do not know how I can help you," said he. "I suppose you do fashions." He felt inadequate to discuss fashions. Modern woman's attire was too scant a subject for his formidable intellect.

But he was not asked to discuss fashions and in a wondering, half-admiring and possibly faintly ironical way he expressed his surprise at North American interviewers whether male or female. In England public men mostly gave formal statements. They did not sit for their portraits. But he did not seem to object to sitting for his portrait.

"In England," said he, "the press asked me questions when I left. They will also make inquiries when I return." It was only an occasional tribulation.

Was that true of Lloyd George?

"Lloyd George," said he, "is well aware of the personal prestige that comes from constant appearance in the press, but he prefers to give his opinions formally. He is not too willing to throw himself on the mercies of casual interviewers."

But Lord Birkenhead himself was not formal, not this morning at least. "I haven't any opinions today," said he, "formal or informal. I'm off to play tennis. Do the best you can for me."

This interview, brief and informal as it was, serves at least to dispel three myths about this mystery man of modern English politics: that he is a Prohibitionist, that he had given up smoking and that he is blunt and ungracious to interviewers.

If Lord Birkenhead can be a mental thistle, a political nettle that cannot be interrogated too closely, particularly about Wilsonian idealism, he has nonetheless a gracious exterior. The sting of his wit and irony is well concealed by the debonair down of conversational ease and personal amiability.

But, as he said, it was too fine a day and too early in the morning to talk politics.

Last night he spoke in Massey Hall, roaming about at will through the fields of political history and even dealing to a considerable extent in futures. He was an oratorical stereopticon, exhibiting a series of views on what has taken place, is now taking place, and is about to take place in Britain, and those who have shared, are sharing, and are about to share in the responsibilities of making it happen.

Lloyd George Willing to Address 10,000

☆ THE TORONTO DAILY STAR
October 5, 1923

New York.—Sir Alfred Cope promised the *Star* this morning that Lloyd George would address an overflow meeting either at the [Toronto] Arena Gardens or at the Coliseum. "A wire will be sent to the mayor to make the necessary arrangements as soon as Lloyd George arrives this morning," Sir Alfred said. "If they can get 10,000 people in, all the better. Lloyd George will not be able to speak more than twenty minutes, but we want everyone to hear him. Voice amplifiers should be arranged for."

The Arrival of Lloyd George

☆ THE TORONTO DAILY STAR
October 5, 1923

New York.—While the gigantic *Mauretania*, tall as a cliff, lay off quarantine outside New York harbor today waiting for the early morning fog to lift, a short, thickset, ruddy faced little man with a thick patriarchal mane of white hair was dressing in his cabin before going on deck early.

No one knows what he was thinking about, but one may venture the opinion that as he thought of the new world it must have come into his mind that he, David Lloyd George, is the one great survivor of the wreck of the Old World.

He has been spared for something. Perhaps it is to save the world. He tried that once at an old seaport town called Genoa. All the nations who hate each other met and sat down to the conference table together. When they snarled and refused to discuss world problems, Lloyd George calmed them and brought them together. When France or Russia threatened to go away, Lloyd George talked and they stayed.

I heard him talk there in times of crisis and he was very wonderful. But he could not stay. He had to get back to London and finally "the ship of Genoa," as he always called it, went on the rocks and all the nations went away.

They say that Genoa and the Near East gave him his death blow in politics. But talking with him on the *Mauretania* today I could see that nothing could ever give him a death blow. The political sword that will kill him has not yet been forged. Not yet.

Genoa was a tragic conference. The last of the great conferences. The conference that he dominated. Of the men who sat with Lloyd George there, Walther Rathenau, cold and idealistic, was shot in the back in his town motorcar as he drove to the foreign office in Berlin.

Vorovsky, the Russian, scholarly and kindly, was murdered at the table as he drank his after-dinner coffee in a hotel in Lausanne.

Stambouliski, a roaring bull of a man who worked only for the good of Bulgaria, was hunted down and killed in a field by his own soldiers while he tried to hide in a straw stack.

Gounaris, the Greek premier, was carried from his bed sick with typhoid to stand before the firing squad in a drizzling rain in the courtyard of the military hospital.

All this within a year.

But Lloyd George carries not one scar from that conference. He is the great survivor.

There was Lord Northcliffe too. Northcliffe, who had been a friend of Lloyd George and then hated him and swore to drive him from office.

"I've been in the government for sixteen years," Lloyd George told George Adam one night at Genoa. "I've had a long time of it. But I will not be driven from office by that man Northcliffe."

Adam has written of the incident. That was when the attacks on Lloyd George were at their bitterest. But Lord Northcliffe was dead and buried before Lloyd George ever relinquished the premiership.

He is a fighter, Lloyd George. But he knows the truth of what Gabriele D'Annunzio says, "*Morire non basta.*" "It is not enough to die." You must survive to win.

The Little Welshman Lands

☆ THE TORONTO DAILY STAR
October 6, 1923

New York.—The first sight of Lloyd George was standing high up on the top deck of the *Mauretania* with Dame Margaret and Megan. The *Mauretania* lay at anchor under the bluffs of Staten Island with a tug along each side snuggling close. Then the revenue cutter touched and after a minute's parleying a crowd of newspapermen went over the side like a boarding party.

Lloyd George had disappeared. The pack hunted from deck to deck and finally his secretary appeared. There was a shout "He's coming," and then he came into the after saloon. About fifty newspapermen were standing. One chair had been reserved. Lloyd George seated himself. He smiled. "Ah, so this is the electrocuting chair," he said.

Lloyd George looks older. He is short, thickset, rather heavy with a double chin and that flowing mane of white hair that is getting thin on the very top. When he smiles his face is the face of Puck. A rising sun of wrinkles goes out from each eye. Everyone laughs with him. But he is older. As you stand close to him you see that when he stops smiling the laugh wrinkles remain. Today he wore an old gray four-in-hand tie, a fur-lined black ulster, and a silk hat that sat incongruously on his thick hair.

"Have you any message for Canada?" I asked him.

"No. I have a message that I am most anxious to deliver, but I will not deliver it until we reach Montreal." Lloyd George smiled. "I've been in Canada, you know. I crossed all the way to Vancouver, but they tell me there are great changes now. I am most anxious to visit Canada, and look forward to Toronto.

"I am not coming to the United States to say anything, but to see a good deal," Lloyd George continued. "I've been anticipating this visit for many years but I've been a busy man. I want especially to see the country. That is why I am going to travel as far as I can by daylight."

"What do you think about the European situation?" asked a reporter.

"Well, it is not very good, is it?" Lloyd George answered. His accent is not English but thicker with a Welsh burr.

"I should like very much to have a game of golf on this trip, but—" Lloyd George's face went into that complete smile again. "I'll take jolly good care the press is not around when I have it."

"Do you think the Labor party has about reached its limit?" Lloyd George was asked. "That depends on how it behaves." He shook his head and spoke very considerately. "I think it will have to behave better."

"The anti-Semitic propagandists are remarkably stupid, remarkably stupid," Lloyd George told a Jewish reporter, who asked him what he thought of anti-Semitism as a danger spot.

"Do you think the League of Nations was weakened by the Italian action?" I asked. Lloyd George answered immediately: "Yes, I think it was."

"Mr. George, do you think the world is any better for the Versailles treaty?" a reporter asked. Lloyd George was emphatic. "I don't think the mischief is with the Versailles treaty but rather with the way it is carried out." He paused and considered, then smiled. "That is a long story, a very long story."

A cartoonist brought forward a picture for Lloyd George to sign. Lloyd George took the pencil and then looked at the cartoon. Then he was swept with laughter. He laughed and laughed, holding the picture in his hand. "Hello, hello," he laughed. "Do I really look like that?"

We went up the deck. Down in the harbor below the steep sides of the *Mauretania* was a tug gaily decorated with white and blue, against which was a great banner "Welcome to Lloyd George, great friend of the Greeks" and the band on the tug was playing, "Yes, we have no bananas."

I pointed the boat out to him. "Yes, I have been a great friend to them," Lloyd George said under his breath.

On the top deck the photographers and movie men were massed. Photographers shoved and jostled Sir Alfred Mond, Secretary of Labor Davis, Melville Stone of the Associated Press, Charles Schwab and other notables. It was a jam with all the photographers shouting, "Mr. George, Mr. George, just this way, Mr. George. Look up, Mr. George. Mr. George, just once more. Look this way. Hey you in the gray hat [Mr. Schwab], get out of the way. Now, Mr. George." Finally it was over. But he has been christened. To Americans he is Mr. George.

"Do you think the League of Nations can be a going concern without the United States?" a reporter shouted at Lloyd George as he walked along the deck. "No," Lloyd George said over his shoulder.

His secretaries, the official welcomers, including Acting Mayor Hulbert, who is substituting for Mayor Hylan, who is sick at his home in Brooklyn, got him off the *Mauretania* on to the mayor's boat of welcome, where the reporters who had not got up at five o'clock to be sure and be aboard the revenue cutter were still waiting.

The Greek boat of welcome followed just behind the mayor's boat, bands playing, people waving and with Mr. Lloyd George and his wife and daughter in the pilot house, the mayor's boat steamed down the bay. The little boat forged through the choppy harbor past the anchored ships until on the left the oxidized green Statue of Liberty came in sight. An old four stacker was riding at anchor and a row of coal barges that had once been white-sailed ships slipped along. On the right were the low sheds of Governors Island and through the smoke the great town looking high and dim and ghostly.

Lloyd George watched it all with eager interest. Various volunteer guides gave him information of various degrees of accuracy. Then the smoke and mist cleared and the buildings became harder and clearer. New York from the harbor is as beautiful as Constantinople but with a hard, high, white cubic beauty of its own. The bands played. There was a great crowd of people massed on shore. It was the greatest welcome any Britisher has ever received in America. The Battery was black with people.

Through a solid mass of people, held back by cordons of police, Lloyd George and his party in motorcars rode up the sunless canyon of lower Broadway to the city hall, where he was met by Acting Mayor Hulbert and given the proverbial keys of the city. All the way along the route the white streamers of ticker tape that are Manhattan's accolade shot down from the tall buildings.

A few paraders with signs and banners branding Lloyd George as an undesirable alien and objecting to his presence in New York were arrested by police and their signs taken away. Just before the Lloyd George party reached the old brown City Hall that stands in a green square in the heart of the new city, incongruous with its brown striped awnings and its wide porch in the midst of the great buildings, another rush was made by members of an Irish society to get their banners into position before the hall, but the banners were seized and torn up by the police. Meanwhile on the pavement boys were selling big stacks of German marks at five cents the thousand-mark bill and doing a thriving trade.

From the City Hall Lloyd George went to the Waldorf to rest a moment before going to the Biltmore, where he is being entertained by the United Press at a luncheon.

Seeing the three of them together, it is impossible to say who look the most alike. For they all look alike. Lloyd George, Dame Margaret and Megan. Lloyd George is the tallest and Megan the shortest but Dame Margaret is the only one in the family with a title.

Megan Lloyd George is twenty-one years old and a very pretty girl. She is petite, smiles shyly, talks very low, very softly and very intelligently. She does not photograph well because her features are small, but that is a family trait. Neither her father nor her mother takes good pictures.

"I'm so glad to be here in New York and to be going to Canada," she told the *Star* on the *Mauretania* this morning. Asked if she would take up a political career, she said: "I love the life, but I am much too young to decide."

"How do you like being a sidelight to your father?" asked the *Star*. "Oh, I don't feel like a sidelight at all," Megan answered.

Miss Megan does not smoke, "but," she told the *Star*, "I don't care if other people do. I adore going with my father and love seeing the different cities. At the different conferences I have had such a good time dancing. I love to dance."

"How do you like American girls?" asked the *Star*. "I know several American girls," Megan answered, "and like them tremendously, and I don't believe they have a bit too much freedom."

Miss Megan was dressed in a black velvet suit with a white blouse with red buttonholes and a red collar, a tight-fitting black hat, light stockings and black strapped slippers. Her hair is not bobbed but she wears it as though it were.

She told the *Star* she had been to two schools in London and one in Paris and is glad she doesn't have to go to any more. She does not use cosmetics. She is a good sailor and did not miss a meal on the boat in spite of a moderate gale.

"How about marriage?" asked the *Star*. "Oh, I am much too young to think about that," Megan answered.

Miss Megan had been her father's constant companion on all his conferences—Cannes, Spa, Genoa and at Versailles—and has probably seen the making of more history than any girl in the world.

"Is it very good?" she asked the *Star* when told that it had been arranged for all the Lloyd George family to go to Irving Berlin's *Music Box Revue* tonight.

Dame Margaret Lloyd George is very motherly, very wholesome, and very Welsh. "I am most anxious to come to Canada," Dame Margaret told the *Star*. "I know and like so many Canadian people and I look forward to meeting the many Welsh people that I know are there."

While the *Star* was talking with Dame Margaret, Secretary of Labor Davis came up and greeted her in Welsh. The *Star* could not follow this conversation but the secretary explained that he was trying to get a maid to travel with Dame Margaret. There are no servants in the Lloyd George retinue.

Dame Margaret told the *Star* she has five children, three sons and a married daughter living in India, and Megan. Dame Margaret smiled at this. Everybody in the Lloyd George family smiles when Megan's name is mentioned. And by the way Megan is pronounced Maygin.

"Of course I have no impressions yet," she told the *Star*, "but with the sun out and the beautiful day, everything is in our favor, isn't it? We have planned to do no shopping in New York and we have no social program outside of traveling with Mr. Lloyd George. That will keep us occupied, rather."

Dame Margaret wore a black moiré silk hat with a pleated ruffle in the front, a black coat of pressed fur looking like seal, with a kolinsky stole and a string of pearls. Her dress was black.

Lloyd George's Wonderful Voice

☆ THE TORONTO DAILY STAR
October 6, 1923

New York.—Yesterday afternoon in the banquet hall on the nineteenth floor of the Biltmore, the *Star* heard Lloyd George make his first real speech in America.

It was a big luncheon given by the United Press for the former prime minister and until the speeches began all the reporters present were under a pledge not to send any messages. Lloyd George was to speak but his speech was not a private one. At the last moment the reporters were informed that it had been decided the speech was for publication.

The *Star* watched Lloyd George finish a hearty luncheon at the head one of the six tables on the banquet floor, Newton D. Baker introducing the famous statesman.

While Mr. Baker was speaking, Lloyd George leaned forward and toyed with his spectacles. It is his old trick while getting ready to speak. There was a thin sputter of applause several times during Baker's speech, but the audience was impatient with the preliminaries. They wanted Lloyd George. Lloyd George who sat there grave and dignified playing with his spectacles and making phrases in his mind.

The Lloyd George who rose to speak was not the "Mister George" of the "Hey this way, Mister George" of the photographers.

It was the Lloyd George of the great days who spoke, and as he spoke the *Star* tried to analyze what it is that makes him the really wonderful orator he is. While you are writing his words on the paper they die and lose their greatness. If you remember them they move you, but once they have been reduced to lead marks on paper they are far less effective. True, he said very fine and very strong things, but in type the essence of them is gone.

It is his wonderful voice combined with his Gaelic gift of prophecy that strikes one. When he talks, you feel he is a prophet and prophets have a way of their own. He talks much as Peter the Hermit must have talked about the Crusades. If Sarah Bernhardt's voice was golden, and it was,

Lloyd George's is hammered gold. He must love to use it. His preaching voice is very different from his speaking voice, which is rather ordinary, although with a strain of richness in it.

"Canada sent 400,000 troops to fight for our flag," he told his audience. "Not one of those would have come in response to a decree from Downing Street. They were the fruit of the independence you taught us. We could not have enrolled a single company of Canadians if we had issued an order that [they] should be impressed for the support of the British Empire. They came of their own free will on the appeal of their own ministers, supported by their own Parliament, elected by their own people and the lesson you taught us in the eighteenth century has been the salvation of the British Empire, as we know it today.

"The real founder of the British Empire as we know it was George Washington. Washington taught us to make it a democratic empire. Canada is as free from any interference with her own affairs from Downing Street as America.

"In London at this hour we have representatives of the great dominions of the British crown, all sitting under conditions of perfect equality.

"Among them is General Smuts who twenty or thirty years ago fought against the British forces for the independence of his native land and afterwards signed a treaty to become an independent partner in the Empire. We have Mr. Cosgrove, the head of the Irish Free State, sitting there as the result of a treaty representing a free people with the most complete independence as far as their internal affairs are concerned. We owe that something that is of strength to us, something that is a source of power to us, a something that is a source of might to us—we owe that entirely to the lessons from you, the free people of this great country, and so far from any resentment, from any feeling of regret in British hearts, we have nothing but a feeling of gratitude for the great men who founded this great republic and in doing so taught Britain how to govern free people."

That was the best part of his speech. But it was not what held his audience most. A certain way of saying "Empire," a bite in his voice when he spoke of military domination and the great feeling of the prophet held them tight with him.

Later the *Star* met Lloyd George at his evening press conference. Lloyd George sat tipped back in a chair in a ballroom in the Waldorf before a huge mirror and answered questions [as] fast as they were asked.

"Do you think Liberal reunion is coming?" brought the answer, "Oh yes, it's coming, like all good things, it's coming."

"Would you like to see more women in politics?" He answered, chuckling, "That depends on the kind of women."

The *Star* asked Lloyd George about the Imperial Conference, but he said he had heard nothing except fragmentary reports by wireless and could not discuss it as yet.

As he stepped into the elevator, he said: "I'm going to get an hour's sleep now before dinner." The elevator shut.

Miss Megan George a Hit

☆ THE TORONTO DAILY STAR
October 6, 1923

New York.—Miss Megan George is the idol of the ship news reporters. These hard-boiled men, who are used to greeting the early-morning faces of famous movie stars and visiting foreign beauties, were completely knocked over by the youngest of the Lloyd George family.

"She doesn't have to tell us she doesn't use cosmetics," one reporter said. "We've seen them come off at seven o'clock in the morning before. She's a wonder, I tell you."

Luis Angel Firpo was in the crowd that met Lloyd George at the City Hall. He had a ticket for the mayor's boat, but there was a celebration dinner last night, to celebrate his re-embracing his Argentine citizenship, and the boat left a little early.

The *Star*, after talking and walking with Lloyd George about the Mauretania for nearly an hour, stepped with the former premier on board the Macon to go ashore. The *Star* had gotten up at an early hour on the morning to attend to the welcoming business aboard the revenue cutter for which, fortunately for many newspapermen and -women, official government passes were necessary.

At the Theater with Lloyd George

☆ THE TORONTO STAR WEEKLY
October 6, 1923

New York.—Lloyd George attended the *Music Box Revue* last night. In front of the theater the street was jammed solid with people waiting to see him. Police had difficulty in keeping the entrance open.

When Dame Margaret entered the box first in a light-purple evening gown, no one recognized her. Then came Megan, her hair parted in the center and drawn low over her ears. A sputtering of handclapping broke out. Lloyd George followed Megan into the box wearing a big cape, his hair hanging over his collar in the back, one of his four double chins resting on the high collar in front. With his silvery hair and his keen face, he looked in the big cape like some retired medieval fencing master.

There was a storm of applause in the theater and then the party seated themselves. There were twelve others in the box, including Sir Alfred Mond, Mrs. Charles Dana Gibson, Thomas Lamont. The curtain rose. The music began and Lloyd George leaned forward, his chin on his hand, one finger pressing into his cheek. He chuckled at each real joke and caught them all. Megan had wrapped a Spanish shawl, a souvenir of last winter's trip to Algeciras, around her shoulders, and both she and her mother never took their eyes from the stage. They did not laugh quite as quickly as Lloyd George at some of the jokes but enjoyed the show tremendously.

On the stage a man was supposed to be having a dream in which he is married to an absolutely charming and beautiful wife. "God pity the poor bachelors on a night like this," he cried, and Lloyd George rocked with laughing.

A moment later the man's real wife awakens him rudely. This also was good for a laugh.

Then a tenor in a shiny satin dinner coat came out and began to sing. While he sang, the girls he sang of appeared back of a film and gracefully postured into sight and out again. It was very pretty.

Sir Alfred was enthusiastic about the Zionist movement and talked with a boyish enthusiasm. "You know when they mention Lloyd George's name at a meeting everybody goes crazy," he said. "They're absolutely wild about him."

Irish Republican sympathizers had little luck with Lloyd George in New York. While the George party were in the Music Box Theater last night, about forty men and women made a demonstration outside, but were shooed on by the police without any arrests being made. Most of them returned and stood in the dense crowd that packed the opposite side of Forty-fifth Street. When the former prime minister and his party came out of the theater, the hecklers started to shout and threw a few eggs, but their range was from ten to twenty yards short. Flanked by motorcycle police and the friendly crowd, Lloyd George's car rolled away untouched. The hysterical women among the de Valera agitators were cheered ironically by the crowd, which took the whole affair as a joke.

Hearst Not Paying Lloyd George

☆ THE TORONTO STAR WEEKLY
October 6, 1923

Aboard Lloyd George's Special.—In the special car "Ottawa" attached to a special train provided by the Canadian National Railways, Lloyd George is speeding toward Canada today.

The train is guarded by state constabulary armed with pistols, who patrol each station as the train stops. Lloyd George is wearing a flowing artist's tie, an old hat and has discarded his ulster. He is enjoying the trip immensely. He is traveling by day in order to see the country and has a perfect October day for the trip past the Palisades and through the historic Vermont country.

There was some talk this morning that Lloyd George will extend his Canadian trip to Vancouver.

"It seems a shame that he should get up to Canada and not go to the coast," Sir Henry Thornton, whose private car precedes Lloyd George's on the train, told the *Star* today.

Lloyd George will be strongly urged to make the Vancouver trip.

Sir Alfred Cope [Lloyd George's secretary] told the *Star*, however, he believed Lloyd George's program would make the extension impossible.

Lloyd George made platform appearances for crowds who came to see him at Albany, Troy, North Bennington, Vermont, Manchester, Vermont, and Rutland. The special train is due to arrive at Montreal at 9:15 tonight and in addition to the dignitaries will be met by a reception committee in Welsh costume.

Lloyd George and his party lunched today as the guests of Sir Henry and Lady Thornton aboard the C.N.R. president's private car. Sir Henry, wearing a cap, looks very much like Babe Ruth. Miss Ann Thornton [his daughter] and Megan George are becoming great friends. G. H. Ingalls, vice-president of the New York Central, and J. E. Dalrymple, vice-president of the Canadian National, were also luncheon guests.

After leaving Troy the train has been winding through the green hills of upper New York State. The trees are all turning, the beeches yellow, the maples red. It is a glorious landscape and a perfect day for the trip. Lloyd George has been enthusiastic about the beauty of the country.

A current like an electric wire of human sympathy stretches across the seas between England and America, Lloyd George told a crowd of five hundred people at Troy, while his special train, which arrives in Montreal [Saturday], stopped for five minutes.

"No man took a greater part in settling the ago-old dispute between Britain and Ireland than your fellow townsman and ex-governor, Martin H. Glynn," Lloyd George told an audience of three thousand people gathered to hear him at Albany today. "He explained to me the views of an Irishman and I told him the aims of Britain in rather a dingy room in the House of Commons."

A strong cordon of police, around the platform Lloyd George spoke from, attempted to keep Sir Henry Thornton from getting near the speaker. Lloyd George was introduced by the ex-governor, an old Downing Street acquaintance who traveled to Albany with him aboard the special car "Ottawa." The street below the Albany station was full of people. A band played "Men of Harlech" and then "Auld Lang Syne" as the train pulled out after a ten-minute halt.

Albany, N.Y.—Sir Alfred Cope, speaking for Lloyd George, made the following statement to the *Star* this morning in answer to an editorial in the *London Morning Post*, which was reprinted in the *New York Times* this morning:

"Mr. Lloyd George is not here for the Hearst press nor for the United Press or any other newspaper organization. He is here as a private citizen and is paying his own expenses except in Canada, where he is the guest of the Canadian government, and some expenses that are paid in the United States by Corsedd. I have refused offers of three and four thousand dollars for him to lecture, making only a 20-minute speech. All journalists who accompany him must make their own arrangements with the railway companies. Peter B. Kyne was engaged by me to help handle Lloyd George's tour in the States. He was not hired as a Hearst man, but as a man with practical experience, a novelist and author and a man who is free to sell his work wherever he wishes. As a matter of fact, he tells me his contract with Hearst expired a few days ago.

"Lloyd George is urged to speak several times in each town he will stop at, but in return for his speech he wants the rest of his time to get the American and Canadian views. That is what he is here for. To see the country and to know the people. He is not here on a lecture tour."

"A Man of the People"

☆ THE TORONTO DAILY STAR
October 8, 1923

Montreal.—"I am a man of the people and I have fought all my life for the people. I have had more sympathy and support from Americans in my fight for democracy than from almost any other country," Lloyd George told the crowds who gathered around the rear platform of his car on Saturday at Troy, N.Y., and North Bennington and Manchester, Vt., to see and hear the famous wartime prime minister.

Although Lloyd George is universally popular with Americans, some of them seem just a bit confused as to who he is. One New Yorker said to the *Star*: "I guess there wasn't anybody else could take the helm the way he did. I have just finished reading his book, *Men Like Gods* [by H. G. Wells]. I guess things would be pretty good all right if we had that Utopia, eh?"

It was a very impressive moment when David Lloyd George met the son of Abraham Lincoln. A crowd of villagers pressed around but stood a little back from the two. "Just a moment. I want to have Megan here to shake your hand," Lloyd George said. Megan came out from the car and stood demure and shy before the white-haired, bearded old man. "I am most glad to meet you, my dear," said Mr. [Robert Todd] Lincoln.

"How old were you when your father died?" Lloyd George asked. "Just twenty-one," Mr. Lincoln said. "I was away at college when he was killed." Mr. Lincoln is eighty-four now. The special train only had four minutes allowed it to stop and while Lloyd George and Mr. Lincoln were still talking the whistle blew for the departure.

"My principal recollection of Toronto [in 1889] was being got up in the middle of the night by some newspaperman who wanted my opinion as to whether there was going to be war [in South Africa] or not," Lloyd George told the *Star* as his train neared Montreal. "Yes, I attended my first cabinet meeting there too. Ross was premier then. Yes, that was the very first cabinet meeting. That was before the Boer War.

"From Toronto I went out on the prairie, out in Saskatchewan," he said, leaning back in his seat in his private car and smoking. "I remember a town there called Rapid City. And another called Carlyle. It was near

Carlyle that I saw a coyote. He was loping along ahead of us." Continuing his reminiscences of that trip of thirty-four years ago, "Yes, it was near Carlyle that there was a meeting going on one Sunday morning. People had come for miles to go to the church."

He gave several reminiscences of the great anti-war meeting in Birmingham at the time of the Boer War when he was nearly mobbed. "They really had me if they had known it. The man who was inciting the mob stood on the window ledge just outside the room I was in. He could have gotten me by simply smashing the glass." His eyes twinkled. "But they didn't know I was in there hearing all these passionate denunciations of myself. No, I did not escape wearing a policeman's coat. I simply marched out with the police. No one knew me then and I was not recognized."

Lloyd George seldom prepares his speeches in advance.

"I have a pretty good idea what I am going to say, so it is never written out in advance," he explained to the *Star*.

Count Apponyi and the Loan

☆ THE TORONTO DAILY STAR
October 15, 1923

Count Albert Apponyi, 77 years old, for fifty years one of Hungary's greatest statesmen, head of the Hungarian peace delegation at Paris, and one of the few surviving idealists of Europe, arrived in Toronto this morning.

Count Apponyi is tall, a head taller than ordinary men, and looks like a combination of Colonel [George Taylor] Denison and Anatole France. He has enormous brown hands, a quick smile, a leathery, seamed, aristocratic Magyar face, white hair and beard.

The *Star* brought him the first news that the Inter-Allied Reparations Commission had unanimously adopted a resolution requesting the League of Nations to reorganize Hungarian finances as they had those of Austria, commencing with a loan of £24,000,000 to the stricken country on the international markets.

"This is great news," Count Apponyi said. "It is a matter of the greatest need and urgency. This move marks the turning of the tide for Hungary."

Count Apponyi arrived this morning from Chicago, where he saw Lloyd George. It was a dramatic meeting between the two statesmen.

They met at the speakers' table of the great luncheon given in Lloyd George's honor by the Chicago Association of Commerce at the Hotel La Salle.

Lloyd George, short of stature and dynamic, left his place and walked with hand outstretched to where sat Count Apponyi, tall, venerable of years, an artist's portrait, almost, a product of a culture that is a thousand years old.

Count Apponyi rose, his hand met Lloyd George's in a warm, firm clasp, and with one impulse the audience leaped to its feet in a storm of cheering and applause.

When Lloyd George returned to his seat, he turned to Mayor Dever and Judson Stone, at his right and left, and said: "I consider Count Apponyi one of the most brilliant statesmen of Europe."

The audience cheered for eight minutes.

"I had never heard Lloyd George before," Count Apponyi said. His eyes twinkled. "But he had heard me. It was a great pleasure to hear him. He was received with tremendous enthusiasm."

The occasion referred to by Count Apponyi when Lloyd George had heard him speak was the famous presentation of the cause of Hungary that the count made at Paris during the peace conference, an appeal that has been unmatched for pathos and unrivaled eloquence.

Count Apponyi was met at the station by Col. J. B. Maclean, of Toronto, and Prof. Mavor, of Toronto University, who is an old friend of the Hungarian statesman. He was accompanied by his manager and friend, Dr. M. A. de Josika-Herezeg, Ph.D. His daughter, Countess Marika, is coming direct to Toronto from Newport and will arrive this evening. She will be the guest of Col. and Mrs. Maclean while stopping here.

Count Apponyi's wife, who is a daughter of Count Mendorf and a cousin of His Majesty King George, did not come to Canada on this trip, but will be on his next trip to Canada.

Count Apponyi, who was in Toronto eleven years ago, speaks twice in Toronto today, at luncheon at the Empire Club, and at 8:30 this evening at the university. He will speak in English, one of the six languages he speaks with equal clarity and eloquence.

"I will speak in Canada at least once on the League of Nations," Count Apponyi told the *Star*. "It may be tonight. I never know just exactly what I will say until I see the audience."

Count Apponyi looks his age as you stand close to him. But [he] has a super-vitality. His white hair is close-cropped, his features huge, and through the wiry, white haze of his square-cut beard you see that his chin is really not prominent. In fact, it is rather receding than otherwise.

"I did not touch on the league in the States," the count continued. "It is not a popular subject there. Yes, I am pro-league myself. And I want to talk not on its limitations, but on what it is able to accomplish."

"How do you regard the present German crisis?" asked the *Star*.

"It is not for me to discuss the causes of that condition but unless something is done to check it there will be chaos."

Count Apponyi was rolling down his sleeves, dressing in his room at the York Club before going out to speak. As he talked his accent grew clearer and less cloudy. He was in deadly earnest. "Unless something relieves the tension in Germany, chaos will come—and then perhaps Ludendorff."

"You think there will be a return to the monarchy?" the *Star* questioned.

"No, not necessarily, but there will be the uniting of all the policies of despair. The despair will unite. It may be aid from Russia. Yet the statesmen of Europe seem to be blind to this." Count Apponyi spread out his great, brown, freckled hands. "They seem to be blind to it all.

"There is no present prospect of the restoration of the legitimate monarchy in Hungary," Count Apponyi told the *Star*. "I saw the queen, who is in exile."

"The Empress Zita?" suggested the *Star*.

Count Apponyi has spent a lifetime in the Magyar cause, often ranged against the Austro-Hungarian Empire.

"We prefer to call her the Queen Zita. She was only interested in educating her children. She was not thinking of any attempted restoration."

"To you, an outsider," smiled the count, "she is the ex-empress. To us she is the queen."

Hungary has only two alternatives, according to Count Apponyi. To maintain the present government or to restore the legitimate monarchy. That is, the son of the late King Karl and Queen Zita, who is living on the Basque coast near San Sebastian.

"The people of Hungary are fundamentally opposed to the idea of a republic," Count Apponyi stated.

"There is [a] great deal of talk sometimes that Admiral Horthy will be made king?" the *Star* said.

"It is absolutely impossible," Count Apponyi said forcefully. "If there was ever a king, he would have to be of the legitimate monarchy. Imagine a king with only fifteen majority in the chamber. Pauf. The next week I might be in." Count Apponyi smiled.

"Have you any official position now, Count?" asked the *Star*.

"None at all. I am a member of the opposition in a small way. But opposition is not a product for export. I believe the present government is doing its very best and if it gets the loan it may last a very long time. I would not overthrow it if the overthrowing rested with me. Because I have no better government to put in its place."

Count Apponyi is in the position in speaking on Europe as a whole of having to speak most carefully.

"England has been most friendly to Hungary," he said. "France has not been unfriendly. But, of course, she has her relations with the Little Entente. The Little Entente seems an integral part in her conception of world policy.

"When I talk today on the general situation in Europe I will not attempt to lay blame for the effects we have, but rather to tell what the conditions are and what remedies we have."

Count Apponyi smiled his big, broad, deep-wrinkled, very wise smile.

"As I am only to speak for twenty minutes you see I must now work and select my themes very carefully. It is not as though one had three hours."

Years ago popularity among all classes of Hungarians was a factor in Count Apponyi's doing away with all headgear. In that way he eliminated the need of constantly doffing his hat for public appearances. He has resumed a hat, however, for his Canadian appearances.

Bullfighting a Tragedy

☆ THE TORONTO STAR WEEKLY
October 20, 1923

It was spring in Paris and everything looked just a little too beautiful. Mike and I decided to go to Spain. Strater drew us a fine map of Spain on the back of a menu of the Strix restaurant. On the same menu he wrote the name of a restaurant in Madrid where the specialty is young suckling pig roasted, the name of the pensione on the Via San Jerónimo where the bullfighters live, and sketched a plan showing where the Grecos are hung in the Prado.

Fully equipped with this menu and our old clothes, we started for Spain. Our objective—to see bullfights.

We left Paris one morning and got off the train at Madrid the next noon. We saw our first bullfight at 4:30 that afternoon. It took about two hours to get tickets. We finally got them from scalpers for twenty-five pesetas apiece. The bullring was entirely sold out. We had barrera seats. These, the scalper explained in Spanish and broken French, were the first row of the ringside, directly under the royal box, and immediately opposite where the bulls would come out.

We asked him if he didn't have any less distinguished seats for somewhere around twelve pesetas, but he was sold out. So we paid the fifty pesetas for the two tickets, and with the tickets in our pockets sat out on the sidewalk in front of a big café near the Puerta del Sol. It was very exciting, sitting out in front of a café your first day in Spain with a ticket in your pocket that meant that rain or shine you were going to see a bullfight in an hour and a half. In fact, it was so exciting that we started out for the bullring on the outskirts of the city in about half an hour.

The bullring or Plaza de Toros was a big, tawny brick amphitheater standing at the end of a street in an open field. The yellow and red Spanish flag was floating over it. Carriages were driving up and people getting out of buses. There was a great crowd of beggars around the entrance. Men were selling water out of big terra-cotta water bottles. Kids sold fans, canes, roasted salted almonds in paper spills, fruit and slabs of ice cream. The crowd was gay and cheerful but all intent on pushing toward the entrance. Mounted civil guards with patent-leather cocked hats and carbines slung over their back sat their horses like statues, and the crowd flowed through.

Inside they all stood around in the bullring, talking and looking up in the grandstand at the girls in the boxes. Some of the men had field glasses in order to look better. We found our seats and the crowd began to leave the ring and get into the rows of concrete seats. The ring was circular—that sounds foolish, but a boxing ring is square—with a sand floor. Around it was a red board fence—just high enough for a man to be able to vault over it. Between the board fence, which is called the barrera, and the first row of seats ran a narrow alleyway. Then came the seats which were just like a football stadium except that around the top ran a double circle of boxes.

Every seat in the amphitheater was full. The arena was cleared. Then on the far side of the arena out of the crowd, four heralds in medieval costume stood up and blew a blast on their trumpets. The band crashed out, and from the entrance on the far side of the ring four horsemen in black velvet with ruffs around their necks rode out into the white glare of the arena. The people on the sunny side were baking in the heat and fanning themselves. The whole sol side was a flicker of fans.

Behind the four horsemen came the procession of the bullfighters. They had been all formed in ranks in the entranceway ready to march out, and as the music started they came. In the front rank walked the three espadas, or toreros, who would have charge of the killing of the six bulls of the afternoon.

They came walking out in heavily brocaded yellow and black costumes, the familiar "toreador" suit, heavy with gold embroidery, cape, jacket, shirt and collar, knee breeches, pink stockings, and low pumps. Always at bullfights, afterward the incongruity of those pink stockings used to strike me. Just behind the three principals—and after your first bullfight you do not look at their costumes but their faces—marched the teams, or cuadrillas. They are dressed in the same way but not as gorgeously as the matadors.

Back of the teams ride the picadors. Big, heavy, brown-faced men in wide flat hats, carrying lances like long window poles. They are astride horses that make Spark Plug look as trim and sleek as a King's Plate winner. Back of the pics come the gaily harnessed mule teams and the red-shirted monos, or bullring servants.

The bullfighters march in across the sand to the president's box. They march with easy professional stride, swinging along, not in the least theatrical except for their clothes. They all have the easy grace and slight slouch of the professional athlete. From their faces they might be major league ball players. They salute the president's box and then spread out along the barrera, exchanging their heavy brocaded capes for the fighting capes that have been laid along the red fence by the attendants.

We leaned forward over the barrera. Just below us the three matadors of the afternoon were leaning against the fence talking. One lighted a cigarette. He was a short, clear-skinned gypsy, Gitanillo, in a wonderful gold brocaded jacket, his short pigtail sticking out under his black cocked hat.

"He's not very fancy," a young man in a straw hat, with obviously American shoes, who sat on my left, said.

"But he sure knows bulls, that boy. He's a great killer."

"You're an American, aren't you?" asked Mike.

"Sure," the boy grinned. "But I know this gang. That's Gitanillo. You want to watch him. The kid with the chubby face is Chicuelo. They say he doesn't really like bullfighting, but the town's crazy about him. The one next to him is Villalta. He's the great one."

I had noticed Villalta. He was straight as a lance and walked like a young wolf. He was talking and smiling at a friend who leaned over the barrera. Upon his tanned cheekbone was a big patch of gauze held on with adhesive tape.

"He got gored last week at Málaga," said the American.

The American, whom later we were to learn to know and love as the Gin Bottle King, because of a great feat of arms performed at an early hour of the morning with a container of Mr. Gordon's celebrated product as his sole weapon in one of the four most dangerous situations I have ever seen, said: "The show's going to begin."

Out in the arena the picadors had galloped their decrepit horses around the ring, sitting straight and stiff in their rocking-chair saddles. Now all but three had ridden out of the ring. These three were huddled against the red painted fence of the barrera. Their horses backed against the fence, one eye bandaged, their lances at rest.

In rode two of the marshals in the velvet jackets and white ruffs. They galloped up to the president's box, swerved and saluted, doffing their hats and bowing low. From the box an object came hurtling down. One of the marshals caught it in his plumed hat.

"The key to the bullpen," said the Gin Bottle King.

The two horsemen whirled and rode across the arena. One of them tossed the key to a man in torero costume, they both saluted with a wave of their plumed hats, and had gone from the ring. The big gate was shut and bolted. There was no more entrance. The ring was complete.

The crowd had been shouting and yelling. Now it was dead silent. The man with the key stepped toward an iron-barred, low, red door and unlocked the great sliding bar. The door swung open. The man hid behind it. Inside it was dark.

Then, ducking his head as he came up out of the dark pen, a bull came into the arena. He came out all in a rush, big, black and white, weighing over a ton, and moving with a soft gallop. Just as he came out the sun seemed to dazzle him for an instant. He stood as though he were frozen, his great crest of muscle up, firmly planted, his eyes looking around, his horns pointed forward, black and white and sharp as porcupine quills. Then he charged. And as he charged, I suddenly saw what bullfighting is all about.

For the bull was absolutely unbelievable. He seemed like some great prehistoric animal, absolutely deadly and absolutely vicious. And he was silent. He charged silently and with a soft, galloping rush. When he turned he turned on his four feet like a cat. When he charged the first thing that caught his eye was the picador on one of the wretched horses. The picador dug his spurs into the horse and they galloped away. The bull came on in his rush, refused to be shaken off, and in full gallop crashed into the animal from the side, ignored the horse, drove one of his horns high into the thigh of the picador, and tore him, saddle and all, off the horse's back.

The bull went on without pausing to worry the picador lying on the ground. The next picador was sitting on his horse braced to receive the shock of the charge, his lance ready. The bull hit him sideways on, and horse and rider went high up in the air in a kicking mass and fell across the bull's back. As they came down the bull charged into them. The dough-faced kid, Chicuelo, vaulted over the fence, ran toward the bull and flapped his cape into the bull's face. The bull charged the cape and Chicuelo dodged backward and had the bull clear in the arena.

Without an instant's hesitation, the bull charged Chicuelo. The kid stood his ground, simply swung back on his heels and floated his cape like a ballet dancer's skirt into the bull's face as he passed.

"Olé!"—pronounced Oh-Lay!—roared the crowd.

The bull whirled and charged again. Without moving, Chicuelo repeated the performance. His legs rigid, just withdrawing his body from the rush of the bull's horns and floating the cape out with that beautiful swing.

Again the crowd roared. The Kid did this seven times. Each time the bull missed him by inches. Each time he gave the bull a free shot at him. Each time the crowd roared. Then he flopped the cape once at the bull at the finish of a pass, swung it around behind him and walked away from the bull to the barrera.

"He's the boy with the cape all right," said the Gin Bottle King. "That swing he did with the cape's called a veronica."

The chubby-faced Kid who did not like bullfighting and had just done the seven wonderful veronicas was standing against the fence just below us. His face glistened with sweat in the sun but was almost expressionless. His eyes were looking out across the arena where the bull was standing making up his mind to charge a picador. He was studying the bull because a few minutes later it would be his duty to kill him, and once he went out with his thin, red-hilted sword and his piece of red cloth to kill the bull in the final set it would be him or the bull. There are no drawn battles in bullfighting.

I am not going to describe the rest of that afternoon in detail. It was the first bullfight I ever saw, but it was not the best. The best was in the little town of Pamplona high up in the hills of Navarre, and came weeks later. Up in Pamplona, where they have held six days of bullfighting each year since A.D. 1126, and where the bulls race through the streets of the town each morning at six o'clock with half the town running ahead of them. Pamplona, where every man and boy in town is an amateur bullfighter and where there is an amateur fight each morning that is attended by 20,000 people in which the amateur fighters are all unarmed and there is a casualty list at least equal to a Dublin election. But Pamplona, with the best bullfight and the wild tale of the amateur fights, comes in the second chapter.

I am not going to apologize for bullfighting. It is a survival of the days of the Roman Colosseum. But it does need some explanation. Bullfighting is not a sport. It was never supposed to be. It is a tragedy. A very great tragedy. The tragedy is the death of the bull. It is played in three definite acts.

The Gin Bottle King—who, by the way, does not drink gin—told us a lot of this that first night as we sat in the upstairs room of the little restaurant that made a specialty of roast young suckling pig, roasted on an oak plank and served with a mushroom tortilla and vino rojo. The rest we learned later at the bullfighters' pensione in the Via San Jerónimo, where one of the bullfighters had eyes exactly like a rattlesnake.

Much of it we learned in the sixteen fights we saw in different parts of Spain from San Sebastian to Granada.

At any rate bullfighting is not a sport. It is a tragedy, and it symbolizes the struggle between man and the beasts. There are usually six bulls to a fight. A fight is called a corrida de toros. Fighting bulls are bred like racehorses, some of the oldest breeding establishments being several hundred years old. A good bull is worth about $2,000. They are bred for speed, strength and viciousness. In other words a good fighting bull is an absolutely incorrigible bad bull.

. . .

Bullfighting is an exceedingly dangerous occupation. In the sixteen fights I saw there were only two in which there was no one badly hurt. On the other hand it is very remunerative. A popular espada gets $5,000 for his afternoon's work. An unpopular espada though may not get $500. Both run the same risks. It is a good deal like Grand Opera for the really great matadors except they run the chance of being killed every time they cannot hit high C.

No one at any time in the fight can approach the bull except directly from the front. That is where the danger comes. There are also all sorts of complicated passes that must be done with the cape, each requiring as much technique as a champion billiard player. And underneath it all is the necessity for playing the old tragedy in the absolutely custom-bound, law-laid-down way. It must all be done gracefully, seemingly effortlessly and always with dignity. The worst criticism the Spaniards ever make of a bullfighter is that his work is "vulgar."

The three absolute acts of the tragedy are first the entry of the bull when the picadors receive the shock of his attacks and attempt to protect their horses with their lances. Then the horses go out and the second act is the planting of the banderillos. This is one of the most interesting and difficult parts but among the easiest for a new bullfight fan to appreciate in technique. The banderillos are three-foot, gaily colored darts with a small fishhook prong in the end. The man who is going to plant them walks out into the arena alone with the bull. He lifts the banderillos at arm's length and points them toward the bull. Then he calls "Toro! Toro!" The bull charges and the banderillero rises to his toes, bends in a curve forward and, just as the bull is about to hit him, drops the darts into the bull's hump just back of his horns.

They must go in evenly, one on each side. They must not be shoved, or thrown or stuck in from the side. This is the first time the bull has been completely baffled, there is the prick of the darts that he cannot escape and there are no horses for him to charge into. But he charges the man again and again and each time he gets a pair of the long banderillos that hang from his hump by their tiny barbs and flop like porcupine quills.

Last is the death of the bull, which is in the hands of the matador who has had charge of the bull since his first attack. Each matador has two bulls in the afternoon. The death of the bull is most formal and can only be brought about in one way, directly from the front by the matador, who must receive the bull in full charge and kill him with a sword thrust between the shoulders just back of the neck and between the horns. Before killing the bull he must first do a series of passes with the muleta, a piece of red cloth about the size of a large napkin. With the muleta, the torero must show his complete mastery of the bull, must make the bull miss him again and again by inches, before he is allowed to kill him. It is in this phase that most of the fatal accidents occur.

The word "toreador" is obsolete Spanish and is never used. The torero is usually called an espada, or swordsman. He must be proficient in all three acts of the fight. In the first he uses the cape and does veronicas and protects the picadors by taking the bull out and away from them when they are spilled to the ground. In the second act he plants the banderillos. In the third act he masters the bull with the muleta and kills him.

Few toreros excel in all three departments. Some, like young Chicuelo, are unapproachable in their capework. Others like the late Joselito are wonderful banderilleros. Only a few are great killers. Most of the greatest killers are gypsies.

Pamplona in July

☆ THE TORONTO STAR WEEKLY
October 27, 1923

In Pamplona, a white-walled, sun-baked town high up in the hills of Navarre, is held in the first two weeks of July each year the world series of bullfighting.

Bullfight fans from all Spain jam into the little town. Hotels double their prices and fill every room. The cafés under the wide arcades that run around the Plaza de la Constitución have every table crowded, the tall Pilgrim Father sombreros of Andalusia sitting over the same table with straw hats from Madrid and the flat blue Basque caps of Navarre and the Basque country.

Really beautiful girls, gorgeous, bright shawls over their shoulders, dark, dark-eyed, black lace mantillas over their hair, walk with their escorts in the crowds that pass from morning until night along the narrow walk that runs between inner and outer belts of café tables under the shade of the arcade out of the white glare of the Plaza de la Constitución. All day and all night there is dancing in the streets. Bands of blue-shirted peasants whirl and lift and swing behind a drum, fife and reed instruments in the ancient Basque Riau-Riau dances. And at night there is the throb of the big drums and the military band as the whole town dances in the great open square of the Plaza.

We landed at Pamplona at night. The streets were solid with people dancing. Music was pounding and throbbing. Fireworks were being set off from the big public square. All the carnivals I have ever seen paled in comparison. A rocket exploded over our heads with a blinding burst and the stick came swirling and whishing down. Dancers, snapping their fingers and whirling in perfect time through the crowd, bumped into us before we could get our bags down from the top of the station bus. Finally I got the bags through the crowd to the hotel.

We had wired and written for rooms two weeks ahead. Nothing had been saved. We were offered a single room with a single bed opening onto the kitchen ventilator shaft for seven dollars a day apiece. There was a big row with the landlady, who stood in front of her desk with her hands on her hips, and her broad Indian face perfectly placid, and told us in a few words of French and much Basque Spanish that she had to make all her money for the whole year in the next ten days. That people would come and that people would have to pay what she asked. She could show us a better room for ten dollars apiece. We said it would be preferable to sleep in the streets with the pigs. The landlady agreed that might be possible. We said we preferred it to such a hotel. All perfectly amicable. The landlady considered. We stood our ground. Mrs. Hemingway sat down on our rucksacks.

"I can get you a room in a house in the town. You can eat here," said the landlady.

"How much?"

"Five dollars."

We started off through the dark, narrow, carnival-mad streets with a boy carrying our rucksacks. It was a lovely big room in an old Spanish house with walls thick as a fortress. A cool, pleasant room, with a red tile floor and two big, comfortable beds set back in an alcove. A window opened on to an iron-grilled porch out over the street. We were very comfortable.

All night long the wild music kept up in the street below. Several times in the night there was a wild roll of drumming, and I got out of bed and across the tiled floor to the balcony. But it was always the same. Men, blue-shirted, bareheaded, whirling and floating in a wild fantastic dance down the street behind the rolling drums and shrill fifes.

Just at daylight there was a crash of music in the street below. Real military music. Herself was up, dressed, at the window.

"Come on," she said. "They're all going somewhere." Down below the street was full of people. It was five o'clock in the morning. They were all going in one direction. I dressed in a hurry and we started after them.

The crowd was all going toward the great public square. People were pouring into it from every street and moving out of it toward the open country we could see through the narrow gaps in the high walls.

"Let's get some coffee," said Herself.

"Do you think we've got time? Hey, what's going to happen?" I asked a newsboy.

"Encierro," he said scornfully. "The encierro commences at six o'clock."

"What's the encierro?" I asked him.

"Oh, ask me tomorrow," he said, and started to run. The entire crowd was running now.

"I've got to have my coffee. No matter what it is," Herself said.

The waiter poured two streams of coffee and milk into the glass out of his big kettles. The crowd were still running, coming from all the streets that fed into the Plaza.

"What is this encierro anyway?" Herself asked, gulping the coffee.

"All I know is that they let the bulls out into the streets."

We started out after the crowd. Out of a narrow gate into a great yellow open space of country with the new concrete bullring standing high and white and black with people. The yellow and red Spanish flag blowing in the early-morning breeze. Across the open and once inside the bullring, we mounted to the top looking toward the town. It cost a peseta to go up to the top. All the other levels were free. There were easily twenty thousand people there. Everyone jammed on the outside of the big concrete amphitheater, looking toward the yellow town with the bright red roofs, where a long wooden pen ran from the entrance of the city gate across the open, bare ground to the bullring.

It was really a double wooden fence, making a long entry from the main street of the town into the bullring itself. It made a runway about two hundred and fifty yards long. People were jammed solid on each side of it. Looking up it toward the main street.

Then far away there was a dull report.

"They're off," everybody shouted.

"What is it?" I asked a man next to me who was leaning far out over the concrete rail.

"The bulls! They have released them from the corrals on the far side of the city. They are racing through the city."

"Whew," said Herself. "What do they do that for?"

Then down the narrow fenced-in runway came a crowd of men and boys running. Running as hard as they could go. The gate feeding into the bullring was opened and they all ran pell-mell under the entrance levels into the ring. Then there came another crowd. Running even harder. Straight up the long pen from the town.

"Where are the bulls?" asked Herself.

Then they came in sight. Eight bulls galloping along, full tilt, heavyset, black, glistening, sinister, their horns bare, tossing their heads. And running with them, three steers with bells on their necks. They ran in a solid mass, and ahead of them sprinted, tore, ran and bolted the rear guard of the men and boys of Pamplona who had allowed themselves to be chased through the streets for a morning's pleasure.

A boy in his blue shirt, red sash, white canvas shoes, with the inevitable leather wine bottle hung from his shoulders, stumbled as he sprinted down the straightaway. The first bull lowered his head and made a jerky, sideways toss. The boy crashed up against the fence and lay there limp, the herd running solidly together passed him up. The crowd roared.

Everybody made a dash for the inside of the ring, and we got into a box just in time to see the bulls come into the ring filled with men. The men ran in a panic to each side. The bulls, still bunched solidly together, ran straight with the trained steers across the ring and into the entrance that led to the pens.

That was the entry. Every morning during the bullfighting festival of San Fermin at Pamplona, the bulls that are to fight in the afternoon are released from their corrals at six o'clock in the morning and race through the main street of the town for a mile and a half to the pen. The men who run ahead of them do it for the fun of the thing. It has been going on each year since a couple of hundred years before Columbus had his historic interview with Queen Isabella in the camp outside of Granada.

There are two things in favor of there being no accidents. First, that fighting bulls are not aroused and vicious when they are together. Second, that the steers are relied upon to keep them moving.

Sometimes things go wrong, a bull will be detached from the herd as they pile through into the pen and with his crest up, a ton of speed and viciousness, his needle-sharp horns lowered, will charge again and again into the packed mass of men and boys in the bullring. There is no place for the men to get out of the ring. It is too jammed for them to climb over the barrera or red fence that rims the field. They have to stay in and take it. Eventually the steers get the bull out of the ring and into the pen. He may wound or kill thirty men before they can get him out. No armed men are allowed to oppose him. That is the chance the Pamplona bullfight fans take every morning during the Feria. It is the Pamplona tradition of giving the bulls a final shot at everyone in town before they enter the pens. They will not leave until they come out into the glare of the arena to die in the afternoon.

Consequently Pamplona is the toughest bullfight town in the world. The amateur fight that comes immediately after the bulls have entered the pens proves that. Every seat in the great amphitheater is packed. About three hundred men, with capes, odd pieces of cloth, old shirts, anything that will imitate a bullfighter's cape, are singing and dancing in the arena. There is a shout, and the bullpen opens. Out comes a young bull just as fast as he can come. On his horns are leather knobs to prevent his goring anyone. He charges and hits a man. Tosses him high in the air, and the crowd roars. The man comes down on the ground, and the bull goes for him, bumping him with his head. Worrying him with his horns. Several amateur bullfighters are flopping their capes in his face to make the bull charge and leave the man on the ground. The bull charges and bags another man. The crowd roars with delight.

Then the bull will turn like a cat and get somebody who has been acting very brave about ten feet behind him. Then he will toss a man over the fence. Then he picks out one man and follows him in a wild twisting charge through the entire crowd until he bags him. The barrera is packed with men and boys sitting along the top, and the bull decides to clear them all off. He goes along, hooking carefully with his horn and dropping them off with a toss of his horns like a man pitching hay.

Each time the bull bags someone the crowd roars with joy. Most of it is home-talent stuff. The braver the man has been or the more elegant pass he has attempted with his cape before the bull gets him, the more the crowd roars. No one is armed. No one hurts or plagues the bull in any way. A man who grabbed the bull by the tail and tried to hang on was hissed and booed by the crowd and the next time he tried it was knocked down by another man in the bullring. No one enjoys it all more than the bull.

As soon as he shows signs of tiring from his charges, the two old steers, one brown and the other looking like a big Holstein, come trotting in and alongside the young bull, who falls in behind them like a dog and follows them meekly on a tour of the arena and then out.

Another comes right in, and the charging and tossing, the ineffectual cape-waving, and wonderful music are repeated right over again. But always different. Some of the animals in this morning amateur fight are steers. Fighting bulls from the best strain who had some imperfection or other in build so they could never command the high prices paid for combat animals, $2,000 to $3,000 apiece. But there is nothing lacking in their fighting spirit.

The show comes off every morning. Everybody in town turns out at five thirty when the military bands go through the streets. Many of them stay up all night for it. We didn't miss one, and it is *quelque* sporting event that will get us both up at five thirty o'clock in the morning for six days running.

As far as I know, we were the only English-speaking people in Pamplona during the Feria of last year [July].

There were three minor earthquakes while we were there. Terrific cloudbursts in the mountains and the Ebro River flooded out Zaragoza. For two days the bullring was under water and the corrida had to be suspended for the first time in over a hundred years. That was during the middle of the fair. Everyone was desperate. On the third day it looked gloomier than ever, poured rain all morning, and then at noon the clouds rolled away up across the valley, the sun came out bright and hot and baking and that afternoon there was the greatest bullfight I will perhaps ever see.

There were rockets going up into the air and the arena was nearly full when we got into our regular seats. The sun was hot and baking. Over on the other side we could see the bullfighters standing ready to come in. All wearing their oldest clothes because of the heavy, muddy going in the arena. We picked out the three matadors of the afternoon with our glasses. Only one of them was new. Olmos, a chubby-faced, jolly-looking man, something like Tris Speaker. The others we had seen often before. Maera, dark, spare and deadly looking, one of the very greatest toreros of all time. The third, young Algabeno, the son of a famous bullfighter, a slim young Andalusian with a charming Indian-looking face. All were wearing the suits they had probably started bullfighting with, too tight, old fashioned, outmoded.

There was the procession of entrance, the wild bullfight music played, the preliminaries were quickly over, the picadors retired along the red fence with their horses, the heralds sounded their trumpets and the door of the bullpen swung open. The bull came out in a rush, saw a man standing near the barrera and charged him. The man vaulted over the fence and the bull charged the barrera. He crashed into the fence in full charge and ripped a two-by-eight plank solidly out in a splintering smash. He broke his horn doing it and the crowd called for a new bull. The trained steers trotted in, the bull fell in meekly behind them, and the three of them trotted out of the arena.

The next bull came in with the same rush. He was Maera's bull and, after perfect cape play, Maera planted the banderillos. Maera is Herself's favorite bullfighter. And if you want to keep any conception of yourself as a brave, hard, perfectly balanced, thoroughly competent man in your wife's mind, never take her to a real bullfight. I used to go into the amateur fights in the morning to try and win back a small amount of her esteem but the more I discovered that bullfighting required a great quantity of a certain type of courage of which I had an almost complete lack, the more it became apparent that any admiration she might ever redevelop for me would have to be simply an antidote to the real admiration for Maera and Villalta. You cannot compete with bullfighters on their own ground. If anywhere. The only way most husbands are able to keep any drag with their wives at all is that, first there are only a limited number of bullfighters, second there are only a limited number of wives who have ever seen bullfights.

Maera planted his first pair of banderillos sitting down on the edge of the little step-up that runs around the barrera. He snarled at the bull and as the animal charged, leaned back tight against the fence and as the horns struck on either side of him, swung forward over the brute's head and planted the two darts in his hump. He planted the next pair, same way, so near to us we could have leaned over and touched him. Then he went out to kill the bull and, after he had made absolutely unbelievable passes with the little red cloth of the muleta, drew up his sword and as the bull charged, Maera thrust. The sword shot out of his hand and the bull caught him. He went up in the air on the horns of the bull and then came down. Young Algabeno flopped his cape in the bull's face. The bull charged him and Maera staggered to his feet. But his wrist was sprained.

With his wrist sprained, so that every time he raised it to sight for a thrust it brought beads of sweat out on his face, Maera tried again and again to make his death thrust. He lost his sword again and again, picked it up with his left hand from the mud floor of the arena and transferred it to the right for the thrust. Finally he made it and the bull went over. The bull nearly got him twenty times. As he came in to stand up under us at the barrera side, his wrist was swollen to twice normal size. I thought of prizefighters I had seen quit because they had hurt their hands.

There was almost no pause while the mules galloped in and hitched on to the first bull and dragged him out and the second came in with a rush. The picadors took the first shock of him with their bull lances. There was the snort and charge, the shock and the mass against the sky, the wonderful defense by the picador with his lance that held off the bull, and then Rosario Olmos stepped out with his cape.

Once he flopped the cape at the bull and floated it around in an easy graceful swing. Then he tried the same swing, the classic "veronica," and the bull caught him at the end of it. Instead of stopping at the finish, the bull charged on in. He caught Olmos squarely with his horn, hoisted him high in the air. He fell heavily and the bull was on top of him, driving his horns again and again into him. Olmos lay on the sand, his head on his arms. One of his teammates was flopping his cape madly in the bull's face. The bull lifted his head for an instant and charged and got his man. Just one terrific toss. Then he whirled and chased a man just in back of him toward the barrera. The man was running full tilt and as he put his hand on the fence to vault it the bull had him and caught him with his horn, shooting him way up into the crowd. He rushed toward the fallen man he had tossed who was getting to his feet and all alone Algabeno met him with the cape. Once, twice, three times he made the perfect, floating, slow swing with the cape, perfectly, graceful, debonair, back on his heels, baffling the bull. And he had command of the situation. There never was such a scene at any world series game.

There are no substitute matadors allowed. Maera was finished. His wrist could not lift a sword for weeks. Olmos had been gored badly through the body. It was Algabeno's bull. This one and the next five.

He handled them all. Did it all. Cape play easy, graceful, confident. Beautiful work with the muleta. And serious, deadly killing. Five bulls he killed, one after the other, and each one was a separate problem to be worked out with death. At the end there was nothing debonair about him. It was only a question if he would last through or if the bulls would get him. They were all very wonderful bulls.

"He is a very great kid," said Herself. "He is only twenty."

"I wish we knew him," I said.

"Maybe we will some day," she said. Then considered a moment. "He will probably be spoiled by then."

They make twenty thousand a year.

That was just three months ago. It seems in a different century now, working in an office. It is a very long way from the sunbaked town of Pamplona, where the men race through the streets in the mornings ahead of the bulls to the morning ride to work on a Bay-Caledonia car. But it is only fourteen days by water to Spain and there is no need for a castle. There is always that room at 5 Calle de Eslava, and a son, if he is to redeem the family reputation as a bullfighter, must start very early.

Game-Shooting in Europe

☆ THE TORONTO DAILY STAR
November 3, 1923

In a popular conception Europe is a very overcrowded, overcivilized, altogether decadent place where what shooting is done is committed by fashionably dressed languid members of the aristocracy who shoot hundreds of braces of protected grouse or woodcock driven past them by beaters, between pauses for cups of tea and snapshots by the photographers for the leading illustrated weeklies.

Hunting, to be never confused with shooting under pain of social ostracism, consists of these same popular social figures donning pink coats and remaining in an upright position on top of a horse as long as possible as near as practicable to the rear of a pack of dogs who pursue a fox across the fields and meadows of the loyal and cheering peasantry.

Not so on the continent. Hunting is the great national sport of France, Belgium, Italy, Germany, Czechoslovakia and points east. It is called hunting, "*la chasse*," and it means shooting. And there is plenty to shoot. Right now you would have extreme difficulty getting inside of any local train leaving Paris in any direction on Saturday or Sunday because of the thousands of hunters, their shotguns slung over the shoulders, leaving for a weekend in the country.

There is probably more game within twenty miles of Paris, France, than within twenty miles of Toronto, Ontario. There is good deer hunting in Germany, good snipe and plover shooting in the Ruhr, good partridge and rabbit shooting in almost every department of France and dangerous big-game hunting in France, Belgium and Germany.

It is a moot question whether there is any dangerous big-game hunting in Ontario, excluding the skunk and porcupine. The hunter in the woods is in fully as much danger from the moose as though he were stationed in the members' enclosure at the Woodbine taking potshots at the favorite. The black bear wants just one thing from the hunter, distance. Wolves, I understand, are a tender subject.

But there is scattered all over Europe a really dangerous game animal. He is the wild boar and every year incautious hunters are killed by him.

Last year there were two hunters killed in France alone by wild boars. During the war when there was almost no shooting game flourished unchecked all over Europe. One of the best little flourishers of them all was the wild boar.

In some districts, like the wild Auvergne country and parts of the wooded slopes of the Côte d'Or down below Dôle, boars became so numerous that they destroyed crops and were a public menace. One farmer last winter had shot eighteen on his place in less than a year. The nineteenth was a big, chunky, viciously built fellow that the farmer saw out of his window one snowy morning. He took down the old shotgun and fired from the back door. The boar went into a thicket. The farmer followed him and the boar charged with a squealing grunt of rage and bowling the farmer over, savaged him with his tusks. A wild boar's tusk is like a razor and about three to six inches long. It makes a ghastly wound and once a boar gets a man down it keeps driving into him in an insane rage until the man is dead. The farmer's wife finally killed the boar.

A wild boar will weigh up to 200 pounds and ounce for ounce and pound for pound is about as fierce and vicious an animal as there is. It is also one of the very finest things to eat in the world and as "sanglier" and "marcassin," the latter young boar, is one of the reasons that make Dijon the place that all good eaters hope to go when they die.

An American pal of mine named Krebs decided to go boar hunting. He went down to a little town in the Côte d'Or in the foothills of the blue wall of the Jura where the boars were reported to be tearing up the crops and intimidating the population.

All the hunters in the place turned out. The reputation of the little town, we can call it Cauxonne, was at stake. Speeches were made in the local café. Impassioned appeals. An American had come all the way to Cauxonne to hunt boars. Such a thing. Further, he was an American journalist. If Cauxonne revealed itself as the great boar-hunting center that every citizen assembled knew it to be, Tourists, with a capital T, would flock in from all over the world. What an opportunity! The American must get boars. It was an affair touching the honor, the future, and the prosperity, above all, brothers, the prosperity of Cauxonne. The excitement lasted until well into the night.

Krebs was wakened before daylight. The boar hunters were assembled at the café. They were waiting for him. He arrived half asleep. Inside the café were about twenty men. Bicycles were stacked outside. Hunting the boar was nothing to be undertaken on an empty stomach. They must have a small drink of some sort. Something to warm the stomach.

Krebs suggested coffee. What a joke. What a supreme and delightful joker the American. Coffee. Imagine it. Coffee before going off to hunt the sanglier. What a thing. Drôle enough, eh?

Marc. Marc was the stuff. No one ever started after the wild boar without first a little marc. Patron, the marc.

The marc was produced.

Now marc, pronounced mar as in marvelous, is one of the three most powerful drinks known. As an early-morning potion it can give vodka, douzico, absinthe, grappa, and other famous stomach destroyers two furlongs and beat them as far as Zev beat Papyrus. It is the great specialty of Burgundy and the Côte d'Or and three drops of it on the tongue of a canary will send him out in a grim, deadly, silent search for eagles.

The marc was produced. It passed from hand to hand and from hand to mouth. Cauxonne was practically already famous. They must celebrate. Had not the American all but already shot dozens, nay hundreds, of wild boars? There was no doubt of it. Cauxonne was one of the great tourist centers of France. But had not the terrific slaughter of boars soon to be accomplished destroyed one of her greatest assets? No. It was no matter. Nothing mattered. Another bottle of marc, Patron.

At nine o'clock in the morning the boar hunters mounted their fleet of bicycles and tore at a terrific clip in a northerly direction out of town. Stragglers and bent and damaged bicycles were found along the road all day. The main body of hunters slept very comfortably in a stretch of woods about four miles north of town, their heads pillowed on their bicycles. Krebs hunted hard all day and shot a large crow. He left for Paris that night, afraid that if he stayed the boar hunters would want to repeat the hunt next morning.

Germany is full of game. In tramping through the Black Forest, I have time and again seen deer, browsing on some little hillside just out of the edge of the forest, or in the evening coming down to drink at a little trout stream way back in the hills. Nearly every well-to-do German with sporting proclivities in the Schwarzwald or the mountainous, forest country of South Germany has one or two staghounds and I have a standing invitation to hunt any fall with Herr Bugler of Triberg.

There are lots of snipe, plover and woodcock all down through the Rhineland and around the Ruhr and good duck shooting along the Rhine in the spring. Last spring, coming down the river from Mayence to Cologne, we passed great rafts of ducks. The British officers in the garrison at Cologne had very good pheasant, grouse and quail shooting in the country within sight of the great cathedral towers.

Switzerland is the home of the chamois. I have never come any closer to the chamois than in the form of a gasoline strainer. He produces a very fine grade of celluloid horn, however, which is used to ornament the alpenstocks that are sold to tourists. So he cannot be regarded as extinct. But as a popular sporting animal he is about on the same plane as the wooden carved bears that are sold in Berne.

There are still chamois but they live very high and far off and are very rarely shot and only then by an expert mountaineer and climber who works with field glasses and a telescope sight. Switzerland is a good game country though. Full of rabbits, big snow hares, partridges and the giant black cock. Black cock, or capercailzie, are a sort of glorified partridge with glossy, iridescent plumage. They are larger than a big orpington chicken, terrific flyers, and live in the forests of Switzerland and nearly all central and western Europe.

Italy is probably the only country in the world where they not only shoot but eat foxes. In the fall in Milan you will see hanging outside the door of the butcher's shop two or three deer, a long line of pheasants and quail, and one or two red foxes. Everybody who can get a license and get out hunts in Italy. The shooting is probably poorer than in any other country in Europe, because no sorts of birds seem to be protected and all day long in the hills you hear the boom of the black-powder fowling pieces and in the evening see the hunters coming into town with their game bags full of thrushes, robins, warblers, finches, woodpeckers and only an occasional game bird. Next day in the marketplace you can see long lines of songbirds of every sort hung up for sale. Even sparrows are sold.

To get a license to shoot in Italy you must have a certificate that you have never been in jail signed by the chief of police and the mayor of your hometown. This gave me some difficulty when I first applied for a shooting license. In the Abruzzi, the wild, mountainous part of Italy lying up in the country from Naples, there are still bears. There are wolves too, in the wild wastes of the Campagna, within thirty miles of Rome. It is a safe statement that there will be wolves in Italy long after they are exterminated in Ontario. For the Roman wolves have existed since long before the Christian religion first came to Rome, while less than five hundred years ago the American continent was undiscovered.

Belgium is a good shooting country and the Ardennes forest is one of the greatest wild-boar-hunting parts of Europe.

In the Pyrenees, in the south of France and north of Spain, there is perhaps the wildest country of western Europe. Every year hunters kill dozens of bears in the Pyrenees mountain fastnesses.

What is the reason for the continued existence of game in good numbers in the most highly civilized and well-settled centers of the world while in many of the United States, like Indiana, Ohio and Illinois, game is rapidly being exterminated? It is careful protection, rigidly enforced closed seasons, and the fact of government-owned forests, which are really farmed for timber rather than cut over and denuded of trees. Indiana was once a timber country. So was the Lower Peninsula of Michigan. Today there is hardly a patch of virgin timber in the Upper Peninsula of Michigan. Michigan deer hunters are already going north into Ontario. Ontario's supply of game seems inexhaustible. But wait until the steady hunting, the destruction of timber and the forest fires have kept up for fifty years. See the result that has been obtained in the States by the motorcar that allows a party to hunt over a hundred miles where they used to be able to hunt over five. The prairie chicken, one of the finest game birds, has been practically wiped out. Quail have been practically exterminated in many states. The curlew has gone. The wild turkey has gone.

But France will always be a game country. For there are forests in France that were there in Caesar's time. More important still, there are new forests in France that were not there in Napoleon's time. Even more important, there will be new forests, a hundred years from now, where today M. Poincaré has looked on only scarred hillsides. And all the forests will be full of game.

The Frenchman likes to hunt. If the game falls off he wants to know the reason why.

The Lakes Aren't Going Dry

☆ THE TORONTO STAR WEEKLY
November 17, 1923

Water in the lakes is low. Rocks are exposed in the St. Lawrence near Montreal that are not remembered to have appeared before.

The Canada Steamship Lines, which run steamers through the St. Lawrence rapids, say they have run no boats since the end of July and report that they must dynamite rocks at several places before their steamers resume their runs next summer.

Vessels with a capacity of 500,000 bushels of wheat have been coming through from Lake Superior 50,000 bushels short because of the low water.

All the external signs point to lower water in the lakes than ever before.

But in the basement of the Harbor Commission building on the waterfront at the foot of Bay Street there is a little copper cylinder that slides up and down on the rising and falling water like a monkey on a stick. This copper cylinder takes no account of signs, rocks that the oldest inhabitant has never seen before, bear stories, bull reports or weather conditions. It merely measures the height of water in Toronto harbor, Lake Ontario. And it has been measuring steadily since 1854.

According to its figures, the bay, and consequently Lake Ontario, are nowhere near a low-level record.

This copper float that shifts a slide up and down a graduated scale measures the rise and fall of the water in Toronto's harbor exactly. Zero, the starting point from which the measurements are taken, is 246 feet above the sea level at New York. It just happened to be that. Sea level has nothing to do with the measurement.

Captain Hugh Richardson, Toronto's first harbormaster, fixed the zero point in 1854. He wanted a standard to measure the rise and fall of the water by and found a flat rock on the bottom of the bay where the Queen's Wharf used to be. Captain Richardson dropped a weighted line to the rock and found after several measurements that the depth averaged 9 feet.

In other words, 9 feet was the average height of the water at this particular place. The water at his measuring point would rise and fall correspondingly with the deepest water in the bay. The measuring spot was not far enough out to be affected by winds or waves.

The part of the bay where Captain Hugh Richardson established the first measuring gauge is now solid land. Only a line of willows marks the outlines of the old Queen's Wharf. When the harbor was filled in the measuring gauge was moved to the new pierhead at the foot of Bathurst Street in 1912. There zero was set at 245 feet above New York sea level. The gauge remained fixed there until 1917, when it was established in the basement of the Harbor Commission building, where it remains at present.

In addition to the old rise-and-fall copper cylinder there is a modern Haskell gauge where the rising and falling of the harbor waters are shown by a line traced on a cylinder of paper which revolves by clockwork and is only removed once a month. This gauge is so delicate that even the passing of a vessel and consequent displacement of water is registered.

Both the old and the new gauges are set in wells in the basement of the harbor building. The old gauge is still used for daily readings and is checked by the Haskell gauge at the end of the month.

Right now the water is six and a half inches below the zero mark. But this is no lower than it was last year. While in 1897 it was 21 inches below zero and in 1900 was 16 inches below the measuring point.

Since the first measurements were made in 1854 the highest level the water ever reached was in 1870, when it rose to 47 inches above the zero point of 9 feet. The next highest level was sixteen years later, in 1886, when the bay flooded to 46 inches above zero.

The lowest level ever recorded was in 1895, when the water of the bay dropped to 26 inches below the average. The next shallowest period came two years later, in 1897, when the water fell to 25 inches below zero.

There is a definite fluctuation in the depth of water in Lake Ontario. Starting in 1854, when the water rose to 36 inches above the measuring point, it fell away steadily but surely until 1870, when the high level was a record-smasher. Then the level dropped again until 1876, when it rose for another high tide and then fell again until the high water of 1886.

Since then it has fallen until 1901, when it started to mount again and rose until 1908, when it hit forty-six and one-half inches above zero, flooding Center Island and causing great property damage.

From the record floods of 1908, the water level fell steadily until in 1911 it was the lowest since 1874. In 1911 the ferry boat Trillium ran aground and lay for fifty-eight minutes, stuck fast on her way to the city from the Toronto-Tecumseh lacrosse match at Hanlan's Point.

The Island Queen went to her rescue, took off 600 passengers to lighten the Trillium—and went aground herself. Launches, sailboats, rowboats, canoes rescued the 2,000 stranded people of the two boats. And that summer, ferryboats had a hard time dodging the shoals and sandbanks caused by the shallow water.

Again in 1913 the old reaction came, and on April 13 of that year the water in the harbor was rising at the rate of 2 inches a day. Hundreds of feet of land on the lagoon at the island were under water and property was being damaged. The water kept on mounting until it reached 36 inches above the zero mark on April 16. The harbor board was extremely anxious and property owners on the island were panicky. At the same time Lake Superior was falling steadily.

The northwest gales came along and lowered the dangerously mounting flood. On May 10 an east wind piled the water, in the harbor up to the 39-inch mark. But that was the highest it reached and from then on fell away.

The drop back commenced the next year, 1914, when the water only got up to 24 inches above the zero mark. In 1915, only two years after the threatened flood, the lake level could not rise above 9 inches and remained almost stationary.

The water-level measure records the strange rise and fall of the water in the Great Lakes, but it does not explain it. Are there tides in the Great Lakes?

One theory is that as the molten mass in the interior of the earth cools it causes the surface of the earth to slowly contract. It may expand occasionally in a sort of bubbling motion.

All over the world this motion would be going on and other bodies of fresh water rise and fall just as Ontario does. As the earth contracts the water would fall. As it expands, the water would rise. These tides are well known on the Swiss lakes, which rise and fall with regularity.

Lake Ontario is usually deepest in June, and then falls away in depth until it becomes shallowest in November, January or February. That is the local movement, caused probably by the great flow of water which comes down the chain of lakes from Superior to Ontario, causing the level to rise in each lake until the flood has passed.

But there is no satisfactory explanation for the big controlling movement that causes periods of floods and terms of shallow water following one another in a mysterious and unaccountable movement which makes June sometimes the shallowest month in spite of the local causes that work to make it the deepest. Hot summers, evaporation, snowfall play their part, but do not explain all.

After two years of resting the floods had another try in 1916, when in June the water level set out for a record. Every day in June the waters of the harbor rose until on the tenth it was up to 36½ inches above the zero. Thousands of dollars of damages were done to the island, boathouses swept away, beaches destroyed, property flooded. The friendly northwest gale came along though and lowered the dangerously mounting level.

After 1916 the water level stayed fairly high. In 1919 it mounted to 39½ inches above zero, or near the flood level. But in 1920 the highest it could climb to was 12 inches above the zero mark. In 1921 it only got up to 24½ inches above, and last year started to climb again to 27 inches. This year the highest water has been 15 inches above zero, measured on June 24. The lowest measured was in February, when the harbor waves were down to 11½ inches below the measuring point. Just now it is 6½ inches below zero.

From previous indications there may be a spell of several years of low water before a climb again. But the water level is tricky and knows no regular rules, and there is nothing in the past performances of the harbor to prevent another flood next spring.

Trout Fishing in Europe

☆ THE TORONTO STAR WEEKLY
November 17, 1923

Bill Jones went to visit a French financier who lives near Deauville and has a private trout stream. The financier was very fat. His stream was very thin.

"Ah, Monsieur Zshones, I will show you the fishing," the financier purred over the coffee. "You have the trout in Canada, is it not? But here! Here we have the really charming trout fishing of Normandy. I will show you. Rest yourself content. You will see it."

The financier was a very literal man. His idea of showing Bill the fishing was for Bill to watch and the financier to fish. They started out. It was a trying sight.

If undressed and put back on the shelf piece by piece, the financier would have stocked a sporting-goods store. Placed end to end his collection of flies would have reached from Keokuk, Ill., to Paris, Ont. The price of his rod would have made a substantial dent in the interallied debt or served to foment a Central American revolution.

The financier flung a pretty poisonous fly, too. At the end of two hours one trout had been caught. The financier was elated. The trout was a beauty, fully five and a half inches long and perfectly proportioned. The only trouble with him was some funny black spots along his sides and belly.

"I don't believe he's healthy," Bill said doubtfully.

"Healthy? You don't think he's healthy? That lovely trout? Why, he's a wonder. Did you not see the terrific fight he made before I netted him?" The financier was enraged. The beautiful trout lay in his large, fat hand.

"But what are those black spots?" Bill asked.

"Those spots? Oh, absolutely nothing. Perhaps worms. All our trout here have them at this season. But do not be afraid of that, Monsieur Zshones. Wait until you taste this beautiful trout for breakfast!"

It was probably proximity to Deauville that spoiled the financier's trout stream. Deauville is supposed to be a sort of combination of Fifth Avenue, Atlantic City, and Sodom and Gomorrah. In reality it is a watering place that has become so famous that the really smart people no longer go to it and the others hold a competitive spending contest and mistake each other for duchesses, dukes, prominent pugilists, Greek millionaires and the Dolly sisters.

The real trout fishing of Europe is in Spain, Germany and Switzerland. Spain has probably the best fishing of all in Galicia. But the Germans and the Swiss are right behind.

In Germany the great difficulty is to get permission to fish. All the fishing water is rented by the year to individuals. If you want to fish you have first to get permission of the man who has rented the fishing. Then you go back to the township and get a permission, and then you finally get the permission of the owner of the land.

If you have only two weeks to fish, it will probably take about all of it to get these different permissions. A much easier way is simply to carry a rod with you and fish when you see a good stream. If anyone complains, begin handing out marks. If the complaints keep up, keep handing out marks. If this policy is pursued far enough the complaints will eventually cease and you will be allowed to continue fishing.

If, on the other hand, your supply of marks runs out before the complaints cease you will probably go either to jail or the hospital. It is a good plan, on this account, to have a dollar bill secreted somewhere in your clothes. Produce the bill. It is 10 to 1 your assailant will fall to his knees in an attitude of extreme thanksgiving and on arising break all existing records to the nearest, deepest and woolliest German hand-knitted sock, the South German's savings bank.

Following this method of obtaining fishing permits, we fished all through the Black Forest. With rucksacks and fly rods, we hiked across country, sticking to the high ridges and the rolling crests of the hills, sometimes through deep pine timber, sometimes coming out into a clearing and farmyards and again going, for miles, without seeing a soul except occasional wild-looking berry pickers. We never knew where we were. But we were never lost because at any time we could cut down from the high country into a valley and know we would hit a stream. Sooner or later every stream flowed into a river and a river meant a town.

At night we stopped in little inns or gasthofs. Some of these were so far from civilization that the innkeepers did not know the mark was rapidly becoming worthless and continued to charge the old German prices. At one place, room and board, in Canadian money, were less than ten cents a day.

One day we started from Triberg and toiled up a long, steadily ascending hill road until we were on top of the high country and could look out at the Black Forest rolling away from us in every direction. Away off across country we could see a range of hills, and we figured that at their base must flow a river. We cut across the high, bare country, dipping down into valleys and walking through woods, cool and dim as a cathedral on the hot August day. Finally we hit the upper end of the valley at the foot of the hills we had seen.

In it flowed a lovely trout stream and there was not a farmhouse in sight. I jointed up the rod, and while Mrs. Hemingway sat under a tree on the hillside and kept watch both ways up the valley, caught four real trout. They averaged about three-quarters of a pound apiece. Then we moved down the valley. The stream broadened out and Herself took the rod while I found a lookout post.

She caught six in about an hour, and two of them I had to come down and net for her. She had hooked a big one, and after he was triumphantly netted we looked up to see an old German in peasant clothes watching us from the road.

"Gut tag," I said.

"Tag," he said. "Have you good fishing?"

"Yes. Very good."

"Good," he said. "It is good to have somebody fishing." And went hiking along the road.

In contrast to him were the farmers in Oberprechtal, where we had obtained full fishing permits, who came down and chased us away from the stream with pitchforks because we were Auslanders.

In Switzerland I discovered two valuable things about trout fishing. The first was while I was fishing a stream that parallels the Rhône River and that was swollen and gray with snow water. Flies were useless, and I was fishing with a big gob of worms. A fine, juicy-looking bait. But I wasn't getting any trout or even any strikes.

An old Italian who had a farm up the valley was walking behind me while I fished. As there was nothing doing in a stream I knew from experience was full of trout, it got more and more irritating. Somebody just back of you while you are fishing is as bad as someone looking over your shoulder while you write a letter to your girl. Finally I sat down and waited for the Italian to go away. He sat down, too.

He was an old man, with a face like a leather waterbottle.

"Well, Papa, no fish today," I said.

"Not for you," he said solemnly.

"Why not for me? For you, maybe?" I said.

"Oh yes," he said, not smiling. "For me, trout always. Not for you. You don't know how to fish with worms." And spat into the stream.

This touched a tender spot, a boyhood spent within forty miles of the Soo, hoisting out trout with a cane pole and all the worms the hook would hold.

"You're so old you know everything. You are probably a rich man from your knowledge of fishworms," I said.

This bagged him.

"Give me the rod," he said.

He took it from me, cleaned off the fine wriggly gob of trout food, and selected one medium-sized angleworm from my box. This he threaded a little way on the number ten hook, and let about three-fourths of the worm wave free.

"Now that's a worm," he said with satisfaction.

He reeled the line up till there was only the six feet of leader out and dropped the free-swinging worm into a pool where the water swirled under the bank. There was nothing doing. He pulled it slowly out and dropped it in a little lower down. The tip of the rod twirled. He lowered it just a trifle. Then it shot down in a jerk, and he struck and horsed out a fifteen-inch trout and sent him back over his head in a telephone-pole swing.

I fell on him while he was still flopping.

The old Italian handed me the rod. "There, young one. That is the way to use a worm. Let him be free to move like a worm. The trout will take the free end and then suck him all in, hook and all. I have fished this stream for twenty years and I know. More than one worm scares the fish. It must be natural."

"Come, use the rod and fish now," I urged him.

"No. No. I only fish at night," he smiled. "It is much too expensive to get a permit."

But by me watching for the river guard while he fished and our using the rod alternately until each caught a fish, we fished all day and caught eighteen trout. The old Italian knew all the holes, and only fished where there were big ones. We used a free wriggly worm, and the eighteen trout averaged a pound and a half apiece.

He also showed me how to use grubs. Grubs are only good in clear water, but are a deadly bait. You can find them in any rotten tree or saw-log, and the Swiss and Swiss-Italians keep them in grub boxes. Flat pieces of wood bored full of auger holes with a sliding metal top. The grub will live as well in his hole in the wood as in the log and is one of the greatest hot-weather baits known. Trout will take a grub when they will take nothing else in the low-water days of August.

The Swiss, too, have a wonderful way of cooking trout. They boil them in a liquor made of wine vinegar, bay leaves, and a dash of red pepper. Not too much of any of the ingredients in the boiling water, and cook until the trout turns blue. It preserves the true trout flavor better than almost any way of cooking. The meat stays firm and pink and delicate.

Then they serve them with drawn butter. They drink the clear Sion wine when they eat them.

It is not a well-known dish at the hotels. You have to go back in the country to get trout cooked that way. You come up from the stream to a chalet and ask them if they know how to cook blue trout. If they don't, you walk on a way. If they do, you sit down on the porch with the goats and children and wait. Your nose will tell you when the trout are boiling. Then after a while you will hear a pop. This is the Sion being uncorked. Then the woman of the chalet will come to the door and say, "It is prepared, Monsieur."

Then you go away and I will do the rest myself.

Gargoyles as Symbol

☆ THE TORONTO STAR WEEKLY
November 17, 1923

It would be difficult to find a detail of architecture that is more popular with the European tourists than the gargoyles of Notre Dame in Paris. Thousands have climbed the weary stone stairs to examine them in detail and then examine, from above, the magnificent panorama of the French capital. But the gargoyles are pleasant fellows to meet, with their grinning faces and elfish profiles; all pleasant but two. And those two are located on the northeastern aspect of the tower that looks out toward Germany. These two are the hungry gargoyles. The one is swallowing a long, luckless dog, while its companion gazes greedily down toward the land where France is now encamped.

But, the tourists will remonstrate, Notre Dame was built centuries ago. How could the present-day attitude of France be veiled in their horrible visage?

Truly the cathedral was built more than six hundred years ago, but these gargoyles were executed and placed in position there by order of Napoleon the Third, a short time before the outbreak of the Franco-Prussian war. The cathedral is old; but these monstrosities are not. They belong to modern history and the commencement of French hatred toward the eastern neighbor.

These world-famed gargoyles were placed on Notre Dame by E. E. Viollet-le-Duc, who died in 1879. He was an intimate friend of Napoleon the Third, and was employed in the restoration of many ancient buildings that had suffered during the French Revolution. In that connection he was engaged with his Notre Dame gargoyles for eleven years. Other buildings which he restored with figures do not exhibit the horror and rapacity of these two gargoyles which face Germany. Did he here express, in stone, the thoughts of the French leaders which are now current history?

The Sport of Kings

☆ THE TORONTO STAR WEEKLY
November 24, 1923

The friend who calls up over the telephone.
The horse that has been especially wired from Pimlico.
The letting in of the friends in the office.
The search for ready money.
The studying of the entries.
The mysterious absence from the office.
The time of suspense and waiting.
The feeling of excitement among the friends in the office.
The trip outside to buy a sporting extra.
The search for the results.
The sad return upstairs.
The hope that the paper may have made a mistake.
The feeling among the friends in the office that the paper is right.
The attitude of the friends in the office.
The feeling of remorse.
The lightened pay envelope.

Wild Gastronomic Adventures of a Gourmet

☆ THE TORONTO STAR WEEKLY
November 24, 1923

Last night we were cooking venison.

As the meat sizzled in the pan it brought back adventures in eating. Wild gastronomic adventures.

In order that this may be a full confession, the author writes under a pseudonym. But it is all true. Every word of it is true.

I have eaten Chinese sea slugs, muskrat, porcupine, beaver tail, birds' nests, octopus and horse meat.

I have also eaten snails, eels, sparrows, caviar and spaghetti. All shapes.

In addition I have at one time and another eaten Chinese river shrimps, bamboo sprouts, hundred-year-old eggs, and lunch-counter doughnuts.

Finally I must confess to having eaten mule meat, bear meat, moose meat, frogs legs and fritto misto.

It is better to keep foreign names out of this. They will only complicate it.

Once upon a time I lived for almost three weeks on goat's milk. That was when my face was yellow as a Chinaman's with mountain jaundice and they used to drive the goats up to the door of the hospital. I will never willingly take another drink of goat's milk.

Of the other delicacies named above, the most toothsome are bamboo sprouts and beaver tail. Unfortunately, due to climatic exigencies, it is almost impossible to combine them in the same dish.

The least to be commended is mule meat. There is very little one can say for mule meat. It makes little appeal to either the esthetic sense or the palate. In ranking foods it should be placed somewhere between boiled moccasin and the more toothsome of the tallow candles.

That is unless it is a young mule. I have never eaten young mule. It may be very good.

Before the confessional is over I must admit that I have frequently eaten goat. Young goat, that is. It is a delicacy in Italy and the skinned young goats hang in the marketplaces like rabbits. Stewed it is very good.

My real gastronomic adventures began at the age of ten. A number of us kids had a shack in a run-down cherry orchard back of our house. We were all mighty hunters. We all pulled pretty deadly slingshots.

We read Ernest Thompson Seton's *Two Little Savages* and decided that the only proper thing to do was to eat whatever game you killed.

This ideal proved a boon to the cats of the neighborhood. If a cat has nine lives, that ruling must have saved hundreds of lives. It brought me, however, into contact with sparrows as game birds.

The sparrow may not be as strong a flyer as the quail. Fewer sportsmen shoot him than pursue the partridge. He will never rank with the wild turkey. But he is a mighty fine bird to eat. Try it some time and see.

It was about this time in my gastronomic career that I was led into what I can now look back on as a gastronomic excess. On a bet I ate a fair-sized quantity of poison ivy.

My father is immune to the effects of poison ivy. He is also, by the way, immune to mosquitos. I boasted of the fact to a collection of the gang that poison ivy would not harm my old man. They doubted me.

I therefore declared that poison ivy wouldn't hurt me either. Some doubt as to this was expressed.

I thereupon offered to eat some poison ivy to prove my point. A good deal of doubt of my actual willingness to eat any poison ivy was freely expressed.

A wager involving, I think, ten thousand dollars was made that I would not eat the ivy. I thereupon ate the ivy.

It did not harm me in the least. I never collected the wager. But I acquired a certain social standing among the other boys by my ability and willingness to eat poison ivy at any time to silence scoffers or win bets.

I do not know whether I still have the ability to eat poison ivy. It has not been tested for many years.

Chinese sea slugs I first ate in Kansas City. During a winter spent as police reporter on the *Kansas City Star*, I continued my epicurean education by eating steadily through the menu of a Chinese restaurant. Not one of these short-order Canadianized Chinese restaurants, but a real chop suey, chow mein place with teakwood tables and a fan-tan game going in the back room.

At this time I had discovered chow mein which, when properly made, has much the same game edge on any occidental dish you can name as Mr. Dempsey has on Mr. P. Villa.

Somehow I felt that chow mein couldn't be the only Chinese dish. Somewhere in that un-understandable menu there doubtless was listed a dish that would make chow mein look like chow mein made everything else in the world look to me.

So I determined to eat my way completely through the menu. It was a large menu of almost seven pages. It took me all winter. But I made some wonderful discoveries.

No one has to tell me how Dr. Banting felt when he discovered insulin. I have known the thrill of scientific gastronomic research.

There were several drawbacks though. In the first place I could get no one to eat with me after the first few weeks. Then there were sea slugs. I encountered nearly half a page of sea slugs. Sea slugs in every known form. They nearly stopped me. Even now the word sea slug, or its Chinese equivalent, makes me shudder.

Just after sea slugs on the menu came ancient eggs. One-hundred-year-old eggs. Dark green in color. If you want instruction as well as amusement from this article, let me give you a straight tip. Lay off ancient eggs. They aren't worth it.

In the first place they are very expensive. In the second place they don't taste good.

I was constantly in debt to various police sergeants, pugilists and wrestling promoters that winter. It cost a lot of money to keep to my eating program. Finally the Chinese restaurant keeper got enthusiastic over my eating. He laid himself out. He did his best. But he never extended me credit. I think he was afraid I might die on him.

For years I used to get a postcard from that Chinese restaurant keeper every Christmas.

Kansas City was a great eating town. In those days the favorite newspapermen's eating house was just up Grand Avenue from the *Star* plant. One night at midnight three of us went in and sat at the counter.

One reporter ordered milk toast. This order sounded like an insult to the waiter, who had been celebrating the successful ending of the week, and he made a pass at the reporter with a large knife he had been using to slice ham.

The reporter swung at the knife wielder and fortunately connected. The knife wielder took a dive through the plate-glass cigar case. As the other waiters refused to regard the incident as closed we were forced to eat at the all-night lunch wagons.

Kansas City was a live town in those days, and the glory of its nocturnal life was the all-night lunch wagon. Many a night I have stood in the shelter of an all-night lunch wagon while the blizzard swept down from the great cold funnel of the Missouri River valley and eaten chili con carne, brown, red and hot all the way down, and real chilmaha frijoles while I learned about life and Mexican home cooking from the keeper of the wagon. To be invited inside an all-night lunch wagon was a great honor only accorded to the elect. The owners were all wonderful cooks, too.

It was the cook and conductor of an all-night lunch wagon that first loaned me a copy of Stephen Crane's *The Red Badge of Courage.*

The worst food I have ever eaten over a period of three days was in Kingston, Ont. On the third day I had time to locate a good Chinese restaurant where they could cook Chinese food. But they used too much bean oil.

There is a good Chinese restaurant in Cobalt, Ont. Everybody that has ever been there knows the one I mean.

Toronto restaurants I have found uniformly dull. The food is there and it is cooked, and that is about all you can say. On the other hand there is excellent food and good cooking in many of the Toronto hotels. Especially on Sunday.

Toronto has good cafeterias. The variation in prices in different cafeterias is amazing. In one it will be impossible to get any sort of a meal under 75¢ or 85¢. The same meal, exactly as well cooked in a cafeteria exactly as centrally located, will cost 40¢ or 45¢.

You can have adventures in eating in Toronto. But you have to go into the Ward to get them.

Snails I first ate in Dijon, France. Somehow I had never hankered after snails ever since the morning I saw a hawker pushing a wheelbarrow-load of them through the narrow streets of the Montagne Ste. Geneviève quarter shouting "Escargots! Escargots!" at the top of his lungs and pausing to chase the little fellows that wriggled off out of the gutter.

There was something about that live mass in the wheelbarrow. A snail in every shell and two horns on every snail. Somehow it didn't stimulate the appetite.

But in Dijon you are no man if you don't eat escargots. So I ate them. I don't know that I'm any more of a man now. But I know what snails taste like.

The thing they remind you most of is an inner tube. Cross an inner tube with a live frog, and make the product slippery, and you have the texture. There are few snails sold now though. For the past years there has been a small famine. Seventy percent of the snails exported from Burgundy have been made of beef, cut snail-shape, cooked and packed in the snail shells. There is no lack of snail shells.

Frog legs are no exotic dish. Most people have eaten frog legs. They taste like the white meat of chicken except the meat is more tender and delicately flavored.

There are two common animals that taste like very good young pork. One is the opossum or just plain possum, who trims coat collars, eats persimmons, and was beloved of ex-President Taft, of reciprocity memory.

The other is the common porcupine or quill pig.

Porky will eat anything from a canoe paddle to a barrel of salt pork, barrel and all, but his meat is nearly as tender and delicious as the possum's. He looks hard to skin, but by nailing his carcass up to a tree by the front paws he is very easy to work with.

I have had some very fine meals of porcupine in the bush.

Muskrats are good eating, too, as any Indian can tell you. The meat is as tender as chicken. In preparing both muskrat and porcupine, when skinning them you must cut out the little kernels of scent glands which lie along the inside of the forelegs.

Beaver tail is another strictly Canadian delicacy. It is becoming increasingly hard to obtain. I have eaten it once. Then it was prepared by a very fine cook and struck me as about the best thing I'd ever sunk a tooth into.

Deer liver fried with back bacon is another wonderful article of food that Canadians have a better chance at than anyone else. You have never had the real venison flavor until you eat fresh deer liver fried over a wood fire with good back bacon crisping in the pan with it.

Octopus is a great article on the menu of all the seaports of the Mediterranean. The tentacles are cut into manageable lengths, breaded and fried in butter. It varies in appeal. Sometimes it is good and sometimes it is very tough and leathery.

When I first ate it on a waterfront restaurant in Geneva, I was not aware it was octopus. That always makes a difference. About halfway through the dish I noticed the little vacuum cups on a piece that had lost its batter. It was a shock. But then the adventurer in eating gets used to shocks.

There was horse meat for example. For weeks I ate horse meat before I discovered it. It is not bad eating. Except artillery horses and steeplechasers. The meat is like beef, but stringy.

Opposite where I lived in Paris there was a "Boucherie Chevaline" with a big golden horse's head above the door and a sign that announced that the proprietor was prepared to proceed to the place and elevate horses, mules or donkeys at any hour of the day or night. Except for the golden horse's head outside it looked like any other butcher shop. All the usual cuts of meat were on display. It did a good day-in-and-day-out business among the housewives of the quarter.

After years of adventurous eating there are only a few things that I dislike. One of them is parsnips. Another is the doughnut. Another is Yorkshire pudding. Another is boiled potatoes.

There are articles of food, like the sweet potato, that I can no longer eat because I once made a pig of myself about them. There are other things, like spaghetti, that I cannot eat so well now that my hand is losing its cunning.

But I have discovered that there is romance in food when romance has disappeared from everywhere else. And as long as my digestion holds out I will follow romance.

The Big Dance on the Hill

☆ THE TORONTO STAR WEEKLY
November 24, 1923

The arrival.
The vast crowd on the floor.
The encounter with the boss.
The man-to-man smile from the boss.
The feeling of elation.
The doorkeeper from the office who is serving out.
The whisper from the doorkeeper.
The long journey down the hall.
The closed door.
The clink of glasses.
The opening of the door.
The imposing array of glassware.
The sight of the host.
The look on the host's face.
The sight of the boss with the host.
The look on the boss' face.
The sight of several other distinguished-looking men.
The look on the distinguished-looking men's faces.
The atmosphere of disapproval.
The request from the attendant.
The giving of the order.
The silence kept by the host, the boss and the distinguished-looking men.
The uncomfortable feeling.
The increase of the uncomfortable feeling.
The retreat.
The journey down the long hallway.
The chuckles from the doorkeeper.
The statement from the doorkeeper that he had been instructed to admit only the family and old friends.
The renewed chuckles of the doorkeeper.
The desire to kill the doorkeeper.
The sad return to the dance floor.

Wolfe's Diaries

☆ THE TORONTO STAR WEEKLY
November 24, 1923

Three years ago it looked as if the faded brown pages of General Wolfe's own diaries covered with his clear copper-plating penmanship and tracing the events of one of Canada's times of greatest crisis had been lost to the Dominion. It was an inestimable historic loss.

Included in the historic collection of Monckton papers, the diaries were offered for auction sale in London. Ottawa had set aside a sum for the purchase. But Sir Leicester Harmsworth, the late Lord Northcliffe's brother, outbid the Dominion government.

Now Sir Leicester has presented the entire collection of books and documents to Canada as a memorial to Lord Northcliffe, and in a short time they should arrive at Ottawa.

The collection is called the Monckton Papers. But it is General Wolfe's own documents, papers and his personal order book covering a period of eleven years, between the time when he was a major in the 12th of Foot to the eve of his death in the attack on the Heights, that are the greatest in popular interest.

Wolfe's order-book is a revelation of both the man and the soldier. Anyone who has ever enjoyed the protection of artillery fire will relish this passage:

> Officers of artillery and detachments of gunners are put on board the armed sloops to regulate the fire, that in the hurry our own troops may not be hurt by our artillery. Captn. York and the officers will be particularly careful to distinguish the enemy, and to point their fire against them. The frigates will not fire until broad daylight, so that no mistake can be made.

A new light upon Wolfe's own opinion of the battle that was to give him his death wound is shown by this extract.

> . . . The rest march on and endeavor to bring the French and Canadians to battle.

> The officers and men will remember what their country expects from them and what a determined body of soldiers are capable of doing against five weak battalions mingled with a disorderly peasantry.

Then to conclude the order, written in the same copper-engraving script:

> The soldiers must be attentive to their officers and resolute in the execution of their duty.

It was the last order Wolfe ever wrote.

A new side to Wolfe, the admirer of Gray's "Elegy," is given in his orders where he declares that he must have young and vigorous officers to lead the troops in "the never-ceasing war that should be made upon the Indians till they are totally exterminated or driven to a distance. Young officers armed and dressed for the service of the woods would spread terror among them and soon root 'em out."

Sir Leicester has had the entire collection bound in polished morocco embossed in gold. Some of the important documents are set out in die-sunk pages with wide margins in order to eliminate friction.

Included in the collection is a series of thirty-three letters written by General Wolfe during the siege of Quebec. Many points about the siege are cleared up by these letters.

Journals of French officers, letters addressed to the French commander, and diaries and maps of the French positions are also numbered in the collection of documents relating to the siege.

The Monckton manuscripts themselves deal with the period from 1752, when Lieut.-Col. Monckton arrived in Nova Scotia until after Monckton assumed the command on the death of Wolfe. They give in detail the story of the siege and capture of old Quebec and reveal all the secret orders of the expedition.

Wolfe's own papers and documents passed into General Monckton's hands on his death. To this collection have been added thirty volumes of rare books dealing with the time and many priceless manuscripts by Sir Leicester Harmsworth to make the collection as complete as possible.

General Wolfe was no believer in the soldier marrying. In one order he states, "The lieutenant-colonel recommends to the soldiers not to marry at all. The long march and the embarkation that will soon follow must convince them that many women in the regiment are very inconvenient, especially as some of them are not so industrious nor so useful to their husbands as a soldier's wife ought to be."

A threatened invasion of England from France is also revealed in Wolfe's orders, when his regiment was brought down from Scotland and stationed in Canterbury. Wolfe orders that the men "should fix bayonets and make a bloody resistance" if the enemy makes a landing.

From England the regiment went out to the colonies, and how the entire struggle between the British and the French in Canada looked to the man on the job is set forth in Wolfe's daily orders. In Wolfe's own papers is a series of conditions for the French surrender and a first draft of a scheme for governing and administering Canada, "if God's blessing rest upon the success of our arms."

Old French maps of Canada, one of which shows "The New Discoveries in the West of Canada," being especially interesting, are included in the collection. Hudson Bay is shown in a strange bulging form with a direct connection between it and Lake Superior. The lakes are all in the map, but their size and shape are such as they would appear to a voyageur whose only concern was to traverse them as quickly as possible.

There is also a quaint map of the battles of Lexington and Concord in the American Revolution showing the British regular's version of those affairs.

Tancredo Is Dead

☆ THE TORONTO STAR WEEKLY
November 24, 1923

No. He was neither an opera singer nor a five-cent cigar. He was once known as the bravest man in the world. And he died in a dingy, sordid room in Madrid, the city where he had enjoyed his greatest triumphs.

For many years Tancredo was famous throughout the Latin world. For ten minutes' work he used to get $5,000. And he worked early and often. But a woman impersonator came along and spoiled the whole game for him.

Tancredo's fame was made in the bullring. He was no bullfighter. But he thrilled the crowds that came to the bullfights as nothing else could. His name on the posters meant a packed arena.

Tancredo appeared after the third bull had been killed. Dressed in white, his head bound in a white cloth, his face covered with flour, he walked out from the barrera amid a roar of applause and took his place in the center of the sanded arena, standing like a statue facing the toril from which the bull would be released. The gate of the toril would swing open and the bull dash out into the glare of the bullring. Momentarily blinded by the sunlight, he would then sight Tancredo and charge him.

Tancredo never moved. To move would have been fatal. He simply fixed his eyes on the bull.

Standing stiff as a statue, he gimleted the bull with his eyes. Just as the bull was about to hit him, it stopped, stiffening its short legs and plowing up the sand. Until this moment the audience was in a hush of suppressed excitement. They never knew but what the bull might not stop.

But the bull always stopped, and with its eyes fixed on Tancredo slowly backed away, tossing its head and snorting to make itself believe it was not afraid.

Then a torero would vault over the barrera and attract the bull away with his cape, and Tancredo would break his stiff pose and walk away across the arena while the crowd thundered applause.

The ten-minute appearance was all he had to do, and he could name almost his own price.

Never in all his performances was he gored by a bull. His eyes were all-powerful.

But imitators sprang up in bullrings all over Spain. Tancredo no longer had a monopoly. He could no longer command his high prices, for the imitators had an added advantage. They were not one hundred percent effective.

Sometimes the bull would halt and back away. Sometimes the eye of the amateur Tancredo would waver or he would give an involuntary shiver, and the bull would carry through his charge and the human statue would shoot up into the air in a tangle of gory sheeting.

The thrill of what might happen gave the Spanish crowd the same thrill that sends people of other nations out to automobile road races and the Grand National Steeplechase.

In the end Tancredo's popularity was lost because of his own perfection.

There was no possibility of an accident with Tancredo. Tancredo was too brave.

Then a woman emulator came along. That was the final straw.

According to the *New York Herald* dispatch announcing Tancredo's death, Doña Tancredo was nowhere near perfect. She was thrown sometimes, and this the Spaniards considered unesthetic and called on the authorities to suppress the act.

Tancredos were in operation all over the Spanish peninsula. Some of them were seated in chairs when the bull came out. Some of them would remain standing in the center of the ring throughout the bullfight. Most of them spent a large part of their time in the hospital. And then the woman.

Bullfight fans began to complain that the old formal sport was being made into a burlesque. "No more Tancredos," they shouted.

So the government passed a law barring the act from Spain. With it they barred Tancredo's livelihood.

Don Tancredo himself tried to learn to become a matador. But he found himself up against a competitive profession in which his rivals had been trained since they were five years old. He proved slow on his feet and not particularly graceful.

While he tried to calm the bull with his eye, he found that it was only possible if his body remained absolutely rigid. In the exigencies of the bullring there was no time to acquire this rigidity before the bull appeared. He was a dismal failure in bullfighting.

For years he was a familiar figure around the cafés of the Puerto del Sol in Madrid and then he disappeared. It takes money to sit in a café.

Now he is dead. To the older generation of bullfight fans he is a memory of a thrill they will never have again: the white-sheeted figure with uncanny flour-covered face standing stiff in the hot glare of the bullring while the bull that wanted only to kill him backed away, cowed by his eye.

To the younger generation he is not even a name.

There is a new generation of bullfight vaudeville acts. Charley Chaplins in costume who allow themselves to be gored for so much per goring. The feeling is turning against these, too. They are only allowed in the informal bullfights of the dog days where the young matadors get their tryouts on young bulls.

Tancredo is dead. Penniless and a failure because he was too perfect.

"Nobelman" Yeats

☆ THE TORONTO STAR WEEKLY
November 24, 1923

They have given the Nobel Prize for literature to William Butler Yeats.

This is highly satisfactory to most literati and to their friends and companions in the cognoscenti.

The man in the street won't know anything about it anyway, and when the publishing houses warm up to their work, everybody six months from now will be reading Yeats.

Clubwomen will discover that Yeats is not dead. "My dear, of course he's not dead, he's just won the Nobel Prize and he writes the most wonderful poetry. Of course, I haven't had time to read it yet but we're going to have a paper on him at the club next Wednesday. There is a Yeats that is dead, though. I'm absolutely sure of it. I remember reading something about him at the time. As a matter of fact, we had a paper on him too at the club and a discussion afterwards."

Yes, there is a Yeats who is dead. That was Bill Yeats' father.

Nobody seems to know much about how the Nobel Prizes are given but they always stir up a lot of discussion.

William Butler Yeats has written, with the exception of a few poems by Ezra Pound, the very finest poetry of our time.

This is a statement that will be instantly challenged by the admirers of Alfred Noyes, John Masefield, Bliss Carman and Robert Service. Let them read what they like. There is little use in attempting to convert a lover of Coca-Cola to vintage champagne.

Only six years ago Yeats' poetry was being published in the States in *The Little Review*, which was being suppressed for publishing Joyce's much-discussed *Ulysses*.

Yeats has also written plays, communed with the fairies, and been elected a senator in the Irish Free State. His hair hangs in a lank sweep on one side of his Celtic face and he makes no attempt to dress like a businessman. He is very shy, rarely speaks above a whisper, and in the same whisper lectured here and in the States.

By giving the Nobel Prize to Yeats, the Nobel Prize–givers had made up for a lot of things.

In 1911 they crowned with the $40,000 accolade M. Maurice Maeterlinck of Belgium and the Côte d'Azur. Lately, people don't seem to think so much of the writings of M. Maeterlinck.

Again, in 1913, the $40,000 laurel wreath was ensconced on the lofty and serene brow of Rabindranath Tagore, the Hindu poet. Of late years, a good many find something a little syrupy about the poetry of Tagore.

Neither Maeterlinck nor Tagore has successfully stood up as great literary figures.

In the next-to-the-last year of the war, the 40,000 paper ones were divided between Karl Gjellerup and M. Pontoppidan. These gentlemen are modestly described in the records as Danish authors. Authors of what is not stated.

Anatole France waited until he was well into his eighties when he had attained a height where neither rewards nor honors could mean anything to him, and was finally presented with the Nobel award. He received the distinction of being placed on the Index by the Pope in the same year.

While Anatole was only in his seventies, however, the Nobel awarders singled out Verner Heidenstam, the Swedish poet, for the prize. You have doubtless read Verner's powerful pieces? Yes, neither have I.

In 1920 the award went to a real writer, Knut Hamsun of Norway. It was said to be awarded to him because of his epic novel, *The Growth of the Soil*. This is one of the few great novels since *Madame Bovary*.

Immediately Hamsun received the prize, publishers made a rush for translation of his works. They appeared one after another. Not in the sequence in which they were written but often going straight back so that his earliest and most imperfect books were issued to a waiting public which had read *The Growth of the Soil*, and wanted to go on from there. As the result of the flood of Hamsun's failure and pot-boilers that have been brought out in English, he has been killed off to many people that will thus never read his masterpiece.

And yet no American author has won the Nobel Prize. It once looked as though Sherwood Anderson was headed in that direction, but he has swerved a long way off now.

It is an Englishman that is the ghost that must haunt the Nobel Prize–givers' consciences. That Englishman is Thomas Hardy.

Thomas Hardy is too old now for the prize to do him any good. But he could do a great deal of good to the prize.

It is a last chance for the Nobel Prize-winners [judges] to honor the greatest living English writer. Year after year, he has been passed over while the Tagores, the Maeterlincks, the Heidenstams, the Gjellerups, and, last year, Benavente, the Spanish dramatist, were given the coveted award.

One Pole has received the Nobel Prize. He was Henryk Sienkiewicz, the author of *Quo Vadis?*

Another Pole who has not received the prize is Joseph Conrad, the author of *Lord Jim*, *Typhoon*, *The Nigger of the Narcissus*, *Falk*, *Victory*, and other books which let him share with Hardy the honor of being the greatest writer writing in English.

Perhaps if Conrad had decided to write in French at the period when he gave up the sea, and was undecided in which language to write, French or English, he might have won the Nobel Prize long ago.

It has just occurred to me that perhaps the Nobel committee don't read English very well. That would account for the omission of Hardy quite easily.

There is also a chance that Yeats' new honor [as senator] may have had more to do with determining his choice than the poems he published in *The Little Review*.

Changed Beliefs

☆ THE TORONTO STAR WEEKLY
November 24, 1923

Before coming to Canada I believed many things about the country. Some of these came from reading books, some from magazines, many from newspapers. Some of them were hearsay from people who had been in Canada.

Now I have changed many of these beliefs. It is a good thing to confess when you have been wrong.

These are the beliefs I have changed:

1—*That all Canadians are in a wild political ferment about the Dominion's status in the Empire, and are either ardent Imperialists or anxious to break loose altogether.*

This is not true. They are almost uninterested. For one Torontonian who could explain what Imperial preference means there are ten who could tell you the score of the Argos-Queen's game.

2—*That in the first week of November all Toronto businessmen, newspaper reporters, politicians, artists, coal dealers, coal heavers and pugilists left en masse for the north to go deer hunting.*

This has not proven true. A few men who are sure of their jobs go deer hunting. The average citizen of deer-hunting age and proclivities takes it out in cleaning his rifle and kicking himself for having bought that new car instead of sticking to the old Ford.

3—*That in the great open spaces where men are men, the inhabitants wore the kind of costumes that are used in illustrations in James Oliver Curwood stories.*

Another error. The drummers and young men who stand around in front of the Hudson Bay Company's store wear Classy Campus Cut Clothing. Men who work wear overalls.

4—*That all Indians in the great north wore their hair bobbed.*

Only the squaws do. Most of them, on late reports from Paris, are letting it grow out.

5—*That there was a great amateur athlete in Canada named Lionel Conacher.*

It seems that there was a great amateur athlete named Conacher in Canada, but that he is now, at the age of twenty-three years and six months, playing football in the States for an academy of the scholastic ranking of Upper Canada College.

6—*That the average man in a Canadian city was a great lover of all sorts of sports.*

He loves to watch games and to read about them. The playing of them seems to be left to a small minority. Since motorcars have become universal most Torontonians have even given up walking.

7—*That Toronto streetcars were overcrowded, badly run, and altogether unsatisfactory.*

This is all wrong. No city in the world has a better-run and more comfortable streetcar system than Toronto.

8—*That Toronto has the finest police force in the world.*

I know nothing about this from personal experience. But something seems to have happened to the belief.

9—*That living in Toronto would be much cheaper than in the States.*

It is if you keep house. If you eat at restaurants it is about twenty-five percent more expensive.

10—*That there are no great Canadian writers. Writers, that is, of the first rank, such as Hardy, Conrad, Fielding, Smollett and Joyce.*

There is one. Thomas Chandler Haliburton, of Nova Scotia. Although I do not believe his works are widely read.

Bank Vaults vs. Cracksmen

☆ THE TORONTO STAR WEEKLY
December 1, 1923

Shortly after midnight on a Sunday morning, five mounted bandits rode into the little town of Ville Marie on the Quebec side of Lake Temiskaming twenty-five miles south of Haileybury.

They rode in Wild West style. Shooting out the lights as they galloped up the main street and putting the citizens of the town into a panic.

It was just like the movies. Except it was deadly real.

Two young clerks named Damonte and Chener were sleeping over the Quebec branch when the masked riders pulled up and began shooting into the building.

In their nightclothes, the two young clerks escaped from the building and rushed to the Bayview Hotel. When the proprietor of the hotel tried to call Haileybury on the phone to give the alarm, he found there was no answer. The telephone was dead.

As they rode into town, the bandits had cut the telephone and telegraph wires. Ville Marie was isolated from the outside world.

While two robbers worked inside the bank, three others kept guard outside, armed with rifles.

The hotel proprietor, two guests and the bank manager ran toward the bank, but the masked men standing in the doorway with their rifles warned them back.

A woman showed a lamp in a window opposite the bank building and a shot extinguished the lamp.

Inside the bank there was a muffled roar. But the men inside did not come out. The guards at the door were nervous. They did not know what was keeping their pals. The town was rousing. In a deer country the men have rifles and the bandits did not know how long it would be before they would have to face a posse.

Then there was a terrific explosion. A burst of flame outlined the whole scene in a sudden glare of white and black and the men inside came rushing out. The bank building was on fire. All the men mounted and rode out of the town.

As the two men who had been working inside at blowing the safe swung into their saddles, the horses were jumping from the smell of the smoke from the burning building. A twelve-year-old boy ran toward them. Afraid he would be able to identify them from the glare of the building, which was beginning to flare up, they shot him twice. Both bullets went into the boy's ankle. No one else came out and the bandits rode away through the town.

But what had happened inside the bank?

The desperadoes had blown open the vault door. But when they attempted to blow open the safe, they had blown it clear out through the back of the bank building. There it was found, unopened, by the citizens of Ville Marie when they came out in the glare of the burning bank building to look at the scene of the crime. Next day, June 26, 1916, the safe was brought across the lake to Haileybury. The robbers had obtained a few thousand dollars worth of bonds, which prove more of a liability than an asset to yeggmen, from the vault. All the cash was in the safe. And they didn't get any of it.

With variations this robbery has appeared again and again through the annals of Canadian crime.

It is the story of unsuccessful safe-blowing. Safe-blowing is supposed to be a thing easy to accomplish. But year after year it becomes increasingly hard.

There have been great bank robberies in Canada, and Toronto has recently suffered. But they are an entirely different thing. The "stick-up" or payroll jobs.

In them the banks have been attacked at the weakest link in their chain of money-guarding. The time when their money must be temporarily exposed for the purpose of transferring large sums through messengers.

There is no mechanical device that can protect them there except the pistol or the sawed-off shotgun. And opposed to them is a very efficient mechanical device that has changed the entire aspect of crime. That device is the automobile. It plays its part in nearly every robbery, holdup or crime of violence in Canada.

But while the banks must expose their funds occasionally, during a transference they take good care that there should be no chance of any robbery during the time that the funds are in the care of the bank itself.

There are electrical systems installed in banks that automatically give the alarm to the police and set off a siren and gong outside to give a local alarm if any burglary is attempted.

This system is not altogether popular with Toronto banks.

An officer of one Toronto bank told the *Star Weekly* that people were in almost every day with some safety system or other.

A favorite system they have to sell is one whereby the teller steps on a button if anyone comes in to hold him up. That sets off an alarm outside. The idea is for the button to be where he can reach it in his usual position if he is forced to throw up his hands. As a result, it is right under his feet and he is setting it off all the time. "We can't afford to cry wolf in a bank," the bank officer explained.

Then there was the rumor that a certain Toronto bank was protected by machine guns. Just how the machine guns were to be cut loose on the robbers was never explained.

The origins of this rumor are the two German Maxims, war souvenirs, that flank the entrance to the vault of the Canadian Bank of Commerce.

In many banks there are supposed to be secret watching-places built into the building near the eaves where an armed guard can observe every move made below and himself remain unseen.

"That is a very primitive measure," a Toronto bank officer told the *Star Weekly*. "When I was young I once had the job of watching through a hole in the floor down into the vault below. In those days, too, a vault was once protected from burglars by an iron bar that fitted into the door from another vault and the place of entrance covered with plaster. That was the real old days."

In those days, the hours when the bank was shut and the cash and bonds locked in the vault were the most dangerous of all. Now they are the safest.

It is the wonderful supervaults and mammoth safes that guard the money of Canadians that have made the head offices of all the banks absolutely cracksman-proof. A safe-builder told the *Star Weekly* that no head office of a Canadian bank had ever had its safe blown. A bank officer confirms this statement.

To break into a modern big safe and yegg-proof vault, the burglar would need a motortruckload of tools and a college graduate in engineering to handle them.

When banks are robbed and the safes blown, it is always a little branch that suffers. Then even when the robbers cut the communications and give themselves a free hand, they are often foiled.

Take the attempted bank robbery last year in Carleville, Saskatchewan.

On August 23, three robbers entered the bank, held up the clerks, tied them up, and fired seven charges of nitroglycerine in the safe. But they couldn't open it. Finally they gave up and went off in a motorcar.

On September 17, 1920, a gang of safe-blowers attempted to use an oxyacetylene blowtorch and other modern steel-cutting equipment to break into the Merchants' Bank at Beachville, Ont. The equipment was so bulky it had to be transported by truck and the men fled when a young employee of the bank who was inside awakened and fired his revolver through the window. The equipment was left behind.

How safes were brought to the point of perfection where cracksmen, if they are to enter, must use tools that it would be almost impossible for them to transport, and the dramatic history of the constant struggle between the safe-builder and the safe-blower is told in an article by Edward H. Smith, published in *The Scientific American*, from which the following extracts were taken:

On a memorable Monday morning in 1878—October 28, to be precise—the cashier of the old Manhattan Savings Institution turned his key in the lock of the street door, walked nonchalantly into the banking room and fainted. Men will do stranger things in the face of miracles, and one had been wrought here. The door to the great iron vault gaped open, torn and twisted on its hinges, as though a Titan had wrenched it with the weight of mountains and the power of tides. On the floor was a litter of papers, account books, coins, pieces of shattered iron and ends of broken tools. From the interior of the huge metal box, long considered beyond the strength and ingenuity of men, was missing a total of $2,747,700 in cash and bonds. The greatest bank robbery in history had been committed between Saturday night and that sticky dawn.

The cashier revived, summoned the other officers in haste, closed the doors and put up a sign relating that the bank had been forced to suspend because of robbery. Policemen came in droves; crowds gathered and tried to storm the entrance; the news spread through the city and across the country; runs on other banks began and were checked with difficulty. The corner of Broadway and Bleecker Street, where the bank stood, was obstructed for many days with crowds of curious people who had come to see where this astounding thing had taken place. The doings of a small gang of cracksmen became a piece of history.

To this burglary, just forty-five years ago, is to be traced the beginning of modern developments in the protection of our great banks against criminal attack, so it may be worth while to glance at some of the facts concerning it.

A gang of notorious professional bank burglars, headed by the famous Jimmie Hope, had laid plans for the attack on the Manhattan Savings Institution and consumed all of three years in working out their scheme. They had eventually corrupted one Michael Shevelin, the bank watchman, gained entrance to the place with his collusion and worked on the vault door with wedges, powerful jackscrews and explosives, through the nights of Saturday and Sunday, finally reaching the bonds and cash about 3:30 o'clock on Monday morning. Their loot consisted of $2,506,700 in registered bonds, $73,000 in coupon bonds and a fortune in cash. To save the bank from disaster and foil the robbers, the Congress and the state legislature passed acts cancelling the stolen registered bonds and causing fresh securities to be engraved and issued in their stead. To such lengths the nation had to go to protect its finances against a few bold and clever men.

It must not be assumed that such a burglarious raid as that on the Manhattan Savings Institution had happened without precedent or that the banks had not done what they could to prepare for such attacks. The burglary of large banks was an old story in 1878, and great quantities of inventive energy and of bank money had then already been expended in the quest of some method of vault construction that could be relied upon. It is interesting to note some of the ideas that then appplied.

The vault of the old National Park Bank, when it was finally dismantled some years ago, to make room for a modern substitute, was found to have been built of solid slabs of granite closely fitted together. The edges of each such slab had been incised with a series of hemispherical depressions, which fitted precisely to similar scoopings from the adjacent granite blocks, thus forming globular holes, five or six inches in diameter. Into each of these holes a cannon ball had been placed, so that if a burglar tried to enter the vault by digging at the joints of the stones, he would encounter the loose cast-iron balls.

It must be remembered that nitroglycerine was then unknown and that the burglar had to drill holes to get at the tumblers of the locks or to blow in the gunpowder which was then his only explosive agent.

But all such precautions were not of much avail, for the reason that the better bank burglars of the day understood how to attack the strongest vault doors then in existence. Invention had provided nothing better than heavy close-fitting doors of cast iron, chilled and later case-hardened, but iron doors after all. We shall have a word to say about the evolution of the vault door. For the present it is enough to observe how burglars, without such weapons as they now possess, ripped their way through the no-doubt formidable defenses of the old banks.

Another New York City feat of the same Jimmie Hope will illuminate the matter. In the fall of 1868, Hope rented a basement under the rooms of the Ocean National Bank at the corner of Fulton and Greenwich streets, and opened a carpet business. In front was his showroom; in the rear his workroom. To divide these and keep passersby from intruding on his privacy, he had a partition erected, dividing the two parts of the establishment. In reality, this ceiling-high screen was put in place to mask his operations against the bank, whose vault he had carefully studied.

On the night of June 27, 1869, nine years before the greater feat at

Manhattan bank, Hope and several assistants, including the famous old robbers, Ned Lyons, Mark Shinborn and George Bliss, reached the banking rooms by means of a hole they had been slowly cutting through the ceiling of their carpet store and the floor of the bank. They went to work on the door of the vault with wedges. First a fine wedge, no thicker than the blade of a knife, was hammered into the crack of the door near the lock. A slightly thicker wedge was next pounded into place with sledges, and then a still heavier tool took its place. Gradually the burglars worked their way up to wedges two or more inches thick at the base. These were forced home with big jackscrews, which got their purchase from heavy iron bands or cables which had been passed around the vault or secured to its back by heavy hooks. Gradually the jacks were turned until the thick edges forced their way in and pried the door from its iron jamb. The bolts were now forced back and the work was done. Explosives and heavy crowbars were then used on the inner iron door. This robbery totalled $1,200,000, of which, fortunately, the larger part was in non-negotiable bonds.

As a consequence of this mode of attack, the construction of doors came to be the matter of chief concern with the vault-builder. The first heavy doors in use had been straight-edged, like the end of a square-sawed board. Then, in order to get a door that would close more tightly, came the beveled or sloping edge, the inner face of the door being narrower than the outer. But the wedges of the burglars soon put this pleasant scheme to rout. Then came the stepped edge, which is still in use on all ordinary safes. The steps were designed to stop the wedges from penetrating beyond an inch or two. Wedges backed by powder formed the burglar's answer to this scheme. Then came the tongue-and-groove edge, which did good service until nitroglycerine came along. The grooves now proved to be a happy circumstance for the cracksman. His liquid explosive lodged in them and he got wonderful results for the minimum of "soup." Faced with this peril, the vault-builders went back to a battleship or armor-plate door, which was soon found worthless.

The construction of such doors is one of the marvels of modern vault engineering. Entirely aside from its complicated multiple time-locks, its numerous powerful bolts, its intricate inner locking devices and its other mechanical intricacies, such a door is a first-class piece of engineering. It seems to the eye to be a solid piece, yet it consists of many layers; it is a composite in more than one sense. The layers, to mention only some of n, are ordinary strain-resisting steel; reinforced concrete, used against t-resisting metal, to delay burglars operating with the cutter-burner resisting metals; at least one and often two layers containing foils of electric burglar alarm systems, and so on.

n & Company door weighs about 50 tons and that of al Reserve Bank, the thickest if not the largest ever built, is said by its makers to achieve a total weight of almost two hundred thousand pounds.

The vaults must be designed to foil any possible or conceivable method of assault. In addition, they must be constructed to resist fire and tremendous heat likely to be developed when a great building comes into conflagration. In consideration of this risk, the roofs or tops of the big vaults of today must be even stronger than the floor, sides and front or door, for the roof must be additionally reinforced against the impact of falling bodies from above, in case of the collapse of a building through fire or earthquake.

What kind of engineering is required for the achievement of such prodigious strengths may be guessed when the dimensions of really big bank vaults are understood. For instance, in the new Federal Reserve Bank in New York there are three such vaults, one on top of the other. Each vault measures about 125 feet in depth and about 55 feet in the average width. The bottom of the nethermost room rests on bedrock and the walls of the vaults are in part under the waters of the harbor. The main door of each of these vaults weighs about 90 tons and each of the three rooms has a second or emergency door used for ventilation during business hours. The vault doors of this bank are not of the plug type, another and unique design having been employed to suit the needs of the building in which the vaults were placed.

In describing the structure of the walls, floor and roofs of our great vaults, it is to be remembered that no standard has yet been arrived at, that a number of engineers entertain conflicting ideas about certain details of construction and that experiment is constantly being carried forward. Again, the chief difficulty in arriving at a perfected type of vault, and one that is not likely to be overcome in the future, is the matter of the constant development of tools useful in attacks on such structures. There has not been a successful burglary committed upon the vault of any great metropolitan bank since 1878. Nevertheless, industry and the arts have gone ahead and perfected a number of tools which might at any time be employed by burglars of sufficient skill and daring to seize the opportunity. To this class belong the electric arc, the electric and pneumatic chisel, the electric drill and the oxyacetylene torch in its latest development.

This last-named tool is of special peril and interest. I have previously written of its effectiveness against the safes and vaults employed in rural or suburban banks and the defeats met by the manufacturers of strongboxes made for this clientele. It now appears that the cutter-burner tool, as it is preferably called by vault engineers, is a decided menace to the gre banks and their ponderous equipment, so that much reconstructio endless experiments are in progress. To date nothing has been f can be called a genuinely effective resistant.

The effort to find metals which would foil the withering flame of the torch is not without its note of romance. When the oxyacetylene cutter-burner was first employed, there was a great scamper after heat-resisting metals and a number of compositions were produced which withstood the fiery tongue of the torch fairly well. [. . .]

Inflation and the German Mark

☆ THE TORONTO STAR WEEKLY
December 8, 1923

"Now if any gentleman needs his quarter for a meal or a bed—"

The barker stood in a narrow alley opposite Osgoode Hall, Toronto. In front of him was a soapbox with a few envelopes of foreign money.

In front of the soapbox stood a crowd of out-of-workers, shifting from foot to foot in the mud, and listening dull-eyed to the spellbinder.

"As I say," went on the barker, moistening his lips under his gray mustache, "if a gentleman has an immediate need for his quarter, I don't want it. But if he is prepared to make an investment, I am offering him the chance to make himself rich for life.

"Only a quarter, gentlemen. Just one Canadian quarter, and Russia is bound to come back. A quarter buys this 250,000 Soviet ruble note. Who'll buy one?"

Nobody seemed on the point of buying. But they all listened to him perfectly seriously.

It was the Russian ruble, the Austrian kronen and German mark, not worth the paper they are printed on, making a last stand as serious money in Toronto's Ward.

"In normal times this note I hold here is worth about $125,000. Suppose it goes up to where the ruble is worth only one cent. You will have $2,500. You can walk right into the bank and get $2,500 for this one note."

One man's eyes shone and he moistened his lips.

The barker lifted the little pink bit of worthless paper up and looked at it lovingly.

"And Russia is coming back, gentlemen. Every day her money gets more valuable. Don't let anyone tell you Russia isn't coming back. Once a country gets to be a republic she stays that way, gentlemen. Look at France. She's been a republic a long time."

A man in the front row in an old army coat nodded. Another man scratched his neck.

The barker drew out a big blue-green bill and laid it alongside the Russian ruble note.

No one explained to the listening men that the cheap-looking Russian money had been printed in million-ruble denominations as fast as the presses could work in order to wipe out the value of the old imperial money and in consequence the money-holding class. Now the Soviet has issued rubles backed by gold. None of these are in the hands of the barkers.

"To the first man that pays a quarter for this 250,000-ruble note I am going to give free this German mark note for 10,000 marks."

The barker held both notes up for inspection.

"Don't ever think that Germany is through. You saw in the paper this morning that Poincaré is weakening. He's weakening, and the mark will come back, too."

He was Coué-izing the crowd. A man pulled out a quarter.

"Gimme one."

He took the two bills, folded them and put them in his inside coat pocket. He smiled as the spieler went on. He had a stake in Europe again.

The foreign news would never be dry to him now.

Four or five more men bought a half million rubles for a quarter. The rubles are not even quoted on the exchange any more—yet they and the worthless German marks have been sold all over Canada as investments.

Then the money seller leaned over and picked up an envelope of thousand-mark notes. They were the well-printed pre-war notes that were in common use in Germany until the exchange tumbled from 20,000 marks to the dollar this spring down the toboggan where you can almost name the number of billions you want on a dollar and get them. None of these marks are worth any more than any others. Except as pieces of paper for wallpapering or soap wrappers.

"These are special," the money seller said. "I'm selling these at a dollar apiece. They used to be fifty cents. Now I've raised the price. Nobody has to buy them that doesn't want them. They're the real pre-war marks."

He fondled them. The real pre-war marks.

Worth 15 cents a trillion before the New York banks refused to quote them any more last week.

"What makes them any better than those marks you gave away?" asked a gaunt man leaning against the wall in the alley. He was one of those who had invested a quarter in Europe and was jealous of this new mark being sprung on him.

"They're all signed for in the Treaty of Vairsails," the barker said confidentially. "Every one of these is signed for in the peace treaty. Germany has thirty years to redeem them at par."

The men standing in front of the soapbox looked respectfully at the marks that were signed for in the treaty. They were obviously out of reach of investors. But it was something to be near them.

On the wall of the one-story shack that bounded the alley, the tall youth who smoked a pipe and stood in the background while the vendor of money talked had tacked a number of clippings and samples of foreign money.

The clippings were mostly about the economic comeback made by Soviet Russia and various other foreign dispatches of an optimistic tone.

With his forefinger the money vendor traced out the story of a dollar loan to some Austrian bank.

"Now, who wants to buy 10,000 Austrian kronen for a dollar?" he asked the crowd, holding up one of the big purple bills of the old Hapsburg currency.

In the banks today the Austrian crown is worth .0014½ cents. In other words, about 14 cents for 10,000 kronen. At one dollar for 10,000 kronen, the men in the alley were invited to take a flyer in Austrian currency.

"Now, personally, I only keep enough Canadian money to pay the bills," the spellbinder went on. "You can't tell what is going to happen to Canadian money. Look at these different currencies today. A wise plan is to keep a little Russian money, a little German money, a little Austrian money, and a little British money."

Most of the men looked as though even the smallest amount of Canadian money would be exceedingly welcome. But they listened on, and every lot offered, after the spellbinder had talked long enough, found a quarter produced by somebody, and the hope of getting rich quick implanted in some man.

"Take these Austrian bills, for example," the money seller went on. "There's a bill I sold for two dollars. Now I'm selling it for only a dollar. And I'll give a million-ruble Soviet note away with it."

At this announcement, some of those who had bought the rubles for two bits a quarter-million looked sullen.

"Oh, these are different rubles," the vendor assured them. "There are some of these rubles here I wouldn't take ten dollars for. Let some gentleman offer me ten dollars and see if he can get them."

"I won't deny I have rivals," the speaker proceeded. "They try and undersell me. They cut prices on me. But now I'm going to cut prices on them. My big rival asks 40 cents for a million-ruble note. I'm going to undercut him to the limit. He's started this competition. Let's see if he can stick in it. Gentlemen, I will give this million-ruble note away with an Austrian note for 10,000 crowns. All for one dollar."

No one seemed to have a dollar. So the reporter bought.

"There's a gentleman that can size up an investment," the spieler said. "Now, you other gentlemen. You know Austria is coming back. She's got to come back. Say the Austrian crown gets up to only half a cent in value. You have fifty dollars right off the bat."

But a dollar was out of the class of the investors present.

Reluctantly the soapbox merchant went back to the more moderate amounts.

"Now if a man want to invest a quarter," he commenced, and held up one of the pink quarter-million ruble notes.

Again his audience was with him. This was all right. There were still a few quarters to be invested. What was just one more meal in the face of a chance for a quarter-million dollars?

War Medals for Sale

☆ THE TORONTO STAR WEEKLY
December 8, 1923

What is the market price of valor? In a medal and coin shop on Adelaide Street, the clerk said: "No, we don't buy them. There isn't any demand."

"Do many men come in to sell medals?" I asked.

"Oh, yes. They come in every day. But we don't buy medals from this war."

"What do they bring in?"

"Victory medals mostly, 1914 Stars, a good many M.M.'s, and once in a while a D.C.M., or an M.C. We tell them to go over to the pawnshops where they can get their medal back if they get any money for it."

So the reporter went up to Queen Street and walked west past the glitering windows of cheap rings, junk shops, two-bit barber shops, second-hand clothing stores, and street hawkers, in search of the valor mart.

Inside the pawnshop it was the same story.

"No, we don't buy them," a young man with shiny hair said from behind a counter of unredeemed pledges. "There is no market for them at all. Oh, yes. They come in here with all sorts. Yes, M.C.'s. And I had a man in here the other day with a D.S.O. I send them over to the secondhand stores on York Street. They buy anything."

"What would you give me for an M.C.?" asked the reporter.

"I'm sorry, Mac. We can't handle it."

Out onto Queen Street went the reporter, and into the first secondhand shop he encountered. On the window was a sign, "We Buy and Sell Everything."

The opened door jangled a bell. A woman came in from the back of the shop. Around the counter were piled broken doorbells, alarm clocks, rusty carpenters' tools, old iron keys, kewpies, crap shooters' dice, a broken guitar and other things.

"What do you want?" said the woman.

"Got any medals to sell?" the reporter asked.

"No. We don't keep them things. What do you want to do? Sell me things?"

"Sure," said the reporter. "What'll you give me for an M.C.?"

"What's that?" asked the woman, suspiciously, tucking her hands under her apron.

"It's a medal," said the reporter. "It's a silver cross."

"Real silver?" asked the woman.

"I guess so," the reporter said.

"Don't you know?" the woman said. "Ain't you got it with you?"

"No," answered the reporter.

"Well, you bring it in. If it's real silver maybe I'll make you a nice offer on it." The woman smiled. "Say," she said, "it ain't one of them war medals, is it?"

"Sort of," said the reporter.

"Don't you bother with it, then. Them things are no good!"

In succession the reporter visited five more secondhand stores. None of them handled medals. No demand.

In one store the sign outside said, "We Buy and Sell Everything of Value. Highest Prices Paid."

"What you want to sell?" snapped the bearded man back of the counter,

"Would you buy any war medals?" the reporter queried.

"Listen, maybe those medals were all right in the war. I ain't saying they weren't, you understand? But with me business is business. Why should I buy something I can't sell?"

The merchant was being very gentle and explanatory.

"What will you give me for that watch?" asked the reporter.

The merchant examined it carefully, opened the case and looked in the works. Turned it over in his hand and listened to it.

"It's got a good tick," suggested the reporter.

"That watch now," said the heavily bearded merchant judicially, laying it down on the counter. "That watch now, is worth maybe sixty cents."

The reporter went on down York Street. There was a secondhand shop every door or so now. The reporter got, in succession, a price on his coat, another offer of seventy cents on his watch, and a handsome offer of forty cents for his cigarette case. But no one wanted to buy or sell medals.

"Every day they come in to sell those medals. You're the first man ever ask me about buying them for years," a junk dealer said.

Finally, in a dingy shop, the searcher found some medals for sale. The woman in charge brought them out from the cash till.

They were a 1914–15 Star, a General Service Medal and a Victory medal. All three were fresh and bright in the boxes they had arrived in. All bore the same name and number. They had belonged to a gunner in a Canadian battery.

The reporter examined them.

"How much are they?" he asked.

"I only sell the whole lot," said the woman, defensively.

"What do you want for the lot?"

"Three dollars."

The reporter continued to examine the medals. They represented the honor and recognition his King had bestowed on a certain Canadian. The name of the Canadian was on the rim of each medal.

"Don't worry about those names, Mister," the woman urged. "You could easy take off the names. Those would make you good medals."

"I'm not sure these are what I'm looking for," the reporter said.

"You won't make no mistake if you buy those medals, Mister," urged the woman, fingering them. "You couldn't want no better medals than them."

"No, I don't think they're what I want," the reporter demurred.

"Well, you make me an offer on them."

"No."

"Just make me an offer. Make me any offer you feel like."

"Not today."

"Make me any kind of an offer. Those are good medals. Look at them. Will you give me a dollar for all the lot?"

Outside the shop the reporter looked in the window. You could evidently sell a broken alarm clock. But you couldn't sell an M.C.

You could dispose of a secondhand mouth organ. But there was no market for a D.C.M.

You could sell your old military puttees. But you couldn't find a buyer for a 1914 Star.

So the market price of valor remained undetermined.

European Nightlife: A Disease

☆ THE TORONTO STAR WEEKLY
December 15, 1923

Nightlife in Europe is not simply a list of cafés. It is a sort of strange disease, always existent, that has been fanned into flame since the war. Its flame is burning an entire generation.

Paris nightlife is the most highly civilized and amusing. Berlin is the most sordid, desperate and vicious. Madrid is the dullest, and Constantinople is, or was, the most exciting.

Paris goes to bed the earliest of any big town in the world. Promptly at twelve-thirty o'clock the last omnibuses leave on their crosstown trips, the last subway train roars along the Metro, and the streets around the Opéra empty as though a curfew had sounded. Taxis leave the streets to drive home, and the final trains are jammed with Parisians on their way home. Paris is dead.

Hours before, shutters have been up and the residential quarters tight asleep. There remain only the nighthawks. Where do thy go?

There are three oases of light in the tight-shuttered darkness of a Paris night.

One of them is Montparnasse. Here the Latin Quarter cafés keep open a couple of hours more. There is no place in the world deader than a Montparnasse café unless you know the crowd. If you know the people, it is a club and a center for gossip, a common meeting place.

Where is the really gay Paris nightlife we hear so much about? Where are the young people who never go to bed at night? The people that do not exist before ten o'clock at night?

They are probably packed into a little place around the corner from the Hôtel Crillon in the staidest, most respectable, un-Bohemian quarter of Paris. In the Rue Boissy d'Anglais is the café of the Boeuf sur le Toit or the Bull-on-the-Roof, Jean Cocteau's bar and dancing, where everyone in Paris who believes that the true way to burn the candle is by igniting it at both ends goes. By eleven o'clock the Boeuf is so crowded that there is no more room to dance. But all the world is there. Sitting at tables, talking and drinking while the jazz plays.

But French nightlife is so civilized that it is not exciting to the outsider. Nightlife is a sort of state of mind. Either you are in it or you are out of it. It is in Cocteau's bar that nightlife in the highest sense—that of living at night—is brought to the boiling point.

The Boeuf, though, closes at two in the morning. Sometimes before. And two in the morning is when the true nightlifer is just getting under way. So in a taxi the nightlifer starts up the slopes of Montparnasse.

Montmartre is the famous Paris place for night activity, It is compounded of the garish tourist traps around the Place de Clichy, with red-painted doors and thousands of electric light globes. These have fantastic names and fake artists who are hired to come in and sit at the tables to give a Bohemian atmosphere. They are run for the purpose of getting Americans, both North and South, to buy champagne.

Champagne is the great symbol of nightlife to the uninitiated. And the tourist traps make the most of it. They sell champagne and champagne only. If the visitor tries to order anything else, he is given the choice of champagne or the street door. It ranges in price from six to eight dollars a bottle. While it is being drunk, the tourist can look around at other tourists and the hired artists who are dressed in Greenwich Village costumes.

Champagne, by the way, is a sacred name in France. The only wine allowed by law to be called champagne wine comes from a certain defined district around Rheims in the Champagne province. Other fake champagne must be labeled Epernay, mousseux or whatever district they come from. There is a terrific fine for selling these wines from just outside the champagne district as the veritable wine. The real champagne vintners have important government connections.

A patriotic-minded journalist heard that a certain Montmartre resort was selling mousseux as champagne. With a witness, he went into the place and ordered a single glass of champagne. He was served a sparkling liquid, the bubbles hopping and jumping to the surface. He paid a champagne price. The waiter went away.

The journalist tasted the glass. "Mousseux!" he shouted. "The camel has served me with mousseux and I ordered champagne. What an outrage. Not only an outrage, but a breaking of the law. Bring the proprietor. Bring the proprietor instantly before I send for the police."

The proprietor is reported to have settled the case for 20,000 francs.

Numberless other journalists and men-about-town ordered glasses of champagne after that, hoping for such a chance, but the mousseux sellers were wise. It was not worth the chance. It is costly business mistaking a Frenchman for a tourist.

The famous Moulin Rouge on Montmartre is an enormous dancing place where shop girls, their gentlemen friends, and a certain number of tourists go to dance on a large and slippery floor in the glare cast by a spotlight that is supposed to give romance through different-colored celluloid disks that make a red, orange, or green glow. It is cheerful and innocuous, and one of the few places in Paris where the foreigners come into contact with French people taking their pleasure.

The real nightlife places do not open up until after three o'clock in the morning. At present the two most notable of these are the Caucasian, a very smart Russian place, and Florence's. Florence is an American Negress who has made a tremendous vogue for herself in Paris as a dancer.

When I first met her some time ago, she was a typical Negro dancer, jolly, funny and wonderful on her feet. Until you had seen Florence dance the "Everybody Steps," you had seen nothing.

Then a section of the French nobility took her up. She danced at the home of the Princesse de This and the Comtesse de That. Late last summer we wandered into Florence's dancing place to get some corn-beef hash with poached egg and buckwheat cakes at two-thirty in the morning. It was absolutely dead. No one had come in yet. The Negro staff were not overeager to serve us. They thought we ought to buy champagne.

Now the mark of a real student of nightlife is that he should be considered so much of an asset to a place that the compulsory-consumption-of-champagne rule should be suspended in his favor.

"We're old friends of Florence," I explained.

"Suah, boss. What'll you all have? Beeah? Anythin' you say, boss."

We had a good meal, and then Florence came in. Florence was changed. She had acquired an English accent and a languid manner.

"Oh. Hulloa," she said. "Yes, I'm dawncing private now. But do drop in on us sometime heah. So jolly to see you again."

It wasn't jolly at all. Another of the really amusing after-midnight places had been ruined by prosperity.

"Miss Flawnce she ain't a Niggah no mo. No suh. She done tell customahs mammy's an Indian lady fum Canada," a waiter explained. "Ah'm luhnin' to talk that English way, too. Ah'm goin' tuh tell people my mammy's an Indian lady fuhm Noble Scotia. Yes, suh. We'll all be Indiums this tahm nex' yeah. Yes, suh."

There are other famous nocturnal places in Paris—Zelli's, where the newspapermen all used to go, the very dressy *dancings* in the Rue Caumartin, where one would find Peggy Joyce and other famous ladies of the front page, and sleek-haired Chileans and Argentineans dancing to American jazz music.

Berlin's nightlife is a great contrast to that of Paris. Berlin is a vulgar, ugly, sullenly dissipated city. After the war it plunged into an orgy that the

Germans called the death dance. There is nothing attractive nor gay about the nightlife of Berlin. It is altogether revolting.

If champagne is the deus ex machina of the after-hours existence of Paris, cocaine takes its place in the German capital. Cocaine peddlers get short shrift from the Paris police. But in Berlin they sell their wares openly all over the city. In some cafés cocaine is served at the tables by the waiters.

Berlin is the home of the nightclub. Riding or walking along the street at night, a ragged-looking man will run up to your cab and try to get you to go to a nightclub. A fine new nightclub. All the nightlife of the city.

There is no nightclub in Berlin that is not disgusting, heavy, dull and hopeless. The gaiety is as forced as it is real in Paris on the 14th of July, when the entire city dances in the street for two nights steady and the streets are roped off to shut out taxis and autobuses.

If anyone has any doubt that the Germans lost the war and realize they lost it, all they need would be a session of after-midnight Berlin.

Madrid is another business. Nobody goes to bed in Madrid. On the other hand, they don't do anything to amuse themselves. They just stay up and talk.

All of the downtown district of Madrid is at its very busiest at two o'clock in the morning. Cafés are crowded. The streets are jammed with people. Theaters start in Madrid at ten o'clock at night. Matinees commence at 6:30 in the afternoon.

There are two big downtown dancing places. One called Maxim's. The other, two or three doors up the street, I have forgotten the name of. It makes no difference. They are both alike.

Always beware of a place called Maxim's. It means imitation Paris. Now Paris is a very fine thing. But it doesn't imitate well. And there are Maxim's all over the world.

Even the original Maxim's in Paris is a dull enough place. It has a bar as you go in and then a big room full of tables, with a dancing floor at the far end. It is always full of profiteers, American buyers, and the inevitable sprinkling of South Americans. The music plays loudly and the prices are high. The lights are bright. It is a good place to get a headache.

All the imitation Maxim's are reproductions on a small scale of the original.

In Madrid I asked a bullfighter where the really gay life of the city was. Where he went himself, for example.

"Me? I go to bed," he smiled shyly. "I don't like to talk and I don't like to drink. Since I have learned to read, I read a little every night in bed before I go to sleep."

"What do you read?" I asked.

"Oh, the bullfighting papers," he said.

He is a very serious young man, makes $15,000 a year, and probably has half the girls in Madrid in love with him. But he doesn't believe in nightlife.

Constantinople before the Mudania armistice was probably the most hectic town in the world. Mustapha Kemal had announced that when he came into town it was going to be shut tight up—and everybody believed him. He had done everything he ever said he would up till then.

Nobody slept much during the day and nobody slept at all during the night. No good restaurants opened up before ten at night and the theaters opened at midnight. The followers of the prophet spent their waking hours trying to make absolutely sure there would be none of the product of Constantinople's Bavarian breweries left to dump into the Golden Horn when Kemal arrived.

The breweries tried to keep pace with the Moslem demand. It was a great race. Along toward evening, the crews of the British, American, Spanish, Italian and French fleets would come ashore and rush to the aid of the Mohammedans in their struggle with the breweries. It was a great battle, with the brewers always a little ahead. In spite of their smaller numbers, their organization was better.

As the evening advanced fights would break out among the sailors of the different nationalities in the various Galata beer emporiums. This no doubt slowed up their efficiency. Especially when there were shootings or knifings, which occasionally resulted in pitched battles.

All of Constantinople was in a feverish sort of wildness. It had nothing of the sullen ugliness of the Berlin pleasure resorts.

There is the famous incident of the captain of a cruiser of a neutral nation, not the United States, whose vessel was anchored in the Bosporus. The incident came very near to being of tremendous international gravity.

One night at three o'clock in the morning, the commander came aboard his ship. His manner was distrait. His eyes were rolling.

"Clear the ship for action," he commanded.

The commander paced restlessly up and down the bridge. The ship was as busy as only a warship with its crew suddenly roused at three a.m. can be. Men rushed in every direction. Guns were trained for a broadside.

"Commence firing on the city," the captain shouted down his telephone from the bridge. "War has been declared."

Somebody had sense enough to grab him and take him below. Constantinople had been a little too much for him.

The captain was said to have been drinking douzico straight. It has a faculty of making people go crazy at odd times. It is prepared with some sort of strange Turkish ingredients, but its base is grain alcohol imported from the United States in large steel drums. It was never served without some crackers, cheese or radishes to give it something to work on in addition to the lining of the stomach.

From Stamboul across the Golden Horn to the high barren plain at the top of Pera, Constan stayed up all night. Every big newspaper story that broke came after midnight in the nightclubs of Pera. It was in one of these, the Pele Mele, in some way derived from Pall Mall, that an excited young officer just back on a destroyer from Mudania confided the news of the signing of the armistice to a Russian countess who was acting as a waitress.

The officer, who had been present at the signing, told the countess in greatest secrecy because he had to tell someone. He was so excited. She recognized the value of the story and told an American newspaperman whom she liked much better than she did the officer.

In an hour, through means of his own, the newspaperman verified the report, and put it on the cable to New York, where it arrived in time for the morning papers. The signing was not announced officially until next morning at eleven o'clock. By that time the correspondents of the other papers, whose correspondents did not know the countess, were getting cables from New York asking them why they were scooped on Mudania.

Italy is a strange country for nightlife. Nightlife must be taken to mean, not dissipation or dancing places necessarily, but merely that strange, feverish something that keeps people up and about during the hours they would normally sleep.

Milan, the largest city in the north of Italy, with about 800,000 inhabitants, goes to bed almost as early as Toronto does. Verona, not a third as big, is alive and gay at two-thirty in the morning. I remember hiking into Verona with a pack long after midnight expecting to find everything closed tight, and finding the city as alive as Paris at 9:30 in the evening.

Turin is another late town, and a very pleasant town. Rome is very dull at night. Rome, to my mind, is very dull nearly all of the time. It is the last city in the world I would ever want to live in.

Marseilles has one of the most variegated, interesting and toughest night sides in Europe.

Seville, too, is late to bed. So is Granada.

Nightlife is a funny thing. There seems to be no reason or rule that controls it. You cannot find it when you want it. And you cannot get away from it when you don't want it. It is a European product.

Goiter and Iodine

☆ THE TORONTO STAR WEEKLY
December 15, 1923

Should a whole city be dosed for the ills of a few of its inhabitants?

Across Lake Ontario, Rochester, N.Y., is answering that question in the affirmative by introducing iodine into the city's water supply in an effort to combat goiter by mass medication.

Rochester is in the heart of the goiter belt that stretches across the fresh-water reaches of the North American continent. Goiter, or enlargement of the thyroid gland, is caused according to physicians by a lack of iodine. Most of the iodine of the world is found in the sea. People living near the sea are immune from goiter, the scientists say.

Rochester's experiment, which is being carried out under the direction of Dr. George W. Goler, health officer, consists in dosing the Kodak City's water supply with 16.6 pounds of soluble iodine daily over a period of three weeks twice a year. This is fifty parts of iodine to a billion parts of water.

It is said to be such a small amount of the drug that its presence cannot be determined even by chemical analysis. But the scientists conducting the experiment believe it will successfully prevent goiter.

When the wholesale dosing was decided on, a notice was posted in the city schools of Rochester stating: "We are putting fifty parts of iodine per one billion parts of water in the Hemlock water supply for prevention of goiter. If you are under twenty years of age, drink three or four quarts of water a day and see your goiter disappear."

Toronto, although it is in the goiter belt and has as large a percentage of cases of the disease as Rochester, has no intention of adopting the mass method, according to Dr. C. J. O. Hastings, of the Department of Public Health.

Dr. Hastings would not comment on the Rochester experiment beyond stating that it had not been tried and was not contemplated in Toronto. Dr. Hastings believes the treatment of goiter among children should be handled by the family physician.

"Goiter is a deficiency disease," Dr. Hastings stated. "It is due to insufficient iodine content in our food and drink. This has been shown by demonstration that enlargement of the thyroid gland can be readily produced by entirely eliminating iodine from our food and water supply. Another proof is the demonstration that goiter can be prevented and cured by the proper administration of iodine in a form that can be assimilated by our system. That is, by giving a small medicinal dose of some officinal preparation of iodine such as syrup iodide of iron or iodide of sodium for a period of say two weeks in spring and fall."

A year ago Dr. Hastings stated the percentage of goiter in Toronto schoolchildren was as high as fifteen to twenty percent in one school ranging down to two percent in another. Since then no new survey has been made so the increase or decrease of the disease can only be conjectured.

Since earliest times medical men have faced the problem of goiter. Out of the age-long struggle certain facts have emerged.

Goiter, or thick neck, is an enlargement of the thyroid gland that lies across the front of the neck. The thyroid is necessary for the growth of children. If it cannot get iodine in some form or other, this gland swells and enlarges.

It is the great preventive of goiter. The sea is where the iodine of the world is stored. In other days our table salt came from the sea and contained all the iodine that was needed by the human body. Now it often comes from inland salt mines.

People who live in high mountainous countries, where whatever iodine may have been deposited when the waters receded from the earth has been almost completely washed away by melting snow and glaciers, are the most gravely affected with goiter. In Switzerland the disease is almost universal among the men and women of the mountains. In the Canton of Zurich one district was found to be one hundred percent goiterous.

The further one gets from the sea the more prevalent does goiter become.

Along the seaboard, on the other hand, the disease almost never appears.

The North American continent is, by some students of the goiter problem, divided into four goiter belts. These run across from east to west. The southern and eastern coast has practically no goiter. North in the plains and Ohio valley there is a certain amount of the disease. Then comes a belt where it is more frequent, including the middle and western states.

In the high ground of the Great Lakes, in cities such as Chicago, Buffalo, Rochester, Toronto and Detroit and in the mountainous regions of the West, goiter is most prevalent.

All water contains a certain amount of iodine, except in the most goiter-ridden parts of the world such as the Swiss, Tyrolean and Trentino Alps. In parts of these districts, the natives drink from glacial streams which contain nothing but snow water.

Dr. J. P. McClendon, professor of physiological chemistry in the University of Minnesota Medical School, says that eating seafood on Fridays and holidays at the seashore is a goiter preventive. All marine animals and plants contain iodine and the necessary anti-goiter drug can be obtained through eating fish, according to the professor.

He advises the inhabitants of the goiter belt to give children a little powdered kelp, seaweed, or other iodine-containing material mixed with their food, water or salt.

Dwellers along the seacoast escape goiter because of the way the seawater is thrown into spray in great storms and blown inland great distances. Iodine in sea salt is sometimes blown landward a distance of 200 miles, scientists state.

Dr. H. A. Stevenson, of London, is a pioneer in advocating iodine treatment as a public health measure in Ontario. Prominent Ontario physicians have pointed out the numberless bad effects from thyroid enlargement. Nervousness, irritability, lack of balance, and various conditions are the result of overdevelopment of the thyroid gland, which could be controlled by iodine administration.

Dr. Stevenson, in 1921, while an M.P.P., advocated regular treatment in the public schools in order to secure a normal development of the thyroid gland to commence with a survey of schoolchildren of the province. His proposal seemed too new and did not meet with instant approval.

Human beings are not the only sufferers from goiter. Sheep, cattle, hogs, dogs and fish are all liable to the disease.

Dr. Hastings tells of one of the first practical demonstrations of goiter prevention in Michigan. A large flock of sheep were afflicted with goiter. Their condition seemed hopeless. But they found in a new pasture a bed of crude salt and after licking it soon recovered. No further cases of goiter developed. The salt was analyzed and found to contain a great quantity of iodine.

Brook trout have been heavy sufferers from goiter. At one time the malady became so prevalent among government hatcheries and the fish died off to such an extent that it was believed artificial trout raising would have to be abandoned.

Investigators discovered that the artificial food the trout were getting was free from iodine content. When a small amount of iodine was added, the fish became normal again.

Rochester's experiment in goiter prevention by mass medication was only undertaken after consultation with the leading scientists and authorities of the city. Investigation showed that Rochester used 24 million gallons of water a day. There was already two parts of iodine in a billion parts of water.

Difficulty was encountered in diffusing the iodine properly through the city's entire water supply but the fact that the water fed through ten miles of pipes from one reservoir to another helped this out.

"The amount of iodine taken is so small that it cannot be harmful to a normal person," Dr. Goler, the Rochester health officer, told a reporter for a New York paper. "But in this region, where iodine is not obtained in either water or salt, everyone is deficient in iodine. This deficiency does not manifest itself in everyone in the same manner.

"In some it causes goiters but we do not know how greatly this lack of iodine may affect our health in other ways. There is not the slightest danger of getting too much iodine during the six weeks of the year it is in the water, even if one drinks it who comes from a region where there was enough iodine in the water and who consequently has plenty of iodine in his system."

About 300,000 people get their drinking water in Rochester from the city waterworks. A private water company supplies about 37,000 people with water from Lake Ontario. So far no iodine has been placed in Lake Ontario.

"We have in this country caused many diseases to disappear, including typhus, cholera, yellow fever and smallpox," Dr. Goler is reported to have stated.

"Other diseases are in the process of disappearing. These include malaria, typhoid and diphtheria.

"We know that iodine will prevent goiter. When a million pigs died from goiter, they began feeding them iodine. Should we not do as much for ourselves and our children as we have already done for fish and pigs by adding a little iodine to their drinking water?"

I Like Americans

☆ THE TORONTO STAR WEEKLY
December 15, 1923

I like Americans.
They are so unlike Canadians.
They do not take their policemen seriously.
They come to Montreal to drink.
Not to criticize.
They claim they won the war.
But they know at heart that they didn't.
They have such respect for Englishmen.
They like to live abroad.
They do not brag about how they take baths.
But they take them.
Their teeth are so good.
And they wear B.V.D.'s all the year round.
I wish they didn't brag about it.
They have the second-best navy in the world.
But they never mention it.
They would like to have Henry Ford for president.
But they will not elect him.
They saw through Bill Bryan.
They have gotten tired of Billy Sunday.
Their men have such funny haircuts.
They are hard to suck in on Europe.
They have been there once.
They produced Barney Google, Mutt and Jeff.
And Jiggs.
They do not hang lady murderers.
They put them in vaudeville.
They read *The Saturday Evening Post.*
And believe in Santa Claus.
And they make money.
They make a lot of money.
They are fine people.

I Like Canadians

☆ THE TORONTO STAR WEEKLY
December 15, 1923

I like Canadians.
They are so unlike Americans.
They go home at night.
Their cigarettes don't smell bad.
Their hats fit.
They really believe that they won the war.
They don't believe in Literature.
They think Art has been exaggerated.
But they are wonderful on ice skates.
A few of them are very rich.
But when they are rich they buy more horses
Than motorcars.
Chicago calls Toronto a puritan town.
But both boxing and horse racing are illegal
In Chicago.
Nobody works on Sunday.
Nobody.
That doesn't make me mad.
There is only one Woodbine.
But were you ever at Blue Bonnets?
If you kill somebody with a motorcar in Ontario
You are liable to go to jail.
So it isn't done.
There have been over 500 people killed by motorcars
In Chicago
So far this year.
It is hard to get rich in Canada.
But it is easy to make money.
There are too many tearooms.
But, then, there are no cabarets.
If you tip a waiter a quarter
He says "Thank you"

Instead of calling the bouncer.
They let women stand up in the streetcars.
Even if they are good-looking.
They are all in a hurry to get home to supper
And their radio sets.
They are fine people.
I like Canadians.

The Blind Man's Christmas Eve

☆ THE TORONTO STAR WEEKLY
December 22, 1923

To all but one of the half million inhabitants of Toronto it was Christmas Eve. To the blind man it was only the twenty-fourth of December.

The blind man leaned against a building out of the sharp edge of the wind, and shifted from one foot to another on the sidewalk, while the city flowed by him in a last rush of Christmas preparation. He had come a long way to this town, by many different stages.

Through the soles of the blind man's shoes the cold from the wet stone sidewalk was numbing. It was snowing. The blind man could tell because the flakes struck his face for an instant touch of damp cold. The crowd kept moving past.

It was a strange city the blind man had come to. The policemen were all giants. He knew they were giants because their voices came from high above his head and they talked a strange thick accent. The streets were full of people. But there was no jollity. Just a crowded river of people all moving somewhere. And it was cold.

The blind man was not sure that he was not dead. He had been standing up against the building a long time. He was going to keep on standing there. After a while something would happen. Something always had happened.

As a matter of fact if he stood there long enough he was sure to be taken up by one of the big policemen and would probably eat a very good Christmas dinner at the station house.

But the blind man did not realize this. He was not thinking any more. He was just standing and it was very cold and very wet.

As he stood looking out at all the things he could not see, some music started suddenly just beside him. It was an Italian organ-grinder, his coat collar turned up, his cap turned down, who had taken advantage of the shelter of the building against the wet snow and the crowd. He did not like the town either. But he had wine and garlic on his breath and a family in the Ward and he spat on the pavement for Canada and ground away.

Although it was coming from just behind him, the music seemed to the blind man to come from a long way off. At first he did not notice the tune. But somewhere inside him it reached something. The blind man began to see.

He saw a low, white-pillared house set far back in the trees at the end of a long, sandy drive. He saw a boy come riding up the drive on a pony and swing off at the horse block.

"Christmas gift, Aunt Lucy," the boy shouted to someone on the wide porch of the house.

The music kept on. It wasn't a very good hand organ and the wet had gotten into it.

The blind man did not notice that the music was second-rate. He didn't even notice that there was music. He was feeling a strange tight feeling inside himself and he was seeing things.

He saw broad fields sloping away and he smelt the odor of bacon being fried early in the morning. He heard the pounding that thoroughbred horses' hoofs make as they sweep down in a pack toward a fence and he saw that glimpse of a pleasant country that a man gets as he is on rises over a fence full in a pounding gallop. He saw a big square bed with linen sheets and a small boy tucked in the bed listening while someone sat on the bed and stroked his head and talked to him. And he saw a small boy rising early in the morning and going downstairs to start out across the frost-rimed fields with his dog and his gun. He saw many far-off forgotten things.

Then the music stopped.

"Would you mind playing that piece over again?" asked the blind man turning his face toward the Italian.

"You like him? I like him, too. He's a good piece, eh?" The Italian adjusted a button on the machine and commenced to grind out again, "Oh, the sun shines bright on my old Kentucky home."

He looked up at the blind man while he ground, studying him critically and then grinding away like an artist.

The blind man seemed to be absorbing the music. Suddenly he seemed to have enough. He did not look blank or sodden now. His ear was busy sorting out the traffic on the busy street. A policeman's whistle shrilled. The blind man started calmly forward into the traffic.

The Italian did not see him go. His head was bent low over the organ.

Twenty minutes later the ambulance drove off with its gong clanging.

"Did you hear what he said, Joe?" queried one attendant on the front seat.

"Something about the old dumhicky home," answered the other.

"Sometimes it catches them cuckoo that way at the last," observed the other attendant sagely.

In the back of the ambulance a rough blanket covered the stretcher and under the blanket the face of the blind man was smiling. He had seen very clearly for some time.

Christmas on the Roof of the World

☆ THE TORONTO STAR WEEKLY
December 22, 1923

While it was still dark, Ida, the little German maid, came in and lit the fire in the big porcelain stove, and the burning pinewood roared up the chimney.

Out the window the lake lay steel-gray far down below, with the snow-covered mountains bulking jagged beyond it, and far away beyond it the massive tooth of the Dent du Midi beginning to lighten with the first touch of morning.

It was so cold outside. The air felt like something alive as I drew a deep breath. You could swallow the air like a drink of cold water.

I reached up with a boot and banged on the ceiling.

"Hey, Chink. It's Christmas."

"Hooray!" came Chink's voice down from the little room under the roof of the chalet.

Herself was up in a warm, woollen dressing robe, with the heavy goat's-wool skiing socks.

Chink knocked at the door.

"Merry Christmas, mes enfants," he grinned. He wore the early morning garb of big, woolly dressing robe and thick socks that made us all look like some monastic order.

In the breakfast room we could hear the stove roaring and crackling. Herself opened the door.

Against the tall, white porcelain stove hung the three long skiing stockings, bulging and swollen with strange lumps and bulges. Around the foot of the stove were piled boxes. Two new shiny pairs of ash skis lay alongside the stove, too tall to stand in the low-ceilinged chalet room.

For a week we had each been making mysterious trips to the Swiss town below on the lake. Hadley and I, Chink and I, and Hadley and Chink, returning after dark with strange boxes and bundles that were concealed in various parts of the chalet. Finally we each had to make a trip alone. That was yesterday. Then last night we had taken turns on the stockings, each pledged not to sleuth.

Chink had spent every Christmas since 1914 in the army. He was our best friend. For the first time in years it seemed like Christmas to all of us.

We ate breakfast in the old, untasting, gulping, early-morning Christmas way, unpacked the stockings, down to the candy mouse in the toe; each made a pile of our things for future gloating.

From breakfast we rushed into our clothes and tore down the icy road in the glory of the blue-white glistening Alpine morning. The train was just pulling out. Chink and I shot the skis into the baggage car, and we all three swung aboard.

All Switzerland was on the move. Skiing parties, men, women, boys and girls, taking the train up the mountain, wearing their tight-fitting blue caps, the girls all in riding breeches and puttees, and shouting and calling out to one another. Platforms jammed.

Everybody travels third class in Switzerland, and on a big day like Christmas the third class overflows and the overflow is crowded into the sacred red plush first-class compartments.

Shouting and cheering, the train crawled alongside the mountain, climbing up toward the top of the world.

There was no big Christmas dinner at noon in Switzerland. Everybody was out in the mountain air with a lunch in the rucksack and the prospect of dinner at night.

When the train reached the highest point it made in the mountains, everybody piled out, the stacks of skis were unsorted from the baggage car and transferred to an open flatcar hooked on to a jerky little train that ran straight up the side of the mountain on cogwheels.

At the top we could look out over the whole world, white, glistening in the powder snow, and ranges of mountains stretching off in every direction.

It was the top of a bobsled run that looped and turned in icy windings far below. A bob shot past, all the crew moving in time, and as it rushed at express-train speed for the first turn, the crew all cried, "Ga-a-a-a-r!" and the bob roared in an icy smother around the curve and dropped off down the glassy run below.

No matter how high you are in the mountains there is always a slope going up.

There were long strips of sealskin harnessed on our skis, running back from the tip to the base in a straight strip with the grain of hair pointing back, so that you pushed right ahead through the snow going uphill. If your skis had a tendency to slide back, the slipping movement would be checked by the sealskin hairs. They would slip smoothly forward, but hold fast at the end of each thrusting stride.

Soon the three of us were high above the shoulder of the mountain that had seemed the top of the world. We kept going up in single file, sliding smoothly up through the snow in a long upward zigzag.

We passed through the last of the pines and came out on a shelving plateau. Here came the first run down—a half-mile sweep ahead. At the brow the skis seemed to drop out from under and in a hissing rush we all three swooped down the slope like birds.

On the other side it was thrusting, uphill, steady climbing again. The sun was hot and the sweat poured off us in the steady uphill drive. There is no place you get so tanned as in the mountains in winter. Nor so hungry. Nor so thirsty.

Finally we hit the lunching place, a snowed-under old log cattle barn where the peasant's cattle would shelter in the summer when this mountain was green with pasture. Everything seemed to drop off sheer below us.

The air at that height, about 6,200 feet, is like wine. We put on our sweaters that had been in our rucksacks coming up, unpacked the lunch and the bottle of white wine, and lay back on our rucksacks and soaked in the sun. Coming up we had been wearing sunglasses against the glare of the snowfields, and now we took off the amber-shaded goggles and looked out on a bright, new world.

"I'm really too hot," Herself said. Her face had burned coming up, even through the last crop of freckles and tan.

"You ought to use lampblack on your face," Chink suggested.

But there is no record of any woman that has ever been willing to use that famous mountaineer's specific against snow blindness and sunburn.

It was no time after lunch and Herself's daily nap, while Chink and I practiced turns and stops on the slope, before the heat was gone out of the sun and it was time to start down. We took off the sealskins and waxed our skis.

Then in one long, dropping, swooping, heart-plucking rush, we were off. A seven-mile run down and no sensation in the world that can compare with it. You do not make the seven miles in one run. You go as fast as you believe possible, then you go a good deal faster, then you give up all hope, then you don't know what happened, but the earth came up and over and over and you sat up and untangled yourself from your skis and looked around. Usually all three had spilled together. Sometimes there was no one in sight.

But there is no place to go except down. Down in a rushing, swooping, flying, plunging rush of fast ash blades through the powder snow.

Finally, in a rush we came out onto the road on the shoulder of the mountain where the cogwheel railway had stopped coming up. Now we were all a shooting stream of skiers. All the Swiss were coming down, too. Shooting along the road in a seemingly endless stream.

It was too steep and slippery to stop. There was nothing to do but plunge along down the road as helpless as though you were in a millrace. So we went down. Herself was way ahead somewhere. We could see her blue beret occasionally before it got too dark. Down, down, down the road we went in the dark, past chalets that were a burst of lights and Christmas merriment in the dark.

Then the long line of skiers shot into the black woods, swung to one side to avoid a team and sledge coming up the road, passed more chalets, their windows alight with the candles from Christmas trees. As we dropped past a chalet, watching nothing but the icy road and the man ahead, we heard a shout from the lighted doorway.

"Captain! Captain! Stop here!"

It was the German-Swiss landlord of our chalet. We were running past it in the dark.

Ahead of us, spilled at the turn, we found Herself and we stopped in a sliding slither, knocked loose our skis, and the three of us hiked up the hill toward the lights of the chalet. The lights looked very cheerful against the dark pines of the hill, and inside was a big Christmas tree and a real Christmas dinner, the table shining with silver, the glasses tall and thin-stemmed, the bottles narrow-necked, the turkey large and brown and beautiful, the side dishes all present, and Ida serving in a new crisp apron.

It was the kind of a Christmas you can only get on top of the world.

A NORTH-OF-ITALY CHRISTMAS

Milan, the sprawling, new-old, yellow-brown city of the north, tight-frozen in the December cold.

Foxes, deer, pheasants, rabbits, hanging before the butcher shops. Cold troops wandering down the streets, from the Christmas leave trains. All the world drinking hot rum punches inside the cafés.

Officers of every nationality, rank and degree of sobriety crowded into the Cova Café across from the Scala Theater, wishing they were home for Christmas.

A young lieutenant of Arditi, telling me what Christmas is like in the Abruzzi, where they hunt bears, and the men are men, and the women are women.

The entry of Chink with the great news.

The great news is that up the Via Manzoni there is a mistletoe shop being run by the youth and beauty of Milan for the benefit of some charity or other.

We sort out a battle patrol as rapidly as possible, eliminating Italians, inebriates and all ranks above that of major.

We bear down on the mistletoe shop. The youth and beauty can be plainly seen through the window. A large bush of mistletoe hangs outside. We all enter. Prodigious sales of mistletoe are made. We observe the position. We depart, bearing large quantities of mistletoe, which we give to passing charwomen, beggars, policemen, politicians and cabdrivers.

We re-enter the shop. We buy more mistletoe. It is a great day for charity. We depart, bearing even larger quantities of mistletoe, which we present to passing journalists, bartenders, street-sweepers and tram conductors.

We re-enter the shop. By this time the youth and beauty of Milan have become interested. We insist that we must purchase the large bush of mistletoe outside the shop, an empty bank building. We pay a large sum for the bush, and then, in plain sight of the shop window, we insist on presenting it to a very formal-looking man who is passing along the Via Manzoni wearing a top hat and carrying a stick.

The very formal gentleman refuses the gift. We insist that he take it. He declines. It is too great an honor for him. We inform him that it is a point of honor with us that he accept. It is a little Canadian custom for Christmas. The gentleman wavers.

We call a cab for the gentleman, all this within plain sight of the shop window, and assist him to enter and place the large mistletoe tree beside him on the seat.

He drives off with many thanks and in some embarrassment. Many people stop to stare at him.

By this time the youth and beauty of Milan inside the shop are intrigued.

We re-enter the shop and in lowered voices explain that in Canada there is a certain custom connected with mistletoe.

The youth and beauty take us into the back room and introduce us to the chaperones. They are very estimable ladies, the Contessa di This, very large and cheerful, the Principessa di That, very thin and angular and aristocratic. We are led away from the back room and informed in whispers that the chaperones will be going out for tea in one-half an hour.

We depart bearing vast quantities of mistletoe, which we present, formally, to the headwaiter of the Grand d'Italia Restaurant. The waiter is touched by this Canadian custom and makes a fitting response.

We leave, chewing cloves, for the mistletoe shop. Under the small remaining quantity of mistletoe, we demonstrate the sacred Canadian custom. Eventually the chaperones return. We are warned by a whistle up the street.

Thus the true use of mistletoe was brought to Northern Italy.

CHRISTMAS IN PARIS

Paris with the snow falling. Paris with the big charcoal braziers outside the cafés, glowing red. At the café tables, men huddled, their coat collars turned up, while they finger glasses of grog *Americain* and the newsboys shout the evening papers.

The buses rumble like green juggernauts through the snow that sifts down in the dusk. White house walls rise through the dusky snow. Snow is never more beautiful than in the city. It is wonderful in Paris to stand on a bridge across the Seine looking up through the softly curtaining snow past the gray bulk of the Louvre, up the river spanned by many bridges and bordered by the gray houses of old Paris to where Notre Dame squats in the dusk.

It is very beautiful in Paris and very lonely at Christmastime.

The young man and his girl walk up the Rue Bonaparte from the Quai in the shadow of the tall houses to the brightly lighted little Rue Jacob. In a little second-floor restaurant, The Veritable Restaurant of the Third Republic, which has two rooms, four tiny tables and a cat, there is a special Christmas dinner being served.

"It isn't much like Christmas," said the girl.

"I miss the cranberries," said the young man.

They attack the special Christmas dinner. The turkey is cut into a peculiar sort of geometrical formation that seems to include a small taste of meat, a great deal of gristle, and a large piece of bone.

"Do you remember turkey at home?" asks the young girl.

"Don't talk about it," says the boy.

They attack the potatoes, which are fried with too much grease.

"What do you suppose they're doing at home?" says the girl.

"I don't know," said the boy. "Do you suppose we'll ever get home?"

"I don't know," the girl answered. "Do you suppose we'll ever be successful artists?"

The proprietor entered with the dessert and a small bottle of red wine.

"I had forgotten the wine," he said in French.

The girl began to cry.

"I didn't know Paris was like this," she said. "I thought it was gay and full of light and beautiful."

The boy put his arm around her. At least that was one thing you could do in a Parisian restaurant.

"Never mind, honey," he said. "We've been here only three days. Paris will be different. Just you wait."

They ate the dessert, and neither one mentioned the fact that it was slightly burned. Then they paid the bill and walked downstairs and out into the street. The snow was still falling. And they walked out into the streets of old Paris that had known the prowling of wolves and the hunting of men and the tall old houses that had looked down on it all and were stark and unmoved by Christmas.

The boy and the girl were homesick. It was their first Christmas away from their own land. You do not know what Christmas is until you lose it in some foreign land.

W. B. Yeats a Nighthawk

☆ THE TORONTO STAR WEEKLY
December 22, 1923

William Butler Yeats, the Irish poet, who was this year awarded a Nobel Prize for literature, is remembered with something akin to terror by a Toronto man whom he compelled to keep a very unwelcome vigil. This gentleman was his host at the time of his last visit to Toronto [February 2, 1920]. He expected that after the fatigue of his lecture at Hart House the poet would be ready to slumber, but Yeats proved to be a real Dublin nighthawk. Perhaps it would be more appropriate to call him a nightingale.

Anyway, his lecture had made him thoroughly wide-awake and put him in a wonderful conversational mood. He told literary anecdotes. He crooned Erse sagas. One o'clock struck. Two o'clock struck. Yeats grew fresher than ever, but his host was yawning, hollow-eyed, on his chair. He was not accustomed to late sessions with the muses.

The only thing that kept him awake was a terrible fear that he might fall off his chair and disgrace himself forever. At last, about four in the morning, either the poet became exhausted or he observed his host's somnolent condition. Anyway, he called the seance off and went to his bedroom.

He must have passed an exceedingly restless night, for in the morning it looked like ex-Premier Nitti's house after the Fascisti had got through with their visit. The bedclothes were strewn everywhere in great confusion. When it was all sorted out it was found that the poet had left behind his hairbrush and pajamas and a few other articles indispensable to his toilette.

The host had to send these articles by special delivery to New York, so that Yeats might present his usual immaculate appearance to his audience. In spite of the honor of entertaining a genius, this Toronto admirer of poetry in future will prefer for domestic comfort one of our more sedate Canadian poets.

Yeats recently received the Nobel Prize in person at Stockholm. But

Sweden's capital is famous for its nightlife. It may be that his Swedish host easily beat him in an all-night contest. In Toronto at any rate the poet was an easy winner. His host remembers him not as a nightingale but as a nighthawk and a nightmare.

Young Communists

☆ THE TORONTO STAR WEEKLY
December 22, 1923

Three hundred children of Toronto will never again know Christmas.

No. They are not dead.

Although they are nearly all very poor children they have no need for the *Star*'s Santa Claus Fund. They have renounced Santa Claus.

Christmas for them is only going to be the twenty-fifth day of December. For they have set their feet on the stern, flinty path of communism. And on the road that they must go Christmas is regarded as an objectionable survival of a barbaric custom. There is no Christmas in the good Communist's calendar. Toronto's three hundred young Communists are not due for another holiday until March 18, the anniversary of the Paris Commune.

Who are the three hundred child Communists of Toronto?

Some time ago a local minister charged from his pulpit that there were four "red Sunday Schools" holding meetings in Toronto every Sunday. No details were given.

There are five of these so-called "Sunday Schools" at present in Toronto. Communist leaders make no attempt to conceal their existence.

They are divided into Ukrainian, Finnish and English sections and are in reality groups where children can be directed in their development into Communists. Every effort is made to do away with the usual school idea. There is no teacher and no pupil. Development is aimed at rather than instruction.

Now what are Communists? Most Toronto people lump Socialists, Syndicalists and Communists vaguely together as Reds and let it go at that.

Roughly speaking the Communists believe in the abolishing of capital, the dictatorship of the proletariat or laboring class, and the necessity of a revolution to bring these ends about.

Communists are not to be confused with Socialists, Social Revolutionaries, Syndicalists or any milder believers. These children's groups in Toronto are Communist groups.

The Finnish group, which is directed in its activity by Mrs. F. Custance, who spent four months of last year in Moscow studying the Young Communist work, is the most highly organized. It has fifty children as members. They call themselves the Don Hall Young Comrades Club and hold their meetings at the Don Hall, 957 Broadview Avenue, each Sunday.

There are thirty children in the English group. It is known as the Young Communist League Group and holds its meetings each Sunday at Denison Avenue and Queen Street.

Ukrainian children are organized into three different groups in east, west and center Toronto. There are 188 children in the Ukrainian organization, which is under the same direction as that which is under fire at present in Port Arthur, Ont.

This gives only 268 children altogether, but the figure of 300 was furnished by Communist headquarters and may be accounted for by other organizations on which data has not yet been obtained.

A green-covered, paper-bound book with a five-pointed Russian Soviet star in black on which are seated five little children on the cover gives the aims and methods of procedure in forming the groups of Communist children.

It is headed, "Manual for Leaders of Children's Groups," published by the executive committee of the Young Communist International.

It starts by declaring, "The Communist children's groups must be neither party kindergartens nor children's homes. They must be live organizations of the children of the workers, organizations to counteract the poison of the bourgeois education."

Then comes the manner of attack outlined. In big black type the book asks "HOW DO WE BEGIN!"

"Nothing in the world is easier than to attract children. Where there is a will there is a way. Youths, boys and girls of the Young Communist Leagues go in a group to the places where children are—on the streets in the evening, in parks, public playgrounds, or at some outdoor celebration. They watch the children at play and gradually and tactfully join in their games, perhaps teaching them a new circle game which all can join. Other children are attracted and approach to play the new game. After a while when the children are a little tired, "Shall we learn a new song?" At first the little ones may be suspicious, then they will be shy, but eventually they will all join in 'The Red Flag,' 'The Internationale,' or some other revolutionary song."

That is a quotation from the manual for use here among the children of Toronto. That is the method advocated for making Young Communists.

The manual continues. "Or one may go among the proletarian parents. In this trade union hall, or that clubhouse, or some other room or park or garden we meet on these days. Let your children come. The children will beg their parents for permission to attend and they will bring their friends and playmates. Children are naturally excellent agitators.

"Of course, there will be cases where the parents will refuse to permit the children to come. The mass of the adult proletariat is extremely petty bourgeois in its home life. These parents must be made the subject of special attention by the Communist leaders.

"There will be instances where the adults will use coercive measures. If the child is determined and energetic it will oppose the will of reactionary or backward parents and will attend the meetings despite the prohibition of the parents. More sensitive children will endure great internal conflicts, and with these, especially, great understanding and patience must be used. The active measures to be used by the leaders will depend upon whether the parents are merely backward proletarians or conscious reactionaries and social patriots."

There is a quotation that the average conscious reactionary of a parent can chew on for some time.

We can now shut the green manual for a little while for a trip out to Dovercourt Road and Queen Street to watch young "Reds" in the making.

It is Saturday night. The meeting is to be held in the Templar Hall. In the hallway outside the door is a board table selling pink and green pop. There is a sentry at the door. He is serious-eyed and perspiring.

Inside the hall is dark except for the stage at one end, where there are two green canvas pillars and a backdrop painted with trees that look like the illustrations of trees in the coal age. The dark hall is filled with parents, relatives, and friends. All Ukrainian. All dressed up.

On the brightly lighted stage against the poisonous green backdrop sits a triple row of children. They all have mandolins and are playing away with terrific childish seriousness. An exceedingly thin Bulgarian, spectacled, sat at the end of the front row and led the playing.

In the hall stolid faces, intelligent faces, tired faces looked up at the stage, and on the stage sat the children. The child Communists. The young "Reds."

They didn't look very dangerous. One little girl was about nine years old, with hair the color of rice straw and rosy pink cheeks. She turned her toes in as she played and kept her eyes on her mandolin.

One little boy had big glasses that made him look like a frog.

There was one really beautiful child, dark, quick-eyed, childish beauty.

But most of them were just ordinary-looking kids. Blondes predominating, since they came from Little Russia, all cheerful-looking and all deadly serious in their playing.

"Easy," hissed the Bulgarian music leader in English as they played their piece over again softly.

They gave a long program of mandolin and violin music and folk choruses. The folk choruses were delightful, the mandolin playing was not bad, and the violin playing was absolutely terrible.

Then they went off the stage and up into the gallery, and a gaunt-faced, handsome, dark young man with sideburns, and the light of revolution in his eye, came out and made a long speech. He was the leader of the group.

He spoke in Ukrainian, which sounds like low German spoken by a man with a hot potato in his mouth.

His speech was to the effect that before the war eastern and western Galicia were two of the most illiterate and backward countries in the world. Now the part of Galicia under Polish domination is more backward and illiterate than ever. But in the part under Soviet rule excellent schools have been established and Galicians from Poland constantly run away into Soviet Russia to get an education.

It was a very long speech, and during it nearly everyone in the audience became restive. The children in the gallery temporarily abandoned communism for the study of the woes of that noble proletarian, B. Google, and his class-conscious jockey Sunshine. They all seemed much more interested in comics than communism.

There was an intermission, then more music, several recitations, one from Zchewchenko, the Ukrainian national poet, and then a very fat man with a receding forehead and a big jaw made another speech. This was shorter, and announced that classes would be instituted for grown-ups as well as children in history, geography and grammar. History to be taken up from the revolutionary standpoint. The fat man, whose face was very pleasant when he smiled, but would curdle milk if he frowned, is a truck driver in his working hours and one of those very active in the groups.

Finally, the united mandolin, violin groups and choruses sang and played the march of the Red Army and the "Internationale." The first is a good, stirring march. The second is the most uninspiring tune I know.

They used to say in Italy that if the Reds had possessed any tune as good as the Fascisti hymn "Giovanezza," Italy would have gone Bolshevist for good when the workers seized the factories. But nobody can fight or feel like dying to the strains of the "Internationale!"

As a whole the Ukrainian meeting seemed very much as any Ukrainian Nationalist organization would have been whether there had been anything Communistic about it or not. One felt that if the Ukraine had not happened to have been one of the federated Soviet republics of Russia, the meeting would have been the same except that the quality of the music would have been a little better.

The reason for this is that the parochial organization was all there for the Communists to take over. It is in starting an absolutely new organization that the manual of the Young Communist League aims. Some of its sections are much more startling.

On page 12 the green manual states: "The children's groups are the militant community of children. They are the nuclei of the militant proletariat of the future. But they cannot be made militant communities by commands. They must become so, naturally, through experience and reason applied to experience. Communist education is not—as its opponents accuse it of being—the teaching of children to repeat ready-made formulae, the committing to memory of the A.B.C. of communism. It is neither the rational system commended in France nor yet the dogmatic system used in Great Britain. The children who are being educated in the Communist children's groups are not having their mental food served to them already prepared and semi-digested."

Later on it states on page 16: "We Communists assert that the child must be enrolled as a fighter in the struggle of its class and must share the fate of its class. The petty bourgeois reformist pedagogues, the humanitarian Utopians, and the social reformers are shocked almost to the fainting point by this, or else they are outraged at the idea. Dogs may bark, but the train goes on just the same."

Trouble is forecasted in this paragraph on page 13: "It is perfectly true that many features of our Communist children's groups are not agreeable to the parents, especially to those who have the bourgeois ideology. The children who comes to us gain in self-confidence, in independent initiative, and in the development of their critical faculties. Their observation becomes more keen and espies the weaknesses and inconsistencies of their parents, and naturally the parents do not relish this. Being themselves the slaves of machinery during the day, they prefer to play the role of small gods at home. In their petty bourgeois egotism, in their desire for peace and comfort, they do not see the great progress the child is making. Their vanity is hurt—and no pain is more severe than hurt vanity—by the pitiless criticisms of the child."

What is the child to be made by all this? What is the end in view?

In "Can a Child Be a Fighter?" the manual states, "The Communist children's movement has already obtained a quantity of valuable material dealing with the militant abilities of children. This is especially true in Germany where more than 30,000 children are organized.

"The children understood, however, how to maintain their rights and to defend themselves. They declared that they had a right to distribute their papers as long as nationalist, religious, and other literature was distributed in the schools. When prohibited from wearing soviet badges they replied they would wear these badges as long as monarchist, nationalist, and religious badges are permitted to be worn. When the teacher proceeded to the use of violent methods the children declared a school strike."

The children are also to be taught how to engage the teacher in argument with the end of confusing the teacher and turning the schoolroom into a discussion. To the history lesson the child learns in school the local Communist group must oppose the proletariat version. While the child is learning one version of history in his day school he must learn another on Sunday in the "Red" Sunday School.

On page 27 the manual states, "To the history of the bourgeois we oppose the history of the proletariat. In the matter of religion, we must not oppose religious teaching by ridicule. Instead we must enlighten the children on the origin of religion and on the history of its development into an instrument of power—a tool of the rich against the poor, the ruling against the subject classes."

The Young Communist's International strongly recommends games and sports not as an end in themselves, but to build bodies for fighters. The advantages of rambles and open-air hikes are also shown. Girls are urged to participate in games as well as the boys. "The Red army needs women fighters as well as men," their manual states on page 40.

The Young Communists are also urged not to ignore the Boy Scout movement, but to build up a similar organization of their own. They are urged to retain the methods of the scouts but reject their aims.

"We give the children actual military tasks," the book of instructions to leaders declares on page 42. "It is also necessary to train the children for conspirative or illegal work, the transportation of literature, courier service, the use of codes or secret signals for conveying information or for communication."

"Enlightenment," "Our Hikes and Rambles," "Propaganda on Excursions," are other topics in the handbook.

Then there is a chapter on fairy tales. "Unfortunately," writes the author, "there are only a few real proletarian fairy tales and the folk tales are difficult to use, even if the brave prince is called a 'worker' and the enchanted princess is a 'factory' girl who is released by the noble prince-proletarian."

The noble "prince-proletarian" is an entirely new and altogether wonderful conception.

As a substitute for the fairy tales the children are guided into acting out and making up their own tales, such as this one which was given in Berlin and is contained in the book for Toronto leaders.

"A door in the rear of the hall opened and a number of children entered, holding a demonstration with red flags and singing the song, 'We Are the Young Guards.' The demonstration marched to the platform, while the boys and girls detached themselves from the march and sold their papers to the audience. Suddenly one of these children was arrested and brought to the police station. His papers were taken away from him and as he refused to go away without them he had to remain in police headquarters.

"In a school at the right of the stage, the children told their teacher of the arrest. The teacher commented, 'That is quite right. He had no business to be selling such a paper.'

"Then the children hold a meeting. They decide to strike until their young comrade is released. The teacher comes into the almost empty room and asks the few 'scabs' who have remained where their schoolmates are. They tell him that there is a strike. The teacher goes to the police on the left of the stage and begs them to give up the little prisoner. He is released and his papers are returned to him. Then all the children join in a procession of triumph, singing the 'Internationale' and all the others join in."

The Young Communist groups are only two months old in Toronto. The most advanced is the Finnish group under Mrs. Custance, who was for fourteen years a teacher in the English public schools before she went into communism by way of woman's suffrage and social reform work. Mrs. Custance is a kindly faced, earnest woman, very full of her subject.

At present her group is studying the life of the bee and contrasting it with the life of human beings.

"They study the communal life of the bees and all their different workers and contrast that with the artificial life of human beings," Mrs. Custance said. "The bees kill their non-producers. Of course we do not teach the children how the useless members of society should be disposed of. They are too young for that. We let them make their own inference."

The conduct of the schools under Mrs. Custance is decided by the children themselves as much as possible.

"The children must realize and appreciate this freedom without it becoming simply play," Mrs. Custance declared. "Our idea is that every one should be useful. The usefulness of the individual should be not for his own benefit, but for the benefit of all of society. There should be no very, very rich and no very, very poor."

"How about Christmas?" I asked.

"No. Of course the children will not celebrate Christmas. It is really a survival of barbarism. We teach that nearly all the old holidays are survivals of old pagan feast days."

"What holidays do the Communist children observe, Mrs. Custance?" I asked.

"March 18th, the anniversary of the Paris Commune, May 1st, Labor Day, and November 7th, the anniversary of the Russian Revolution."

That's all. There isn't any Christmas. And, as yet, there isn't any Thanksgiving.

Betting in Toronto

☆ THE TORONTO STAR WEEKLY
December 29, 1923

On the Mexican border there is a tough dusty town. It has saloons, "queer" hotels, gambling houses and short-order restaurants on both sides of a dusty street. High-powered motorcars stand wheel to wheel at the curb with battered Fords, and Mexican ponies are hitched in between.

On the edge of this tough town is a tough racetrack where twelve horses are standing, taut, jerky and nervous, in front of an elastic barrier while a jockey tries to bring up a horse that is wearing a strange-looking hood like a Ku Kluxer to his place in line facing the elastic.

"Come on son. Bring that thing with the blinders up," the starter orders from his perch overlooking the line of horses restlessly footing in the sand.

"Bring him up, I tell you. Move over. Don't crowd there. Hey you! It's you I'm talking to. Move that dog over. Move him. Now bring him up, son. Now!"

The barrier snaps up in its awkwardly angled jerk. A bell rings. And the horses are off in a pounding mass topped with color that stretches out into a race as they line out at the first turn.

The horse with the hood on, that made all the trouble at the barrier, is running last, hopelessly beaten and going steadily back in the dust while the race pulls away ahead of him and the jockey flogs with his whip in disgust.

Another good thing has gone wrong.

"Ten on The Dictator in the sixth at Juarez," he says to a neighbor in a bowler hat.

"On the nose?" asks the man in the Christy [hat] without turning around.

"On the nose," says the man with the racing paper.

Two thousand miles to the north a group of men stand against the wall of a building across the street from the City Hall in Toronto. One man is reading a racing paper.

Two thousand miles to the south at that very moment, The Dictator is galloping doggedly through the dust that is raised in a cloud by the twelve horses that are far out ahead of him. His jockey is saying to himself, "This is a swell skate. This is the thing Charley said he'd put a nice bet on for me if I'd ride him."

Meantime in Toronto bets will continue to be placed on The Dictator, or Flying Frog or Runyan's Onion or whatever the particular good thing's name happens to be, until some time after the horse has been led back to the stall.

The particular form of betting that has been described is called betting on the nod. It requires no apparatus, receipts, betting slips or tickets. All it requires is confidence, a feeling of mutual trust between the bettor and the bet-taker. It goes on year in and year out to the extent of thousands of dollars a day in Toronto's regular betting public, and it is almost impossible to check. There is no evidence.

But the small bettors on the nod are the smallest part of the public that have been hit by The Dictator's defalcation. They form one percent of Toronto's betting public.

A well-known Toronto horseman who is on the inside in racing affairs states that there are 10,000 people in Toronto who bet on the races every day, month in and month out.

A former bookmaker puts the figure at from nine to ten thousand. Both men know their business.

Over $100,000 is played each day in Toronto with bookmakers the year around according to one of these men. For years Toronto has been known all over the world as the biggest betting town in North America.

"But that is changing now," the horseman states. "The big-money players are leaving. They are driven out by the pari-mutuel machines and the government tax."

Ten or fifteen years ago, A. M. Orpen's place operated in the Coffin Block, opposite the Peacock Hotel. With Moylett and Baillie's, it was the biggest of the old Toronto betting places. Commissions of $5,000 were not uncommon in those golden days of Toronto betting.

Now there is no bookmaker in Toronto who will handle a $5,000 bet. But you can still lay a bet of $1,000 or $2,000 although the bookmaker will place it out of town. Practically all the big money bet in Toronto is wired to Montreal, according to those in the know.

The man who bets with a bookmaker in Toronto is up against a stiff game. The bookmakers pay the pari-mutuel prices as telegraphed in from the outside tracks—with a limit. When you read in the paper that O'Grady's Lady won at the odds of $52.50 for a $2.00 ticket at Latonia, you may have registered the wish that you had bet on the Lady and idly wondered how it was done.

But no matter how much you had bet on the estimable female you could not have collected more than $15.00 for your $2.00 bet.

The bookmakers have a working agreement that they will make a limit of $15.00 to win on a $1.00 bet, $6.00 to place, and $3.00 to show, no matter what the horse pays. If the horse you bet on won at 200 to 1 you could not collect more than $30 on a $2.00 bet in Toronto.

As a matter of fact if you only bet $2.00, you would have to deal with one of the smaller bookmakers and these have a $10.00, $4.00, and $2.00 limit.

The bookie's answer to any protest on this limit is that nobody has to bet if he doesn't want to. You can accept the conditions or leave them. As a result, really long shots are absolutely eliminated.

In addition the bettor is up against the handicap of not being able to bet an entry. In other words, when two or more horses are coupled in the betting, the man who is betting must name the horse he expects to win with. If any other horses in the entry win, he has lost his bet.

A bettor cannot play the field either. No bookmaker in Toronto accepts bets on the field. If he places a bet on a horse which is in the field, and a field horse other than the one he has named wins, he loses his money even though he would have to accept reduced odds if his horse should win.

It is a rocky road for the bettor. But the bookmakers are more or less organized, they are doing an illegal business with constant risk and they figure on making things as much in their favor as they can. And as they say, "Nobody has to bet with us that doesn't want to."

Some bookmakers have been known to relax some of their rules in favor of old clients, or men prominent in betting who object to the entry and field rules as absolutely unjust.

Who are the 10,000 regular bettors of Toronto?

According to the men who know, they are of all classes. Professional men, doctors, lawyers, clerks, secretaries, truck drivers, office boys, businessmen and laborers.

Toronto bookmakers have few women customers. The old hackneyed cliché: "You know stenographers are the bookmakers' biggest clients," does not apply here. If it applies anywhere.

"Women are heavy bettors at the Woodbine," a man high up in racing affairs told me. "But they do not like to bet on the horses when they are out of town."

Few Toronto bookmakers like to handle bets from women. None of the big commission men who handle bets for Montreal books will accept a bet from a woman.

Most of the key operators in Toronto at present are commission men. They work on the basis of two and one-half percent commission on the bet. Eighty percent of these commissions are placed in Montreal.

Ninety-nine percent of the betting that is done in Toronto today is done on a cash basis. The old halcyon days of Abe Orpen and Moylett and

Baillie, when bookmakers' statements were only rendered once a week on Monday morning, are gone.

"Of course, I could still get a $500 bet down in five minutes without putting up a cent," a widely known turfman explained to me. "But the old credit days are gone. It would be done to me as a favor. Not as a matter of business."

It is a great web of wire that stretches from the southern racetracks all over North America at this time of year. It has been estimated that more men are employed in the betting business in North America than work in the steel business. And it goes on under the surface.

Toronto is a famous betting town. But if you do not follow the races, you never see any betting. If you happen to be a bettor, you see betting everywhere. That is, if you look for it. Rather, you see signs of betting.

At the corner of Adelaide and Bay streets, a shiny sedan stops against the curb. The driver sits unconcernedly at the wheel. Beside him on the front seat is a lantern-jawed man in a soft hat. They are evidently waiting for someone.

If you watch long enough, you will see a man detach himself from the passing lunch-hour crowd and step up to the window of the sedan. He steps away and goes on. Another man steps up, then hurries along.

Perhaps fifteen people pay the car a visit. Then it moves along to another corner. There the process is repeated.

That is the rolling bookmaker. He has done and still does a good business in Toronto. But it is a piker's business, and the police have spotters out who take the car numbers. A number of these betting shops on wheels have been arrested during the last year.

Then there are the bookmakers who operate behind the cigar counters of certain restaurants, in certain cigar stores, ice cream parlors and poolrooms. These men are mostly accepting commissions for larger bookmakers.

The bulk of the bookmaking betting done in Toronto is done right in the offices, factories or stores. Every office building where any number of men are employed has its own bookmaker's agent. He is an employee in the building and gets a commission of two and one-half to five percent on every bet he accepts.

When a bookmaker's agent accepts a bet, he gives a receipt for it and then telephones the bet in to the bookmaker, who at present, if he is an operator of any magnitude, is probably located in a private house where he can conduct his business undisturbed.

Sometimes an agent for a bookmaker calls at an office or factory regularly each day. But oftener the agent is an employee. That cuts down overhead expenses. They are the bane of the bookie.

New Orleans is the track where most Toronto people play the money.

"That is because you have the books there and the prices are much better than on the mutuel machines," an old-time turfman who has the reputation of being one of the shrewdest horsemen in Canada stated.

"Toronto bettors are nearly all form players. In the old days this had the reputation of being the town where the most short-priced winners came in of any in the country. It is the money that is bet that makes them favorites. This has always been a shrewd betting town," continued the man on the inside.

"How many of Toronto's betting public have made money on this last year's wagering, then?" I asked.

"None of them," he answered positively. "Not a one makes money on the year. They can't do it."

"How about racing information?" I asked.

"It is almost entirely false," he answered. "I have had the people who are putting out sure tip information come to me at the Woodbine and ask me for a horse in a certain race. Just for my opinion. Then this same information would come back to me as being special inside stuff from the stable."

As far as I was able to discover there is no one selling tips on races in Toronto at present. Toronto bettors like to do their own selecting.

There are plenty of touts after the Toronto trade, though. Their usual form of procedure is to write a letter to some person whose name they have obtained. The letter says that the writer has a brother in the So-and-So stable and this stable has a real horse that is going to be sent out for the money in a field of palsied selling-platers some day next week. The man who gets the letter is urged to play $10 for the writer on this certainty.

On the day of the race a wire comes giving the horse's name. The tout usually has at least three horses in the same race and sends out about thirty wires.

The trick has varying forms, but the principle is the same—get somebody else to bet money for you just because you tell them to. There is always someone willing to do it.

All big betting is doomed in Ontario, according to the horseman quoted before.

"Three years from now there won't be a fifty-dollar machine at the Woodbine," this man said sadly. "The big tax of ten and one-half percent is putting the big bettors right out of business. They can't buck it. Attendance at the Windsor track has fallen off forty percent. Money bet has fallen off fifty percent and handbooks in Detroit have increased one hundred percent."

Racing for the big bettor, the man who bet his hundreds and thousands at a crack seems to be doomed in Ontario. The giants of the old days are passing. But the 10,000 remain faithful in spite of what they are up against.

McConkey's 1914 Orgy

☆ THE TORONTO STAR WEEKLY
December 29, 1923

New Year's Eve is gone.

No one knows just where it is gone.

But the general opinion seems to be that it has gone over the border in bottles, barrels and cases.

New Year's Eve dies harder in the States.

Two nights from tonight the time-honored custom of drinking the old year out and watching the new year come in out of a bottle will still be carried on. New Year's Eve is still celebrated as one great national orgy on the other side of the line.

The writer has attended orgies in all parts of the world. Always they have been dull.

The dancing dervishes of Stamboul are amiable old men who jiggle around as long as the money drops.

The wild dancing of gypsies in the cave in the hill above the Alhambra in Granada is a dull peseta-catching tourist trap.

The average Parisian orgy is a certain soporific.

But a New Year's Eve in any big city in the States is something else again.

Where else will you see a beautiful young lady dive into a hotel fountain out of pure joy of living?

Where else, if the beautiful young lady took this dive, would she be applauded by the police?

Where else would you see another young lady and her escort fishing in another hotel fountain for goldfish, using their slippers as scoops while the police hold back the crowd to see that there is fair play, and a procession of young men run about the crystal room with their hands on one another's shoulders, shouting that they were the wild Princetonian shoehorns and that tonight was tonight?

New Year's Eve as an orgy in Toronto met its death at the hands of Colonel [George Taylor] Denison in February of 1914.

The exact words of the colonel which placed the lid on New Year's Eve-ing on the American plan in Toronto were uttered in the police court.

"There is plenty of evidence to support the charge," the colonel summed up. "I think the whole thing was a disreputable affair. As far as I can gather from the evidence, it was just a drunken revel, called an orgy. It was certainly not a respectable thing for thirty or forty women to stagger out of the place and for two or three to have been carried out. We have got the evidence of people who did not want to give evidence. We have got evidence that there was not only noise, but drunkenness, and men kissing their wives and other people's wives. It was just a revel that should not have been allowed in any respectable house. You could not call it an orderly house independent of the offense of selling liquor. The license will be suspended for sixty days."

In these words the colonel put the final touch on the New Year's Eve party in Toronto. That made a terrific stir in numberless families.

It is all legendary now. There are many different versions of what happened at McConkey's "Tavern" that night and morning. The tale has assumed Homeric proportions with the lapse of the years.

In those days McConkey's had a lunchroom on the ground floor at King Street where the Bank of Nova Scotia stands now. The lunchroom ran through to Melinda Street and was an eating place famous throughout Canada. It was a daily part of the lives of many Toronto men to drop into McConkey's for a sandwich and a glass of something or other.

Upstairs were six or seven bedrooms, and on the third floor a ballroom. It was in the ballroom that the party occurred.

Reservations were made for 250 guests. They were to see the old year out and the new year in. Champagne and wine were to lubricate the passage of the discarded year. There was no necessity to pay for the wine. It could all be charged and the bill sent the following week.

A dinner was served sometime early in the evening. This was an established fact. Of the people who testified, a number remembered the dinner.

Just what happened at the party will never be fully established. It is not safe yet to go into the matter. The amazing thing which came out in the police court was that no one had drunk more than three or at most four glasses of champagne. Witness after witness testified to this fact. No one had seen anyone else drunk either.

It seemed there was some doubt as to what constituted being drunk.

One witness said that he had seen no drunkenness and nobody under the influence of liquor.

"When is a man drunk?" was the question.

"When he is incapable of standing, walking or talking," was the answer.

It seemed to be the general definition.

At any rate Colonel Denison accepted the testimony of the constable who watched McConkey's disgorge revelers at various hours during the morning.

Policeman John Boyd was the second witness called. He said he came on duty at eleven o'clock, at which hour a good many people, seemingly theater patrons, were entering McConkey's.

"Between twelve and three o'clock I saw between forty and fifty intoxicated women come out of the restaurant. Two women were carried out and many were led."

"Did you ever see a woman escorted?" Mr. H. M. Ludwig, K.C., who appeared for Mr. McConkey, asked the constable.

"Yes," answered Boyd, "but not staggering. There was a great deal of noise, women laughing. Stragglers were coming out of the place at 4 a.m."

"Weren't they waiting for their motorcars?" asked Mr. Ludwig.

"They may have been," answered the constable. "There were a great number of taxicabs lined up."

Walter Richards, then McConkey's headwaiter, said he saw no one drunk or even under the influence of liquor, no women acting queerly and heard only a very little noise.

Crown Attorney Corley suggested that Richards was an admirably deaf and dumb waiter.

One of the guests said, "I saw no one drunk but many exhilarated. I left very early after having a fight. On a dance floor a man bumped into a lady with whom I was dancing and I objected. He said he would see me downstairs. I went down with him and, after arguing with him, we had a mild fight."

Even the fights were mild that night, according to the witnesses.

"I received a crack on the mouth," concluded the witness.

The other participant in the mild fight said he had heard a good deal of noise, but that was just at midnight when the company sang "Auld Lang Syne," rattled the windows and blew horns.

"There was a little spasmodic blowing of horns after that," said he.

In answer to a question of Colonel Denison's as to when a man is drunk, the witness said, "When he can't get on a streetcar."

Still another witness stayed until 1:30. He saw no fighting nor anybody carried out.

"Did you see any kissing?"

"No."

"Any fighting?"

"No."

"Anybody under the influence of liquor?"

"Not while I was there."

"Was there any noise?"

"Not much. Just a good joyful evening."

One witness, more frank than the others, saw people slightly under the influence of liquor.

"Did you see anyone staggering?"

"Yes."

"Where?"

"A man was trying to get in."

"That was not Mr. McConkey's fault," Mr. Corley said.

In spite of all that testimony, the colonel did not like the party. He did not like it at all. He liked it so little that there has never been another New Year's Eve of the sort since in Toronto.

Toronto still has a modified New Year's revel. Tables are still engaged at downtown hotels and it is said that lawless people still bring certain quantities of forbidden beverage with them to be consumed at their own tables.

The ghost of McConkey's 1914 party still approaches those tables. But it starts away in alarm. It is a very timid ghost. It is afraid of Colonel Denison and his successors on the bench.

Our Modern Amateur Impostors

☆ THE TORONTO STAR WEEKLY
December 29, 1923

Last September in Montreal I chanced to go to a prizefight. The fights were not much. None of the fighters got much of a hand. But there was one popular figure.

"Gentlemen and ladies, allow me to introduce to you Kid Lavigne, former lightweight champion of the world," the announcer bellowed. The Kid, short, middle-aged, looking like a pocket edition of Gentleman Jim Corbett under the lights, bowed at ease, his hands on the ropes. "One of the greatest fighters of all time," finished the foghorn voice.

Crash! came the applause.

"Kid Lavigne, ladies and gentlemen, has consented to referee the next bout," megaphoned the announcer.

More applause.

I felt that even if the bouts were dull, I had at least seen Kid Lavigne. It is something to see a champion of the world. So he was stored away in memory, a short, competent-looking little man, the lights above the ring shining on his smoothly brushed hair.

A few weeks ago came the announcement in the paper that the former lightweight champion of the world, Kid Lavigne, had been granted a marriage license in Detroit. Mr. Lavigne, the dispatch said, was employed in the Ford plant.

That seemed funny.

Last week a wire from Montreal brought the information that a referee's license which had been issued to a man posing as Kid Lavigne had been canceled upon the discovery that the former lightweight champion was in reality living in Detroit and working in the Ford plant. The man claiming to be Kid Lavigne had photographs, letters and clippings to prove he was the real Kid, but his story had been discredited by a sportsman who had seen the real Saginaw Kid in action in the old days.

Why do they do it?

What is the impulse in a man that makes him pass himself off as someone else, often to make himself believe he is someone else, facing in the end almost sure detection?

This article does not deal with the bad-check passers, the fakers, the sordid swindlers, but with the amateur impostor, that strange type of man who has some queer kink in his imagination that makes him give himself the personality and adventures of some other person. This kink may be the same that in another man would make a Joseph Conrad or a great painter.

You encounter these amateur impostors often enough. One summer we were playing baseball in northern Michigan. A slight-built young fellow appeared one day in front of the grandstand out at the Petoskey fair-grounds and started to warm up with the regular pitchers. He was Dixie Davis of the St. Louis Browns, he told the gang.

Naturally, he obtained plenty of attention. He threw a nice curveball and seemed to have plenty of stuff. He wasn't cutting loose, he explained. He was up in Petoskey because he had disputed one of Umpire Billy Evans' decisions, and been suspended. It was too hot in St. Louis and he was taking a vacation during his suspension.

On the following Sunday, we played Traverse City at our home grounds in Charlevoix. I was assigned to persuade Dixie Davis to pitch for us. It was not a very difficult task. He would be glad of the workout. Sure. He'd be there all right. It would help him keep in shape.

All we had to do was send a motorcar to drive him over and get him a uniform.

We sent the car. But at the hotel they declared he had already left to go to Charlevoix.

"He's pitching there this afternoon," the hotel clerk said. "I wish I could have got off for the game."

Dixie didn't show up. Two days later we read in the papers that Dixie Davis had shut out the New York Yankees that very same Sunday in St. Louis.

It may seem a long jump from an imitation Dixie Davis back to George Psalmanazar. But the line runs straight back to 1704 in the city of London. On its way back it takes in Jacques Richtor, of the Great North. Jacques is too recent in memory to need explanation.

George with the funny last name arrived in London, a dark, swarthy young man, obviously a foreigner. He could speak no word of English, but learned quickly.

As soon as he could speak any English, he started enlisting the aid of England for his native land of Formosa, from which he had come by many perilous adventures. He wanted missionaries there. The Bishop of London was one of his most ardent supporters.

He published a book which was received with great acclaim. It was called *A Historical and Geographical Description of Formosa*. It recounted the habits, language, dress and character of the inhabitants of that distant land. It also described the Formosan scenery, buildings, wars, politics, poets and statesmen. There was no doubt about it. It was an important work.

Psalmanazar filled his books with drawings of the Formosan royal family and illustrations of its buildings. He constructed a language and a grammar and taught English students to understand them. He appeared before scientists and gave lectures on the Formosan language at Oxford.

This wonderful book was dedicated to the Bishop of London. Formosa was as much the topic of conversation then as King Tut's tomb was last year.

When the crash finally came, Psalmanazar admitted he was a native of Languedoc, France. He had come to England as an immigrant. He was exposed by a few hardy doubters who had mistrusted him from the start.

Dr. [Frederick A.] Cook was a piker beside Psalmanazar, although many people feel that the doctor's mountain-climbing adventures in the West, including his ascent of Mount McKinley, were much more finished and delicate bits of work than the North Pole business.

Captain J. A. Lawson was a splendid forerunner to Cook and Richtor. The captain wrote *Wanderings in New Guinea* in 1875. There was nothing coarse about this work. Deftly and one-by-one, the navigator got rid of his traveling companions. You hardly notice they have gone until you reach the last page and there is no one to return with the adventurous captain.

Tooloo the Lascar goes mad and shoots himself with Captain Lawson's rifle by putting the muzzle in his mouth and pulling the trigger with his toe. Hostile natives slay Joe, the splendid young Australian. Danong, the courageous Papuan, dies by the same hands. Aboo, another guide, disappears a little later. Billy, the Australian aborigine, the last survivor, deserts the captain at Singapore.

There is only the courageous captain. And what a welcome he received. He discovered it. He had been to the top of the world on Mount Hercules, a smile higher than Mount Everest. Everest, you remember, was unscalable to a British exploring party last year. They could not get sufficient oxygen.

Lawson, as he neared the summit of Mount Hercules, also encountered difficulty. "The cold now became excessive," he wrote. "My hands were so numb I could not feel whether I had fingers or not. The water in our bottle was a mass of ice. We had very little extra clothes with the exception of our blankets. Aboo became quite lethargic, and several times sat down and fell asleep."

Still they climbed.

Poor Lawson's downfall came when a certain Captain Moresby, a British naval officer, who at the time of the publication of the captain's book happened to be out in his old stamping ground. The gallant captain gave certain latitudes and longitudes in his book. Captain Moresby had charted those waters and was able to prove that the explorer's principal village was situated in the middle of Torres Strait.

No one ever learned whether Captain Lawson had ever been in New Guinea or not. He wouldn't tell.

Two years ago Louis de Rougemont died in a London poorhouse. To the poorhouse authorities he was plain Louis Redmond. But Louis was one of the greatest of them all.

The year the Boer War started the *Wide World Magazine* announced with pride the publication in serial form of the "Amazing Adventures of Louis de Rougemont," as recounted by himself. Louis had just arrived in London on a vessel straight from New Zealand. He talked with conviction. His story still makes good reading.

Louis was no piker. For thirty years he had wandered among the cannibals. It started in the West Indies in a pearling expedition. There was action from the start. After a thrilling battle with an octopus, who had sucked down a native diver, Louis is left alone on board the pearler one day and blown out to sea.

He is cast away on a sandy island and makes himself a sort of super Emperor Jones. He acquires the wonderful Wamba. There was never anyone so wonderful as that dusky spouse.

She fights with him and nurses him. Louis was a fighter, too. His wonderful charge is an epic. He even wields a hefty spear as well as a long bow.

Toward the last of the narrative two girls from the homeland are washed up on the island. Like Louis they are castaways. They like Louis, too.

Whether Wamba became jealous is not stated but the good old sea takes the girls for its own. It is a sad loss. But Louis has Wamba to console him.

Then comes the cry of "A Sail! A Sail!" And the long homeward voyage. Thus it was that the great story of thirty years among the cannibals came to be told.

It sounds fishy? But de Rougemont was invited to tell the story to a British scientific society.

The *Daily Chronicle*, which exposed Dr. Cook, burst Louis de Rougemont's bubble. His thirty years with the cannibals had been spent with Swiss bankers. His tropical island had been the dull streets of London. Louis' thirty years had been spent in the routine of a London banking house.

Still, at the age of 67 he made a comeback and married a brilliant young woman who tells how he entertained her for some time with his wonderful imagination.

There is one case in the annals of the great impostors where the impostor was honestly deceived.

While the science of geology was still in the hands of its earliest pioneers,

Professor Beringer lectured at the University of Würzburg. In his old class were a number of bright young men who knew the haunts of the genial old man in his hunt for fossils that would develop his theories about the origins of life. These students paid nocturnal visits to the professor's favorite hunting grounds.

Shortly after, the professor's hammer and bright eye discovered evidence of a totally new kind of extinct life. He found fossil frogs, snakes and insects galore.

The students were inspired by his enthusiasm.

There was almost nothing the professor couldn't find. One day he found a cast of a spider in its web and not one strand disturbed although it had come through the grinding of hundreds of thousands of years. Then came another fossil of a spider in the act of catching a fly.

The professor went around like a man who had seen a vision. He was exalted in his classroom. Finally he unearthed a rock on which was inscribed the Hebrew word for Jehovah. "No," said Professor Beringer. "I am right. My opponents who uphold the false doctrine of slow evolution are wrong. All life is the work of a creator. He has not only been kind enough to leave evidence here but has appended his signature to make it official."

On this basis, the professor published his book, profusely illustrated. The title page presented a pyramid of the fossils surmounted by the stone with Jehovah written on it. He dedicated the book to the Prince of Würzburg.

When one of the students raised the shout of derision that grew and swept Germany when the book appeared, the poor professor destroyed all the copies of his book he could reach, tried to buy up the others and died shortly after of a broken heart.

There is no record of any other exposed impostor dying of a broken heart from Count Berty Gregory, who posed in Toronto years ago as an Austrian nobleman and was discovered to have been a stable groom, down to Jacques Richtor, the boy wanderer of the north, who duped reporters and bush authorities with his tale until he was unmasked as a runaway lad from the States. They don't die of broken hearts, these impostors.

For there is some strange force inside of them that forces them to be impostors. They might die of a broken heart if they could not live their lives of the imagination.

Swiss Avalanches

☆ THE TORONTO STAR WEEKLY
January 12, 1924

Far below in the valley town André heard the great roar.

It came in a loud crack and then a terrible roar like the end of the world.

"Up your way, André," said the postmaster sagely.

Two men standing in the post office looked at André queerly.

"I would not live up there for all the money in the canton," one man said.

The postmaster laughed.

"There is no one fears the mountains like a mountaineer."

He handed André his pile of papers and weighed out two pounds of sauerkraut from the barrel. "I hope you will find everything well, André."

"Don't worry about me," André said, and slinging his rucksack on his back, opened the door out into the bright Alpine sunshine.

Towing his skis behind him on a cord about his waist, André started in his bent-kneed, mountaineer's stride up the steep, icy road that wound up the valley. He was very worried. He knew what that roar meant. It was an avalanche.

In the spring the avalanches fall with a certain regularity. They have their established paths. You see these paths in the summer, bare swaths cut through the forests on a steep hillside. Many of the spring avalanches fall the same date almost each year. Nearly all of the big ones have familiar names—nicknames given to them because of the familiarity that breeds contempt.

But winter avalanches have no nicknames. They come suddenly and terribly and they bring death.

So André trudged up the road until it swung off in a direction that did him no good. Then he stamped into his skis, shot down the clamps and thrust along, up the valley, holding just that upward grade he could make comfortably without slipping back.

For miles he went steadily up in the tireless, thrusting climb that makes the ski for the mountaineer what the canoe is to the Indian or the snow-shoe to the trapper of the barren lands of the north. Suddenly he came around a bend in the valley onto the work of the avalanche he had heard in the town. He thanked God he had not yet married Helza in the village.

The valley was wiped out. Instead there was the most snow André had ever seen in his life. It rose sheer ahead of him, two hundred feet high. A gigantic rubble of snow, like the crest of a flood, towering, frozen, immovable. Trunks of trees projected from it.

On the right, the side of the mountain was bare. There had been a sharp slipping crack and all the snow had roared away from the side of the mountain with the same instantaneous rush that snow sliding off the roof has, to pour down into the valley its weight of thousands of tons, turning over and over and finally piling up and up into this mass.

André looked up at it from below and felt very small. Where was his house, he wondered. It had been directly in the path of the avalanche. His heart was heavy. It would be a long time now before he could marry.

He started to climb up the left side of the valley. This was a great avalanche. It had wiped him out completely. He might as well have a look at it.

Up he zigzagged until he was level with the height of the avalanche. Then he saw something. About a hundred yards above him, on the opposite side of the valley from where he had left it, was his house! It looked a little tipsy, it was true. But it was right side up. There it was. No mistake.

André was frightened. He did not know whether to start down the valley in a long rush to town or to go down on his knees. He compromised. He crossed himself and started for the house. There it was. All right. Everything inside. Just a little crockery broken.

"It was evidently a sign to me," thought André, "that this side of the valley is better. In the spring I will dig new foundations here. But I wish the Bon Dieu had also removed my barn in safety."

What had happened was the great wind from the falling avalanche had lifted the house on it as though the rush of air were a solid thing and deposited it on the far side of the valley three hundred yards away.

Avalanches seldom do good deeds like that. I have seen an iron bridge, weighing I do not know how many tons, that had been lifted two hundred feet up the side of an Alpine valley by the rush of wind from a great falling snowslide. Again I have seen a swath of forest that had been scoured bare, the tree trunks cut off at the base as though they were matchsticks.

Kipling wished the name of "Our Lady of the Snows" on to Canada, and Canadians have been stepping out from under it ever since. There is plenty of snow in Canada. Or rather there has been until this winter. But east of the Rockies there are no avalanches.

Other countries regard snow as a blessing, not as a libel. In the mountains, it makes it possible to skid the timber down. It makes hard, smooth roads, it makes it possible to bring the mountain meadow hay, cut and cured in the summertime, down on big sledges with turned-up runners that the sledgeman runs between and leans against to make the hay sled turn to left or right.

Finally snow brings tourists. It brings them by the hundreds and thousands. So while Canada indignantly denies that she is "The Lady of the Snows," we have the spectacle of five different countries in Europe all loudly clamoring that they have the most and the deepest snow in the civilized world. They spend thousands of dollars advertising their snowy claims too. But none of them ever mention the avalanches.

Avalanches are the skeleton in the winter sport's closet. They cause ninety percent of the deaths in mountain skiing. If you have ever sat in the house and heard the sharp, rattling roar as a big chunk of snow slides off the roof, you know how quick an avalanche starts. They go off like a steel trap.

Skiers used to be advised, if they got into an avalanche, to try and turn and run directly down the slope and get ahead of it. That advice was written by some fireside-hint counselor.

You might exactly as well try to outrun a burst from a Lewis gun fired directly at your back as try to ski ahead of an avalanche. There is only one thing to do. Swim in it as though you were in the water and try and keep your head from being buried. If you can kick off your skis you will have a better chance of staying up. The whirling snow will seize on your skis and drag you under by them.

If the avalanche is from the side of a hill and spreads out into a flat valley, you have a good chance of coming through all right. But if it goes down into a steep gulch or steep valley, it will pile up and the unlucky skier who is caught is smothered if he is not crushed.

Although winter avalanches are much more tricky and difficult to figure than those that fall in the spring in the mountains, the person who is caught in one has a much better chance of surviving. For new-fallen winter powder snow weighs only about 150 pounds a cubic yard while old, wet, spring snow weighs about three-quarters of a ton per cubic yard.

Powder snow too is full of air. You can live for some time without suffocating if overwhelmed by a winter avalanche. But the heavy, wet, spring snow contains almost no air. All its weight is water, and if you are not crushed you are very liable to be drowned.

Plenty of skiers have escaped unhurt although carried down thousands of feet by an avalanche if they had been able to keep on the surface and if the snow has spread out onto a gradual slope. But last winter a young man was killed not far from where we were skiing by an avalanche which carried him only about fifty feet. In that rush, though, it took him over a precipice.

Your first avalanche is a terrific thing. It is the deadly suddenness of it that puts you out. You may be skiing down a slope running parallel with a mountain side when there is a C-R-A-C-K! The side of the mountain seems to drop sideways out from under you, the snow piles up in a rushing flood of sliding cakes and over and over you go.

That is a "wind-board" avalanche. Wind-board is treacherous stuff to ski on. It is a hard layer of snow that lies precariously on the main field. It has been hardened by the wind and often lies over pockets or bubbles that make patches that only need to be cut by the running blade of the ski to start avalanching.

It is not, of course, as dangerous as the great "ground avalanche," such as played a trick on André's house. But you cannot tell what it may carry you over if you are skiing in difficult country. It may be fatal to be carried twenty-five feet by a little windslab snowslide in the high Alps, whereas on some of the long ski slopes of the Dolomites you might be able to survive a half-mile avalanche ride.

One day last January, after a championship bob race on the Sonloup Les Avants course in which we had smashed our bob and lost the race through hitting a rut just at the final ice turn before the homestretch, when everybody felt sore and disappointed, and our one desire was to avoid commiserations and "better-luck-next-times," young George O'Neil and I started off for the Dent de Jaman on skis.

Before you get to where skiing is possible, you have to hike, toting or towing your skis, up one of the stiffest, straight-up-and-down, heartbreaking stretches of road in the world. We got up into the open country above the shoulder of the mountain, crossed several avalanches, having a hard time picking our way over the huge snowfalls and then reached the long snowfields of the col, or saddle, of the mountain. By the time we were up under the edge of the Dent, a blunt, granite tooth like a miniature Matterhorn, it was dark and we had to run down in the dark.

The open fields were all right. But once we got into the descending road we made a beautiful mess of things. In the dark on the icy road we fell about every twenty yards. We fell hard and handsome. We fell into trees, each other, over the bank, on our faces, on our backs, and in several new styles.

Ultimately George's ski came off in a fall and shot over the edge and down into a steep gulch below. He saw it strike the roof of a cabin below, in the faint moon that was now up, and skid on off and down. We made the rest of the trip on foot.

Next morning George was laid up and I started up the trail alone in a blinding snowstorm. I mushed on as fast as I could make it uphill, for the only chance of getting the ski lay in reaching the hut where it had hit in falling and see the direction the mark had made. Hadley [Hemingway] and Isabelle Simmons were following me up with a lunch.

As I reached the edge of the road where the ski had gone over, the snow turned to rain. Now the only reason more people do not get killed skiing is because the dangerous avalanches all fall during the rain—and anybody that has any sense doesn't go out in the rain.

There was a faint crease in the high piled snow on the roof of the hut about two hundred feet down the steep slide. I knew it must be the snowed-in mark made by the ski. As I sighted along it, I figured the ski would light below and run straight down until it hit a clump of willows that stuck up out of the bed of a mountain torrent that ran under the snow about a half a mile below.

Straight up above the road was a regular avalanche funnel of a valley. A narrow funnel of a valley rising almost straight up from the road to Cape au Moine. Furthermore I had heard that avalanche come down the year before. We had crossed it later and it has spread out right into this same mountain torrent's bed.

It looked like a bad bet. But after thinking it over, I decided it was probably safe enough if I took off my skis and wallowed down. Any slope over 25 degrees will avalanche. But chamois tracks will sometimes cut across a slope of 40 or 50 degrees. Their legs sink in instead of setting the snow loose as a pair of skis do.

There is nothing chamois-like about size 11 skiing boots but the principle seemed the same. So I went down into the bed of the stream and there sure enough was the ski stuck in the bushes.

It was only about a half a mile climb up but it seemed like a hundred years wallowing up through the wet snow armpit deep. What made it seem so long was that wonderful super-avalanche trap all ready to spring, hanging straight up above as far as you could see. All the way up I kept thinking that the ski was only worth about fifteen francs anyway.

The girls were at the top, on the safe side of the road, soaked to the skin by the warm rain. We went into a hay barn built into the side of the mountain out of the avalanche track and put on dry sweaters out of the rucksacks and brought out the thermos bottle and the sandwiches.

While we sat in the dark hut, leaning back against the hay packed solid up to the roof and watching the rain through the open door fourteen avalanches came down. I counted them. No one else had such a personal interest in them as I had. But we were all very glad to get home. It was the warm rain's doing. The mountaineers call the warm wind-rain Föhn. It sometimes comes in the midst of the coldest winter weather. It comes from nowhere and it goes back the same place. Sometimes it lasts for days.

Other times for only an hour or so. But it always brings avalanches and it can be death to be out in.

After you have lived a long time in the mountains you see the mountain dwellers' standpoint. I remember once in the spring we were crossing the St. Bernard Pass before it was open. In Bourg St. Pierre we wandered around the little town halfway up the pass while Hadley had a nap in the inn. Bourg is just below the snow line. There was a little cemetery with many graves. On most of the graves was this inscription, "Victim of the Mountain."

"That's odd," said Chink. "Victim of the mountain. Sounds as though the mountain were a person."

"How is it, Father?" I asked a priest. "Victim of the mountain?"

"He is the great enemy of the mountain-dwelling people," answered the priest, looking down into the gorge the river cut below us. "It is different from the sea. The mountain does not help the mountain man. He is not his livelihood."

"It is very strange, Father," Chink said.

"Yes, it is very strange," the priest said. "When one is young one goes always into the high mountains. These are all young men." He pointed at the crosses. "But when one is older one knows better." He smiled. "It is better to avoid an enemy such as the mountain. Yet we can never leave him. Perhaps in this, too, he shows he is our enemy."

So This Is Chicago

☆ THE TORONTO STAR WEEKLY
January 19, 1924

Seven miles of dirty, wooden houses all alike stretching out on the great West Side.

* * *

Three fat men in the canyon of LaSalle Street painted like Indians, war bonnets on their heads, shivering in the cold wind and shouting, "Buy a string of beads. Real Indian beads. Make somebody happy."

* * *

All the best-looking debutantes at a dance with their hair cut like members of the Brooklyn National League ball team.

* * *

The boys who went into LaSalle Street when you first went on the newspaper now all driving their own cars, all members of the club, and asking gloomily if you think there is any possible way they could make a living in Paris.

* * *

Michigan Avenue, the most beautiful street in the world, smooth, dark and slippery, a skyline on one side through the snow and the gray lake on the other. The red and green lights of the signal towers winking the traffic forward or stopping it.

* * *

A poll of ten different Chicagoans on the subject of the drainage canal diverting the water necessary for Hydro revealing the general opinion, "Sure. You may be right. But what do the Canadians think they can do about it?"

* * *

One of the best-selling records in Chicago homes, the reproduction of the voices of King George and Queen Mary broadcasting a speech to English children with "God Save the King" and "Home Sweet Home" on the reverse side, played by the band of the Coldstream Guards.

* * *

Two cases of Scotch from the Atlantic seaboard delivered by express to a broker's office marked as "Books" and opened and served by the special policeman of the brokerage firm, dressed in his blue uniform and wearing a star.

* * *

The cop who volunteered the information that the present mayor had closed up the beer saloons tight and seemed anxious to enter into conversation on the subject.

* * *

The Italian news dealer who refused to accept a Canadian quarter saying, "Us Americans ain't got no use for them things."

* * *

The Negro lady on the dining car coming home who ordered a plain steak, had it explained to her by the headwaiter that it would be $1.65 and she was sure when the turkey dinner was only a dollar. Had it re-explained to her by the waiter at the headwaiter's request, "Here, Jim, make this lady understand that steaks cost a dollar sixty-five." And finally paid her bill with a $50 note.

The Freiburg Fedora

☆ THE TORONTO STAR WEEKLY
January 19, 1924

There is one thing Toronto demands in clothes. That thing is conformation.

This does not mean conformation in the same sense as it is applied to a horse at the Royal Winter Fair.

No. Far from it. It means conformation; to conform.

Take my soft felt hat, for example. There is nothing wrong with the hat. It is a good hat. It sheds the rain and keeps the sun out of my eyes. But the first time I wore it in Toronto was the last time. Nothing could induce me to wear it again.

In the first place, I hadn't meant to wear it. But we live out in the country and I had been on a walk in the country and then decided to go downtown.

As I got on the car the conductor looked at me suspiciously. He seemed relieved when I produced a ticket.

The car was full and I had to stand up. Two girls started to giggle.

"What do you think he is?" asked one.

"I don't know," said her friend. "Maybe it's Red Ryan [a bank robber]."

At this mirth became general.

"No," said the first girl. "I think he's Harold Lloyd."

This remark was good for laughs halfway down the car.

"Where do you suppose he got a hat like that?" asked the second young lady.

"Maybe that's what they're wearing now in the States," the first young lady warned. "I saw [Rudolph] Valentino wear a hat something like that in a film once."

I removed the hat and bowed low.

"Observe the color of my hair, ladies," I said. "I am not Red Ryan."

The girls seemed somewhat taken aback.

"One glance at this Roman nose," I continued, "will prove to you that I am not Harold Lloyd. Will you favor me with a glance at the nose?"

But the girls did not look up.

"As for this hat," I said, "they are not, as far as I know, wearing them in the States at present. I am not absolutely sure on this point, not having been in the States for some time. This hat was given to me by the late Emperor Charles of Austria. I always wear it on his birthday."

I replaced the hat on my head.

"Say," said a gentleman in a cap who had been observing me truculently for some blocks, "what do you mean getting fresh with a couple of girls?"

But the car by now had reached the corner of Queen and Bay streets.

"I am very sorry, sir, but I cannot detain you longer." I bowed. "But I must leave the streetcar here. I have an appointment with the new mayor."

"For two bits I'd give you a sock on the jaw," observed the gentleman in the cap.

"I couldn't think of it for a moment," I said. "My dear fellow, it would be quite impossible. I could not think of accepting a gift of hosiery from a chance acquaintance, no matter how pleasant."

I bowed again and descended from the car. The gentleman in the cap was comforting the two young ladies.

"I'd have poked him in a minute," said the gentleman.

"He had no right to talk to a decent working girl like that," sobbed one of the girls.

"I'd have poked him," comforted the gentleman in the cap.

On the sidewalk, I removed the hat and looked at it. There was no doubt but that it differed from the other hats that passed and re-passed me in front of the city hall. It was old and green and it flopped down on one side like the hats that Robin Hood and his merry men wore. It had changed greatly since I bought it two years before in Freiburg im Breisgau for a hundred marks.

Then, for fifteen marks extra, I had bought a clip with a leather tab on it that buttoned over a suspender button and held the hat in the jaws of the clip when one wished to hike bareheaded.

Since then the old hat seemed to have lost a little something in every country it had shed rain and wind and sun in. The hot sun of the Thracian desert had burned most of the green out of it, it had been chafed by heavy snow glasses strapped to it, and it had gained nothing by being sailed down into the sunbaked sand of the bullring.

It was obviously a disreputable and, no doubt, a funny-looking hat. So I folded it up and stuck it in my hip pocket and walked to the nearest hat store bareheaded.

"What kind of a hat do you want, sir?" asked the clerk, ignoring gracefully the fact that I was bareheaded.

"Oh," I said, "give me one of the kind that everyone is wearing."

I have one of that kind now. But I know very well that if I ever try and wear it in Europe, somebody will want to take a poke at me.

Index

D

G

H

N

O

U

V

SUN
– Bretts wrinkling up her eyes
– prizefighter in Vienna